THE
IRISH
REGIMENTS

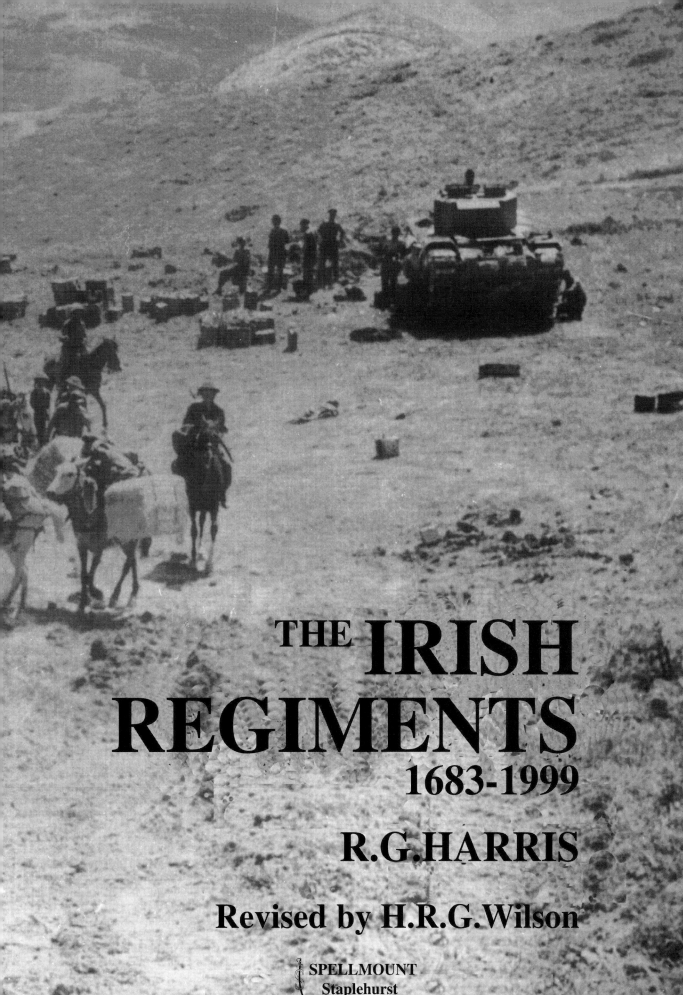

THE IRISH
REGIMENTS
1683-1999

R.G.HARRIS

Revised by H.R.G.Wilson

SPELLMOUNT
Staplehurst

For Dorothy, George and Helen

Also published by Spellmount

The Irish Guards in the Great War: The First
  Battalion/The Second Battalion – Rudyard Kipling
The History of British Military Bands Vol 3 (Infantry &
  Irish) – Turner & Turner
The Scottish Regiments – Mileham
English & Welsh Infantry Regiments – Westlake
The Art of Warfare in the Age of Marlborough – Chandler
Marlborough as Military Commander – Chandler
Sedgemoor 1685 – Chandler
Wellington's Military Machine – Haythornthwaite
Napoleon's Military Machine – Haythornthwaite
Wellington's Regiments – Fletcher
Rorke's Drift – Bancroft
The Devil's Adjutant: Jochen Peiper, Panzer Leader –
  Reynolds
Steel Inferno: 1st SS Panzer Corps in Normandy –
  Reynolds
The Unforgettable Army: Slim's XIVth Army in Burma –
  Hickey

First published in the UK in 1989
New Edition 1999 published by
Spellmount Ltd
The Old Rectory
Staplehurst
Kent TN12 0AZ

10 9 8 7 6 5 4 3 2 1

The right of R G Harris to be identified as the author of
this work has been asserted by him in accordance with the
Copyright, Designs and Patents Act, 1988

© R G Harris 1989, 1999

British Library Cataloguing in Publication Data
A catalogue record for this book is available from the
British Library

ISBN 1–86277–026–0

Printed in Singapore

*Pipe-Major Rosborough and Drum-Major Strawbridge, Royal
Inniskilling Fusiliers, c1929.*
THE PARKER GALLERY

*Frontispiece:
An interesting photograph showing an unidentified Rifleman in
greatcoat and caubeen, c1940.*
R. J. MARRION

Contents

Foreword

General Sir Roger Wheeler GCB CBE ADC Gen
Chief of the General Staff

I am delighted to commend this updated version of R.G. Harris' history of the Irish Regiments to readers, both military and civilian alike. The contribution of the Irish to the British Army over the past three centuries cannot be overstated and must never be overlooked. At the highest level a wholly disproportionate number of Field Marshals proudly claim Irish ancestry and, as this splendid book demonstrates, there are countless examples of the Irishman's resilience, resourcefulness and selfless sacrifice in the service of the Crown.

The numbers of Irish Regiments in existence today may be greatly reduced from that at the beginning of this turbulent century but I know from my own experience that those serving are worthy successors of their illustrious predecessors.

This book sets out in an attractive and informative manner the origins and often interwoven histories of the Irish Regiments right up to the present. It balances accounts of operational achievements with details of many changes of uniforms, interesting facts and amusing anecdotes. After all, as anyone who has been privileged to serve alongside the Irish Soldier knows, life is never dull and humour never far from the surface, no matter what the circumstances.

Colonel, The Royal Irish Regiment

Author's Note

To the casual observer the laying up of Colours of the Southern Irish regiments in 1922 may have been an event of little consequence, more so as it followed hard on the heels of one of the most savage wars in the history of mankind. That casual observer may, of course, be forgiven for considering the event the end of a chapter or the final curtain, but not for those who knew the Irish soldiers. Hence, the purpose of this book is an attempt to place between one pair of covers the stories of all the Irish regiments of the British Army, from the Battle of the Boyne and Vinegar Hill, Peninsula and Waterloo to South Africa and India and on until the 36th Division on the Somme – to 1922. Subsequently, the story of the Northern Irish regiments, although still with a good sprinkling of Southern men, both in the ranks and also up to highest command – to the Western Desert, Normandy, Korea, Goose Green and all the other many places between.

It is my hope that by the inclusion of anecdotal material, uniform notes and with some emphasis on bands and pipers, that just a little more than the abridged story of a regiment may emerge. It would also be nice to think that here and there the Irish character appears, with possibly a gleam of Irish humour showing through.

Pipes and drums. Belfast, 1960s.
CENTURY NEWSPAPERS LTD, BELFAST

I regret that before setting pen to paper I could not arrange a tour of the museums in Northern Ireland and Eire, but I have been compensated by spending many pleasant hours in research at the Army Museums Ogilby Trust Library and Archives Office through the very kind permission of Colonel P. S. Newton, MBE, and I am more than grateful to him for this privilege.

During the years before the mechanisation of the horsed regiments in the British Army, the Irish love of horses was self evident by the number of Irish cavalry regiments; four – a fact which displayed a degree of one-upmanship over the Scots who could only boast one. (The few remaining horses in the army today, ie those for the Mounted Squadron of the Household Cavalry and for the Royal Horse Artillery, are often purchased in Ireland.) In my text I use the term trooper when referred to a cavalry soldier, although the correct term was private until 1923. Similarly, the infantry soldier was generally referred to as private, although there were of course, guardsmen, fusiliers, riflemen and rangers amongst the Irish foot regiments.

Occasional mention is made of 'a note by an observer'. In most cases this would refer to an observation recorded by my friend and mentor, the late Lionel E. Buckell, whose records and files are preserved by the Ogilby Trust and contain invaluable material on uniform, dress and other military historical matters. Many of these regimental files also contain some notes and sketches by Robert Ebsworth. He was a 19th century wine and spirits salesman who travelled the country calling at barracks and military camps in pursuit of business. At the same time he managed to make notes and sketches of the soldiers he saw, their dress and accoutrements, which he duly recorded with any scraps of regimental gossip he may have heard. Sad to say the main collection of Ebsworth material is now housed in the Bibliotheque Nationale, Paris, who purchased the collection in England in the 1920s, a circumstance which could not happen today, now this country has its own National Army Museum.

Before I could even commence this book I had to turn to the works of previous historians, those who compiled the full individual histories of the old Irish regiments, although unfortunately such volumes are now long out of print. I acknowledge my gratitude to these writers. I would also stress the value of reference material to be found in the Journals of the Society for Army Historical Research, and the Irish equivalent – The Irish Sword, Journal of the Military Historial Society of Ireland.

A Colonel of the Royal Munster Fusiliers with his Adjutant, crossing the River Somme, near Peronne, March 1917.
IWM

Acknowledgements

I now wish to record my sincere thanks to all those who have so kindly given me their time and expertise, have answered so many of my questions, read through portions of my text and provided supporting collaboration during the months spent in preparing this work. My two Irish colleagues, Glenn Thompson and Tom Heaslip, have found invaluable material for me and I offer my thanks to both. A special word of thanks to John Tamplin and Alf Flatow for their unfailing good humour and help when pointing me in the right direction at the Army Museums Ogilby Trust Library, and to Keith Hook for not only putting his Irish regimental badges at my disposal for the frontispiece but also assisting with a troublesome chapter. Brian Forde, former Royal Hussar, has told me much about his family connection with the Leinster Regiment; and one-time Sergeant-Major of the Royal Ulster Rifles – Jim Cramer – has kindly allowed me full use of his library, whilst Stuart Barr of Worcester has generously helped by checking my material against his own specialised knowledge of the Connaught Rangers. Well known for their own writing, both Michael Barthorp and William Carman have found time to advise me; Bill has, in addition, supplied photographs.

In the field of photography I wish to give particular thanks to my old friend Stan Eagle of Edinburgh for allowing me to use prints from his unique collection, and similar thanks are due to Stanley Kretschmer and Dennis Quarmby. Other friends, William Boag, MA, Laurie Archer, Bob Marrion and Mike Chappell, have all contributed from their picture collections and to all these gentlemen I am greatly indebted.

Lastly, I give special thanks to my wife. Without her work as typist, photographer and provider of sustenance, this book would never have been completed.

R. G. HARRIS
SOUTHSEA 1988

Updating this work to reflect the changes that have affected The Irish Regiments since 1988 would not have been possible without the co-operation of the Regiments themselves. I am extremely grateful to all who promptly answered my queries, checked revisions and provided recent photographs.

I must single out Colonel Robert Rowe and Lieutenant Colonel Charles Linford of Headquarters The Royal Irish Regiment, not least as their Regiment has undergone the most fundamental reorganisation of any in the British Army during the period.

It has at all times been my aim to retain the style and character of R.G. Harris' original work.

H. R. G. WILSON
SOUTH COLLINGHAM 1999

PART ONE ■ EARLY AND DISBANDED REGIMENTS

Cavalry and Fencibles

CAVALRY

23rd Light Dragoons This regiment was an Irish corps, raised 1794 and disbanded in 1802. It did see some service under General Lake against Irish rebels. There is a known painting by George Morland showing a Light Dragoon private of this corps, Colonel William Fullerton's Regiment.

24th Light Dragoons Another of the short-lived Irish cavalry corps raised in 1794 and disbanded in 1802. Known as Colonel William Loftus's Regiment, it had a skull and crossbones as badge and the motto 'Death or Glory'.[1]

33rd (Ulster) Light Dragoons The last of the Light Dragoon regiments with an Irish connection was the 33rd (Ulster) Regiment, with an even shorter existence, 1794-1796. This regiment was raised by Lt-Col Blackwood and saw no service abroad.

[1] See J.S.A.H.R. Vol XX, pp72-92 and accompanying sketches Nos 37 and 39.

Badges of the Irish Regiments
1. 4th (Royal Irish) Dragoon Guards
2. 5th (Royal Irish) Lancers
3. 6th (Inniskilling) Dragoons
4. 8th (King's Royal Irish) Hussars
5. Irish Guards
6. The Royal Irish Regiment
7. The Royal Inniskilling Fusiliers
8. The Royal Irish Rifles
9. Princess Victoria's (Royal Irish Fusiliers)
10. The Connaught Rangers
11. The Prince of Wales's Leinster Regiment (Royal Canadians)
12. The Royal Munster Fusiliers
13. The Royal Dublin Fusiliers
14. North Irish Horse
15. South Irish Horse
16. The Royal Irish Rangers
17. Ulster Defence Regiment
18. 18th (County of London) Bn The London Regiment (London Irish Rifles)

(The badges and photograph kindly supplied by Lt Cmdr K. B. Hook, RN, Rtd)

FENCIBLES

Fencible Regiments were first raised in 1756 for a seven year period until 1763 when disbanded. Consisting of cavalry and infantry units they were defined as regular troops but were not liable for overseas drafting. Later, fresh regiments were raised in February 1793 and most were disbanded by 1801. Hamilton Smith's notebooks at the Victoria and Albert Museum list 35 of these regiments with an accompanying chart of uniform colours, followed by a smaller list of those regiments raised in 1799. The Fencible Cavalry Regiments appear separately with the note that 'when serving in Ireland blue uniforms will be worn. All regiments have the Light Dragoon uniform with crested helmet, all lace silver, feather – white over red'. Formed in 1794, but not on Hamilton Smith's list, the Irish regiments are as follows:
Lord Roden's or 1st Irish, bright blue uniform with white facings.
Lord Glenworth's or 2nd Irish, bright blue uniform with yellow facings.
The Loyal Irish Fencibles are recorded as raised by Col W. Handcock, but no uniform details are supplied.

Two interesting units on the 1799 list are the Ancient Irish Fencibles, Col J. Fitzgerald, and the Tarbert Fencibles, Col Sir Edward Leslie. In Fortescue's Volume 4 of the *History of the British Army*, there is an entry concerning Fencible Cavalry in general and the Ancient Irish in particular. 'But by March 1800 the greater part of the cavalry had been disembodied so it would not be wise to reckon the Fencibles as exceeding at their highest figure 20-25,000 men. Several of the Fencible Regiments volunteered for service abroad and that the Ancient Irish found their way to Egypt. Most, if not all of the Fencible Infantry was disbanded in May 1801 before the preliminaries of peace.' This regiment was among reinforcements from, possibly, Minorca and reached the force in Egypt between May-July 1801. The implication is that they were Infantry, not Cavalry, as they formed part of Blake's

6 Brigade for the operation against Alexandria, 9-26 August 1801. Corps disbanded in 1802. A button of this regiment is known, an Irish harp in relief with the title around the rim.[1]

The Tarbert Fencibles. It has always been assumed that this was a Scottish Regiment but the Letters of Service to raise the regiment were issued on 27 July 1798 and the first commissions are dated 19 March 1799. It was raised by Sir Edward Leslie whose seat was in Tarbert, County Kerry. The regiment moved to the south of England and it is known that they took a route which marched through Gloucester, Poole and Ringwood to Southampton. In 1800 they moved to Winchester, then later the same year to Fort Cumberland in Portsmouth and in January 1801 they moved to Guernsey in the Channel Islands where they remained until 1802. Whilst in Hampshire in 1800 a soldier of the regiment was hanged for murder, details of the crime recorded on a plaque upon a stone at Botley, Hants, subsequently removed to Southsea Castle Museum. The Scottish United Services Museum possesses a medal presented to a John Moore of the regiment, as best shot.[2] There is also an oval shoulder-belt plate in a private collection, which shows a simple design, crown above G R and title around the rim. The regiment is thought to have had a scarlet uniform with blue facings. Disbanded in 1802 with colours believed to be laid up in Kilkenny Cathedral, Ireland.

[1] Article by Major H. G. Parkyn, OBE, *Connoisseur*, March 1922.
[2] Data kindly supplied by W. G. F. Boag, MA, of the Scottish United Services Museum.

N.B. Whilst dealing with early Military Regiments (Reign of James II) it should be noted that C. C. P. Lawson in his Vol I of the *History of the Uniforms of the British Army*, records the regiments in the service of France and known by the names of the Colonels: Fitzjames, Dorington, Bulkeley, Clare, Lally and Dillon.

EARLY AND DISBANDED REGIMENTS

Infantry   *Yeomanry*

76th Foot   1756-63. Raised as a two battalion regiment in Ireland 1756, George, Lord Forbes, its Colonel. Designation established on 20 June 1759 as 76th Regiment of Foot, one battalion in Ireland, one in Africa. Disbanded 1763.[1]

83rd Foot   See 83rd Regiment (Royal Irish Rifles).

90th Irish Light Infantry   Raised by Hugh Morgan in Ireland 1759. Said to be a regiment of fine appearance when first brought over to England. Served at the Siege of Belle Isle, 1761 and capture of Havana 1762. Disbanded in England 1763. Joshua Reynolds painted a portrait of Colonel H. Morgan.[2]

96th (Queen's Royal Irish) Regiment of Foot   Raised in Ireland in 1793, Col J. Murray. Fought in West Indies but broken up at Halifax, Nova Scotia, 1795-6.

97th (Earl of Ulster's) Regiment of Foot   This regiment eventually became the 2nd Bn The Queen's Own (Royal West Kent Regiment). When raised in 1824-5 was entitled 97th (Earl of Ulster's) Regiment and regarded as an Irish corps, the Earldom of Ulster being the Irish title of the Duke of Cambridge. Facings were sky blue and consequently the regiment was known as the 'Celestials', 'harp with silver strings'. This regiment *not* disbanded.

99th Prince of Wales's Tipperary Regiment of Foot   1805-18. Raised in Ireland in 1805. Served in Bermuda and North America. Renumbered 98th (Prince of Wales's Tipperary) Regiment of Foot and disbanded at Chatham in 1818. A miniature of an officer of the 99th Regiment is known, showing an oval shoulder-belt plate with the numerals 99 upon it. He wears a scarlet coat with yellow facings. The Earl of Landaff was its first Colonel in 1805 and Hugh Montagu Mathew Colonel from 1811 until disbandment.

100th Prince Regent's County of Dublin Regiment of Foot   1805-18. See Leinster Regiment.

101st (Irish) Regiment of Foot   1794-5. The National Army Museum own a fine miniature by Buck of an officer of this regiment. He wears a scarlet uniform with yellow facings and has an oval shoulder-belt plate with the numerals 101 upon it. See Royal Munster Fusiliers.

101st The Duke of York's Irish Regiment   1806-17. See Royal Munster Fusiliers.

102nd (Irish) Regiment of Foot   1793-5. See Royal Dublin Fusiliers.

103rd (King's Irish Infantry) Regiment of Foot   1781-3. Raised by Sir Ralph Abercrombie in 1781 but disbanded in 1783.

105th Regiment   Raised in 1777 at Philadelphia by Lord Rawdon, later Earl of Moira and Marquess of Hastings, regiment known as the 'Volunteers of Ireland'. Believed to have been composed of Irish and New York Loyalists. Saw much active service in the American War of Independence and before disbandment in 1783 was entitled 105th (King's Irish) Regiment of Foot.

124th Foot The Waterford Regiment   Raised in August 1794 by Col Carr Beresford. Disbanded September 1795, the men drafted to other regiments. A shoulder-belt plate is known, brass, the word Waterford around the top rim, Regiment around the bottom rim and a crown in the centre.[3]

134th (Loyal Limerick) Regiment of Foot   1794-5. Raised in 1794 as a 2nd Bn/83rd Regiment, but broken up the following year and the soldiers drafted to other regiments.[4]

135th Limerick Regiment   This regiment was raised by Sir Vere Hunt, Bt, but there is some confusion about the date. First noted in the Army List as 4 February 1796 but also recorded as having been inspected at Poole, 22 July 1795. In any event the regiment was disbanded in 1796.[5]

The Yeomanry in Ireland was formed about 1796 and had no connection with the earlier Volunteers, Light Dragoons or bodies of Horse, all of which had disappeared by 1793. The Yeomanry title suggests mounted men but this was not necessarily so, as a so-called Yeomanry regiment could, and did, consist of both cavalry and infantry, but its officers were appointed by the Government who financed and controlled it. Many Yeomanry units did serve during the Irish Revolutionary War, but were stood down in 1798 and did not reappear. Troops were needed again in 1803 and various new bodies were formed, but after 1815 most Yeomanry Cavalry disappeared, although remnants of the Force survived until about 1832-4.

Uniform pieces of the Yeomanry are as scarce today as those of the Volunteers, but shoulder-belt plates are known and a fine Tarleton head-dress of the Tipperary Light Dragoons is preserved at the National Museum of Ireland in Dublin.

It was to be another 65 years before Yeomanry units were re-raised in Ireland for the war in South Africa – 1899.

[1] J.S.A.H.R. Vol V, p134.
[2] J.S.A.H.R. Vol XXXVI, p9.
[3] See illustration in J.S.A.H.R. Vol XV, p184.
[4] Chichester and Short. (Much other data about these high numbered regiments to be found in this work.)
[5] See J.S.A.H.R. Vol XXXIII. Notes by T. H. McGuffie. This title, 135th Limerick, given in a list by the Marquess of Cambridge.

EARLY AND DISBANDED REGIMENTS

Volunteers

Under threat of invasion towards the close of the 18th century and with little or no protection expected from the Government, the general unease prompted many land owners and gentry as well as large sections of the populace, to form their own military bodies. From about 1776, and lasting until 1782-3, (but in some cases lingering on until 1793), almost every Irish city or town and down to the smallest village, formed independent companies, either volunteer Infantry or Horse and even Artillery. These armed associations elected their own officers and purchased arms (but with some supplied from the militia), and were also responsible for uniform.

No complete records of units or uniforms were ever kept, although several Irish historians have compiled lists for the provinces of Munster, Ulster, Leinster and Connaught.[1] These lists have been republished and are of such historical importance that it has been considered appropriate to reprint here.[2] There is still a wide field of research in

this connection, open to any student with stamina and enthusiasm. It cannot be expected that many pieces of uniform are still in existence but fortunately there are museums in Ireland today rich in the number of metal shoulder-belt plates which have survived, whilst some still appear at auction. These belt plates, the first identifying badges of units, do at least prove the existence of such a unit, however short its history may have been and provide us with a name for that unit, or its initials, and often a crest or badge. The present museum of the Royal Irish Rangers can boast a magnificent collection of these plates, whilst the Ulster Museum, Belfast, has in addition to shoulder-belt plates – buttons and medals of the Irish Volunteers, Yeomanry and Militia. The Dublin Museums also possess some fine pieces, together with paintings etc.

(The names of these Volunteer units do not appear in the General Index, the List being an Index in its own right.)

Helmet worn by a trooper of a Light Dragoon Corps, Irish Volunteers c1780. Helmet of brass with iron bands at the sides, painted black, leopardskin turban, the front has the letters T.L.D. etc.
NATIONAL MUSEUM OF IRELAND

---

[1] The Munster Volunteer Registry, 1782.
The History of the Volunteers, 1782 by Thomas MacNevin. Also J.S.A.H.R. Vol XVII, p208.
[2] The copy in the possession of this writer is enhanced with several small illustrations of medals awarded for shooting or swordsmanship. One example: To Edward Leach by Col R. U. Fitz-gerald for best swordsman in the Imokilly Blue Horse. 19 September 1779.

CAVALRY

County Cork

TRUE BLUE, CORK, 1745 (Col Richard, E of Shannon) – One troop. Uniform: Blue, laced silver epaulettes, white buttons; (Horse) furniture: goatskin.

MITCHELSTOWN LIGHT DRAGOONS, July 1744 (Col Viscount Kingsborough) – One troop. Uniform: Scarlet, faced black, silver epaulettes, yellow[1] helmets, white buttons; Furniture: goatskin, edged black.

BLACK POOL HORSE, 1776 (Col John Harding) – One troop. Uniform: Green, laced gold, ditto epaulettes, buff waistcoat and breeches; Furniture: goatskin.

YOUGHALL CAVALRY, 1776 (Capt-Comdt Robert Ball) – One troop. Uniform: Scarlet, faced white.

BRANDON CAVALRY, 6 May 1778 (Col Sampson Stawell) – One troop. Uniform: Dark olive green jacket, half lapelled, crimson velvet cuff and collar, silver epaulettes; Furniture: White cloth housing and holster caps, embroidered; device BC, harp and crown.

MUSKERRY BLUE LIGHT DRAGOONS, 1 June 1778 (Col Robert Warren) – One troop. Uniform: Blue lapelled, edged white, silver epaulettes, white jacket, edged blue; Furniture: goatskin.

DUHALLOW RANGERS, 1778 (Col Hon Charles Percival) – Uniform not given. Mr Day's note: 'I am indebted to Capt J. Harris of Annabella Villa, Mallow, for the loan of some interesting mementoes of this regiment, that enable me to fill the blank and give its uniform, which was blue, trimmed with silver lace, silver epaulettes and gilt gorget. This gorget is of the usual regulation pattern, crescentic in form, of copper, plated with gold and engraved in the centre with the Royal cypher GR crowned, between two sprays of laurel. It has its old leather lining of sheepskin and is suspended by its original ribbon from two rosettes of blue silk. The shoulder-belt or, more correctly, the collar, is of blue cloth 4in wide with silver lace borders of 1in at each side, and between these a silver band of ⅜in, 'forming a continuation of chevrons from end to end, the length being 4ft 10in, or 2ft 5in at each side when doubled. It is lined with buff leather. The silver epaulettes are of the same pattern to those at present used in the Royal Navy. But of surpassing interest is the regimental banner, which measures 3ft in extreme length by 1ft 9in in width. It is made throughout of satin, rose colour on·one side and purple on the other. The first has, richly worked with threads of gold, the device of a harp crowned, and over it "Duhallow Cavalry", the whole encircled by a wreath of shamrocks. Upon the purple ground in raised silk embroidery is a Volunteer in scarlet uniform upon a bay charger and in the foreground a seated figure of Hibernia with a harp; over all, the motto of the Volunteers, "Pro Aris et Focis", surmounted wtih shamrocks. This banner was carried by the grandfather of Captain Harris, who held a commission in the Rangers as Cornet. All are well preserved and in excellent condition, and free from the ravages caused by moths and damp.'

IMOKILLY HORSE, 1778 (Col Edward Roche) – One troop. Uniform: Scarlet, faced black, yellow buttons, gold epaulettes, yellow helmets, white jackets edged red; Furniture: goatskin, trimmed red.

KILWORTH LIGHT DRAGOONS, July 1779 (Col Stephen, Earl Mountcashel) – Uniform: Scarlet, faced green, gold epaulettes, yellow buttons and helmets; Furniture: goatskin, trimmed green.

IMOKILLY BLUE HORSE, 1779 (Col Robert Uniacke FitzGerald) – Uniform: Blue, faced red.

DONERAILE RANGERS LIGHT DRAGOONS, 12 July 1779 (Col St Leger, Lord Doneraile) – One troop. Uniform: Scarlet, faced green, edged white, gold epaulettes, yellow buttons and helmets, green jackets, faced red; Furniture: goatskin.

GLANMIRE UNION, 27 August 1779 (Col Henry Mannix) – One troop. Uniform: Deep green, faced black; Furniture: goatskin, trimmed green.

CORK CAVALRY, (Col Wm Chetwynd) – One troop. Uniform: Scarlet, faced blue, silver laced, silver epaulettes, white buttons; Furniture: black cloth, laced gold.

MALLOW CAVALRY, 1782 (Col Cotter) – Uniform: Green jackets.

GREAT ISLAND CAVALRY, 24 June 1782 (Capt Wallis Colthurst) – One troop. Uniform: Scarlet, faced green, gold epaulettes, yellow buttons, white jackets edged black;[2] Furniture: goatskin.

County Clare
COUNTY CLARE HORSE, 24 July 1779 (Col Edward Fitzgerald) – Two troops. Uniform: Scarlet, faced dark green, silver epaulettes and buttons, white jackets, green cape; Furniture: goatskin.

SIXMILEBRIDGE INDEPENDENTS, (Col Francis McNamara).

County Kerry
KERRY LEGION CAVALRY, January 1779 (Major Comdt Rowland Bateman) – One troop. Uniform: Scarlet, faced black, edged white, silver epaulettes, white buttons; Furniture: goatskin, edged black.

WOODFORD RANGERS, (Col Wm Townsend).[3]

County Limerick[4]
KILFINNAN LIGHT DRAGOONS, 1777 (Capt Chas Coote) – One troop. Uniform: Scarlet jackets, faced pomona green, laced silver and epaulettes; Furniture: goatskin.

COUNTY LIMERICK HORSE, 8 June 1779 (Col John Croker) – Two troops. Uniform: Scarlet, faced black, yellow buttons, buff waistcoat and breeches, yellow helmets; Furniture: goatskin, edged black.

CONNAGH RANGERS, June 1779 (Col Robert, Lord Muskerry) – Uniform: Scarlet, faced black, yellow buttons; Furniture: goatskin.

COUNTY LIMERICK ROYAL HORSE,[5] (Col Hon Hugh Massey) – Two troops. Uniform: Scarlet, faced blue; Furniture: goatskin.

SMALL COUNTY UNION LIGHT DRAGOONS, (Col John Grady) – Uniform: Scarlet, faced green.

TRUE BLUE HORSE, (Col Wm Thos Monsel).

CONNELL'S LIGHT HORSE, (Col Thos Odell) – One troop. Uniform: Scarlet, faced goslin green, dark green jackets.

RIDDLESTOWN HUSSARS, (Col Gerald Blennerhasset) – One troop. Uniform: Scarlet, faced blue, silver epaulettes, white buttons, white jacket, faced blue; Furniture: goatskin.

County Tipperary
TIPPERARY LIGHT DRAGOONS, 1 May 1776 (Capt Benjamin Bunbury) – One troop. Uniform: Scarlet, faced black, white buttons, silver epaulettes.

TEMPLEMORE LIGHT DRAGOONS, 1776 (Col John Craven Carden) – One troop. Uniform: Scarlet, faced black, white buttons; Furniture: goatskin.

SLEIVERDAGH LIGHT DRAGOONS, September 1778 (Col Jas Hamilton Lane) – One troop. Uniform: Scarlet,

faced white, laced silver, white buttons, silver epaulettes, green jackets; Furniture: goatskin.

CLANWILLIAM UNION, July 1779 (Col John, Lord Clanwilliam) – One troop. Uniform: Scarlet, faced blue, laced silver, silver epaulettes, white buttons, white jacket, faced blue; Furniture: goatskin, trimmed blue.

LORA RANGERS, 1779 (Col Francis Mathew) – One troop. Uniform: Scarlet, faced green, yellow buttons, gold epaulettes; Furniture: goatskin, edged black.

MUNSTER CORPS CAVALRY, (Col John Lap Judkin) – Uniform: Scarlet, faced blue, gold laced, gold epaulettes, buff waistcoat and breeches, yellow buttons, buff jackets; Furniture: goatskin.

CLOGHEEN UNION, 6 January 1781 (Col Cor O'Callaghan) – One troop. Uniform: Scarlet, faced light blue, edged silver lace, white buttons, silver epaulettes, white jackets, edged red; Furniture: goatskin, turned red.

ORMOND UNION CAVALRY, date united with and same as INFANTRY, (Capt Chas Jas Bury) – Uniform: Scarlet, faced white, silver epaulettes, white buttons.

NEWPORT CAVALRY, date united with, same as INFANTRY, (Col see INFANTRY). Uniform: Scarlet, green collar and cuffs, yellow buttons and gold epaulettes.

County Waterford
LISMORE BLUES,[6] 1 July 1778 (Capt Comdt Richard Musgrave) – Uniform: Scarlet, faced blue, white buttons, silver epaulettes, white jackets, edged blue; Furniture: goatskin.

CURRAGHMORE RANGERS, 1 November 1779 (Col Geo, Earl Tyrone) – Uniform: Scarlet, faced white, silver epaulettes, white buttons, white jackets, faced red, half lapelled; Furniture: goatskin.

WATERFORD UNION, (Capt Jno Congreve, junr) Uniform: Green jackets, crimson velvet cuffs and collar, silver epaulettes, white buttons; Furniture: goatskin, edged black.

NUMBER OF TROOPS IN THE PROVINCE		
	Corps	Troops
County Cork	16	16
County Clare	2	3
County Kerry	2	2
County Limerick	8	10
County Tipperary	9	9
County Waterford	3	3
	40	43

INFANTRY

County Cork

CORK ARTILLERY, (Capt Richard Hare, junr) – One company, two pieces, 4-pounders. Uniform: Blue, faced scarlet, yellow buttons, gold lace.

IMOKILLY BLUE ARTILLERY, (Col Robert Uniacke FitzGerald) – One company, two 4-pounders. Uniform: Blue, faced scarlet.

TRUE BLUE, CORK, 1745 (Col Richard, Lord Shannon) – Four companies, viz: one grenadier, two battalion, one light. Uniform: Blue, laced silver, white buttons.

CORK BOYNE, 1776 (Col Jno Bagwell) – Four companies, one grenadier, two battalion, one light. Uniform: Blue, faced blue, yellow buttons, gold epaulettes and lace.

MALLOW BOYNE, May 1776 (Col Sir Jas Laurence Cotter, Bt) – One grenadier company, one battalion. Uniform: Blue, edged buff, buff waistcoat and breeches, yellow buttons.

BANDON BOYNE, 1777 (Col—) – One company. Uniform: Blue, edged buff, yellow buttons, buff waistcoat and breeches, gold epaulettes.

CARBERY INDEPENDENTS, 20 May 1777 (Capt Comdt Wm Beecher) – One company. Uniform: Scarlet, faced green, yellow buttons.

AUGHRIM OF CORK, 1777 (Col Richard Longfield) – Three companies. Uniform: Scarlet, faced scarlet, edged white.

LOYAL NEWBERRY MUSQUETEERS, June 1777 (Col Adam Newman) – Two companies, one grenadier, one light. Uniform: Scarlet, faced black.

CORK UNION, March 1776 (Capt Comdt Henry Hickman) – Four companies, one grenadier, two battalions, one light. Uniform: Scarlet, faced green, yellow buttons.

CULLODEN VOLUNTEERS OF CORK, 23 March 1778 (Col Benjamin Bousfield) – Three companies, one grenadier, one battalion, one light. Uniform: Blue, faced scarlet, yellow buttons; officers: gold epaulettes.

ROSS CARBERY VOLUNTEERS, (Col Thos Hungerford) – One company. Uniform: Scarlet, faced blue.

PASSAGE UNION, 29 March 1778 (Major Comdt Michael Parker) – three companies, one grenadier, one battalion, one light. Uniform: Scarlet, faced deep green, white buttons.

BANDON INDEPENDENTS, 29 March 1778 (Col Francis Bernard) – One company. Uniform: Scarlet, faced black,

The Baltsagh Volunteers. The initials C.Mc.C. are those of the original owner, an officer in the corps – Conolly McCausland.

gold epaulettes, yellow buttons, green jackets, faced black.

YOUGHAL INDEPENDENT BLUES, 1778 (Col Robert Uniacke) – Two companies. Uniform: Blue, faced scarlet, edged white.

YOUGHAL RANGERS, 19 April 1778 (Lt-Col Comdt Meade Hobson) – Two companies, one grenadier, one light. Uniform: Grass green, faced scarlet, gold lace and yellow buttons.

KINSALE VOLUNTEERS, 1 May 1778 (Col Jas Kearney) – Two companies, one battalion, one light.

HANOVER SOCIETY, CLOUGHNAKILTY, 1 May 1778 (Col Richard Hungerford) – Two companies. Uniform: Scarlet, faced buff.

KANTURK VOLUNTEERS, 1 May 1778 (Col John James, Earl of Egmont) – One company. Uniform: Scarlet, faced light blue.[7]

HAWKE UNION OF COVE, 9 May 1778 (Capt Comdt Wm Dickson) – Uniform: Blue, edged and lined buff, yellow buttons, buff waistcoat and breeches.

BLACKWATER RANGERS, (Col Richard Aldworth) – One company.

BLARNEY VOLUNTEERS,[8] (Col Geo Jeffreys) – Uniform: Scarlet, faced black, white buttons.

NEWMARKET RANGERS, (Col Boyle Aldworth) – Uniform: Blue, faced blue.

CURRIGLASS VOLUNTEERS, April 1779 (Capt Comdt Peard Harrison Peard) – One company.

CASTLEMARTYR SOCIETY, May 1779 (Capt Wm Hallaran) – One company. Uniform: Scarlet, faced pale yellow.

INCHIGEELAGH VOLUNTEERS, 1 June 1779 (Capt Comdt Jasper Masters) – One light company. Uniform: Blue, edged buff, buff waistcoat and breeches.

MUSKERRY VOLUNTEERS, 19 June 1779 (Capt Comdt Thos Barter) – One company. Uniform: Blue, edged buff, buff waistcoat and breeches.

DONERAILE RANGERS, 12 July 1779 (Col St Leger, Lord Doneraile) – One company. Uniform: Scarlet, faced green, yellow buttons, gold epaulettes.

BANTRY VOLUNTEERS, 12 July 1779 (Col Hamilton White) – One company. Uniform: Scarlet, faced white.

KILWORTH VOLUNTEERS, July 1779 (Col Stephen, Earl Mountcashel) – One company. Uniform: Scarlet, faced green, yellow buttons.

MALLOW INDEPENDENTS, 1779 (Col Jno Longfield) – One company. Uniform: Scarlet, faced green, yellow buttons.

YOUGHAL UNION FUSILIERS, 1779 (Major Comdt Thos Green) – Two companies. Uniform: Scarlet, faced blue, edged white, white buttons.

DUHALLOW VOLUNTEERS, October 1779 (Col Broderick Chinnery) – One company.

KINNELEA AND KERRECH UNION, December 1779 (Col Thos Roberts) – Three companies. Uniform: Blue, edged white, white buttons.

CHARLEVILLE VOLUNTEERS, (Col Chidley Coote) – Uniform: Blue lapelled, edged red.

IMOKILLY BLUE INFANTRY, (Col Robert Uniacke Fitzgerald).

CASTLE LYONS VOLUNTEERS, (Col—).

County Clare

ENNIS VOLUNTEERS, 12 September 1778 (Col Wm Blood) – Three companies, one grenadier, one battalion, one light. Uniform: Scarlet, faced blue.[9]

INCHIQUIN FUSILIERS, 12 February 1779 (Col Murrough, Earl of Inchiquin) – One company. Uniform: Scarlet, faced light blue, silver buttons, braided wings and shoulder straps, hat cocked one side, large plume of black feathers.

KILRUSH UNION, 11 June 1780 (Col Croften Vandeleur) – Two companies, one grenadier, one battalion. Uniform: Scarlet, faced light blue.

County Kerry

ROYAL TRALEE VOLUNTEERS, 4 January 1779 (Col Sir Barry Denny, Bt) – Two companies, one grenadier, one light. Uniform: Scarlet, faced deep blue, edged white, yellow buttons, gold lace epaulettes and wings.

KERRY LEGION, January 1779 (Col Arthur Blennerhasset) – Seven companies, one grenadier, five battalion, one light. Uniform: Scarlet, faced black, edged white, white buttons.

KILLARNEY FORESTERS, 1779 (Capt Comdt Thos Galway).

GUNSBOROUGH UNION, 1779 (Col Geo Gun).

MILTOWN FUSILIERS, (Major Comdt Wm Godfrey).

LAUNE RANGERS, (Col Rowland Blennerhasset).

DROMORE VOLUNTEERS, (Col Jno Mahoney).[10]

County Limerick

ROYAL GLIN ARTILLERY, June 1779 (Col Jno FitzGerald, Knight of Glin) – Ten officers and staff, 1 Sgt-Major, 1 Sergeant, 4 Bombardiers, 2 Corporals, 60 rank and file, besides a Band of 10; four metal 6-pounders, two small brass grasshoppers (1-pounders). Uniform: Blue, faced gold, gold epaulettes, scarlet cuffs and collar, yellow buttons, gold-laced hat.

KILFINNAN FOOT, 1776 (Col Rt Hon Silver Oliver) – One company. Uniform: Scarlet, faced pomona green.

COUNTY LIMERICK FENCIBLE VOLUNTEERS, (Col Jno Thos Waller) – Uniform: Scarlet, faced light blue.

LOYAL LIMERICK VOLUNTEERS, 10 February 1776 (Col Thos Smyth) – Five companies, one grenadier, three battalion, one light. Uniform: Scarlet, faced white, white buttons.

The Newtown Limavady Volunteer Infantry. Both units were from the Londonderry area. (This shoulder-belt and the one on the previous page are now in the Museum of the Royal Irish Rangers.)
CHRISTIE'S

Note by Mr Day: This regiment, in Fitz-Gerald and McGregor's *History of Limerick*, p447, is called the LOYAL LIMERICK UNION, and has the following reference: 'Soon after the breaking out of the American War the city was frequently left destitute of a sufficient garrison. The Mayor, Mr Smyth, formed an association composed of the principal citizens, which he called "The Limerick Union". It consisted of a troop of Horse and a company of Foot, dressed in blue, faced with buff, and wearing a medal inscribed "Amicitia Juncta". When the Army marched out of Limerick in 1776 the "Union" performed the duty of the main guard. In 1778 the Limerick Union became the LOYAL LIMERICK VOLUNTEERS and changed their uniform to scarlet, faced with white. They increased so much in number that, in 1782, twenty-six corps of Volunteers, belonging to the city and county of Limerick, were reviewed by the Earl of Charlemont.' – RD.

CASTLECONNEL RANGERS, 8 July 1778 (Col Robert, Lord Muskerry) – Battalion and light infantry, four companies. Uniform: Scarlet, faced black, edged white, silver wings.

ADARE VOLUNTEERS, (Col Sir Valentine Richard Quin) – Uniform: Scarlet, faced green.

RATHKEALE VOLUNTEERS, 1 July 1779 (Col Geo Leake) – One grenadier company and one light company. Uniform: Scarlet, faced black, silver wings; officers full laced.

GERMAN FUSILIERS, (Col Jas Darcey).

TRUE BLUE FOOT, (Col Wm Thos Monsel).

LIMERICK INDEPENDENTS, October 1781 (Lt-Col Comdt John Smyth Pendergast) – One grenadier, one battalion and one light company. Two brass field-pieces, 4-pounders. Uniform: Scarlet, faced pomona green, laced, silver epaulettes.

County Tipperary

TIPPERARY VOLUNTEERS, 1 May 1776 (Col Sir Cornelius Maude, Bt) – One light company. Two brass field-pieces, 4-pounders. Uniform: Scarlet, faced black, laced wings.

ROSCREA BLUES, (Col Laurence Panens) – Uniform: Blue, faced blue, edged scarlet.

ORMOND UNION, 1779 (Col Henry Prittie) – Three companies. Uniform: Scarlet, faced white, silver epaulettes, white buttons.

BURRASAKANE VOLUNTEERS, 25 March 1779 (Col Geo Stoney) – One company.

ORMOND INDEPENDENTS, 23 March 1779 (Col Daniel Toler) – Battlion of light infantry, four companies. Uniform: Scarlet, faced black, silver epaulettes and wings.

CLONMEL INDEPENDENTS, 4 June 1779 (Col Richard Moore) – Two companies, one light, one battalion. Uniform: Scarlet, faced black, white buttons.

CASTLE OTWAY VOLUNTEERS, (Col Thos Otway) – Uniform: Scarlet, faced green.

CASHEL VOLUNTEERS, June 1779 (Col Richard Penefather) – Two companies, one light, one battalion. Two field-pieces, 4-pounders. Uniform: Scarlet, faced black, white buttons.

FETHARD INDEPENDENTS, June 1779 (Col Wm Barton) – Two companies, one light, one battalion. Uniform: Scarlet, faced black, white buttons.

NENAGH VOLUNTEERS, 1 July 1779 (Col Peter Holmes) – One battalion, two companies. Uniform: Blue, faced blue,[11] yellow buttons.

THURLES UNION, August 1779 (Col Francis Mathew) – One light, one battalion company.

DRUM DIVISION OF THURLES UNION, August 1779 (Col Theobald Baker[12]) – One battalion company. Uniform of both: Scarlet, faced green, yellow buttons.

KILCOOLY TRUE BLUES, 1779 (Col Sir Wm Barker, Bt) – Uniform: Blue, edged buff, yellow buttons, buff waistcoat and breeches.

NEWPORT VOLUNTEERS, (Col Lord Jocelyn) – Uniform: Scarlet, green collar, yellow buttons.

CARRICK UNION, September 1779 (Col George, Earl Tyrone) – One company, battalion light infantry. Uniform: Blue, faced blue,[13] yellow buttons.

CAHER UNION, 1 January 1781 (Col Hon Pierce Butler) – One light company. Uniform: Blue, faced red, yellow buttons.

Waterford

WATERFORD ARTILLERY, (Capt Joseph Pawl) – One company. Two pieces, 4-pounders. Uniform: Blue, faced red, yellow buttons.

WATERFORD INDEPENDENTS, NCS 1 AND 6, – No 1, March 1778 (Capt Comdt Henry Alcock) – One company, 1st Battalion. 2nd Battalion or No 6, September 1781 (Lt Henry Hayden) – One company, 2nd Battalion. Uniform: Scarlet, faced black, white buttons, silver laced hats.

WATERFORD INDEPENDENTS, NO 2, March 1778 (Capt Robert Shapland

Carew) – One company. Uniform: Scarlet, faced black, silver laced wings, white buttons.

WATERFORD INDEPENDENTS, NO 3, May 1778 (Capt Hanibal William Dobbyn) – One company.[14]

TALLOW INDEPENDENT BLUES, 1 August 1778 (Capt Comdt Geo Bowles) – Two companies. Uniform: Blue, edged white.

ROYAL OAKS, OR WATERFORD INDEPENDENT BLUES, NOS 4 AND 5, September 1779 (Col and Capt Cornelius Bolton) – Two companies, Nos 4 and 5, one light, one battalion. Uniform: Scarlet, faced blue.

DUNGARVAN VOLUNTEERS, 1 November 1779 (Col Rt Hon John Beresford) – Battalion of light infantry, two companies. Uniform: Scarlet, faced black, silver laced wing, white buttons.

CAPPOQUIN VOLUNTEERS, 1779 (Col Jno Kean) – Uniform: Scarlet and white, white buttons.

WATERFORD GRENADIERS, NO 7, June 1782 (Capt David Wilson) – One company. Uniform: Scarlet, faced yellow, wings silver laced, white buttons.

Volunteers of Ulster, Leinster and Connaught

In MacNevin's *History of the Volunteers of 1782*, previously referred to, there is given in an appendix an alphabetical list of Irish Volunteer Corps. These not only include the Munster Volunteers, as shown above, but also the following corps, raised in the other provinces of Ireland:

AGHAVOIE LOYALS, 1 July 1782 (Capt Robert White) – Uniform: Scarlet, faced blue.

ALDBOROUGH LEGION, August 1777 (Col Earl of Aldborough) – Uniform: Scarlet, faced black, silver lace.

ARLINGTON LIGHT CAVALRY, 18 September 1779 (Capt George Gore) – Uniform: Scarlet, faced green, yellow buttons.

ARRAN PHALANX, (Capt Dawson), – Uniform: Scarlet, faced white.

ATHY INDEPENDENTS, September 1779 (Capt Robert Johnson) – Uniform: Scarlet, faced white.

ATHY VOLUNTEERS, September 1779 – Uniform: Scarlet, faced white.

AUGHNACLOY BATTALION, (Col P. Alexander) – Uniform: Scarlet, faced white.

ASHFIELD VOLUNTEERS, (Capt H. Clements) – Uniform: Blue, faced blue.

AUGHRIM LIGHT HORSE, (Col Walter Lambert) – Uniform: Scarlet, faced pea-green.

BALLINTEMPLE FORRESTERS, 12 July 1779 (Capt Stewart) – Uniform: Scarlet, faced blue.

BARONY RANGERS, 17 March 1778 (Col Andrew Armstrong) – Uniform: Scarlet, faced black.

BARONY OF FORTH CORPS, 1 January 1779 (Major Hughes) – Uniform: Scarlet, faced blue.

BALLYLEEK RANGERS, 1779 (Col John Montgomery) – Uniform: Scarlet, faced white, gold lace.

BALLINA AND ARDNAREE (LOYAL) VOLUNTEERS, 1 July 1779 (Col Rt Hon Henry King) – Uniform: Scarlet, faced black.

BELFAST UNION, 12 June 1778 (Capt Lyons) – Uniform: Scarlet, faced blue.

Shoulder-belt plate of Lisburn Volunteers. Brass 3in, engraved with crowned harp, name and motto 'In Pectore Patria', Co Antrim, c1779-93.

BELFAST LIGHT DRAGOONS, 26 March 1781 (Capt Burden) – Uniform: Scarlet, faced green, silver lace.

BELFAST BATTALION, April 1779 (Col Stewart Banks) – Uniform: Scarlet, faced black.

BELFAST VOLUNTEER COMPANY, 6 April 1778 (Capt Brown) – Uniform: Blue, faced blue, laced hats.

BELFAST FIRST VOLUNTEER COMPANY, 17 March 1778 (Capt Waddel Cunningham) – Uniform: Scarlet, faced black.

BURROS VOLUNTEERS, 1779 (Col Kavanagh) – Uniform: Scarlet, faced black.

BURROS IN OSSORY RANGERS, 1 August 1779 (Capt Comdt James Stephens) – Uniform: Scarlet, faced black, silver epaulettes.

BUILDERS' CORPS, 4 November 1781

(Col Read) – Uniform: Blue, faced blue, edged scarlet.

CASTLEBAR INDEPENDENTS, 17 March 1770 (Col Patrick Randal M'Donald) – Uniform: Scarlet, faced deep green.

CASTLE MOUNT GARRET VOLUNTEERS, 1778 (Col D. G. Browne) – Uniform: Scarlet, faced deep green.

CALLAN UNION, 1 April 1779 (Capt Elliott) – Uniform: Green, edged white.

CARLOW ASSOCIATION, 1 September 1779 (Major Eustace) – Uniform: Scarlet, faced black.

CARRICKFERGUS COMPANY, 3 April 1779 (Capt Marriot Dalway) – Uniform: Scarlet, faced pea-green.

CASTLEDURROW LIGHT HORSE, August 1778 (Capt Richard Lawrenson) – Uniform: Green, edged white.

CASTLEDURROW VOLUNTEERS, 1 July 1779 (Capt Bathorn) – Uniform: Green, edged white, silver lace.

CARLOW (COUNTY) LEGION, 1 September 1779 (Col J. Rochfort) – Uniform: Scarlet, faced lemon colour.

CLANRICARDE BRIGADE, June 1782 (Major D'Arcy) – Uniform: Scarlet, faced blue.

CLANE RANGERS, September 1779 (Capt Michael Aylmer) – Uniform: Scarlet, faced white.

CONSTITUTION REGIMENT (CO DOWN), (Capt Ford) – Uniform: Scarlet, faced yellow.

DOWN FIRST REGIMENT (2ND BATTALION, (Col Stewart) – Uniform: Blue, faced orange.

DROGHEDA ASSOCIATION, 1777 (Col Mead Ogle) – Uniform: Scarlet, faced pomona green, gold laced hats.

DUBLIN VOLUNTEERS, 6 October 1778 (Col Duke of Leinster) – Uniform: Blue, faced blue, edged scarlet, yellow buttons.

DUBLIN (COUNTY) LIGHT DRAGOONS, August 1779 (Col Rt Hon Luke Gardiner) – Uniform: Scarlet, faced black.

DUBLIN INDEPENDENT VOLUNTEERS, 24 April 1780 (Col Henry Grattan) – Uniform: Scarlet, faced dark green.

DULEEK LIGHT COMPANY, July 1778 (Capt Thomas Trotter) – Uniform: Scarlet, faced black.

DUNKERRIN VOLUNTEERS, 20 June 1779 (Col J. F. Rolleston) – Uniform: Scarlet, faced black.

DUNLAVIN LIGHT DRAGOONS, 1777 (Col M. Saunders) – Uniform: White, faced black, silver lace.

DUNMORE RANGERS, August 1779

(Col Sir Robert Staples, Bt) – Uniform: Green, edged white.

DUNDALK HORSE, (I. W. Foster, Esq) – Uniform: Scarlet, faced green.

DUNGIVEN BATTALION, 14 June 1778 (Major Thomas Bond) – Uniform: Scarlet, faced black.

ECHLIN VALE VOLUNTEERS, 19 October 1778 (Capt Charles Echlin) – Uniform: Scarlet, faced white.

EDENDERRY UNION, 1 May 1777 (Capt Shaw Cartland) – Uniform: Scarlet, faced black.

EDGEWORTHSTOWN BATTALION, 1779 (Col Sir W. G. Newcomen, Bt) – Uniform: Blue, faced scarlet.

ENGLISH RANGERS, 29 August 1779 (Major Thomas Berry) – Uniform: Scarlet, faced black, silver epaulettes.

EYRECOURT BUFFS, 1 June 1779 (Col Giles Eyre) – Uniform: Scarlet, faced buff, gold epaulettes.

INDEPENDENT ENNISKILLENERS, (Capt James Armstrong) – Uniform: Scarlet, faced black.

FARTULLAGH RANGERS, 1 October 1779 (Col Rochfort Hume) – Uniform: Scarlet, faced blue.

FINEA INDEPENDENTS, 1 May 1779 (Col Coyne Nugent) – Uniform: Scarlet, faced blue.

FINGAL LIGHT DRAGOONS, 27 June 1783 (Capt Thomas Baker) – Uniform: Scarlet, faced white.

FRENCH PARK LIGHT HORSE, June 1779 (Lt-Col Edward M'Dermott) – Uniform: Scarlet, faced black, edged white, gold lace.

GLENBOY AND KILLEMAT REGIMENT, 1 August 1779 (Col Cullen) – Uniform: Scarlet, faced blue, silver lace.

GLIN ROYAL ARTILLERY, April 1776 (Col J. Fitzgerald, Knight of Glin) – Uniform: Blue, faced blue, scarlet cuffs and capes, gold lace.

GLORIOUS MEMORY BATTALION, 1780 (Col T. Morris Jones) – Uniform: Scarlet, faced grass green.

GOLDSMITHS' CORPS, 17 March 1779 (Capt Bejamin O'Brien) – Uniform: Blue, faced scarlet, gold lace.

GRAIGUE (QC) VOLUNTEERS, 1 May 1779 (Col B. Bagnal) – Uniform: Blue, faced scarlet, silver lace.

GRANARD INFANTRY UNION BRIGADE, 1 May 1782 (Capt C. E. Hamilton) – Uniform: Scarlet, faced blue.

FIRST VOLUNTEERS OF IRELAND, 1 July 1766 (Col Sir Vesey Colclough, Bt) – Uniform: Scarlet, faced blue.

IRISH BRIGADE, 5 June 1782 (Capt Charles Abbott) – Uniform: Scarlet, faced grass green, silver lace.

KELL'S ASSOCIATION, 1 November 1779 (Lt-Col Benjamin Morris) – Uniform: Scarlet, faced green.

KILE VOLUNTEERS, 1 August 1779 (Col Charles White) – Uniform: Scarlet, faced blue, silver lace.

KILCULLEN RANGERS, September 1779 (Capt Keating) – Uniform: Scarlet, faced white.

KILKENNY RANGERS, 2 January 1770 (Col Mossom) – Uniform: Green with silver lace.

KILKENNY VOLUNTEERS, 10 June 1779 (Col Thomas Butler) – Uniform: Blue, faced scarlet, gold lace.

Miniature by Buck of an officer, thought to be in the uniform of the Royal Irish Artillery c1800. Uniform blue, facings scarlet, gilt shoulder-belt plate of Harp and Crown.
CHRISTIE'S

LAWYERS' CORPS, April 1779 (Col Townley Patten Filgate) – Uniform: Scarlet, faced blue, gold lace.

LARNE INDEPENDENTS, April 1782 (Capt White) – Uniform: Scarlet, faced blue.

LEAP INDEPENDENTS, 17 March 1780 (Col Jonathan Darby) – Uniform: Blue, faced blue, edged white.

LIBERTY VOLUNTEERS, July 1779 (Col Sir Edward Newenham) – Uniform: Scarlet, faced pea-green.

LIMAVADY BATTALION, 7 November 1777 (Col James Boyle) – Uniform: Scarlet, faced black.

LINEY VOLUNTEERS, 1778 (Major George Dodwell) – Uniform: Scarlet, faced blue.

LISBURNE FUSILIERS, (Lt John Kenby) – Uniform: Scarlet, faced blue.

LONDONDERRY FUZILEERS, 14 June 1778 (Lt A. Scott) – Uniform: Scarlet, faced blue.

LONGFORD LIGHT HORSE, 1779 (Col H. Nisbitt) – Uniform: Buff, faced black.

LOWTHERSTOWN, ETC, INDEPENDENT VOLUNTEERS, 1779 (Col William Irvine) – Uniform: Scarlet, faced black.

MAGHERAFELT (FIRST) VOLUNTEERS, June 1773 (Capt A. Tracy) – Uniform: Scarlet, faced black.

MARYBOROUGH VOLUNTEERS, May 1776 (Col Sir J. Parnell, Bt) – Uniform: Scarlet, faced black.

MERCHANTS' CORPS, 9 June 1779 (Capt Theos Dixon) – Uniform: Scarlet, faced blue, gold lace.

MONIGHAN RANGERS, 10 January 1780 (Col William Forster) – Uniform: Scarlet, faced white.

MONASTEREVEN VOLUNTEERS, October 1778 (Capt Houlton Anderson) – Uniform: Scarlet, faced white.

MOTE LIGHT INFANTRY, 1778 (Col Sir H. Lynch Blosse, Bt) – Uniform: Scarlet, faced pea-green.

MOUNTAIN RANGERS, 15 August 1779 (Col Bernard) – Uniform: Scarlet, faced black.

NASS RANGERS, 10 December 1779 (Capt Comdt R. Neville) – Uniform: Scarlet, faced white.

NEW ROSS INDEPENDENTS, 17 November 1777 (Col B. Elliot) – Uniform: Scarlet, faced black.

OFFERLANE BLUES, 10 October 1773) Col Luke Flood) – Uniform: Scarlet, faced blue, silver lace.

ORIOR GRENADIERS, 13 September 1779 (Capt James Dawson) – Uniform: Scarlet, faced black.

OSSORY TRUE BLUES, 1 July 1779 (Col Edward Flood) – Uniform: Scarlet, edged blue.

PARSONTOWN LOYAL INDEPENDENTS, 15 February 1776 (Col Sir William Parsons, Bt) – Uniform: Scarlet, faced black, silver lace.

PORTARLINGTON INFANTRY, 18 September 1779 (Major Comdt W. H. Legrand) – Uniform: Scarlet, faced yellow, silver lace.

RAFORD BRIGADE (LIGHT CAVALRY), 26 December 1779 (Col Denis Daly) – Uniform: Scarlet, edged blue, gold lace.

RALPHSDALE LIGHT DRAGOONS, (Capt John Tandy) – Uniform: Scarlet, faced yellow.

RAPHOE BATTALION, 1 July 1778 (Lt-Col Nisbitt) – Uniform: Scarlet, faced blue.

RATHDOWN LIGHT DRAGOONS (CO DUBLIN), June 1779 (Col Sir John Allen Johnson, Bt) – Uniform: Scarlet,

Shoulder-belt plate – Bandon Union Yeomanry. Silver, 3¼in c1796.
CHRISTIE'S

faced black.

RATHDOWNY VOLUNTEERS, February 1776 (Col J. Palmer) – Uniform: Scarlet, faced white.

RATHANGAN UNION, 2 August 1782 (Capt William Montgomery) – Uniform: Scarlet, faced white.

ROCKINGHAM VOLUNTEERS, 7 September 1779 (Col Nixon) – Uniform: Blue, faced blue, edged scarlet, yellow buttons.

ROSANALLIS VOLUNTEERS, 1 July 1774 (Col Richard Croasdale) – Uniform: Scarlet, faced blue, silver lace.

ROSCOMMON INDEPENDENT FORRESTERS, 1 May 1779 (Col R. Waller) – Uniform: Scarlet, faced green.

ROSS UNION RANGERS, 1 August 1779 (Col Drake) – Uniform: Scarlet, faced green.

ROSS VOLUNTEER GUARDS, 20 September 1779 (Capt-Lt H. T. Houghton) – Uniform: Scarlet, faced black.

ROXBOROUGH VOLUNTEERS, 1777 (Col William Perse) – Uniform: Scarlet, faced blue, silver epaulettes.

ROYAL 1ST REGIMENT (CO ANTRIM), (Major A. M'Manus) – Uniform: Scarlet, faced blue, gold lace.

SLIGO LOYAL VOLUNTEERS, 25 May 1779 (Lt-Col Ormsby) – Uniform: Scarlet, faced white.

SOCIETY VOLUNTEERS OF DERRY, 17 March 1782 (Capt William Moore) – Uniform: Scarlet, faced blue.

STRADBALLY VOLUNTEERS, 12 October 1779 (Col Thomas Cosby) – Uniform: Scarlet, faced blue, silver lace.

STROKESTOWN LIGHT HORSE, November 1779 (Major Gilbert Conry) – Uniform: Scarlet, faced yellow.

TALBOTSTOWN INVINCIBLES, December 1780 (Col Nicholas Westby) – Uniform: Scarlet, faced deep green.

TRIM INFANTRY, 12 July 1779 (Capt W. H. Finlay) – Uniform: Scarlet, faced black.

TULLAMORE TRUE BLUE RANGERS, 28 October 1778 (Col Charles William Bury) – Uniform: Scarlet, faced blue, silver lace.

TULLOW RANGERS, 10 August 1778 (Capt Whelan) – Uniform: Scarlet, faced black, white buttons.

TULLY ASH REAL VOLUNTEERS, 15 October 1783 (Col J. Dawson) – Uniform: Scarlet, faced black, silver lace.

TYRREL'S PASS VOLUNTEERS, 1776 (Capt Hon Robert Moore) – Uniform: Grey, faced scarlet, silver lace.

TYRONE FIRST REGIMENT, July 1780 (Col James Stewart) – Uniform: Scarlet, faced deep blue.

ULSTER VOLUNTEER TRUE BLUE BATTALION, 3 September 1779 (Major Robert Barden) – Uniform: Blue, faced scarlet.

ULSTER (FIRST) REGIMENT, (Col Earl of Charlemont) – Uniform: Scarlet, faced white.

ULSTER (FOURTH) REGIMENT, (Col R. M'Clintock) – Uniform: Scarlet, faced blue.

ULSTER REGIMENT ARTILLERY, (Capt Thomas Ward) – Uniform: Blue, faced scarlet.

UNION LIGHT DRAGOONS (CO MEATH), (Capt G. Lucas Nugent) – Uniform: Scarlet, faced green.

UNION LIGHT DRAGOONS (CITY OF DUBLIN), 12 September 1780 (Capt Comdt R. Cornwall) – Uniform: Scarlet, faced green.

Officer's shoulder-belt plate. 1st Regt Royal Dublin Volunteers inscribed 1796.

UPPER CROSS AND COOLOCK INDEPENDENT VOLUNTEERS, October 1779 – Uniform: Scarlet, faced black.

WATERFORD ROYAL BATTALION, 25 April 1779 (Major William Alcock) – Uniform: Scarlet, faced blue.

WEXFORD INDEPENDENT LIGHT DRAGOONS, autumn of 1775 (Col John Beauman) – Uniform: Scarlet, faced royal blue.

WEXFORD INDEPENDENT VOLUNTEERS, 4 October 1779 (Capt and Adjt Miller Clifford) – Uniform: Scarlet, faced black.

WICKLOW FORRESTERS, 1 July 1779 (Col Samuel Hayes) – Uniform: Scarlet, faced light blue.

WICKLOW ASSOCIATION ARTILLERY, (Thomas Montgomery Blair, Esq) – Uniform: Blue, faced scarlet.

WILLSBOROUGH VOLUNTEERS, October 1779 (Col Thomas Willis) – Uniform: Dark green, edged white.

---

[1] Presumably means brass.
[2] MacNevin gives: White jackets, edged red.
[3] Colonel Wm Townsend Gunn, in MacNevin's list.
[4] This heading is left out of Day's list.
[5] Dated 28 June 1779, in MacNevin.
[6] Included in previous county in Day's list.
[7] Faced buff (MacNevin).
[8] Dated 13 June 1778, in MacNevin.
[9] Faced black (MacNevin).
[10] MacNevin gives their uniform to be: Scarlet, faced green.
[11] Faced red (MacNevin).
[12] Col Theobald Butler (MacNevin).
[13] Faced red (MacNevin).
[14] MacNevin says: Scarlet, faced green.

EARLY AND DISBANDED REGIMENTS

Royal Irish Artillery

The story of artillery in Ireland really begins in 1756, although there had been a 'traine of artillery of Ireland' recorded as early as 1687. The Royal Regiment of Artillery, Woolwich, sent over a captain and a small detachment of NCOs and men to Dublin in 1755, in order to establish a permanent Company of Artillery in Ireland. This small body was reinforced in 1756 by a major to command, and a further sixty or so NCOs and men. From these small beginnings the Royal Irish Artillery was firmly established and continued to serve, both in Ireland and overseas, until 1801. The officer sent over in 1755 was Captain John Stratton, who remained with the corps throughout its entire history, by 1801 was Colonel commanding the 7th Battalion, and a Brevet General.

There was an expansion to six companies in 1778, brought about by the threat of invasion, whilst at the same time men were sent to man permanent coastal fortifications. The manning of these forts was increased in 1796 by 'additional gunners' from the Irish militia regiments, although the coastline presented an unlimited number of bays and anchorages which made absolute defence by coastal batteries an almost impossible undertaking. Reliance was placed upon the Royal Navy being able to deal with any invasion force at sea.

One invasion fleet in September 1798 was effectively destroyed at sea, only two ships escaping back to France in October. However, another invasion force of four frigates successfully evaded the British fleet and landed on 22 August at Killala Bay, Co Mayo, where there was no coastal fortification. This force, under the French General Humbert, after an initial success at Castlebar, was eventually destroyed, with remnants surrendering to General Cornwallis after the Battle at Ballinamuck on 8 September 1798.

The Royal Irish Artillery, after 46 years, was disbanded in 1801, and the coastal defence became the responsibility of the Royal Artillery.[1]

---

[1] Articles in the *Irish Sword* – Vol XI 1973/4 by F. Forde and Vol XVI 1986 by H. Waller. *The History of Coast Artillery in the British Army* by Col K. W. Maurice-Jones, DSC, late RA, pub RA Institution, 1959.

Painting of an officer c*1805. Signed and dated Dighton 1809.*
M. CANE

4th (Royal Irish) Dragoon Guards

This fine old regiment of 'Horse' dates back to 1685, the nucleus being a troop of Cuirassiers raised in the north of England by the Earl of Arran and popularly known as the Earl of Arran's Cuirassiers, although officially, the 6th Horse. In 1690 the old 5th Horse was disbanded in Ireland, and the 6th was then renumbered 5th. The first uniform was scarlet with white facings and silver lace. The regiment was placed on the Irish Establishment in 1746 with yet another change of title: the 1st Horse or the Blue Irish Horse, blue from the pale blue facings, later changed to dark blue facings in 1768-9. At this time the regiment was ordered to recruit in Ireland, the ranks therefore entirely Irish.

Relics from this period are of course extremely rare, but the National Museum in Dublin has a sword of the 1st Regiment of Horse. On the blade is the inscription '1st Reg Horse' and the name Harvey, the latter thought to refer to Samuel Harvey, sword cutler of High Street, Birmingham.[1]

The artist David Morier selected the mounted drummer for one of his subjects in 1751, no doubt because of the special richness of apparel, and also the horse furniture and drum banners. The Royal Warrant of 1st July 1751 authorised the Clothing of Drummers, Trumpeters and Hautbois as follows:

Colour, facing and lining of the coats – pale blue with red
Colour of waistcoats and breeches – red
Colours of the lace on the clothes of the drummers,
trumpeters, etc – white, with a red stripe.

The coat of red, white and blue carried the Crown and royal GR on the front and the girdle was of silver with two blue stripes running through. The drum banners of light blue with silver fringe top and bottom, with a circular centre-piece of crimson with the monogram in silver lettering – H, this centre-piece surrounded by a wreath of roses and thistles; the drum horse, a grey.[2]

The title changed in February 1788 to the 4th Dragoon Guards, followed a few months later with the addition of the words 'Royal Irish', granted in recognition of long service in Ireland.

In 1811 six troops of the regiment joined the army of Lord Wellington in the Peninsula, although this was not its first active service. From 1691-97 the 5th Horse had served with the Allied army on the continent – Flanders, Steenkirk, the Battle of Landen and at the Siege of Namur.

The regiment's first official battle honour 'Peninsula' was awarded for the two years on campaign in Spain and Portugal, having taken part in the sieges of Ciudad Rodrigo and Badajos in 1812. The defeat of the French at Llerna saw the conclusion of fighting for the 4th, who then returned to Portugal, and was ordered home in 1813 having lost 239 men and more than 400 horses during the campaign.

For the next 40 years the regiment was quartered in various stations in England, Scotland and Ireland. Duties ranged from suppressing riots at

Sheffield, Leeds and Durham, as well as a jail riot at Ayr, and 'aid to the civil power' at Paisley, Cahir, Salford and Preston. There were occasions however when the mere threat of the presence of a troop or two of cavalry, or Yeomanry Cavalry, would be sufficient to deter rioters. In 1839, for example, Charist riots occurred in Birmingham, and so much damage was done to property that an appeal was made by the citizens for protection, when renewed rioting was threatened. A squadron of the 4th Dragoon Guards was sent and the mob was dispersed without bloodshed or damage. Similarly in 1848 at Nottingham much trouble was expected from renewed Charist activities, and the 4th Dragoon Guards and South Notts Yeomanry Cavalry were warned for duty, but owing to the presence of the military the mob dispersed without trouble.[3]

The regiment, after service in Ireland in the 1830s, returned to England and was able to provide guards at the Royal Pavilion at Brighton for King William IV and Queen Adelaide, and in 1838 attended the Coronation of the new Queen. Queen Victoria was graciously pleased to approve the adoption of the Harp and Crown in addition to the Order of St Patrick, with the motto 'Quis Separabit', on standards and appointments.

There are many fine prints and paintings of the regiment showing uniform changes during the 1830s and 1840s. A particularly fine series of paintings was made between the years 1847 and 1850 by the Ferneleys, senior and junior, both working from Melton Mowbray, these paintings now in the possession of the present regiment. All are studies showing the correct uniform of the period. The helmet, introduced in 1847, is the Albert pattern, gilt or brass with black plume, single-breasted scarlet coatee, shoulder scales, white belts, blue overall with red stripes, (the

Left. Miniature painting of Surgeon Robert Pyper MD, 4th (or Royal Irish) Regiment of Dragoon Guards. Army 30 January 1800, Surgeon 3 September 1812 to 3 August 1826.

Portrait of an officer in dismounted review order c1820. Scarlet coatee, dark blue collar, silver lace, gold sash under belt, gold waistbelt plate with silver cypher.
PHILLIPS

shoulder-belts and overalls stripes – gold, or yellow for review), and officers have the black leather sabretache with star badge mounted upon it. One particularly interesting study shows the regiment preparing for the march in the town centre of Devizes, 1847-8. The officers have just emerged from an inn and the regiment is ready to march off, the band is in the foreground. All bandsmen have scarlet helmet plumes and yellow stripes on overalls. The drummer is a bearded man, the drum-horse a grey. It would appear that a design showing a Royal coat of arms on a red centre and a harp in gold is painted on the shell of the drum instead of an actual drum banner.

The 4th Dragoon Guards have had very little written about them, probably due to the fact that the regiment had seen little active service, and spent nearly 100 years in Ireland for most of the 18th century. (The very fine history eventually published in 1982 was well worth waiting for, dealing in the most comprehensive manner with the 4th and 7th Dragoon Guards and the combined regiment of 1922.)[4] One period of history and campaign which was well recorded however was that of 1854-56, the 4th Dragoon Guards in the Crimean War, thanks to the letters and diaries of its Commanding Officer during that period, Lt-Col E. C. Hodge.[5] Hodge was not the usual type of heavy cavalry commander, small in statute, a bachelor without means whose entire capital was tied up in the value of his commission and who was forced to request a loan of £100 from an uncle in order to purchase kit for campaigning. Furthermore, unlike the average cavalry officer of the day, he was conscientious and interested in his profession. He had a poor opinion of most of his own officers and did not approve of his second in command, Major William Forrest. In the two or three months before leaving for the Crimea he had much to do, mainly to see that his regiment was well mounted and to secure fresh horses as well as make sure that many of the old 'heavy' cavalrymen of 13 and 14 stone weight were transferred.

The scene at Dublin when the regiment left on 2 June 1854 can be visualised from a painting by an unknown artist who has managed to capture so well the bustle, excitement and even sadness of the occasion. (There is one serious error in the picture concerning dress. The helmets are shown in the painting with white plumes whereas at this time they were black, except of course for the band and trumpeters. These are shown correctly, as red.)[6]

Hodge's diaries chronicle the voyage to the East and the privations and hardships of the campaign. His entry concerning the all-important charge of the Heavy Brigade on 25 October 1854, including the role of his own regiment, is brief:

> 'a large body of cavalry came into the plain and were charged by the Greys and the Inniskillings. We were in reserve, and I brought forward our left and charged these cavalry in flank. The Greys were a little in confusion and retiring when our charge settled the business. We completely routed the hussars and cossacks, and drove them back.'

A fuller account is given by an eyewitness, Col F. A. Whinyates of the Royal Horse Artillery:

> 'The Inniskilling squadron moved almost simultaneously with the Greys, followed in quick succession by the leading squadron 5th Dragoon Guards and the second squadrons of the Greys and 5th Dragoon Guards. Next the detached squadron Inniskillings, keeping perfect dressing, tore in at a great pace on to the Russian left flank, and took them on their bridle hands with

Bearskin crested helmet c1822-34. Black glazed skull and peak, ornamentation including laurel leaves, gilt, as are scales and lions' heads.

great effect. The going was good and slightly uphill, and as the six squadrons drove deep into the solid mass of Russians, numbers of the latter on foot and some loose horses appeared making off to their left. The two squadrons 4th Dragoon Guards now came up level with the Russian right flank, wheeled into line and charged, followed immediately by both squadrons of the Royals, who came in against the overlapping right front. The Russians, tormented beyond endurance and utterly unable to make head against their aggressors, broke away to their left and tried to rally. They were spread over acres of ground. At once Brandling (Capt J. J. Brandling 'C' Troop RHA) advanced, broke them up with the fire of his guns, and they retreated over the ridge. In eight minutes all was over and a few minutes afterwards the Heavies looked as quiet and formidable as if they had never been engaged.'[7]

Prior to the charge however a curious circumstance arose which, on the one hand had paid a high compliment to Col Hodge from Lord Raglan, and yet caused him acute embarrassment, as it reflected discredit on one of his best friends – Brig-Gen Scarlett. Scarlett had commanded the 5th Dragoon Guards and was duly promoted to Brigadier-General in command of the Heavy Brigade, so Major T. Le Marchant, (Lt-Col from 14 June 1854) was promoted to command of the regiment. He was the son of Maj-Gen J. A. Le Marchant, a distinguished soldier and cavalry General who was killed at Salamanca. Sadly the son's record was disgraceful, he had paid little attention to the welfare of his regiment and actually deserted and quit the Crimea in August 1854. At about the same time as many as 90 men were down with cholera, including some officers also stricken, so the 5th Dragoon Guards were in sad condition. It was then that Lord Raglan ordered that the 5th be attached to the 4th. For the short period before the 5th recovered, the hosts did all in their power to make life tolerable, went unasked to the horse-lines and took on two, or even three horses and saddlery, as well as offering whatever facilities they could for the comfort of their unfortunate guests. It was at this time that Col Hodges acquired the 'title' of 'Commander of the 9th – (4th plus 5th)'. He eventually brought his regiment home with its reputation, and his own,

Sabretaches, full dress and undress patterns, together with dress pouch, all c1834-55.

IV (or Royal Irish) Dragoon Guards, c1834. Print in the Spooner-Eschäuzier Small oblong series, Plate No 7.
THE PARKER GALLERY

Plate for 1822-34 helmet.

enhanced. He continued in the army, becoming a full General before his death, and Colonel of the Regiment from 1874.

Roger Fenton took numerous photographs of the 4th Dragoon Guards during their time in the Crimea,[9] several where named officers appear including one group taken at the entrance of Fenton's marquee, which includes Col Hodge, his Adjutant Capt D. P. Webb and Capt F. R. Forster, whilst another photograph shows Capt Webb outside his own hut. One of Fenton's most well-known pictures is the posed group of the 4th at ease outside a ramshackle hut, and includes two French Zouaves and a British lady. She was Mrs Rogers, wife of a private of the regiment, whose duties included providing food and washing clothes, and who was greatly admired by all ranks. An extract from Col Hodge's diary dated 2 June 1855 reads:

'I have just been informed that a regular official application has been this day sent in by Mrs Duberly of the 8th (Hussars) signed by Col Shewell, applying for the Crimean Medal and clasps for Balaklava and Inkerman. I rather think that Parlby refuses to forward it, but if she gets it I will apply for one for Mrs Rogers who deserves it ten times more than half the men who will get it.'

The Marquess of Anglesey includes in his book a Fenton photograph of Col Hodge's hut (which he had to share with Major Forrest, his second in command, and Forrest's wife), which includes part of the camp of the 4th Dragoon Guards. On the same page as the photograph is

Officer and trumpeter, c1851 by J. Ferneley, Jnr. Painting 21½" × 31", showing black helmet plume, horse throat-plume and black sheepskin saddle cover. Officers' undress sabretache with the gilt star. Officer has red stripe on overalls and the red valise end has lettering $\frac{4}{DG}$ in yellow/gold thread.
AMOT

a reproduction of a watercolour by Richard Simkin of that same hut and scene, obviously based on the photograph and no doubt commissioned by a regimental officer, possibly Col Hodge himself, who would have supplied the detail.

The next active service took place in 1882 when the regiment formed part of the Cavalry Division for Egypt, commanded by Maj-Gen Drury Lowe and consisting of a composite regiment of Household Cavalry, the 4th and 7th Dragoon Guards. It was a short and successful campaign, although the heat, dust and desert conditions made life hard for both horses and men, the former often having to carry a weight of about 18 stone.

On 25 August the regiment, commanded by Lt-Col T. S. Shaw-Hellier, was ordered to intercept a train and cut the railway line. At a steady trot the regiment kept up with the train but found a strong body of enemy cavalry on their flank and came under their fire, whilst the enemy intention was to charge, but when 40 yards away thought better of it and bolted. The train had got away and the Dragoons' horses were too exhausted for further pursuit, so instead an Egyptian camp, full of the most valuable stores, was captured and held until the arrival of the Brigade. In September the regiment took part in the pursuit after the Battle of Tel-el-Kebir, followed by a forced march of 48 hours' duration to reach Cairo before the retreating enemy.

Home once again on 21 October 1882, to be stationed at Brighton, and to be fêted as returning heroes, the whole regiment was wined and dined at the Dome of the Royal Pavilion. Then in 1884 the regiment was called upon to provide a contingent of about 50 all ranks for the Heavy Division of the Camel Corps. An example of the conduct shown whilst in action comes from a cutting from a Brighton newspaper:

'Private Joseph Steel showed great determination and gallantry in action at Abu Klea, when very severely wounded in the neck he was seen to seize his rifle and commence fighting again, until he was knocked down a second time. When placed under the care of the Army Hospital Corps he asked to be allowed to get into the fight again.'[10]

The regiment moved from Brighton to Ireland for a few years, then back to Aldershot in 1892. During this time it was necessary to replace the old drum banners which carried the solitary battle-honour

Senior NCOs, Aldershot 1868. These NCOs wear the scarlet stable jacket, blue pill-box cap with gold band, blue overalls with yellow broad stripe, the NCO seated on mat has the leathered overalls. The figure on chair, second from left, the RSM, has a four bar inverted chevron above right cuff and the embroidered badge on cuff is believed to be St Patrick's Star, the first pattern sleeve badge. Most of these NCOs have Crimean War medal ribbons.

Regimental Band, Aldershot 1868. The Bandmaster, Mr J. Arkell is seated in the centre, identifiable by the gold lace edging at front of stable jacket and he holds his baton in right hand. He was originally a bandsman in the regiment and was eventually appointed Bandmaster after attending Kneller Hall. He held the appointment from 1864-70. The Trumpet-Major leans against the wall at left of group, he has a four bar chevron with crossed trumpets and crown above. The drum banners are much worn, blue with silver embroidered with St Patrick's Star, crown and 'Peninsula' honour above and title scrolls below.

'Peninsula' for a new and richly embroidered pair, with battle-honour scrolls for 'Peninsula', 'Balaklava', 'Sevastopol', 'Egypt 1882' and 'Tel-el-Kebir'.

The regiment embarked for its first tour of duty in India on 12 September 1894, and was stationed at Rawalpindi. That fine old service Journal, the *Navy & Army Illustrated*, for December 1897 has a good photograph showing soldiers of the regiment encamped in the vicinity of one of the frontier forts, one garrisoned by the Khyber Rifles. An interesting feature is that the tents of the Dragoon Guards had been thatched indicating, it is suggested, a long stay. Whilst on frontier patrol in October 1897 Capt T. F. Newcombe-Jones and Cpl Walton and two horses were shot by tribesmen who then disappeared into the hills with no pursuit possible.

The tour of Indian duty lasted until 1906 so the regiment missed the South Africa War entirely. It is fascinating to see how individual soldiers managed to ensure a presence wherever there was any fighting or excitement. Thus we find that the special artist of the *Illustrated London News*, Mr John Schönberg, sending a drawing for the edition of 1 December 1900, showing two important individuals of the Indian Railway Section who accompanied the China Expedition, one of them a Sgt R. White of the 4th Dragoon Guards. The artist clearly shows the brass numerals IVDG on his steel shoulder-chains and the silver St Patrick's star badge worn above the chevrons, this badge having been worn by sergeants and above, certainly from the 1880s but quite possibly well before.

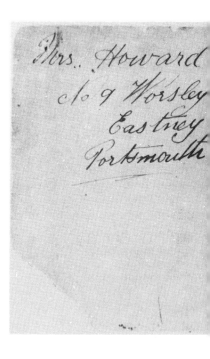

An interesting photograph dated February 1897. A cabinet photograph taken by a Southsea photographer of a private in walking-out dress. This soldier, possibly about to join a draft to the regiment in India, has presumably sent his picture through the post to a lady in Portsmouth, just as it was, without envelope or stamp but having written the address on the reverse side, incurring 2d to be paid instead of the normal 1d postage.

The Drum Horse, Rawalpindi, c1895. Beautifully turned out horse and rider with new drum banners.

During the Indian period the white tropical helmet was worn, mostly with hot-weather white uniform and also with scarlet full dress, but what is unusual is that trumpeters had also worn the white hair plume on the white helmet. Whilst still in India in 1904, a tailor's book describes the forage cap available for officers as dark blue with blue velvet band, the velvet remaining until 18 January 1912 when blue cloth was substituted. The silver cap badge and gilt struck buttons would cost 7s.3d, the cap complete £1.2s.1d, although a field officer's peak would cost 6s. 6d extra.

Having served in India since 1895 the regiment was nicknamed 'The Royal Pindi Dragoon Guards', but eventually sailed for South Africa in 1906. The South African tour was of comparatively short duration and uneventful, and the regiment left Middelburg, Cape Colony, and arrived at Southampton in November 1908 after 14 years abroad. Regimental Headquarters 'B' and 'C' Squadrons proceeded to Brighton and 'A' Squadron to Shrapnel Barracks, Woolwich.

One cannot pass over the Edwardian period without making particular reference to three officers whose names are not only remembered within the regiment but, for differing reasons, throughout the British Army. None were Irish, the first was a Belgian but had an Irish grandmother, his name – Adrian Carton de Wiart. To relate his career in detail would fill a book, indeed his memoirs *Happy Odyssey* makes exciting reading.[11] After joining as a trooper in Paget's Horse he went to South Africa at the outbreak of war there, and was later given a commission in the Imperial Light Horse, then in 1901 was offered a regular commission in the 4th Dragoon Guards, promoted Lieutenant in 1904 and Captain in 1910. During that year he accepted the Adjutantcy of the Royal Gloucestershire Hussars. Just before the war in 1914 he was in Somaliland with the Camel Corps. During fighting against the Dervishes he received a wound in the eye which had later to be removed. From then on he wore an eye patch. Early in 1915 he was back with his own regiment in France, was posted as second in command to the Loyal North Lancashire Regt, next given command of the 8th Bn Gloucestershire Regt, was eight times wounded and received awards for valour and outstanding service: VC, KBE, CB, CMG, DSO as well as Belgian decorations. During the Second World War he reached the rank of Lieutenant General, was Winston Churchill's military representative with General Chiang Kai-Shek, and appointed Colonel of the 4th/7th Dragoon Guards from 1940, a proud distinction he held until his death.

George Tom Molesworth Bridges came to the regiment on his promotion to Major in 1908. He was commissioned in the Royal Artillery in 1892; was serving in East Africa when the South African War broke out and joined the Imperial Light Horse as a Troop Leader. He served in Somaliland as a Special Service Officer 1902-4, was severely wounded and created a Companion of the Distinguished Service Order in 1904. (Actually whilst with the Imperial Light Horse he had been recommended for the Victoria Cross.) He was with his regiment in the early days of the First World War and was in the first cavalry encounters of the war. His actions during the Battle of Le Cateau on 26/27 August 1914 have become legend, made memorable by the poem of Sir Henry Newbolt – 'The Toy Band. A Song of the Great Retreat'. Major Bridges' squadron arrived at the town of St Quentin, where he found to his horror British infantrymen who had marched and marched to the point of near exhaustion when they could fight or retreat no longer, and were prepared to surrender. Bridges found a little toy shop where he bought all the penny whistles and toy drums they had, and arranged an impromptu drum and fife band. At its head he marched round the town, a Pied Piper act, when he put new heart into the demoralised infantry and marched them away from certain captivity. By 1917 he was a Lieutenant General and from 1928 until 1937, as Lt-Gen Sir Tom Bridges KCMG, CB, DSO, was appointed Colonel of the 5th Royal Inniskilling Dragoon Guards.

Robert J. L. Ogilby, a Scotsman, joined the regiment in India as 2nd Lieutenant on 10 January 1900, promoted Lieutenant 26 January 1901. He had to return home in 1904 when his father died and joined the 2nd Life Guards, so his service with the regiment at that stage was brief. He left his polo ponies to his great friend and brother officer Carton de Wiart. At the outbreak of war in 1914 he re-joined the 4th Dragoon Guards and he served with the regiment in France till 1916 when Field Marshal Sir Douglas Haig invited him to take over a battalion of London Scottish, which he commanded until the end of the war. He was awarded the DSO (*London Gazette* 1 January 1918) and Bar (7 November 1918), also Belgian Croix-de-Guerre. In 1954 he founded the Army Museums Ogilby Trust; objectives to preserve the regimental history and traditions of the British Army and to assist regimental museums to equip, maintain and add to their collections. A Robert Ogilby Trust was also formed in 1964. Not only did he remain a faithful friend to all the regiments in which he had served, but has left a permanent organisation for the furtherance of study of British Army history.

The regiment remained at Brighton until 1911 when it moved to Tidworth, the squadron then at Woolwich joining the remainder. Full dress was of course much in evidence during the years at both these stations and so the Dress Regulations of 1911 are provided here. These also serve, in the main, for the 6th Inniskilling Dragoons, uniform differences and badges etc being noted:

Trumpeter Donovan, 4th Dragoon Guards, Delhi Durbar 1902. A State trumpeter was selected from each British cavalry regiment in India, also some from Indian cavalry regiments.

DRAGOON GUARDS AND DRAGOONS
FULL DRESS

Helmet Gilt or gilding metal, bound round the edge. At the top a crosspiece base and a plume socket, 4in high from point of insertion in base. A laurel wreath above the front peak, and an oak-leaf band up the back. Plain burnished chain, 1in wide, mounted on black patent leather, lined with velvet and fastened on each side with a rose ornament. Furniture gilt or gilding metal.

A diamond-cut silver star in front; on the star in gilt or gilding metal, the garter pierced with the motto *Honi soit qui mal y pense* or an elliptical ring with the designation of the regiment. Within the garter or ring the regimental device or number. In the 6th Dragoon Guards the star has plain rays.

Helmet for 1st and 6th Dragoons Of the same pattern as for Dragoon Guards, but of white metal, with gilt or gilding metal oranments.

Plume Horsehair, of the colour stated below for each regiment. The plume rises 2in from point of insertion in socket, and falls as far as the bottom of the helmet. A rose at the top screwed on to the stem of the plume. Steel stem with screw and fly-nut. Colour of plume: white.

Helmet Foreign Service Abroad the white Wolseley helmet, with white pagri is worn instead of the home pattern headdress.

Tunic (except for the 6th Dragoon Guards – Carabiniers) Scarlet cloth; with collar and cuffs of the colour of the regimental facings; in the 1st (King's), 3rd (Prince of Wales's), 4th (Royal Irish), 5th (Princess Charlotte of Wales's), and 7th Dragoon Guards, of velvet; in the 2nd Dragoon Guards (Queen's Bays) and the 1st (Royal), 2nd (Royal Scots Greys), and 6th (Inniskilling), Dragoons, of

cloth. The collar ornamented with ¾in lace (1in for 2nd Dragoon Guards (Queen's Bays), and 1st (Royal) Dragoons, round the top. The cuffs 2in deep at the point and 1¼in at the back, edged with round-back gold cord forming a single Austrian knot, 7¾in deep, traced inside and out with gold Russia braid. Eight buttons in front, and two at the waist behind; a three pointed scarlet flap on each skirt behind, with three buttons, and edged with round-back gold cord, traced inside and out with gold Russia braid. The front edged with the same material and colour as the facings, and the skirts lined with white. Plaited flat gold shoulder cord, lined with scarlet; a small button at the top.

Tunic for and 6th Dragoon Guards   Blue cloth, edged all round, including the top and bottom of the collar, with round-back gold cord. Collar and pointed cuffs of white cloth. The collar laced within the cord, like that for other Dragoon Guards. The cuffs trimmed with an Austrian knot 7½in deep, traced inside and out with gold Russia braid. Eight buttons in front, and two at the waist behind. A three-pointed blue cloth flap on each skirt behind, with three buttons, and edged with round-back gold cord. Plaited flat gold shoulder cord, lined with blue; a small button at the top.

Lace   Gold, of regimental patterns.

Buttons and Badges

Trousers and Pantaloons   Blue cloth, with 1¾in yellow cloth stripes, white stripes in the 2nd and 6th Dragoon Guards (in the latter the stripe is double with a blue light in the centre); primrose in the 6th Dragoons.

Boots   Foot chains instead of foot-straps are worn in the 3rd Dragoon Guards.

Spurs   Steel.

Sword   Cavalry pattern.

Scabbard   Steel.

Sword belt   Web.

Sword Slings   Gold lace, 1in wide, morocco leather lining, and edging of the same colour as the facings, square wire gilt buckles, flat billets and gilt studs.

Girdle   Gold lace, not exceeding 2¼in wide (2½in in the 7th Dragoon Guards), morocco leather lining, edging of the colour of the facings.

Waist Plate   Gilt rectangular plate, with burnished rim.

Sword Knot   White leather strap with gold acorn. In the 7th Dragoon Guards, gold and black cord and acorn. In the 2nd Dragoons, gold cord with gold thistle. In the 6th Dragoons, gold and crimson cord and acorn.

Shoulder Belt   Gold lace, not less than 2¼in or more than 2½in in width (2in in the 6th Dragoon (Guards), with the same lining and edging as the sword slings; gilt buckle, tip, and slide of regimental pattern. In the 6th Dragoon Guards and 6th Dragoons the buckle, tip, and slide are of silver.

Pouch   Black leather, with gold embroidered edging round the top; solid silver flap, 7½in long and 2¾in deep, engraved round the edges. Silver loops and stud. Ornaments regimental pattern.

Gauntlets   White leather.

Great Coat   Universal pattern. Shoulder straps, collar and cuffs, edged with ⅛in yellow cloth.

Church Parade, Review Order, Brighton 1911. The band in the foreground, on the right the Bandmaster, Mr H. Dudley, who remained Bandmaster until amalgamation.

UNDRESS

Forage Cap   Universal pattern. Blue cloth with band and welts of the colour of the facings, except:

> 1st Royal Dragoons – Scarlet band and welts.
> 2nd Dragoons – White cloth band, vandyked, blue welts.

Badges according to regiment.

MESS DRESS

Mess Jacket   Scarlet cloth (6th Dragoon Guards, blue cloth) with roll collar and pointed cuffs of cloth the colour of the facings. Cuffs 6in deep at the points, and 2¾in behind, a 1in slit at the seam. Shoulder straps of cloth the same colour as the jacket, 1½in wide at the base, tapering to about 1in at the point; rounded points fastened with a button; the shoulder straps to be sewn in at the shoulder. Badges of rank in metal. No buttons on the front of the jacket, and no gold braid or piping. Collar badges worn on the lapel.

Mess Vest Scarlet. Open in front, no collar, fastened with four ½in mounted buttons.

Overalls As in full dress.

Boots Wellington, with box spurs.

Regiment	Jackets				
	Colour	Collar	Shoulder Straps	Cuffs	Vest
Fourth (Royal Irish) Dragoon Guards	Scarlet	Blue	Scarlet	Blue	Scarlet

Badges

On Buttons	On Collar of Tunic, Mess Jacket & Frock Coat	On Full Dress Head-dress	On Waist Plate	On the Pouch	On F.S. Helmet and on Forage Cap	On the Service Dress	
						On the Collar in Bronze	On the Cap in Bronze
The Star of the Order of St Patrick, with '4th (Royal Irish) Dragoon Guards' round the star.	In silver, the Star of the Order of St Patrick.	On the Garter star, in gilt or gilding metal, a circle inscribed *Quis separabit* MDCCLXXXIII, on a blue enamelled ground. Within the circle, on a white ground, the Cross of St Patrick in gold and red enamel. On the cross a shamrock leaf in green enamel, with a red enamelled Crown on each petal.	As for 1st Dragoon Guards, but with shamrock instead of oak-leaf wreath. No scroll and motto.	As for 1st Dragoon Guards.	As for collar, but larger, with gilt or gilding metal scroll on on the bottom of the star, inscribed '4th Royal Irish D. Guards'.	As for forage cap.	As for forage cap.

The regiment left Tidworth for France, landing at Boulogne on 16 August as part of the 2nd Cavalry Brigade of the Cavalry Division, with 9th Lancers and 18th Hussars, the same Brigade from Tidworth. For the first few months of warfare they were in the saddle in their proper role as cavalry, and the 4th Dragoon Guards have the distinction of making first contact with the enemy and firing the first shot of the war. The episode is an exciting one and is best described in a Regimental History:

'Early in the morning of 22 August, German patrols were seen on the Soignies road. Two troops of 'C' Squadron were dismounted ready to open fire while the other two troops, under Capt Hornby, drew swords ready to advance and pursue. About six German Uhlans (heavy cavalry) were seen coming down the road towards the ambush. At about 500 yards they must have sensed something, for they stopped and then started to retire slowly down the road. At this moment Cpl Thomas fired the first shot of the war for the British Army. Capt Hornby immediately charged after them with his two troops, and they galloped down the wide pavé road, which had tramlines along it and a ditch on either side. After a mile and a half they came upon the head of the leading German squadron, who turned and fled. At the bottom of a hill they caught them up and drove into them with a cheer and killed and captured about thirty. Capt Hornby was the first officer of the British Army to draw blood with his sword and was awarded a DSO. Many of the Germans tried to throw away their long lances and surrender. Finally the two troops were brought to a halt by rifle fire from dismounted troops deployed across the road. Major G. T. M. Bridges brought up the rest of the squadron in support and, having collected some carts for the prisoners, who had been dismounted, withdrew because the enemy fire was now developing and Major Bridges realised that he was up against the head of a large force. The squadron were given a rousing reception on their return, and the Brigadier issued this order: "The Brigadier desires to congratulate the 4th Dragoon

Warrant officers and sergeants, Cologne, 21 January 1919. The central figure seated, sixth from left as one looks at the group, is believed to be Major E. M. Dorman, DSO, MC. On his left Lieutenant L. E. Misa, Adjutant; RSM G. W. Woodland, DCM and Bandmaster Mr H. Dudley.

Guards on the spirited action of two troops of the squadron on reconnaissance which resulted in establishing the moral superiority of our cavalry from the first over the Germany cavalry.'"[12]

Years later Sgt E. Thomas, MM, gave a much fuller account in an article, illustrated with photographs, in a Journal published between the wars.[13]

(*Note*: Most authors writing about the early clashes of mounted cavalry in the First World War invariably describe the German cavalry as Uhlans. This description is often misleading, Uhlans (Lancers) represented only about one fifth of all German cavalry regiments, and were light cavalry, not heavy as stated in the history. In the case of the 4th Dragoon Guards on 22 August 1914 they came upon soldiers of the 4th Kürassier Regiment, one of the ten regiments of Prussian heavy cavalry, roughly corresponding to the British Household Cavalry. Another misconception, mainly perpetuated by artists and film producers, is to show First World War German aviators wearing the 'ulanka', the tunic worn by Lancer regiments. This was no doubt brought about by the fact that Jagdflieger Rittmeister Manfred von Richthofen, or the Red Baron, was originally a cavalry captain in the 1st Ulanen Regiment and was generally photographed in his Lancer undress or service dress uniform. German flyers in the early days wore the uniform of the regiment or corps, as did British officers in their khaki service dress with regimental badges. When uniform became a consideration in the new Royal Flying Corps, a tunic with a button-over plastron front, known as the 'maternity jacket' was one of the original garments introduced.)

During the remainder of the war the regiment was heavily involved in most actions and lost 72 officers and men killed, with very many more wounded. To recount all the acts of bravery and the battles fought before November 1918 is impossible to compress into a small space, but in the same way that it was first in action in 1914, so in December 1918 it was first over the Hohenzollern Bridge at Cologne as the first regiment of the British Army of Occupation.

Captain Carton de Wiart, DSO, was awarded the VC in 1916, the citation reading as follows:

> 'For most conspicuous bravery, coolness and determination during severe operations of a prolonged nature. It was in a great measure due to his dauntless courage and inspiring example that a serious reverse was averted. He displayed the utmost energy and courage in forcing our attack home. After three other battalion commanders had become casualties, he controlled their commands, and ensured that the ground won was maintained at all costs. He frequently exposed himself in the organisation of positions and supplies, passing unflinchingly through fire barrage of the most intense nature. His gallantry was inspiring to all.'
>
> *London Gazette*, 9 September 1916.

Ten NCOs and men of the regiment were awarded the DCM.

The battle-honours of the regiment during those four years are as follows: 'Mons'; 'Le Cateau'; 'Retreat from Mons'; 'Marne, 1914'; 'AISNE, 1914'; 'Messines, 1914'; 'Ypres, 1914, '15'; 'Somme, 1916, '18'; 'Cambrai, 1917, '18'; 'Pursuit to Mons'.

In 1919 the regiment returned to Ireland, went over to Tidworth in July and in 1921 sailed once again for India, but there were only three officers aboard who had sailed for France in 1914.

The Geddes Axe fell upon the regiment in April 1922 when, by Army Order No 133, an amalgamation with the 7th (Princess Royal's) Dragoon Guards was announced. The single squadron of the 7th, The Black Horse Squadron, sailed from England in September 1922 and joined the two squadrons of 4th Dragoon Guards at Trimulgherry on October 24, the new regiment to be known as the 4th/7th Dragoon Guards.

It will be recalled that as far back as 1746 the title 'Irish' was given to the regiment, and 'Royal Irish' from 1788, whilst in 1768 the composition was entirely Irish. The Order of St Patrick may possibly have been associated with the regiment since 1783, the date of institution of the Order, whilst the Harp and Crown was conferred by Queen Victoria after her Coronation in 1837. From about that time until 1914, however, the Irish presence began to decline. In 1844 the figure of 212 out of a total regimental strength of 360 is given, by 1857 182 out of 458 and in 1886 only 69 out of 461, whilst finally in 1914 there were only 39 out of 561.

It is not entirely surprising therefore that the 4th Dragoon Guards title of 'Royal Irish' was dropped from the new designation, and whilst 'Royal' was restored in 1936 (Army Order No 182) the Irish influences had gradually diminished. The St Patrick's Badge still remains and is worn on cap and collar and NCO's arm, but it is believed that St Patrick's Day celebrations no longer occur.

The last mounted parade was held in Edinburgh in August 1938, the whole scene captured by the artist Lionel Edwards, RI, in a magnificent

Trooper, 4th/7th Dragoon Guards, India 1927. This smart soldier wears khaki-drill service dress, winged breeches with buckskin knee-grips and khaki puttees, black ankle boots with spurs. His helmet has the regimental star badge at front and a white over black brush plume on left, the black to commemorate the 7th Dragoon Guards 'Black Horse'.

painting owned by the regiment. One of the little regimental distinctions of dress is the flash worn by all ranks in service dress upon the left sleeve at the shoulder. This is a black diamond, a chevron of old gold and two of maroon mounted upon it, the whole upon a larger diamond of black. This flash was introduced at the time of Dunkirk.

With the collapse of the Warsaw Pact in the early 1990's the Royal Armoured Corps' structure was radically changed with wholesale amalgamations which few regiments escaped. The 4th/7th Royal Dragoon Guards was no exception and, in 1992, they joined with the 5th Royal Inniskilling Dragoon Guards to form The Royal Dragoon Guards (see page 69) thereby, to some extent, reviving the Irish links.

[1] Full description and photograph supplied by G. A. Hayes-McCoy, MA, PhD, J.S.A.H.R. XXVIII p39.

[2] Many paintings of this drum-horse based on the original Morier, one by C. C. P. Lawson, *History as of the Uniforms of the British Army*. Vol II, 1941. Frontispiece in colour. Another reproduced in Tradition 1960s. Colour-plate by G. A. Embleton. Plate No 35, Edition No 20. A third by R. Simkin. R. Simkin's *Uniforms of the British Army* by W. Y. Carman, c1982. Colour-plates 26 and 28.

[3] *The Yeomanry as an Aid to the Civil Power*. Series of articles by Major O. Teichman, DSO, MC, TD, J.S.A.H.R., Vol XIX.

[4] *A History of the 4th/7th Royal Dragoon Guards and Their Predecessors 1685-1980* by J. M. Brereton. Pub by the Regiment, Catterick 1982.

[5] *Little Hodge*. Edited by The Marquess of Anglesey. Military Book Society 1971.

[6] Reproduced in colour, J.S.A.H.R. Vol LV p63.

[7] J.S.A.H.R. Vol XIX, p102.

[8] *Leaves from a Soldier's Notebook* by Sgt-Major H. Franks, 5th D.Gs. Originally printed 1904. Reprinted 1979. Mitre Publishing, Brightlingsea, Essex.

[9] Reproduced in – *Roger Fenton, Photographer of the Crimean War* by H. & A. Gernsheim, Secker & Warburg, London 1954 and *Crimea 1854-56* by Lawrence James. Hayes Kennedy 1981.

[10] Pasted on the back of a photograph in the author's possession.

[11] *Happy Odyssey*. The Memoirs of Lt-Gen Sir Adrian Carton-de-Wiart. Jonathan Cape 1950.

[12] *Short History of the 4th, 7th and 4th/7th Royal Dragoon Guards* by Major J. A. d'Avigdor-Goldsmid. Gale & Polden 1949.

[13] *I Was There*. Edited by Sir John Hamilton, 1930s. Issued in monthly parts.

THE REGULAR REGIMENTS ■ CAVALRY

5th (Royal Irish) Lancers

Some regiments, like some individual soldiers, are lucky, others not so fortunate, and amongst the less fortunate of cavalry regiments was the 5th (Royal Irish) Lancers.

It was raised in 1689 and fought at the Battle of the Boyne within its first year of existence, as well as fighting in many bloody encounters during those early years in Ireland. By 1702, As Ross's Dragoons, it was sent to the Low Countries and during its time with the Army under Marlborough, gained honours and distinctions and a fine regimental reputation. Subsequently there followed a period of 83 years' stagnation, scattered around Ireland in small troops and parties. The regiment in consequence fell into a state that can best be described as 'unfit for service' and suffered the ignominy of disbandment in 1799.

Re-raised in 1858, as a Lancer regiment commanded by a succession of capable officers, it proved its metal in various actions and battles during Queen Victoria's reign, in Egypt in 1884 and again in South Africa in 1899 made a name for itself by its brilliant cavalry charges. In India in the 1890s it was acclaimed to be, with justification, one of the best, if not the best, in British service. By 1907 and again in 1913 the wheel of fortune had turned in the wrong direction. On the earlier occasion a low point of regimental efficiency was reached and in 1913, along with the officers of two English cavalry regiments, a tug-of-loyalty occurred which the press called the 'Curragh Mutiny', although actually there was no such mutiny. Between 1914 and 1918 it fought and endured the miseries of warfare in France and Flanders and achieved a notable record of service during those years.

In 1921 it suffered once again total disbandment, its soldiers discharged or transferred to other regiments – then in April 1922 there was a change of thinking at the War Office and the 5th Lancers were re-formed at squadron strength, becoming the junior partner of the new 16th/5th Lancers. It serves to this day as an integral part of a Royal regiment, still proudly displaying the badge of the Harp and Crown.

5th Royal Dragoons of Ireland

Wynne's Dragoons was one of the five regiments raised by the Governor of Enniskillen in 1688-9, two of Dragoons and three of Foot. Although at this time these so-called regiments were little more than a rabble-in-arms, they could certainly fight. They were brought on to the establishment of the Regular Army on 1 January 1689, having received horses for the Dragoons, clothing, some arms and, more importantly, training. The regiments eventually emerged as Wynne's Inniskilling Dragoons – afterwards the 5th Royal Irish Dragoons; Cunningham's Inniskilling Dragoons – later 6th Inniskilling Dragoons; Hamilton's Inniskilling Foot; Lloyd's Inniskilling Foot; Tiffan's Inniskilling Foot – later 27th Inniskilling Fusiliers.

At the Battle of the Boyne, 1 July 1690, where Cunningham was

Captain Hon Clotworthy Rowley, 5th Dragoons. Captain 13 February 1792, Major 1776. Officers' waistcoats changed from buff to white 1768.
CHRISTIE'S

Drawing by George Merry showing uniform at disbandment 1799. White out of red plume in cocked hat, scarlet coat – two loops on each side of collar, silver lace and buttons, epaulettes on both shoulders.

killed, Wynne's Dragoons charged the enemy Horse with such vigour that they were themselves in trouble, having galloped too far in pursuit, but rallied and then routed the enemy's infantry. Further desperate fighting occurred during the unsuccessful sieges of Limerick and Athlone during August 1690. An extract from the official history will remind one of the contemporary scene in Northern Ireland today:

'The Grenadiers had now to fall back and regain the covered way, and for three hours did a sharp fight continue, in which the Irish women boldly joined, and when they failed to obtain more deadly missiles, threw stones and broken bottles. At length when the ammunition was spent, while the Irish fire increased, the troops were recalled from the covered way.'[1]

In 1702 six Troops sailed as reinforcementss for Marlborough's Army in Holland, and the other two Troops joined in 1704, the regiment then known as the Royal Dragoons of Ireland, a title conferred by Queen Anne in March that year. At Blenheim on 13 August the regiment was most 'hotly engaged'. During the battle the heavy cavalry and the Dragoons were obliged to make four or five separate charges, the Irish Dragoons suffering casualties, but also capturing three kettle-drums from the enemy. By order of the Duke of Marlborough these were to be carried to the head of the regiment. A curiosity connected with the Battle of Blenheim (which the French call Hochstet after the village of Hochstadt, near Blenheim), is to be found on an old uniform print. This depicts an officer of the 1790s, but in the top corner of the print is displayed a cavalry standard which belonged to the regiment. It is green, carries the Harp and Crown as central device and below a scroll, bearing the word 'Hochstet'. This print is dedicated to General Lord Rossmore, Colonel of the Regiment 1787-9, and was published in March 1800 after the regiment had been disbanded.[2]

Two years later at Ramillies the Irish and Scots Dragoons together captured the entire Regiment du Roi for which both regiments were granted the privilege of wearing Grenadier caps. As General Lunt points out, this method of rewarding a regiment, although an honour, nevertheless cost the government nothing and was of little material benefit to the ordinary soldier.[3] Wearing the Grenadier cap seems to have been a practice which fell into disuse in the Royal Irish Dragoons, although it is known that part of the regiment of Scots Greys wore the cap prior to Ramillies, and again afterwards. These battles were followed by Oudenarde and Malplaquet, the Royal Irish Dragoons fought in both and it has been said that the British cavalry and artillery under Marlborough were second to none.

In 1713 the Royal Irish Dragoons was placed on the Establishment of Ireland and was to be paid for by the revenues of that country. From then until 1799 there was a steady decline due to many varying factors. Although, as in 1744, the regiment sent a detachment for a review on Hounslow Heath, which seems to have gone well enough, most reports were unsatisfactory. In 1774 for example – 'Dress and discipline may be greatly improved.' Throughout the whole of the period up to the Irish Rebellion the regiment was split up in small detachments. Barrack accommodation, if any, was deplorable and troops were often billeted at public houses and on landowners, so there was little control by the officers. In spite of all the circumstances against them, in 1796 when a French invasion was threatened, the whole regiment assembled at Bantry Bay. It received an adverse report the following year but in May 1798, when there was open rebellion in the country, the conduct in general was good. However, the 'fifth column' of that time infiltrated whole regiments and some had enlisted in the ranks of the 5th Dragoons. Several subversives were duly discovered and executed, but the damage

Officers in India c1866. Photo shows most orders of dress. Three or four officers have the Mutiny medal from previous service with other regiments.

Top. First pattern of officers' lance-cap plate 1858-83. Plate gilt, separate silver mounts. Centre. Other ranks' lance-cap plate 1858-83. All one piece. Bottom, Other ranks' lance-cap plate 1883-6. Similar to first pattern but with additional scrolls with honours and title in four parts. Die struck, all in one piece.

was done. It was suggested that the regiment be brought back to England where any remaining Fenians could be dealt with, and the regiment restored to a good state, but King George thought otherwise and ordered total disbandment. The 5th Royal Irish Dragoons returned to England, and during the period from its return and actual disbandment was well behaved, but was disbanded as ordered at Chatham on 10 April 1799.

5th (Royal Irish) Lancers

After a lapse of 59 years the figure 5 returned to fill the gap in the Army List, when the 5th Dragoons were authorised to be re-raised, the authority signified in a General Order dated Horse Guards, 9 January 1858.

'His Royal Highness the General Commanding-in-Chief has much pleasure in communicating to the Army the Queen's Command to cancel the Adjutant General's letter dated April 1799 announcing the Royal determination of His late Majesty George the Third, to disband the 5th Royal Irish Regiment of Dragoons; that letter is cancelled accordingly.

'The Queen commands that the 5th Royal Irish Dragoons be restored to its place among the Cavalry Regiments of the line, and His Royal Highness feels assured that this mark of Her Majesty's grace and favour will be appreciated, and that the 5th Royal Irish Dragoons will emulate other regiments in discipline and loyalty, and vie with them in promoting the glory of the British Arms.

'By Order of His Royal Highness
The General Commanding-in-Chief
(Signed) G. A. Weatherall
Adjutant General'

The title in the Army List of 1858 was 5th (or Royal Irish Light) Dragoons (Lancers). Also restored was the badge 'The Harp and Crown' and motto *Quis Separabit*.

The new regiment was placed under the command of Lt-Col G. A. F. Sullivan from the Royal Scots Greys, with Major Robert Portal from the 4th Light Dragoons as second in command. The regimental officers appointed at the same time were 7 Captains, 9 Lieutenants and 5 Cornets, whilst in addition to the Paymaster, Surgeon and Veterinary Surgeon, there was a Lieutenant and Adjutant, E. F. Weaver from the Royal Dragoons and Quartermaster J. Addy from the Military Train. The officers were a mix – 11 from cavalry regiments, 11 from infantry regiments and 2 from the Military Train; it is interesting to note that the junior Lieutenant and all the Cornets came from the 8th Regiment of Foot. By May 1858 the rank and file numbered 485 Privates, 52 NCOs were transferred in from other regiments, and whilst there were a few of the men who had also transferred in, most were enlisted from recruiting depots in Ireland, England and Scotland. The average height of the men was 5ft 7in and most were lightweight. The horses all came from dealers in Ireland and were of mixed colours, but strong and well bred.

From the Curragh the regiment marched by squadrons from Newbridge to Dublin preparatory to embarkation for Liverpool, en route to Aldershot. A group photograph which was taken before leaving Newbridge shows ten officers and six NCOs in various orders of dress, the uniform described as similar to the 12th Lancers, but with a green plume for the lance cap, the green described as peacock green.

In March 1860 the regiment arrived at Aldershot and was duly inspected on the 12th by the Inspector General of Cavalry, Lord Cardigan, who gave a very favourable report and this was followed by an inspection of the Aldershot Cavalry Brigade by the Duke of Cambridge who is reported to have been 'hugely pleased with the appearance and discipline of the regiment'. Later that month an application was made that the Irish Harp be worn as a badge above the chevrons of NCOs, and this was duly granted on 2 April 1860. A studio portrait of a Sergeant-Major taken in the early 1860s shows this badge in wear on the right arm of his blue stable jacket, above the four chevrons and below the crown.

R. Ebsworth saw the regiment during its sojourn at Aldershot. He describes the lance then in use as the old ash-pole with steel guard, but also comments that the bamboo pole was substituted later. The bandmaster was a Mr Money from the 7th Dragoon Guards, and in the original band there were six Italians from the disbanded British-Italian-Legion.

In 1863 the regiment proceeded to Portsmouth to embark for India, travelling on three separate transports on 22, 25 and 27 July. Ten years were spent in the various cantonments before return home in November/December 1874. It was during the preceding year that officers took into use the black leather sabretache with the crossed lances badge mounted on the outer flap. The regiment at this time was commanded by Lt-Col W. Dunham Massy – a Tipperary man – known throughout the army as 'Redan' Massy. In 1855 whilst serving with his original regiment, the 19th Foot, he led the assault by the Grenadier Company on the Redan, and was so severely wounded was left on the field thought to be dead, but was taken prisoner by the Russians and subsequently rescued by the British. Although his condition was considered hopeless, he eventually pulled through and received the medal with clasp, Legion of Honour and Turkish medal. He was then associated with the 4th Dragoon Guards and Military Train, transferring from the Train as Captain, and was one of the original officers of the 5th Lancers. In 1896, as Lieutenant-General, he was appointed Colonel of the Regiment, which he had commanded from 1871 to 1879.

Prior to 1879 the Regimental Band made do with copper kettle-drums, the old original silver drums captured during Marlborough's campaign having been destroyed by fire at the Tower of London in 1841. Col Massy ordered new drums from George Potter & Co of Aldershot, fine instruments hammered out of sterling sheet-silver and weighing 960oz, regimental crests worked in relief upon the shells and the Irish Harp carved on the stands, whilst the names of the officers concerned with the purchase and presentation to the regiment were also engraved upon the shells. In 1880 Bandmaster A. Robinson transferred to the 3rd Dragoon Guards and Mr J. W. Wood was appointed in his place. It is interesting to record that Mr Wood's son, F. W. Wood, commenced his military and musical career in the band of the 5th Lancers, but after attending Kneller Hall and appointment as bandmaster to the 1st Bn York and Lancaster regimental band, he later went to the Scots Guards and became one of the outstanding Directors of Music in the British Army.

One or two interesting but minor dress changes took place in the 1870s. In March 1875 officers' dress lance caps were ordered to have cock's feathers for wear at leveés and in full dress parades in review order, but on other occasions a hair plume was to be worn. In the same year the leathered overalls went out and NCOs were ordered to wear the silver harp badge on the chevrons instead of above. In April 1882 the battle-honours won by the previous regiment, the 5th Dragoons, 'Blenheim', 'Ramillies', 'Oudenarde' and 'Malplaquet' were returned to the regiment, so the first pattern of lance cap plate introduced in 1858 was replaced in 1883 by one incorporating those honours.

The regiment was called upon in 1884 to furnish two officers and 43 other ranks to serve with the Heavy Divison of the Camel Corps, made up from the three regiments of Household Cavalry, 2nd, 4th and 5th Dragoon Guards, 1st and 2nd Dragoons and 5th and 16th Lancers. The soldiers wore khaki serge jumpers, cord breeches, puttees with ankle-boots and pith sun helmets, the 5th Lancers distinguished by the figure 5 and the letter L cut from red cloth and sewn to the top of the sleeve.

In the action at Abu Klea the Officer Commanding 5th Lancer detachment, Major L. Carmichael, and six of his soldiers were killed, Lt H. Costello and two soldiers wounded. 2151 Pte G. H. Austin of 'A' Troop was eventually awarded the DCM for his bravery at Abu Klea. A coloured photograph of Austin in the author's possession has a newspaper cutting giving the citation above his signature, on the reverse, which reads:

'Private George Austin, 5th Lancers – At the battle of Abu Klea he, with the utmost coolness and bravery, endeavoured to defend a comrade, who was unable to withdraw his bayonet from the body of an Arab, from the fierce onslaught of the enemy; his comrade was killed and Pte Austin continued to stand over him until he had received seven spear wounds before being able to regain the square.'

Private. Dismounted review order. Probably at Cavalry Depot 1890-1.

Private. Mounted review order. Probably at Cavalry Depot 1890-1.

Decisive charge of the 5th Lancers, Elandslaagte 21 October 1899. Painting by H. W. Koekkoek.

In February 1885 two squadrons were formed to take part in the Suakin Expedition. The Cavalry Brigade, consisting of 5th Lancers, 20th Hussars and 9th Bengal Cavalry, and including Royal Horse Artillery and Mounted Infantry, made an initial reconnaissance to Hasheen on March 19. On the following day the 5th Lancers had the opportunity of charging (with lances) the Arabs, which they did, inflicting heavy loss upon the enemy. Major A. B. Harvey commanding, was badly wounded, whilst a Troop Sergeant-Major and four men were killed. The campaign was over by 16 May and the Lancers were back home again by June, having earned the battle honour 'Suakin 1885' (General Order 10/1886) for the regiment, whilst the two squadrons received the Egyptian Medal with clasps 'Suakin 1885' and 'Tofrek'.

Fifteen years later the regiment was back in action, now in South Africa, and once again a squadron charge with lances completely routed the enemy. The terrifying effect of a charge by disciplined cavalry is best related in this extract from the report in *The Times* – 'History of the War in South Africa':

'Major Gore gave the order for which the men had been straining – "Gallop!" – and with levelled lances and bared sabres the two squadrons dashed forward and rode on and through the panic-stricken burghers. As soon as the latter heard the thud of the galloping horses and the exulting cries of the troopers, they opened out and tried to save themselves by flight. But with so small a start their little ponies were no match for the big striding walers, and the cavalry were upon them almost before they realised that they were pursued. Some tried to snap their mausers from the saddle, some threw themselves on the ground, others knelt down vainly imploring for mercy in the agony of their terror. For a mile and a half the Dragoons and Lancers over-rode the flying enemy, then they rallied and galloped back to complete the havoc and to meet such of the fugitives as did escape the central burst. In the second gallop but little sabring or spearing was done, and many prisoners were taken. Then the scattered troops were again rallied. The men fell in and cheered madly. After the action, as usual with British soldiers, "they showed every solicitude for those who had suffered. Though drenched to the skin themselves, many parted with their cloaks and blankets to cover the shivering limbs of the wounded, and some even shared their covering with the unwounded prisoners they were guarding." '

An officer who was principally responsible for the fine state of regimental efficiency was the Commanding Officer from 1894 until his death in 1899, Lt-Col J. J. Scott Chisholm. He exchanged from the 9th Lancers in 1889 and commanded from 1894, taking the regiment from India to Natal in 1898. In September 1899, when it was evident that there was to be a war with the Boers, he was given the task of raising a corps of 500 mounted riflemen, which he did, the regiment – The Imperial Light Horse. It was whilst with this corps that he lost his life, just before his 5th Lancers were about to make their historic charge.

A young trumpeter, J. J. Shurlock, performed an act of great daring during the action at Elandslaagte, taking on and routing three Boers single-handed. The regiment remained in South Africa throughout the war, endured the privations of the siege at Ladysmith and later the long marches, with much more fighting, the Battle of Belfast 1900 just one example. One officer of the regiment was awarded the VC for an act of heroism in 1901 – Lt Frederick Brooks Dugdale:

'On 3 March 1901 Lt Dugdale, who was in command of a small outpost near Derby, having been ordered to retire, his patrol came under heavy fire at a range of about 250yd and a sergeant, two men and a horse were hit. Lt Dugdale dismounted and placed one of the wounded men on his own horse; he then caught another horse, galloped up to a wounded man and took him up behind him and brought both men safely out of action.'

DCMs were awarded to Sgt Hyde and Cpl Smith for individual acts of initiative and bravery.

On return to England after fourteen years abroad, a new Commanding Officer took over, Lt-Col E. H. M. Allenby, CB. The band and one squadron took part in the Coronation procession of King Edward VII, so full dress was back in wear again. Since 1887 the lance cap plume was a darker green and, according to Dress Regulations, the lance cap plate was now to include extra scrolls for 'Suakin 1885' and 'South Africa'.

The Dress Regulations for the Army of 1911 includes this section dealing with the Lancer Regiments:

LANCERS
FULL DRESS

Cap (except for 9th Lancers) Lancer pattern. 6½in high in front, 7in at the sides, and 8½in at the back; 7in square at the top. Skull covered with black patent leather, the upper part and top with cloth of the same colour as the facings. Gold gimp and orris cord across the top and down the angles. On the left side, in front, a gold bullion rosette, with Royal Cypher, embroidered on blue velvet in the 12th and 17th Lancers; on green in the 5th; on scarlet in the 16th; and the Imperial Cypher of the late Queen Victoria on French grey in the 21st; at the back of the rosettes, a ventilated spring socket for the plume stem. A band of inch lace round the waist, with two bands of gold braid below, the upper ½in wide, the lower ¼in; and a similar double band of braid round the bottom of the cap, the ½in braid being the lower; the lace and the several bands of braid to be ⅛in apart. A gilt or gilding metal plate in front, with silver badge of regimental pattern. Black patent leather peak, embroidered with three stripes of gold purl. Plain burnished chain, ¾in wide, mounted on black patent leather lined with velvet, attached to lions' heads at the sides. Rings and hooks on metal leaf at the back of the waist, for the cap line and chain.

Cap for 9th Lancers   Of the size and shape described above. The skull and top covered with black patent leather; the upper part only with blue cloth. Strips of metal covering the angles, with metal ornaments at the corners of the top. On the left side, in front, a metal rosette, with a button in the centre, and a spring socket for the plume stem behind the rosette. A band of metal, an inch wide, round the waist. A ring and hook at the back for the cap-line and chain. Black patent leather peak, with a binding of metal, ¼in wide. Gilt or gilding metal cord chain ¾in wide, mounted on black patent leather lined with velvet, attached to lions' heads at the sides.

Cap-lines   Gold gimp and orris cord, with slide and olive ends, encircling the cap once, passing round the body, and looped on the left breast.

Plume   Drooping swan feathers, length 14in in front and 7in behind from the bend of the feathers, of the following colours:

Lt-Colonel Sir H. F. Guy, Bart, Worcestershire Yeomanry Cavalry and Captain G. McClintock, 5th Lancers, his Adjutant, Blackmore Camp 1908. Both in dismounted review order. (The Adjutancy of a Yeomanry Regiment always considered a pleasant appointment both militarily and socially, particularly good for a hunting man.)
R. J. SMITH

Mounted band. Bandmaster Mr A. J.
Norris (seen on left flank).
S. J. KRETSCHMER

5th Lancers	Green
9th Lancers	Black and White
12th Lancers	Scarlet
16th Lancers	Black
17th Lancers	White
21st Lancers	White

Gilt plume socket with five leaves.

Helmet, Foreign Service Abroad, the white Wolseley helmet with white pagri is worn instead of the home pattern headdress.

Tunic Blue cloth (scarlet in the 16th Lancers), double-breasted, with front, collar and cuffs of the regimental facings; the cuffs pointed, the collar and cuffs ornamented with inch lace round the top, the point of the cuffs extending to 6in from the bottom, two small buttons above the back of the cuffs. Two rows of buttons in front, seven in each row, the rows 8in apart at the top, and 4in at the waist, where the buttons are flat to go under the girdle; two buttons at the waist behind. A three-pointed flap on back of each skirt, edged with square gold cord, three buttons on each flap. A welt of the regimental facings in the sleeve and back seams, down the front, and round the skirts, which are lined with white in the 16th, with black in the other regiments. Gold wire shoulder cords, lined with scarlet in the 16th Lancers; blue in other regiments. Small button at the top.

Lace Regimental patterns.

Buttons and Badges

Trousers and Pantaloons Blue cloth, with two ¾in yellow cloth stripes ¼in apart (white stripes in the 17th Lancers).

Girdle Gold lace, 2½in wide, with two crimson silk stripes; fastened with a small strap and buckle on the inside, and outside with gold Russia braid loops and gold olivets; the loops in three rows, three loops in each row. The girdle to be 3½in larger than the actual waist measurement to allow for lap.

Boots and Spurs

Sword and Scabbard Cavalry pattern.

Sword Belt Web.

Sword Slings Gold lace, 1in, with ⅛in silk stripe; no stripe in the 9th Lancers; Morocco leather lining and edging; oval wire buckles, flat billets and gilt studs. The silk stripes, lining and edging of the colour of the regimental facings.

Sword Knot Gold and crimson cord and acorn.

Shoulder Belt Gold lace, 2in wide, with ¼in silk stripe, Morocco leather lining and edging as for sword slings; silver breast-ornament with pickers and chains, buckle, tip and slide of regimental pattern.

There is no silk stripe in the 9th Lancers, and the ornaments are of gilt or gilding metal.

Pouch Scarlet leather in the 5th, 9th, 12th and 16th Lancers, blue leather in the 17th and black in the 21st; with gold embroidery round the top. Solid silver flap, 7½in long and 2¾in deep. For the 9th Lancers the flap is gilt metal. Silver loops and stud.

Gauntlets White leather.

Great Coat Universal pattern. Shoulder straps, collar and cuffs edged with ⅛in yellow cloth.

UNDRESS

Forage Cap Universal pattern, blue cloth; welts down the quarter seams. Band and welts of the colour of the facings. 12th Lancers, scarlet cloth, band and welts scarlet, except welts down quarter seams which are blue. 16th Lancers, scarlet cloth, blue band and welts.

Frock Coat Universal pattern.

Trousers As in full dress.

Boots Wellington, with box spurs.

Girdle, Sword Slings and Sword As in full dress. Slings are only worn when the sword is carried.

The pouch belt is not worn in undress.

Cap Universal pattern.

Cap Comforter

Jacket Universal pattern. Buttons, gilding metal, die-struck.

Breeches Universal pattern.

Trousers Drab serge mixture.

Leggings Brown, Stohwasser pattern.

Boots Brown ankle.

Spurs Jack, steel.

Belt 'Sam Browne'.

SERVICE DRESS, ABROAD

Khaki Drill Jacket

Khaki Helmet

Khaki Drill Trousers

Remaining Articles As on home service.

MESS DRESS

Mess Jacket Blue cloth with roll collar and pointed cuffs the colour of the facings. Cuffs 6in deep at the points and 2¾in behind, a 1in slit at the seam. Shoulder straps of cloth the same colour as the jacket, 1½in wide at the base tapering to about 1in at the point; rounded points fastened with a button; the shoulder straps to be sewn in at the shoulder. Badges of rank in metal. No buttons on the front of the jacket and no gold braid or piping. Collar badges worn on the lapels. (17th Lancers, no collar badges.) In the 16th Lancers the jacket is of scarlet cloth with collar, cuffs and welting down the back seams and at back of sleeves, of blue cloth.

Mess Vest Cloth the colour of the facings; open in front, no collar, fastened with 4 half-inch buttons.

Overalls As in full dress.

Boots Wellington, with box spurs.

Regiment	Jackets				
	Colour	Collar	Shoulder Straps	Cuffs	Vest
5th (Royal Irish) Lancers	Blue	Scarlet	Blue	Scarlet	Scarlet

Sergeant E. Barratt winning the DCM for conspicuous gallantry, when he repeatedly took supplies to the trenches when under heavy fire and especially on a night when a shell burst over the column and he was hit by shrapnel in fifteen places, but continued to carry on until lifted from his horse. Wash drawing 20" × 14" signed G. D. Rowlandson.
THE PARKER GALLERY

Badges

Regiment	On Buttons	On Collar of Tunic, Mess Jacket & Frock Coat	On Full Dress Head-dress	On the Pouch	On the F.S. Helmet and Forage Cap	On the Service Dress	
						On the Collar in Bronze	On the Cap in Bronze
5th (Royal Irish) Lancers	On crossed Lances a circle surmounted by a Crown, with a shamrock wreath below. On the circle 'Fifth Royal Irish'. Within the circle, the harp.	The Harp and Crown in gilt or gilding metal.	On a gilt or gilding metal plate, universal pattern, in silver, the Royal Arms; below, the harp between sprays of shamrock. Across the bottom of the plate 'Fifth Royal Irish Lancers'. Silver scrolls inscribed with battle honours as per Army List.	In gilt or gilding metal, the Royal Cypher and Crown.	In gilt metal, on crossed lances, a circle inscribed *Quis separabit.* Within the circle the figure '5'. The '5' and the lower part of the pennons in silver.	As for forage cap.	As for forage cap.

G.D. Rowlandson

An officer of the 16th/5th Lancers at the Aldershot Horse Show 1951, in complete and authentic uniform as review order 1914, with correct horse furniture, shabraque etc.
S. D. EAGLE

The regiment moved over to Dublin in 1910 but was represented at the Coronation procession of King George V in London by the mounted band and a mounted detachment. Prior to leaving for Ireland, however, the regiment had transferred from Aldershot to York in 1907. Whilst there they had received, after the annual inspection, the Inspector General's adverse report – 'Unfit for service' – and as this was duly reported in the press an explanatory note followed:

> 'As our announcement with regard to this regiment appears to have given rise to some misapprehension, we desire to state that we believe that the unfitness of the regiment to take the field was mainly, if not solely, caused by the fact that several officers were serving in it who were unsuitable for the cavalry. The removal of the second in command, of two squadron commanders, and of two other officers will, no doubt, enable the regiment to give proof once more of those many soldierly qualities for which it has so long been famous.'[4]

Then in 1914 one of the most unfortunate and badly handled affairs occurred, the so-called 'Curragh Mutiny'. The 3rd Cavalry Brigade in Northern Ireland, 16th Lancers, 4th Hussars and 5th Lancers became involved in the political scene, the refusal of Protestants in Ulster to accept Home Rule and the choice before the British officers – to resign their commissions or to engage, if required, in operations against Ulster and therefore in some cases against fellow Ulstermen. From the three regiments, 59 out of 71 officers preferred to resign and from the 5th Lancers 18 out of 20 opted for resignation. The Commanding Officers of the 5th and 16th Lancers were ordered to the War Office, where fortunately things were settled, although resulting in the political resignation of the Secretary of State for War and the CIGS, Lord Seely and Sir John French respectively. Then of course the war in Europe broke out and full attention was turned to the more pressing matters of the day.

The 3rd Cavalry Brigade sailed for France as part of the Cavalry Division in August 1914. In September the 3rd, 4th and 5th Cavalry Brigades were constituted the 2nd Cavalry Division under Maj-Gen H. Gough, a former 16th Lancer. The regiment was in all the grim fighting of 1914-15 as the battle-honours will testify, but a lighter note was struck by an officer returning to France from leave who brought his foxhounds with him. He managed to keep them for six weeks before the French authorities clamped down.

A Private of the regiment – 6657 Clare, George William, was awarded the VC for his gallantry in action in 1917:

'For most conspicuous bravery and devotion to duty when, acting as stretcher-bearer during a most intense and continuous enemy bombardment, Pte Clare dressed and conducted wounded over the open to the dressing-station about 500yd away. At one period, when all the garrison of a detached post, which was lying out in the open about 150yd to the left of the line occupied, had become casualties, he crossed the intervening space, which was continually swept by heavy rifle and machine-gun fire and, having dressed all the cases, manned the post single-handed till a relief could be sent. Pte Clare then carried a seriously wounded man through intense fire to cover, and later succeeded in getting him to the dressing-station. At the dressing-station he was told that the enemy was using gas shells to a large extent in the valley below, and as the wind was blowing the gas towards the line of trenches and shell-holes occupied, he started on the right of the line and personally warned every company post of the danger, the whole time under shell and rifle fire. This very gallant soldier was subsequently killed by a shell.'

Back on horseback at the end of the war the 5th Lancers took part in the 'Pursuit to Mons'. Whilst attached to the Canadian Corps in November 1918 they were the first British troops to enter Mons, although it is sad to record that very few who had been there four years before were with them then. The re-entry is illustrated by a Caton Woodville painting depicting the welcome received.[5] The principal battle-honours are as follows: 'Mons'; 'Le Cateau'; 'Retreat from Mons'; 'Marne, 1914'; 'Aisne, 1914'; 'Messines, 1914'; 'Ypres, 1914, '15'; 'Cambrai, 1917'; 'St Quentin'; 'Pursuit to Mons'.

Demobilisation took place in 1919 when the regiment, with much reduced ranks, returned from Germany to Canterbury, and was represented in the Victory Parade through London on 21 July. By November the 5th Lancers embarked for India and in March 1921 were stationed at Peshawar when, quite by chance, the Commanding Officer, Lt-Col H. A. Cape, heard that the regiment was to be disbanded, although he did not learn this officially until two months later. The choice was offered to become a Royal Tank Corps Battalion – or disband. The unanimous choice was for the latter and by the end of the year the regiment ceased to exist. Then in April 1922 there was a *volte face*: the War Office had changed its mind and so by Army Order 133 it was announced that the 5th Lancers and 16th Lancers would be amalgamated, the new title to be 16th/5th Lancers. (Because of the break in service between 1799 and 1858 the 5th Lancers were junior to the 16th, and of course most officers and other ranks who wished to 'soldier-on' had transferred to other regiments.) A little story told by Lt-Col A. D. Wintle in his book[6] does however illustrate a kind of esprit-de-corps of an old 5th Lancer who found himself in another regiment, albeit an old soldier of the barrack-room lawyer type:

'About the end of 1921 when I had settled down fairly well in The 18th Hussars and had found my stirrups, as it were, we moved up north from Secunderabad to Risalpur to take over from the 5th Lancers who were being disbanded. We were to take over their barracks, horses, equipment – in fact, everything.

'Amongst other events associated with this move, about half a dozen of their less adaptable troopers were being transferred to our regiment and before long the majority of them were incarcerated in the guardroom.

'Now, every man in close arrest is supposed to be seen every day by his Squadron Leader. And by this time I was back in 'B' Squadron with Old Stuffy Lawrence, VC.[7] So it was before him that I had to parade one of these ex 5th Lancer reprobates soon after our arrival at Risalpur.

'The scallywag was marched in before Major Lawrence and asked what he had to say. Apparently he had a good deal to say. He started off in a strong Irish brogue of remarkable fluency. "Well, ye see, sorr, It was this way, sorr. When The Fift' Ryal Oirish Lansors was in Risalpor, sorr, the King's Rules an' Regulations was known to us all, sorr, but there was some of them we was allowed to bend, sorr, in The Fift' Ryal Oirish Lansors, like. But, ye see,

Band of the 16th/5th Lancers SHAPE (Paris) 8 September 1963. Regimental band giving a concert prior to a sporting event. Note silver harp and crown badge worn on the Band Sergeant's chevrons SHAPE (Paris)

sorr, The 18th Hussars is a different sort of regiment from The Fift' Ryal Oirish Lansors, sorr. They don't do things the same way, sorr . . ." And he went on like this for about ten minutes, explaining the differences between The Fifth Royal Irish Lancers and The 18th Hussars.

'I could see Old Stuffy was getting bored stiff almost to the point of apoplexy with this rigmarole. At last he could stand it no longer.

'He banged his fist on the table. "Half a minute, my man, half a minute," he bellowed. "If we're going to have The Fifth Royal Irish Lancers, let's have The 18th Royal Hussars (Queen Mary's Own). Now, you start your story all over again, see. And, by God, if you so much as get a word wrong I'll have you court-martialled for perjury. Now then, what have you got to say, eh?"

'The man was completely nonplussed and answered: "Nothing, sorr."

'"Well, why the devil couldn't you say so in the first place instead of wasting all our time. Take him away." I did . . . and we had no more trouble with his blarney.'

After the lapse of time it was difficult to make up a 5th Lancer Squadron ('D' Squadron) so 99 men from the 16th Lancers were transferred to it. (One wonders if the 'hero' of Col Wintle's story managed to get back with some of his countrymen.) The marriage, like most others at the time, was not an entirely happy one, but fortunately the 'powers that be' did allow the 16th and 5th to retain some of their own regimental distinctions, ie cap and collar badges of both regiments; 5th Lancer buttons and the Irish harp on the chevrons of NCOs were used by the entire regiment, the latter to this day. Otherwise the 16th Lancers became the dominant partner and in time both settled down as an efficient horsed cavalry regiment.

It was not until 1940 during the Second World War, whilst in India, that the last mounted parade took place and horses were exchanged for tanks. The mechanised regiment eventually joined the 6th Armoured Division in North Africa in 1942.

In 1954 Her Majesty Queen Elizabeth II, the Colonel-in-Chief, confirmed the Regiment's new titles as the 16th/5th The Queen's Royal Lancers. Five years later she presented the Regiment with a Guidon, the first since these were abolished for Lancer Regiments in 1834. The Regiment served in the Armoured and Reconnaissance roles in the United Kingdom and Germany principally during the Cold War years.

In 1993 as a result of the Options for Change defence rationalisation, the Regiment amalgamated with The 17th/21st Lancers to form The Queen's Royal Lancers.

[1] *The Historical Records of the Fifth (Royal Irish) Lancers*, by W. T. Willcox. A. Doubleday, London 1908.
[2] Reproduced in colour in above History.
[3] *16th/5th The Queen's Royal Lancers*, by Maj-Gen James Lunt, CBE, 'Famous Regiments' series. Leo Cooper, 1973.
[4] Report in *The Times*, 8 November 1907.
[5] Reproduced in General Lunt's History.
[6] *The Last Englishman*, by Lt-Col A. D. Wintle. Joseph, 1968.
[7] Major T. Lawrence, VC (formerly 17th Lancers).

THE REGULAR REGIMENTS ■ CAVALRY

6th (Inniskilling) Dragoons

By March 1689 the Ulster towns of Londonderry and Inniskilling were the only remaining garrisons holding out in Ireland against the forces of King James II. Londonderry was undergoing the miseries and privations of siege but in Inniskilling the townspeople strengthened the walls, elected a Governor, formed companies of Foot and troops of Horse, elected officers for these bodies and were eventually strong enough and brave enough to attack the enemy, with some small success. A further success was achieved two months later, whilst in June an attempt was made to relieve Londonderry, but failed. During this attempt they were able to capture a small garrison at Belturbet, with 280 men together with supplies, horses and arms. During those months of 1689, 17 troops of Horse, 30 Foot companies and some Dragoons had been raised. From such beginnings, augmented by officers and later by some troops, regiments of Horse, Dragoons and Foot became the origin of the famous regiments of latter day, the 6th (Inniskilling) Dragoons and the 27th Foot – Royal Inniskilling Fusiliers. These regiments were included in the establishment of the Royal Army of William, Prince of Orange, the Dragoons under the command of Sir Albert Conyngham and to be known by his name.

For the next two years, with the exception of the months in winter quarters, the Inniskillings were continually engaged in marching and fighting, the turning point, of course, the Battle of the Boyne on 1 July 1690. One historian describes the scene during the closing stages of the battle,

> 'The sight of the dreaded grey uniforms was too much for James's country-bred Infantry. "The Horse! The Inniskilliners!" was their panic-stricken cry, and away they went, best pace up the hill to Donore. James himself was the first to fly. He reached Dublin the same night, and the remains of his followers, such of them at any rate as stuck to their colours, dribbled after him in various stages of indiscipline.'[1]

Sir Albert Conyngham was promoted Colonel on 4 September 1691 but was killed that month just before the end of the war. His son Henry was promoted Lieutenant-Colonel and succeeded to command. Earlier on the 12 July the regiment was in battle at Aghrim, suffering casualties, 3 officers and 41 men killed and 27 wounded. The *Cavalry Journal* relates how one of the wounded dragoons turned out to be a female soldier, Christina Davis, her sex had not been detected until then. She recovered and later accompanied the regiment to Flanders where she assisted with the wounded, serving water etc. She married a pensioner at the Royal Hospital Chelsea, her third husband – a man named Welsh. The Hospital made Christina an allowance of one shilling a day for life. She died in 1739 and was buried at the Hospital.

The dragoon of the 17th century was actually a foot-soldier who availed himself of his horse on the march and dismounted whenever

Helmet, 6th Dragoons, 1834-43. All gilt, top portion below the removable bearskin crest is an ornate holder with lion's head. Hanoverian Royal Arms in centre of a pointed rayed plate over regimental title on metal band.
PHILLIPS

Portrait of Cornet Walpole, 6th Dragoons. Edward Walpole born c1737, entered regiment c1755, fought under Marlborough against French, expedition to St Malo and attack on Valencia. Captain 1762. Died of consumption in 1772 aged c34.
THE PARKER GALLERY

Miniature of an unidentified officer, c1790s. Scarlet coat with very pale yellow collar and silver lace loops in pairs. The castle appears on a gold oval on the shoulder wing(s), silver wire fringe.
PHILLIPS

there was any fighting, although towards the end of the century dragoons were changing into cavalry proper. The Inniskilling troops were originally clothed in grey but by 1692 the officers of the mounted regiment were known to have been supplied with crimson cloth for their coats, with crimson shalloon for lining, ash-coloured cloth for waistcoats, the soldiers' clothing almost certainly scarlet. We hear of a wrangle in January 1710 between Col Ecklyn (6th Dragoons) and Col Kerr (7th Dragoons) concerning the precedence of their regiments.

'The Board of General Officers decided "that Ecklyn's appears as well from its ancientness from the first raising of it as from its being brought soonest on the English Establishment to have a right to take post of Colonel Kerr's".'
(WO 71/1.)

The regiment left Ireland in 1708 and was not to return for 100 years, travelling at first to the north of England and, by 1711, Scotland, but with one part of the regiment sent to suppress rioting in Manchester. In 1715 Stair's Inniskillings were engaged against the rebel Highlanders. The King's forces drove the enemy from the field of battle at Sheriffmuir or Dunblane on 13 November, Stair's capturing a standard. The Earl of Stair, Colonel 1715-33, looked after his regiment well during the time in Scotland as recorded in Graham's *Annals of the Viscount and first and second Earls of Stair*:

'According to a custom not uncommon in the army at that time, he provided (by arrangement with the Government) winter quarters and forage for the men and troop-horses, when not on duty, in his grounds at Castlekennedy in Wigtownshire, where fatigue parties of the men were occasionally employed in country labour upon the estate. He had built barracks for them near his

Captain Thomas Fraser Grove, c1846.
Served in regiment, Cornet 1842 – retiring as
Captain 1849. Created Baronet 18 March
1834. Major, Wiltshire Yeomanry 1876-81.
Died 1897. Oil painting by T. M. Joy.
THE PARKER GALLERY

residence in the shire of Galloway, he furnished the horses of the private men with hay and stabling at the moderate rate of two shillings per week through the year; the officers dined with him daily, a dozen at a time by rotation and no dragoon or private man ever came to his house without being hospitably entertained, and what was still more encouraging, he gave eight pence per diem to above 300 of the private men whom he employed in fencing his park, cutting ditches and laying out enclosures.'[2]

It was about this time that the regiment was referred to as the 'Black Dragoons', presumably by reason of their black horses, but were eventually re-mounted on fine Irish bay horses. In August 1742 the regiment embarked for foreign service, landing at Ostend and going into winter quarters in Ghent. Seven years were spent in Flanders, the Battles of Dettingen fought in 1743 and Fontenoy in 1745, and then nine years at home during which we learn something of the dress of the regiment. In the series of paintings by D. Morier of the British Army, there is an excellent portrayal of a mounted private of the regiment, 1751. The facings, ie cuffs, turn-backs on the coats, as well as waistcoats and breeches, agree with the Cothing Warrant of 31 July 1751 – yellow, the hat lace of silver. The lace on shabraque and holster caps, white, with a blue stripe running through. The device on the hind corner of the shabraque was the Castle of Inniskilling, with the word

'INNISKILLING' on a scroll above it, the castle remained the regimental badge throughout its entire history.[3] (The normal spelling is 'Inniskilling' and 'The Iniskilliners' accepted phraseology, also the older title 'Enniskillen', similarly, 'The Enniskilleners'.) Drummers and Hautboys clothed in full yellow coats lined with scarlet and ornamented with silver lace with a blue stripe down the centre, their waistcoats and breeches of scarlet cloth. A light troop or 'hussar' troop was added in 1755 and was with the regiment at St Malo and Cherbourg in 1758. 1758-63 was spent in Germany including action at Minden in 1759, Warbourg and Campen 1760, Kirk Denkern 1761, Wilhelmstahl 1763 and Groebenstein 1763. The light troop was disbanded when the regiment returned home in 1764 and new Clothing Regulations were issued in 1767 bringing a few changes. The following year the yellow waistcoats, the coat linings and breeches were changed to white. Horses of the trumpeters and farriers were to be grey from 1777 and new standards were received in 1781.

The regiment went to Flanders in 1793 under the command of the Duke of York and served before Valenciennes, Dunkirk and Landrecies 1793, and at the Battles of Cateau and Tournay, 1794.

New uniforms were issued in 1812. The helmet was now black leather with brass mountings and a flowing 'horse-tail' plume, the heavy jackboots discarded and replaced by 'Wellington' boots in conjunction with grey overalls. It was the coatee which caused most discontent, short like a shell jacket with tails 8in long at the back, the soldiers complained that their legs became more exposed to the weather and – their version – 'it was the Colonel's economy and done to save the cloth'. For inclement weather a long scarlet cloak with white lining was worn over the uniform, when not in wear and troops in review order, it was rolled

Officer's sabretache and pouch, c1830-7. On a red cloth ground, 2" gold lace edging and buff face, castle in silver with gold gate and trim. 'Waterloo' on metallic silver scroll, 13" high, c8⅜" at top and 11¼" at foot. Pouch same design. Both made Hamburger & Co, 30 King Street, Covent Garden, London, 'Lace Men to the King'.
REAR-ADMIRAL W. WHITESIDE USN

Lt-Colonel Thomas Robert Crawley. A picture appearing in the Illustrated London News *26 December 1863, at the time of his Court Martial at Aldershot, taken from a photograph by J. De Beerski of Aldershot.*

inside out to show the white and carried behind the saddle, but in marching-order rolled red side out. A red valise was introduced in 1815.

Thus clad the regiment, together with the 1st Royal Dragoons and 2nd Dragoons (Royal Scots Greys) formed the famous 'Union Brigade' and made that decisive charge on 18 June 1815 at Waterloo. The Inniskillings and Greys suffered heavy losses, one witness describes how he overtook these regiments in the neighbourhood of Mons and that both corps were mere wrecks. The Lieutenant-Colonel commanding in 1815 was Joseph W. Muter, but on the death of Sir W. M. Ponsonby, he was given command of the 'Union Brigade'. Major F. S. Miller commanded the regiment at the battle. He was bayoneted twice during the action and lost his horse. It appears that he met a Corporal Small of the regiment, who had lost his own horse but was leading one which had belonged to a French officer of Lancers. This was given over to Major Miller who managed to ride it for the remainder of the day, still carrying the French officer's ornate horse furniture. The *Cavalry Journal* also related the remarkable tale of an Inniskilling sergeant, a survivor of the battle, who received 13 sabre wounds in his body, a musket ball passed through his thigh and both arms were broken. In this state he lay on the battlefield, amidst a heap of slain, from the Sunday till the Tuesday following, when persons employed to bury the dead observed signs of life in him and he was conveyed to a hospital and recovered. His story was told to the press in Exeter in 1816.

The regiment returned to England in 1816 and for the next 40-year period of peace before the Crimean War, it was mainly routine soldiering, although sometimes engaged on duty 'in aid of the civil power'. There were various changes in dress which are worth recording: 1821, a return was made to the pattern of coatee as worn before Waterloo with silver braid loops across the chest (which would mean white tape in the case of the men), and an aiguillette of silver cord on the right shoulder for officers, and the 'wings' were shortly afterwards exchanged for silver shoulder cords. The brass mountings of the helmet underwent a slight change about this time and the horse-tail pattern

Captain A. F. Stewart. Dismounted review order c1865. Cornet 1859, Lieutenant 1862, Captain 1864, Major 1879.

Group of officers India c1861-6. It is thought that officer seated at right of table is Lt-Colonel Crawley. Photo by J. Burke.
AMOT

plume was replaced by one of the 'caterpillar' type. In 1831 gold lace was made regulation for the whole army, the Inniskillings had to part with the silver lace and buttons they had clung to since they first wore red coats. These, with the light blue overalls, which had succeeded the grey ones ten years before, had made a very handsome uniform. The new coatee had no lace-holes across the chest, only a single row of gilt buttons down the front; gold epaulettes took the place of the silver ones just introduced (1827) and the silver belts etc, all had to be laid aside for gold ones, as had the silver tapes on the overalls; the men taking to yellow tapes and brass shoulder-scales, whilst later the officers wore on their new pattern of frockcoat, a plain row of buttons displaying the frogs hitherto worn on that garment, although this change may not have been introduced to the regiment. The overalls became dark blue and the officers' shabraques the same colour with gold lace. The musicians are noted in an inspection return of 1834 as wearing Sergeants' lace and an aiguillette, and a helmet, the body of which was white instead of black metal, the crest surmounted with scarlet curled hair instead of black bearskin. A new helmet was introduced about this time, all brass, with a lion for a crest, which was covered, in full dress, with a black bearskin 'caterpillar' plume.

A French artist, A. J. Dubois-Drahonet, was commissioned by King William IV in 1832, to paint 100 pictures illustrating the uniforms of the British Navy and Army, most of these now in the Royal Collection at Windsor Castle. All subjects were apparently drawn from life, painted in oil on card and signed, dated and titled. One of the series is a study of Sgt W. Coper, 6th Dragoons, 1832, showing the new uniform to perfection.[4]

An interesting statistic is available for the year 1831: out of a total strength of 279 rank and file, 226 were Irish. Stationed in southern England in 1837 the Inniskillings received unwelcome publicity in the local press after an affray between a mob on the Dorchester racecourse and men of the regiment. Never known to walk away from trouble, in fact more likely relishing a scrap, the Irishmen on this occasion were

wrongly accused, the newspaper account so one-sided that the Commanding Officer, Lt-Col Henry Madox, felt compelled to write a true account of the affair, which was published in the *United Services Review*, October 1837. It appears that the Dorchester mob was led by a prize-fighter, the local police could not be found (either knocked down or kept out of the way), so a picquet from the regiment arrived on foot. Even though augmented by their own men the dragoons were still not able to match the mob, so a mounted party arrived, which turned the scales in favour of the military, and were able to arrest the ring-leader, who was eventually sent to prison.

Sent to the Crimea in 1854, the regiment disembarked at Varna on 11 July and it was during the early stages of the campaign that the regiment was re-united with old friends when it formed part of the Heavy Brigade of the Cavalry Division. The Brigade consisted of 4th, 5th Dragoon Guards and 1st, 2nd and 6th Dragoons under the command of Brig-Gen Scarlett, the Light Brigade under Lord Cardigan.

One of the decisive actions of the war occurred on 25 October when the Heavy Brigade, numbering about 700 on the day, charged a superior force of about 3,000 Russian cavalry, and routed it. Lord Lucan described the attack as being one of the most successful he had ever witnessed.

Although with the regiment for a short time only, leaving on promotion in March 1855, Assistant Surgeon James Mouat was awarded the Victoria Cross for saving the life of a 17th Lancer officer, after the heroic, but disastrous charge of the Light Brigade on 26 October 1854, the citation reading:

> 'For having voluntarily proceeded to the assistance of Lt-Col Morris, CB 17th Lancers, who was lying dangerously wounded in an exposed situation after the retreat of the Light Cavalry at the Battle of Balaklava, and having dressed that officer's wounds in presence of and under heavy fire from the enemy, and thus, by stopping a serious haemorrhage, assisted in saving his life.'

The Inniskillings' casualties on the day were comparatively light but for the remainder of the campaign had to suffer, along with the whole of the British Army in the Crimea, the most appalling climatic conditions together with the lack of even basic supplies, food, medical, fodder for horses, clothing, etc. By the end of March 1855 the regiment was reduced to a total strength of 70 men, the entire Cavalry Division of 10 regiments being able to muster no more than 300 fit men. Before leaving for home in 1856 conditions had improved and the regiment was in reasonably good shape on arrival at Aldershot, there inspected by Her Majesty The Queen, on 17 July. By this time new uniforms had been issued and described in the records: The Crimean campaign rang the death-knell of the old coatee, and a tunic was substituted for it, as giving the men better protection from the weather. With the coatee went the brass shoulder-scales, cloth straps being introduced instead. This was in 1855, and the same order went on to ordain a white-metal helmet with a white plume (band red and white), the brass helmet and black plume being, presumably, considered by the home authorities, unserviceable. Booted overalls had already been introduced in 1854, perhaps by the regiment going on active service. The end of the war saw blue cloaks replace the old scarlet ones for the cavalry of the line.

Two years at home and the regiment was up to full strength and in

Recruiting Sergeants at Westminster, 1875. A fascinating photograph taken outside the 'Mitre and Dove' at the corner of King Street and Bridge Street. In the immediate foreground nearest camera, is Sergeant McGilney of the 6th Dragoons. Note silver castle above chevrons on right arm. The other recruiters are: with backs to Abbey – in shell jacket, Sergeant Ison, 6th Dragoon Guards, next, Sergeant Titswell, 5th Dragoon Guards, Sergeant Badcock, Royal Scots Greys, Sergeant Bilton, Royal Engineers (cap with peak), Sergeant Minest, 14th Hussars.

peak condition. In July 1858 orders were received for India. In an elite cavalry regiment at that time, receipt of such orders was liable to send shock waves through the commissioned ranks, a proportion of the officers arranging hurried transfers or exchanges, or even deciding to 'sell out'. Each regiment contained a number who had no particular interest in the profession of arms, regarding the regiment simply as an expensive club commensurate with their own social standing, whilst service in foreign parts, particularly India, held no attractions. It was also unfortunate that three splendid senior officers, who had taken the regiment through the Crimean campaign, were coming to the end of their service, Col White, CB, going on half pay before the regiment left and Col Shute, regarded by all who knew him as the 'beau ideal of what a cavalry officer ought to be', commanded for a few months, to be replaced by Lt-Col Crawley, formerly 15th Hussars, by exchange with Lt-Col Fitz-Wygram. His arrival in India during April 1861 marked the beginning of a sad period in regimental history which focused nationwide notoriety upon the regiment. When the regiment left Ahmednugger in November 1861 an inspecting General reported it as being 'as near perfection as it was possible to be', but this was soon to change on arrival at Mhow.

Col Crawley had been in the army since the age of sixteen, although he had seen little combatant service and relied upon an arrogant manner and fiery temper to maintain his brand of discipline. He was soon at odds with many of the officers, in particular a Mr Smales, Captain and Paymaster, who had served in the Kaffir War, 1846-7 and was Chief Paymaster of the Turkish Contingent in the Crimean War, coming to the regiment in September 1858. Captain Smales was placed under arrest for allegedly writing an insubordinate letter to the Colonel and was to be tried by General Court Martial. At the same time the Colonel placed the Regimental Sergeant-Major and two Troop Sergeant-Majors under close arrest; all three were to be witnesses for the defence. The RSM, Mr John Lilley, had held that rank for seven of his eighteen years in the regiment and the previous Commanding Officer, Col Shute, held him in

The Band. Zululand c.1884. The Bandmaster in patrol jacket, stands on left. In the centre the drum-horse and kettle-drummer, the drum banners at that time – blue. To the right the Trumpet-Major, whilst a young officer in frock-coat is in the centre at front on the grass. All bandsmen are in dress scarlet with yellow facings.

high regard, and said so during later proceedings, concluding with these words,

> 'I consider him one of the most straight forward, truthful, and worthy men I ever knew, thoroughly sober and trustworthy, an excellent soldier, and respected by all who knew him.'[5]

Officer, 6th Dragoons. Zululand c.1884. Khaki service dress. Note rank shown on cuff, rings of drab braid terminating with circular design at top, similar in fact to Royal Navy.

The RSM shared a large airy bungalow with his young wife, Mrs Clarissa Lilley. She was desperately ill in the last stages of consumption and had lost two young children a few months earlier, requiring constant nursing. It was shortly after being placed under arrest that the Sergeant-Major and his wife were moved to another bungalow, a one-room building designed to accommodate a single NCO. Conditions of arrest were that the RSM be kept within sight of a sentry at all times, which meant the sentry being inside the bungalow, and that the attentions of any female helper be denied Mrs Lilley. It has to be said that the move from a large bungalow to the small one was nothing to do with the Commanding Officer, although when he did know about it he did nothing to alleviate conditions. It was also said that RSM Lilley was a drinker. He was, of course, a member of a hard-drinking NCOs' mess, but was never known to have himself drunk to excess.

Captain Smales was found guilty at his Court Martial and he was cashiered – although the authorities at home eventually quashed the sentence and he was subsequently re-instated. During this time however, RSM Lilley died, followed a few days later by his wife. Such was the publicity and the outcry concerning this case when it was reported in England, that Col Crawley was ordered home to stand trial by Court Martial, whilst 130 officers and men returned as witnesses. The case was heard at Aldershot between 17 November and 18 December 1862, the Colonel being acquitted. He returned to take up command of the 6th Dragoons once again.[6]

He brought the regiment home from foreign service in January 1867 but his eccentricities soon attracted more unwelcome publicity. At about 2am on the morning of 13 April he paid a surprise visit to the Cavalry Barracks at York and found a horse loose on the square. He promptly ordered 'Boots and Saddles', turning out the whole regiment on a freezing cold night and marching it six miles on the Hull road, and six miles back. This excursion did not endear him to his soldiers, nor to the citizens of York, disturbed from their slumbers by trumpets and a regiment of cavalry clattering through the darkened city.

He was succeeded by Lt-Col The Hon Charles W. Thesiger on 2 December 1868.

In 1878 when Col Thesiger retired, he presented one Royal and three Squadron standards to the regiment. Lt-Col Gore succeeded to command and in 1880 the 6th Dragoons prepared for active service in South Africa. Arriving at Durban in February 1881, peace was declared in the March and so there was no fighting, although two troops had been despatched to Zululand to take part in the celebrations on the restoration of Chief Cetewayo. It is interesting to note that during the nine years spent in South Africa the Inniskillings might claim to have been amongst the pioneers in wearing khaki service dress on active service. Although photographs show that all the normal paraphernalia of a cavalry regiment, ie including all orders of dress, a full band with instruments and drum-horse, were taken to South Africa, an unconventional uniform was introduced, although possibly as an

The officers and senior NCO's. A remarkable collection of photographs thought to show all officers and NCOs who returned with the regiment from Africa in 1891. The officer in the centre is Lt-Colonel F. G. S. Curtis who commanded in Africa 1861-86. Above the castle is a photograph of Lt-Colonel Albert Froom who succeeded Curtis in 1886.

experiment by several officers. A soldier of the 14th Hussars, on service at the same time, had this to say:[7]

> 'Some negotiations had now to be undertaken with the Zulu nation, and General Sir Evelyn Wood was entrusted with them. He took with him three squadrons of cavalry, each consisting of two troops from the three regiments at Ladysmith, and a full band. I was told off to accompany ours (14th Hussars), and as we mustered I could not help observing that the squadrons illustrated two different theories of how a regiment should take the field for active service. We wore serge coats and khaki pants, with Indian puttees in lieu of jack-boots. Our helmets and belts were rubbed over with red clay to harmonise with the colour of the ground, and our steel work was all dulled. The squadrons from the Inniskillings and the 15th Hussars adopted quite a different style; they were as spick and span as could be, helmet and gloves white and clean, and steel and brass work all sparkling in the sun.'

Brighton by the sea made a very welcome station on return in 1890, and before leaving in 1894 the officers gave a ball at the Pavilion, by all accounts a memorable social event. On the occasion of a visit to England by the German Emperor in the summer of 1894, the 1st (Royal) Dragoons sent over a squadron from Ireland to meet their Colonel-in-

Chief, and so it was that the old Union Brigade were to meet again at Aldershot, albeit briefly, the Greys being stationed there and the Inniskillings in camp. In 1897 the regiment took part in the ceremonials for the Diamond Jubilee celebrations, a detachment and the band being sent down from Edinburgh. New yellow drum-banners had been acquired for the occasion, the drum-horse, a magnificent skewbald was

Four soldiers of the 6th Dragoons. Dundalk, 1898. From left to right. Mounted Trooper in review order, (front rank with lances). Trooper in walking-out dress – shell jacket. Trumpeters in dismounted and mounted review order. Band plumes of red.

The Trumpeters, c1905. Wearing the Brodrick cap, blue with yellow piping and inset patch, Trumpet-Major Thewlis on right of group.
D. J. HILL

ridden by Drummer Webb, a large man with handle-bar moustache and looking every inch the ideal heavy cavalryman. The mounted musicians were distinguished from the regimental detachment by their red plumes and yellow band aiguillettes.

On the 22 June that year HRH The Duke of Connaught became the Regiment's Colonel-in-Chief, an appointment he held until 1922. From Edinburgh a return 'home' to Ireland was made in the summer of 1899, the tour interrupted by the outbreak of war in South Africa, the Inniskillings being amongst the first to be warned for service. Two years were spent in South Africa, strenuous soldiering the whole time, although sadly experiencing a bad start before even setting foot ashore, 44 of the 496 horses being lost on the voyage out. One squadron formed the advance guard at the Relief of Kimberley three months after arrival, and from then on the regiment was kept actively engaged in most phases of the war and final stages of the guerrilla war, until 1902. On arrival home at the Curragh on 31 May 1902 HRH The Duke of Connaught was there to meet them.

One of the regimental officers at that time was Major E. H. H. Allenby who was later to become a celebrated General during the First World War. Another was Captain L. E. G. Oates whose life story was written in 1982 by a fellow Inniskilling officer, Lt-Col Patrick Cordingly, under the title *Captain Oates, Soldier and Explorer*. Oates served in Egypt and India, loved horses but became slightly bored with peace-time soldiering and was accepted by Captain R. F. Scott, RN, for his ill-fated expedition to the South Pole, seconded from the regiment in 1910 – the only soldier in an otherwise naval team. The story of Oates's final sacrifice by walking off into an Antarctic blizzard in 1912 so that the remainder might have a better chance of survival is still an inspiration to all ranks of the present regiment. An 'Oates Sunday' is observed on the nearest Sunday to Easter each year.

The Dress Regulations for 1911 couple those for Dragoon Guards and Dragoons; the 6th Dragoons therefore will be found under 4th Dragoon Guards, with the following additions:

Mounted band, Muttra 1913. Bandmaster E. Adams on right of drum horse. Drum banners now yellow, horse throat-plume red. Band horses – greys.
D. J. HILL

Helmet Plume White.

Regiment	Jackets				
	Colour	Collar	Shoulder Straps	Cuffs	Vest
6th (Inniskilling) Dragoons	Scarlet	Primrose	Scarlet	Primrose	Scarlet

Badges

On Buttons	On Collar of Tunic, Mess Jacket & Frock Coat	On Full Dress Head-dress	On Waist Belt	On the Pouch	On F.S. Helmet and on Forage Cap	On the Service Dress	
						On the Collar in Bronze	On the Cap in Bronze
Scalloped edge The Castle of Inniskilling with 'VI' below. For the mess waistcoat the design is in silver.	For tunic and frock coat, the Castle of Inniskilling embroidered in silver. For mess jackets the same but smaller.	On a gilt or gilding metal beaded Garter star, an elliptical ring inscribed 'Inniskilling Dragoons' in burnished letters on a frosted ground. Within the ring, in silver, the Castle over 'VI' on a gilt or gilding metal ground.	On a matted gilt or gilding metal plate with burnished edges in silver, an oak-leaf wreath with a scroll inscribed 'Inniskilling Dragoons' on the lower bend. Within the wreath, the Castle over 'VI'.	In dead gilt or gilding metal the Royal Cypher and Crown. On the Cypher the Castle in silver, with scroll inscribed 'Inniskilling'.	The Castle of Inniskilling in silver, with a scroll below in gilt or gilding metal, inscribed 'Inniskilling'.	As for forage cap, but smaller.	As for forage cap.

A glimpse at the character of the peace-time soldiers of the 6th Dragoons who served in Egypt and India from 1906-14, many with years of solid regimental service before that, and who had taken discharge on completion of their time with the colours and placed on reserve, can be gathered from an account of mobilisation, August 1914. The writer of this narrative was a Southern Irishman serving with the 1st Life Guards.[8] It appears that the three regiments of Household Cavalry had to be built up to war establishment, so it was decided to send all reservists from Dragoon and Dragoon Guard regiments to the 1st Life Guards, Lancers

Officers at the Cologne Races 1920. General Sir A. J. Godley, GOC-in-Chief, BAOR, at top of steps. Officer of 6th Dragoons at bottom of steps – with Gunner officers.

D. J. HILL

to the 2nd Life Guards and Hussars to the Blues. 70% of the reservists sent to the 1st Life Guards were former 6th Dragoons, most were Irishmen but from Liverpool, Glasgow and Tyneside. The rather staid but steady Life Guardsmen whose service life was generally confined to London and Windsor, did not quite know what to make of them. The 'Skins', no doubt finding their short time as civilians dull, were all in high spirits and found it a period for prolonged jollifications and resented being attached to 'The Tins'.

'They lounged about in groups and were always obsessed with a burning desire to get drunk and sing. In this respect they seemed to be remarkably successful. Most of the day and half the night the barracks rang with the song of the Skins, a somewhat melancholy lay, especially when keened in the small hours by a couple of dozen, more or less tipsy Irishmen, in a medley of brogues from the four corners of the kingdom. We Life Guardsmen were scandalised at the continuous carousals of the Dragoons and their complete lack of interest in all our attempts to make them comfortable and promote their welfare. However, with the departure of the service squadron on 15 August, we were able to enjoy more of their society, and got to know them gradually. For all their wild and woolly ways, they were fine soldiers and good fellows, apart from a very small gang of toughs. These were separated in the various squadrons and eventually we came to live, and later to die, with them in perfect harmony and to regard one another as part and parcel of the same unit.'

To revert to the regiment which was, in August 1914, at Muttra, United Provinces, India. By 14 December 1914, with the 2nd Lancers and 38th Horse, Indian Army, as well as X Battery RHA, together

A happy looking group of troopers of 'A', Inniskilling Squadron, V-VI Dragoon Guards, York 1928. These soldiers still wearing the Castle of Inniskilling badge on cap and collar.
D. J. HILL

comprising the Mhow Cavalry Brigade, disembarked at Marseilles. The story of the war years 1914-18 are best illustrated by recording the 10 principal battle-honours – 'Somme, 1916, '18', 'Morval', 'Cambrai, 1917, '18', 'St Quentin', 'Avre', 'Amiens', 'Hindenburg Line', 'St Quentin Canal', 'Pursuit to Mons', 'France and Flanders, 1914-18'. The cost to the regiment had been the loss of 185 brave soldiers, 9 officers and 176 other ranks.

Before returning to York the 6th Inniskilling Dragoons were stationed in the Liège area and later moved to Cologne, but it was at York in 1922 that speculation and ugly rumour were at last proved to be

Presentation of Standard Ceremony, Colchester, 18 March 1938. The Squadron Sergeant-Major holding the Standard, wears the gold lace belt of the 6th Dragoons whilst the Warrant Officer on right wears that of the 5th Dragoon Guards.

Lieutenant A. C. Gibson, officer in charge of the mounted escort at the presentation ceremony, 1938. This officer wears mounted review order, scarlet tunic with royal blue facings and castle badges on collar. A special shabraque of blue with castle and regimental designation on hind sections.

reality. News of the proposed reduction to single squadron strength and amalgamation with another regiment was confirmed, thus heralding the saddest day in the history of the Inniskilling Dragoons.

5th Royal Inniskilling Dragoon Guards

A contingent of 191 all ranks, 6th Dragoons, left York (after a tremendous party which broke up only when the trumpeter sounded reveille), for Southampton, to board ship for Egypt on 14 September 1922. The official existence of the new regiment commenced on 20 November, but the marriage was not a happy one. The new title of 5th/6th Dragoons was unfortunate, upsetting the 5th, who lost their title of Dragoon Guards, and the 6th, who lost the all-important title, Inniskilling. The 6th Dragoons also lost their Colonel-in-Chief, HRH The Duke of Connaught, who relinquished the Colonelcy in favour of HM King Albert of the Belgians, Colonel-in-Chief of the 5th Dragoon Guards since 1915. From the beginning 'A' or Inniskilling Squadron, was in effect a regiment within a regiment, keeping to itself and retaining all its former distinctions, uniform, badges, etc, whilst 'B' and 'C' Squadrons, formerly 5 DGs, retained theirs. In January 1923 when the regiment was inspected by the Commander-in-Chief, Egypt, both regimental Standard and Guidon, with separate escorts, paraded side by side. On other ceremonial occasions when the mounted band was on parade, there were always two drum-horses, each with their own regimental drum banners; this practice continued during the whole period of Indian duty, which commenced in February 1924.

One of the first steps towards integration occurred on 1 January 1927, when the title was changed to 5th Inniskilling Dragoon Guards, a change

One of the first mechanised vehicles of the regiment. Familiarisation of vehicle exercise, Colchester c1938.
RAF (No. 4 Sqn)

brought about by representations to the War Office, made by the two Regimental Colonels, Lt-Gen Sir Michael Rimington (6th Dns) and Maj-Gen Sir Tom Bridges (5 DGs). In consultation with other officers who had served in both regiments, new regulations were drawn up relating to dress and other matters which would, it was hoped, incorporate distinctions of both old regiments. These changes were as follows: Badge of senior regiment as cap badge, and the Castle of Inniskilling badge on collars. Green pantaloons or breeches and overalls to perpetuate the green facings of 5 DGs, and primrose-yellow facings on scarlet dress tunic, mess jacket and band of cap, collar of the blue cloak and stipes on breeches and overalls – primrose the colour of facings, etc, of the former 6th Dragoons. The silver galloping horse badge of 5 DGs was retained for wear over Sergeants' chevrons.

It fell to a new Commanding Officer, Lt-Col R. Evans, MC, formerly Royal Horse Guards and 7th Hussars, to further the work of integration, which he carried out so successfully that during the four years of his command the regiment reached a high peak of efficiency. One of his first moves was to re-introduce the custom of carrying the Salamanca Staff on ceremonial parades, a distinction of the 5th Dragoon Guards which had fallen into abeyance. Having returned to England in October 1928, by July of the following year the regiment was able to turn out in full dress, complete with green riding breeches, a Troop to perform a musical ride and various other trick rides, etc. During the 1930s it was noted for these rides which were performed at tattoos, Royal Tournament and shows throughout the country. New Dress Regulations for the Army were published in 1934 but these soon became out of date as far as the regiment was concerned as, by Army Order 110 of 1935, His Majesty the King was graciously pleased to approve 'that the Regiment, among others, should in future enjoy distinction as a "Royal Regiment". Henceforward their designation was to be "The 5th Royal Inniskilling Dragoon Guards".' This distinction conferred upon the regiment the right to wear facings of royal blue, and in due course, the primrose cloth facings were replaced by others of royal blue velvet (velvet being the traditional material for the facings of Dragoon Guards).[9]

The practice of parading two drum-horses, with respective drum banners, seemed to have ceased after about 1933. A new pair of 5th Dragoon Guards pattern, including the battle-honours of the First World War, had been acquired on return to this country, so although those carrying the old 5th (Princess of Wales's) Dragoon Guards title were then used, it was in conjunction with a shabraque carrying 6th Dragoons title, scroll and Castle.

The Standard and Guidon, however, were still paraded together, but what may be accepted as the final step of integration was the presentation of a new Standard to the regiment. This took place at a colourful ceremonial parade on 18 March 1938 at Colchester, when HRH The Duke of Gloucester, made the actual presentation. The dismounted regiment, in service dress with drawn swords, was formed in line, whilst in the centre of the parade ground was a mounted troop in review order with the old Standard and Guidon. After these were trooped and escorted from the ground the new Standard, which had been placed upon the piled kettle-drums, was presented.

Later that year the last of the horses were replaced by trucks, and so to the commencement of a new phase in regimental history, the Second World War and Armoured Vehicles.

After the withdrawal as part of the BEF from France, via Dunkirk, and re-equipping and training, the regiment landing in Normandy took part in the capture of Mont Pincon, afterwards leading the break-out in the battles of 'Lower Maas' and 'Roer', carrying on until the final surrender of the German Army.

In 1985 HM The Queen approved the appointment of HRH The Prince of Wales as Colonel-in-Chief of the regiment; after the death in 1983 of HM King Leopold III of Belgium the appointment had remained unfilled.

In June that year the regiment celebrated its Tercentenary. During the ceremonial march-past at Tidworth the Regimental Standard was dipped in salute from the turret of a 53-ton Chieftain tank, whilst the band, in full dress, 'rode' past, but mounted – in open vehicles.

The Royal Dragoon Guards

In 1992 as a result of the Options for Change Review, the Regiment was amalgamated with the 4th/7th Royal Dragon Guards to form The Royal Dragoon Guards. This new Regiment effectively embodies the traditions and history of the former 4th, 5th, 6th and 7th Dragoon Regiments.

The Royal Dragoon Guards was originally based at Paderborn, Germany as part of the Allied Command Europe Rapid Reaction Corps and saw active service in Bosnia. It is currently stationed at Tidworth where, on 26 June 1998, it was presented with a new Standard by the Colonel-in-Chief, together with the Duchess Colonel, HRH The Duchess of Kent. The Regiment is due to be re-equipped with Challenger Two tanks in 1999.

Three soldiers of the regiment, Corporal Etheridge, Trooper P. F. Jones and Trooper R. Golding, resting in a battered wood near their tanks on the road to Villers Bocage, on the advance towards Aunay-Sur-Odon, Normandy, August 1944.
IWM

[1] *The Inniskilling Dragoons* by Major E. S. Jackson. Arthur L. Humphreys, 1909.
[2] *History of Ireland*. by Graham. (Graham's grandfather Arthur Graham was a Cornet in Conyngham's Dragoons 1693-1703 and Lieutenant 1703-1706.)
[3] See Plate 45, *Military Drawings and Paintings* in the Collection of HM The Queen. A. E. Haswell Miller and N. P. Dawnay. Vol 1. Phaidon Press, London 1966.
[4] As above – Plates numbers 382-4.
[5] *Last Post at Mhow*. by Arthur Hawkey. Jarrolds, 1969.
[6] Extensive reporting in the *Illustrated London News* December 1862.
[7] *A King's Hussar* by Compton.
[8] *A Trooper in the Tins. Autobiography of a Life Guardsman*. R. A. Lloyd. Hurst c1938.
[9] *The 5th Royal Inniskilling Dragoon Guards* by Maj-Gen R. Evans, CB, MC. Gale & Polden 1951.

THE REGULAR REGIMENTS ■ CAVALRY

8th (King's Royal Irish) Hussars

Between 1958 and 1963 the last of the British Cavalry Regiments were amalgamated. The 8th (King's Royal Irish) Hussars was merged with another former Hussar regiment in Germany on 24 October 1958, thus bringing to a close the separate history of the 8th Hussars which had spanned a period of 275 years, and so commencing a new phase with the new title The Queen's Royal Irish Hussars.

The original regiment was formed in 1693 of Irish Protestants and was to be known by the name of its Colonel, Henry Conyngham, son of Sir Albert Conyngham who had raised at Enniskillen the Regiment of Dragoons which was to become the 6th (Inniskilling) Dragoons. The clothing of Henry Conyngham's Regiment of Dragoons was a scarlet coat, lined and turned up with yellow; with yellow waistcoats and breeches; round hats with broad brims, turned up on both sides and behind; boots reaching above the knee, and yellow horse furniture.[1] The officers were men of experience in battle from the Civil War in Ireland, at Derry and the siege of Limerick. 250 horses were sent over from

Headdress of the 8th Light Dragoons, c1796. The crowned harp authorised in January 1777.
BORIS MOLLO

Miniature of an unidentified officer, c1800. Light blue jacket with scarlet collar and silver lace, sash crimson.
PHILLIPS

Watercolour by H. Martens, c1830-2. At this date still with silver lace but with red pelisse.
THE PARKER GALLERY

England so the regiment had an excellent beginning. Between 1693 and 1751 the title followed each Colonel's name – Bowles's Dragoons, Cathcart's Dragoons, Killigrew's Dragoons, Munden's Dragoons, Neville's Dragoons, Oughton's Dragoons, Pepper's Dragoons, Rich's Dragoons and St George's Dragoons. In 1742 the scarlet uniform was described as having orange facings but the Royal Warrant of 1 July 1751 gives:

'the coat as scarlet; double-breasted; without lapels; lined with yellow; slit sleeves, turned up with yellow; the button-holes worked with narrow white lace; the buttons of white metal, set on three and three; a long slash pocket in each skirt; and a white worsted aiguillette on the right shoulder. Waistcoats and breeches yellow. Hats – three-cornered cocked hats, bound with silver lace and ornamented with a white metal loop and a black cockade. Boots – of jacked leather, reaching above the knee. Cloaks – of scarlet cloth with a yellow collar, and lined with yellow shalloon; the buttons set on three and three upon white frogs, or loops, with a yellow stripe down the centre. Officers – distinguished by silver lace; their coats bound with silver embroidery, the button-holes worked with silver; and a crimson silk sash worn over the left shoulder. Quarter Masters – to wear a crimson sash around the waist. Serjeants – to have narrow silver lace on the cuffs, pockets and shoulder-straps; silver aiguillettes; and yellow and white worsted sashes tied round the waist. Drummers and Hautboys – clothed in yellow coats, faced and lapelled with red, and ornamented with white lace with a yellow stripe down the centre; their waistcoats and breeches to be of red cloth. Corporals – narrow silver lace on the cuffs and shoulder-straps; and a white silk aiguillette.'

Then follows descriptions of the horse furniture and Guidons.

Between the two years 1775 and 1777 many important changes took place, firstly that the regiment was ordered to be made 'light' and in order that this change of status should not involve loss of its distinctions, the officer commanding wrote seeking His Majesty's permission to retain the 'Honourable distinction of wearing Cross-belts', that the coats be faced with blue and that the regiment be called the 8th or King's Royal Irish Light Dragoons. George III, on 28 November 1775 'was graciously pleased to condescend to the request'. Then followed a further application, which should have accompanied the earlier, that being a Royal regiment and Irish, the badge should be The Harp and Crown and the motto *Pirstinae Virtutis Memores*. This was also granted but, now that both badge and motto had been obtained, the cross-belts had to go. In case one wonders about these cross-belts, ie the sword and carbine belts crossing each other on the chest, it should be pointed out that between 1704 and 1713 the regiment fought with distinction in Spain, and that at the Battle of Almenara it took these belts from captured Spanish Horse. This is a story that has never been really established although Lt-Gen John Severne, who claimed 67 years in the army, including 10 commanding the regiment and a further 27 as its Colonel, writing in reply to the new commanding officer of 1781, was able to assure him that:

'In the year 1769 by the King's Order of Regulation of the clothing and accoutrements The Cross Belts are expressly confirmed to the 8th Dragoons

Undated photograph of a private in the uniform of c1854 before leaving for the Crimea.
AMOT

Photograph by Roger Fenton of two sergeants of the 8th Hussars, taken in the Crimea c1855. The sergeants' arm badges are clearly shown, as are the leathered overalls.

Study by Harry Payne, showing a mounted private of the regiment with a Sepoy. India, mutiny period, c1857.

Portrait of a Crimean veteran, Trumpet-Major William Gray. His cavalry cloak is so arranged to show his decorations and medals: Legion of Honour, Crimean Medal with four clasps and Turkish Crimean Medal.
THE PARKER GALLERY

with the addition of carrying their swords like the Regiment of Horse by the Cross Belt which before they carried in waist belts. When Colonel, now Lord Waldegrave, become Colonel he had the Late Duke of Cumberland's (order) to take the Cross Belts from the Regiment. I then remonstrated against it and submitted my reason in writing to his Royal Highness and we were permitted to continue them.'[2]

However, in 1795, after nearly two years of the most rigorous campaigning on the continent, HM George III directed that 'the Royal Irish Dragoons should resume wearing buff equipment as a special mark of royal favour and approbation of their conduct during the period of their arduous continual service.' So this regiment alone was permitted to wear the sword belt on the right shoulder instead of round the waist. It is interesting to note that even after amalgamation in 1958, the title of the Regimental Journal of the new combined regiment remained 'The Crossbelts'.

The first battle-honours were won in India between 1802 and 1822, but prior to 1802 the regiment had served in South Africa, actively employed during the Kaffir War of 1800, and one troop sailed to Egypt in 1801 to join Sir David Baird's force. The regiment in the meanwhile had sailed for India, where it was supplied with white horses and adopted new uniforms of light blue or cavalry grey, with silver lace and red facings. During the siege of Agra the 8th provided working parties together with those of the 27th and 29th Light Dragoons. But it was at Laswari on 1 November 1803 that the regiment, together with two regiments of Native Cavalry and the two other regiments of Light Dragoons, 27th and 29th, made repeated charges, and eventually won the day with the support of British infantry, notably the 76th Foot with Royal Artillery support. The 8th lost 18 killed and 36 wounded that day. Amongst the killed was their Colonel, Thomas P. Vandeleur who rode a black charger, whilst the regiment was mounted on the grey arabs, and consequently their leader was conspicuous and singled out by enemy

Two sabretaches, the one on the right 1856-60, replaced by the sabretache on the left c1870, which in turn was replaced in 1881 by a pattern carrying the 'Afghanistan' battle-honour. Both specimens shown are on red leather backing, scarlet cloth with gold embroidery, silver cypher and lettering on scrolls and bordered with gold shamrock lace.

marksmen. It is reported that the spoils of war were enormous – elephants, camels, 1,600 bullocks, luxurious camp equipment of oriental style, plus 72 cannon and 44 stands of colours. There was further action at Aurungabad, Ferreckabad and Deeg in 1804, and at Bhurtpore in 1805, summed up by the battle-honour 'Hindoostan' following the premier battle-honour 'Leswarree'.

Orders to return to England were received in 1822, but in the intervening years there had been much activity, in the Nepaul War of 1814 where the regiment lost a distinguished commander, Rollo Gillespie, and against the Pindarrees 1816-7. The actual departure took place on 11 January 1823 after 280 men and 616 horses had been handed over to the relieving regiment, the 16th Lancers. On landing at Gravesend on 5 May it was learnt that they were to be equipped as Hussars, the letter with this instruction having been dated 20 August 1822. At first the lace on the new blue Hussar dress and for the shako was silver, but was changed to gold in 1832. The trousers were blue-grey, the pelisse blue and the sabretache face of scarlet with silver lace. A fine watercolour by William Heath[3] shows this uniform of the 1820s, but the change to gold lace and the pelisse changed for scarlet cloth is best shown in the Spooner Upright Series No 24, 1833-6, drawn by St Eschauzier and coloured by C. H. Martin. Capt William Lyon (Cornet in 1823, Lieutenant in 1825 and Captain in 1826, transferred to the 86th Foot as Captain in 1833) was chosen in 1832 as one of the subjects for the paintings by A. J. Dubois Drahonet, the other an unnamed Private.[4]

There were quite a number of good uniform prints of this regiment published during the 1830-50 period, as well as several valuable paintings. During 1840-4 the regiment was in England and one of the finest prints shows an officer and trumpeter in mounted review order, published in the Spooner Oblong Series No 41.[5] The trumpeter wears a scarlet jacket with close yellow braid on chest together with a blue pelisse, the officer and ranks in the background all have the scarlet pelisse. Perhaps the best known print comes from the same series, No 3, which depicts a review of the 1st Life Guards and 8th Hussars, 4 June 1842, by Her Majesty Queen Victoria and Prince Albert on Hounslow Heath.[6] A painting by John Ferneley Jnr shows two grooms with officers' chargers, but on the left of the picture there is a sergeant in mounted review order, this picture one of the first to show a sergeant's arm badge in wear, and it would appear to be an embroidered badge, the harp and crown. Ferneley usually took his subjects 'from life', this example at Melton Mowbray, the regiment at that time distributed by squadrons and troops at York, Newcastle-on-Tyne and Leeds etc.[7]

One of the prints in the Hayes-Spooner Series shows a mounted escort found by the 8th Hussars for a pack-train. Soldiers of the escort have black waterproof covers over the shakos and the pointed hind sections of the shabraque are bent upwards and attached to the valises at rear of saddles. This was no doubt to prevent chafing of horses' flanks when the pointed ends were wet. In June 1844 the regiment embarked at Liverpool and the next six years were spent in many of the various garrisons in Ireland. In this year the busby replaced the shako although the scarlet pelisse had been changed for a blue one after the accession of Queen Victoria, and is shown in the 1842 review picture. A further pair of prints worth mentioning here show both of these changes. Each show officers in mounted review order, the first published in November 1844 in Ackermann's Costumes of the British Army Series and the second in Ackermann's Large Series (of three) published 18 May 1852.[8]

A Victorian family group, c1890. Seated in centre Major-General P. Bedingfeld, (retired) Royal Artillery. On left, Lieutenant E. G. Bedingfeld, 8th Hussars. Centre, Captain H. H. Bedingfeld, 2nd Bn, The Devonshire Regiment. On right, Lieutenant N. N. Bedingfeld, 1st Bn, 60th Rifles.

On return from Ireland the regiment was stationed at Brighton, moving on to Hounslow in 1851 where R. Ebsworth was able to make some notes on the dress of the band, and on other occasions in 1853. In 1851 he states:

> 'that the drum banners are of crimson silk having silver lace border and fringe, the regimental badge, the harp and crown in silver in the centre, the Roman numerals VIII with K.R.I. below also in silver, and on either side of the banner, battle-honours 'Leswarree' and 'Hindoostan' on separate scrolls at top and bottom. (As guidons were ordered to be discontinued from 24 May 1834 the regiment's battle-honours were in future to be displayed on the drum banners.)
>
> 'Bandsmen wear the tall black busby with lines of red and yellow, the same pattern piping on the close braided jacket and pelisse. Sergeants wear the solid silver harp and crown badge on the right sleeve. The band horses are all light chestnut, the drum-horse being distinguished by white patches on the face.'

The mounted band, together with one squadron, formed part of the funeral procession of the Duke of Wellington in October 1852.[9] At Chobham Camp in 1853 Ebsworth noted that on this occasion quite plain blue banners were in use over copper drums, no doubt reserved for drill or for use on the march. At this time the band was under the direction of a German, Adolph Koenig, who left the regiment when it went to India, and was succeeded by a Mr Martin.

Officers and NCOs 'C' Squadron, Norwich 1892. Front row seated, Lieutenant Musenden in stable jacket, Captain Vesey, Captain Wood, Lieutenants Anderson and Thoyts. Note distinctive regimental pattern of patrol jacket worn by Captain Vesey. All NCOs have the silver harp badge above the chevrons.
S. J. KRETSCHMER

The regiment passing through Banbury on manoeuvres, 1894. Note the mixed dress of the officers, ie busbies with plumes, gold lace dress shoulder-belts with blue serge frocks. Leopardskin saddle covers, horse throat plumes. Soldiers on right in marching order.

Narratives by NCOs or private soldiers are few, and those that have survived in print are in consequence of historic value. One such soldier of the 8th Hussars, Pte John Doyle wrote his reminiscences, mainly concerning his Crimean and Indian Mutiny experiences, but also included a brief note on his early days in the regiment – and his last. These were published in 1877 as a small booklet or pamphlet of 36 pages costing a penny or two, and called *An Historical Account of the Famous Charge of the Light Brigade, at Balaclava, October 25 1854.*

'I joined the 8th King's Royal Irish Hussars on the 21st day of February 1850 at Newbridge in Ireland. In May of the same year I was before HRH The Duke of Cambridge concerning my brother, who was then serving in the 73rd Regiment. I made application for a transfer for him to the 8th Hussars, and this would have been granted but he was too tall and too heavy for the 8th. The Duke kindly told me that if I wished to go to him I could do so, but added that he would not advise a young man like me to leave the 8th Hussars to go to an infantry regiment, and if I wished to remain in the 8th Hussars he would give my brother a transfer into the Guards, but before the transfer arrived he was taken out to the Cape of Good Hope in the new steamship *Birkenhead*. The Captain, in trying to cut off a corner, run her on a rock near Table Bay. The women and children were got off before the pilot came on board, or they would all have been lost. The ship was backed off the rock, when she opened from the bottom, and all remaining on board had a very narrow escape; my brother was one who perished in the wreck. In June 1850 we got the route for

Brighton, where we remained for twelve months. In 1851 we marched to Hampton Court and Hounslow, where I was chosen by HRH The Duke of Cambridge and Col Sewell to be one of the Kensington party in London to do Horse Guards' duty, at the time of the 1st Exhibition in 1851, and during that year I had the honour of escorting Her Majesty a great many times. We were relieved at Kensington and in 1852 we got the route for Nottingham; and in 1853 I had the honour of being present at the Duke of Wellington's funeral. (Doyle has mistaken the year, should read 1852 – Author.) In the same year we got the route for Chobham Camp – we remained there about two months. On the day we crossed the pontoon into Windsor Park I was orderly to The Duke of Cambridge; on that occasion a gun went over and two horses were drowned. In the same year we got the route from Chobham to Trowbridge and in 1854 we marched to Exeter to get ready for the Crimean War. Soon afterwards we got the route for Devonport, to embark on board the *Willicanada* for the Crimea.' (Four transports are named in Regimental Records, but not this one – Author.)

The main portion of the regiment disembarked around 20 May 1854 (HQ and remainder arriving mid-June), but were hurriedly re-embarked and towed up the Bosphorus to accompany Lord Cardigan on a reconnoitre in strength. It was during this early period of the campaign that the army began to suffer from those debilitating complaints, diarrhoea and dysentery, whilst two thirds of the troop horses of the Royal Irish Hussars were out of condition.

The regiment was brigaded with the 4th Light Dragoons, 11th Hussars, 13th Light Dragoons and 17th Lancers, to form the famous Light Brigade, commanded by Maj-Gen the Earl of Cardigan. The story of the charge at Balaclava and the events of 25 October 1854 leading up to it, have been told and re-told, whilst Tennyson's stirring poem never fails to thrill. The order to charge at guns a mile or more away meant

Private in mounted review order c1890s.

Corporal and private in hot weather white uniforms, India c1910.
MAJOR A. F. FLATOW TD

The drum-horse, Amballa, India 1914.
S. J. KRETSCHMER

certain annihilation, and out of a total of 600 men only 198 returned. The strength of the 8th, numerically the weakest in the Brigade, was 104 officers and men; 66 were killed or missing and 38 returned. Many brave deeds were performed that day. All ranks were later awarded the Crimean medal although, when conditions were bad, supplies and clothing inadequate and many soldiers almost in rags, one wag is reported to have declared that the medal would be fine providing there would be a coat to fix it to![10]

The photographer, Roger Fenton, was responsible for several pictures of the 8th Hussars, most believed taken in 1855 when supplies, including warm winter clothing, had been received. His photographs of the regiment include the informal group of officers and senior NCOs, the well known cookhouse scene, two sergeants, and another of Paymaster Henry Duberley and Mrs Duberley. Mrs Duberley, one gathers, was not an entirely popular lady, being one of the few wives allowed to accompany their husbands on campaign. Lt-Col Forrest of the 4th Dragoon Guards said of her:

'an odd woman. The French have dedicated a polka to her as "The Amazone". I do not believe she is guilty of that which many say she is, but of course she has many "Followers" as the servant girls say, and her vanity causes her to encourage them.'[11]

The 8th Hussars returned to England and, although due to proceed to Dundalk, were kept back in Portsmouth as HM Queen Victoria wished to see the regiment and came over on 12 May 1856 from Osborne. Accompanied by Prince Albert and Edward, Prince of Wales, they walked down the ranks, although it was a sadly depleted regiment.

Charge of the 8th Hussars during the First World War. Small watercolour 7¼" × 5¼", signed R. Wymer. This is probably intended to show the charge by 'D' Squadron, Villiers-Faucon, 1917.
THE PARKER GALLERY

Trooper R. Marrion, khaki service dress, c1926.
R. J. MARRION

A new pattern uniform had been authorised for Hussars in 1855, said to have been issued whilst in the Crimea, although Fenton's photographs do not show it. In Ireland in 1856 however the much respected artist, Michael Angelo Hayes, made a splendid painting entitled *A Picquet of the 8th Hussars, 1856* where he shows the new dress. The tunic was blue with six rows of chest looping, a pattern which remained in use from that time.[12]

The 8th did not enjoy much time at home. An 'up to strength' regiment of 28 officers and 489 NCOs and men embarked for India on 8 October 1857 where mutiny had broken out in certain sepoy regiments. It was in Central India in 1858-9 that the regiment, in the Field Force under Sir Hugh Rose, saw much hard service and in two furious engagements particularly distinguished itself. Four soldiers were awarded the VC for gallantry, the citation as follows: Heneage, Capt Clement Walker; Ward, No 1584, Sgt Joseph; Hollis, No 1298, Farrier George; Pearson, No. 861, Pte John.

> 'Selected for the VC by their companions. In the gallant charge made by a squadron of the regiment at Gwalior, on 17 June 1858 when, supported by a divison of the Bombay Horse Artillery, and Her Majesty's 95th Regiment, they routed the enemy, who were advancing against Brigadier Smith's position, charged through the rebel camp into two batteries, capturing and bringing into their camp, two of the enemy's guns, under a heavy and converging fire from the fort and town.' (Field Force orders by Maj-Gen Sir Hugh Henry Rose, GCB, commanding Central India Field Force, dated Camp Gwalior, 28 June 1858.)

Later that year Troop Sergeant-Major James Champion was also awarded the VC:

'For distinguished bravery at Beejapore, on 8 September 1858, when both the officers attached to the troop were disabled, and himself severely wounded at the commencement of the action by a ball through his body, in having continued at his duty forward, throughout the pursuit, and disabled several of the enemy with his pistol, also recommended for distinguished conduct at Gwalior.'

The regiment returned home in 1864 where it spent 14 years, in England up to 1867, Scotland in 1868 and to Ireland 1869-75. Hussar dress remained much the same, leopard-skin saddle-covers were authorised for officers in 1868 whilst pants and Hessian boots were introduced for Hussar officers attending levées about 1877. Social activities were not to occupy too much of officers' time as orders were received for service in India – where the regiment arrived in January 1879. It was to be 10 years before ordinary garrison duty at home was resumed; in the meanwhile came a year of frontier service during the Second Afghan War. The official resumé of the regiment's exploits are as follows:

'In December 1879 reinforcements being required in Northern Afghanistan in consequence of the serious aspect of affairs in the neighbourhood of Kabul, the 8th Hussars, then stationed at Muttra, was ordered to the front. Proceeding to Peshawar, the regiment – with the exception of the 1st Squadron, under Major Burke, with Captain Sutton and Lt Fell, which was sent forward to Basawal, detaching a small party under 2nd Lt Duff at Fort Daka – remained at that station till February 1880, when it was moved up to Jamrud; here the Head-quarters and remaining two squadrons were encamped till the latter end of March, when they advanced to Basawal, and were there rejoined by the 1st Squadron. For the next few weeks the duties of

Running Repairs. The drum-horse having shed a shoe whilst taking part in the Lord Mayor's Show, November 1932. The Troop officer on left, kettle-drummer on right, farrier in khaki, at work on rear off-side hoof.

the regiment consisted mainly in escorting convoys and patrolling the line of communications.

'In the middle of April the 8th Hussars marched to Pesh Bolak, and there remained, forming part of the Flying Column under the command of Brigadier-General Gib, for a period of five weeks. At the latter end of May orders were received for the regiment to return to India, and in pursuance of these directions, Head-quarters and the right wing marched down to Basawal, the left wing remaining behind to follow the next day; before it started, however, telegraphic instructions were received by General Gib to proceed on his expedition against the Shinwaris; and marching with the expeditionary force, the left wing took part in the action of Mazina.

HM King George VI inspecting tank crews of the regiment (Cromwell tanks), 7th Armoured Div, 'Somewhere in England' 1940.
IWM

'After being stationed for a short time at Naushahara, and afterwards at Campbellpur, the regiment eventually made its way, at the latter end of September 1880, to Rawal Pindi.'

The *London Gazette* of 7 June 1881 announced the award of the battle-honour 'Afghanistan 1879-80', whilst during that year badges of rank for officers were removed from the collar and affixed to the shoulder straps. The 'Afghanistan' honour was added to the officers' dress sabretache and shoulder-belt pouch (1881-1901). Between 1860 and 1881 the sabretache carried seven battle honours including 'Central India'. The pattern prior to this carried the four Crimean battle honours only, the two earlier honours, 'Leswarree' and 'Hindoostan', being omitted. Sabretaches were not now used by Corporals and below. New drum banners to carry the additional honour were obtained on return to England and were much in evidence at ceremonial parades, including The Diamond Jubilee of Queen Victoria, during the 90s and before embarkation to South Africa.

When the regiment landed at Cape Town on 9 March 1900 it joined the 4th Cavalry Brigade consisting of 7th Dragoon Guards, 8th and 14th Hussars and 'O' Battery, Royal Horse Artillery, under the command of General Dickson, but by the end of the South African War was in a Hussar Brigade, 8th, 18th and 19th Hussars. The clasps awarded for the South Africa medals were: 'Johannesburg', 'Diamond Hill', 'Belfast', 'Orange Free State' and 'Cape Colony', whilst the battle-honour 'South

'Dingo' scout car of the regiment bogged down north of Sittard, Belgium, December 1944.
IWM

Africa 1900-02' appeared in the Army Lists from about 1905, but there was no opportunity to add it to the drum-banners until after the First World War.

Only a comparatively short time was spent at home after return from South Africa in October 1903, as by November 1909 the regiment was back in India. The Dress Regulations of 1911, therefore, had little significance as there was no appreciable difference to those issued in 1904; regulations for Hussar regiments as follows:

HUSSARS
FULL DRESS

Busby   Black sable fur; outside measurement, 6¼in high in front and 7¾in at back; ½in smaller round the top than the bottom. A gold gimp oval cockade, 2in deep and 1½in wide in the centre in front, the top on a level with the top of the busby. A spring socket behind the cockade. A cloth bag covering the top of the busby, and falling down the right side to the bottom; a line of gold braid along the seam of the bag, and down the centre, with a gold gimp button at the bottom; for colour. A hook at the top on the right, to hook up the chain. The cockade is not worn in the 14th Hussars.

Plume   Ostrich feather, 15in high from the top of the busby to the top of the plume; encircled by a ring. Vulture feather bottom in a corded gilt ball socket with four upright leaves.

Busby Chain   Dead and bright gilt corded chain; lined with black morocco leather, white in the 13th Hussars, yellow in the 14th Hussars, and crimson in the 15th Hussars, the leather backed with velvet.

Busby Line   Gold purl cord, with slides and olive ends; encircling the busby diagonally three times, passing through a ring under the bag, then round the body and looped on the breast. A swivel hook on the end of the line. In the 11th Hussars the line is plaited.

Helmet Foreign Service   Abroad, the white Wolseley helmet, with white pagri is worn instead of the busby.

Tunic   Blue cloth, edged all round with gold chain gimp. On each side of the breast six loops of gold chain gimp, with caps and drops fastening with gold-worked olivets. On each back-seam a double line of the same gimp, forming three eyes at the top, passing under a netted cap at the waist, and ending in an Austrian knot reaching to the bottom of the skirt, with a tracing of gold braid all round the gimp. The collar edged along the top with ¾in lace. An Austrian knot of gold chain gimp on each sleeve, reaching to 8in from the bottom of the cuff. A tracing of plain braid below the lace on the collar and round the knot on the sleeve. The skirt rounded off in front, closed behind, and lined with black. Shoulder cords of plaited gold chain gimp, lined with blue; a small button at the top. The 3rd Hussars wear scarlet, and the 13th Hussars buff cloth collars.

Lace   Regimental pattern.

Buttons and Badges

Trousers/Pantaloons   Blue cloth (Crimson cloth in 11th Hussars) with two ¾in yellow cloth stripes, ⅛in apart (buff stripes in the 13th Hussars).

Boots and Spurs   A gold gimp oval boss, 2in long and 1½in wide, is attached to the top of the leg of the boot in front.

Sword   Cavalry pattern.

Scabbard   Steel.

Sword Belt   Web.

Sword Slings   Gold lace, 1in wide, morocco leather lining and edging, crimson in the 11th and 20th Hussars, buff in the 13th and scarlet in the other regiments. Lion head buckles, flat billets and gilt studs.

Sword Knot   Gold and crimson cord and acorn. No crimson in the 13th and 14th Hussars.

Shoulder Belt   In the 10th Hussars, black patent leather, with metal chain ornament; in the other regiments, gold lace, the width not to exceed 2in; morocco leather lining and edging, crimson in the 11th and 20th Hussars, buff in the 13th and scarlet in the other regiments. Regimental pattern buckle, tip and slide; gilt in the 7th, 8th, 10th, 15th and 18th Hussars; in the other regiments the buckle, tip and slide are of silver and silver engraved breast-ornaments with chain and pickers are worn. In the 10th and 18th Hussars the chains and pickers are of special pattern. In the 13th Hussars honours are worn on the shoulder-belt.

Pouch

Regimental Patterns   8th Hussars: Busby bag – scarlet; Plume – red and white; Pouch – scarlet cloth, embroidered in gold. Where the plume is shown of two colours, the first mentioned is the colour of the vulture feather bottom.

The undermentioned regiments have a silk stripe, ¼in wide, in the centre of the shoulder belt; and ⅛in stripe in the centre of the sword slings, of the colours specified for each: 3rd, 4th, 15th Hussars, scarlet; 13th, buff; 14th, gold; 19th, white; 20th, crimson.

Great Coat   Universal pattern. Shoulder straps, collar and cuffs edged with ⅛in yellow cloth.

LEVÉE DRESS

Pantaloons   Blue cloth (scarlet diagonal cloth in the 10th Hussars, and crimson cloth in the 11th Hussars), gold chain gimp down the outside seams.

Boots and Spurs   *Hessian Boots* – Round the top gold gimp lace ⅜in wide, terminating in an oval boss in front, 2in long and 1¼in wide. The height of the boots at the back to reach just above the centre of the calf of the leg, the slope

Air Marshal Sir John Baldwin, Honorary Colonel of the Regiment, with the officers. Exact date of photograph not known but thought to be on return from Korea c1952. All regimental officers wear the tent-cap and the formation sign of 29 Infantry Brigade Group, a white circle on a black ground.

S. D. EAGLE

behind to be 1½in lower than the top of the peak which forms the 'V' cut in front; patent boxes worked into the heels. Straight spurs with dummy rowels, silver plated.

Other articles as in full dress.

MESS DRESS

Mess Jacket Blue cloth with roll collar and pointed cuffs. Cuffs 6in deep at the points, and 2¾in behind, a 1in slit at the seam. Shoulder straps of cloth the same colour as the jacket, 1½in wide at the base, tapering to about 1in at the points; rounded points fastened with a button; the shoulder strap to be sewn in at the shoulder. Badges of rank in metal. No buttons on the front of the jacket and no gold braid or piping. Collar badges worn on the lapels.

Mess Vest Cloth, open in front, no collar, fastened with four ½in buttons.

Overalls As in full dress.

Boots Wellington, with box spurs.

Jacket Colour: shoulder strap, vest – blue. Collar, cuffs – scarlet.

Badges

On Buttons	On Collar of Tunic, Mess Jacket & Frock Coat	On the Pouch	On F.S. Helmet and on Forage Cap	On the Service Dress	
				On the Collar in Bronze	On the Cap in Bronze
Full dome, gilt, burnished.	The Harp and Crown; the Harp in silver, the Crown in gilt or gilding metal.	In gold embroidery the Royal Crest and Harp and Crown, and the Royal Cypher in silver embroidery. Round the Royal Cypher a wreath of shamrocks with scrolls in gold embroidery. The scrolls embroidered in silver, with the honours as shown in the Army List. A similar scroll below the Harp and Crown inscribed *Pristinæ virtulis memores*.	As the collar, but larger, with gilt or gilding metal scroll below, inscribed '8th King's Royal Irish Hussars'.	As for tunic collar.	As for forage cap.

Throat Plume Horsehair, 18in long, red and white. Brass ball and socket.

Leopardskin Universal pattern, edged with cloth of the colour of busby bag. Leopardskins are not used in India.

In 1914 the regiment was stationed in Ambala, so in October, after the outbreak of war in Europe, it embarked as part of the Ambala Cavalry Brigade, 1st Indian Cavalry Division – the Brigade consisting of 9th Hodson's Horse, 30th Lancers and 8th Hussars. The initial change from Indian service was immediately apparent, bad enough for the British but severe suffering for the Indians and for the horses. Eventually horses had to be left in rear areas and all British and Indian soldiers became accustomed to trench life.

The 30th Lancers were replaced by the 18th Lancers in 1916, and from then on the Ambala Cavalry Brigade remained unchanged until February 1918, when the Indian Cavalry left France for Egypt and the 8th Hussars joined the 15th and 19th Hussars on 9 March as part of the 9th Cavalry Brigade (Hussar Brigade) of the 1st Cavalry Division. The last mounted charge took place at Villiers-Faucon in 1917 when 'D' Squadron, 8th Hussars, charged and captured the village. Two machine-guns were captured and kept as trophies of war from that engagement. During the whole war years the regiment had been in many of the major battles as the battle-honours will testify, although the cost was over 100 officers, NCOs and men killed. The battle-honours authorised by the Army Council are as follows, those in capital letters to be emblazoned on the drum banners: GIVENCHY, 1914; SOMME, 1916-18; Bazentin; Flers-Courcelette; CAMBRAI, 1917-18; St Quentin; BAPAUME, 1918; ROSIÈRES; AMIENS; ALBERT, 1918; Hindenburg Line; St Quentin Canal; BEAUREVOIR; PURSUIT TO MONS; FRANCE AND FLANDERS, 1914-18.

During the years between the wars the regiment went back to India in

HRH The Duke of Edinburgh, Colonel-in-Chief, visits the regiment in Luneburg, November 1953. (By this date wearing the Divisional sign of the 7th Armoured Division.) Left to right. Air Marshal Sir John Baldwin, Honorary Colonel, Lt-Colonel Sir William Lowther, Bart, Commanding, HRH and Captain R. W. Piper.
ARMY PUBLIC RELATIONS

1919, saw service in Iraq and to Egypt in 1934. The last mounted parade was held on Armistice Day in Egypt 1935. After service in Palestine 1936, the regiment became a founder member of the 7th Armoured Division. In 1938 the regiment was allied to the 6th Duke of Connaught's Royal Canadian Hussars and the 8th (Indi) Light Horse Regiment of Australia.

During the early part of the Second World War it took part in all the desert warfare of the 7th Armoured Division, the famous Desert Rats. After El Alamein it went to Cyprus to recuperate and reorganise after its heavy losses. It returned to the United Kingdom and from there landed in Normandy and fought its way to Hamburg, still as part of the 7th Armoured Division. After the final victory parade in Berlin it returned to England in 1947, but by October 1950 sailed once again, this time to Korea. Equipped with Centurion tanks the regiment fought at the Battle of the Imjin and the heavy fighting around Seoul and Kowang-San.

Returning home after the Korean War the regiment moved over to Luneburg, Germany, 1952, and it was on 24 October 1958 whilst still in Germany, that the regiment amalgamated with the 4th Queen's Own Hussars to become the Queen's Royal Irish Hussars. At this ceremonial parade the Colonel-in-Chief of the new regiment, Field-Marshal HRH the Prince Philip, Duke of Edinburgh, KG, KT, GBE, presented a Regimental Guidon showing both new and former badges and crests, mottoes of both regiments as well as the combined battle-honours numbering 40 scrolls.

Since the Second World War both regiments formed affiliations and alliances with regiments now known as:

D Squadron (North Irish Horse) The Royal Yeomanry
The Royal Canadian Hussars (Montreal)
8th Canadian Hussars (Princess Louise's)
2nd/14th Light Horse Regiment (Queensland Mounted Infantry)
8th/13th Victorian Mounted Rifles
3rd Battalion The Royal Australian Regiment
2eme Regiment de Lanciers (Belgian)
7eme Regiment de Chasseurs (French)

On 22 October 1941 the then Rt Hon W. L. S. Churchill, had accepted the Colonelcy of the 4th Queen's Own Hussars, in which regiment he had previously served. When, as the Rt Hon Sir Winston Churchill, KG, OM, CH, he died in 1965, officers of the Queen's Royal Irish Hussars in the funeral procession in London, carried his Honours and Decorations and two others the banner of the Cinque Ports and the banner of Spencer-Churchill. The senior Band NCO blew Reveille in St Paul's Cathedral and a bearer party of an officer and senior WOs took the Colonel of the regiment on his last journey from Waterloo Station to Bladon. On this solemn occasion the officers and NCOs wore the scarlet peaked caps, long blue cavalry cloaks, overalls, half Wellington boots and spurs.

The Colonel of the 8th Hussars from 1947-1958 was Air Marshal Sir John Baldwin, KBE, CB, DSO. Commissioned into the 8th Hussars in 1912, he was seconded to the Royal Flying Corps during WWI and left the regiment in 1920 to join the Royal Air Force. On his frequent visits to his old regiment he wore army uniform, khaki service dress or battle-dress and with the officers' tent cap as headwear, a side-cap of green with shamrock pattern interwoven in the gold lace.

In 1990 Saddam Hussein invaded Kuwait and the Regiment deployed with 7th Armoured Brigade, The Desert Rats, to the Gulf. The victorious British advance into Iraq was led by the Regimental Battle Group.

The Queen's Royal Hussars (The Queen's Own and Royal Irish)

This new Regiment was formed in 1993 at Fallingbostel with the amalgamation of the Queen's Royal Irish Hussars and The Queen's Own Hussars. HM Queen Elizabeth The Queen Mother became Colonel-in-Chief and HRH The Duke of Edinburgh Deputy Colonel-in-Chief.

In 1996 the Regiment deployed to Bosnia under command of the Canadian Brigade as part of the NATO Implementation Force. Its performance under appalling operating conditions resulted in the award of the Canadian Forces Commendation.

The Colonel-in-Chief presented the new Regimental Guidon at Catterick on 13 June 1997. The following day the Regiment began training for its Northern Ireland tour October 1997 to April 1998.

The Queen's Royal Hussars are now stationed in Sennelager and are to be re-equipped with Challenger Two Main Battle Tanks in 1999.

Her Majesty Queen Elizabeth The Queen Mother, Colonel-in-Chief, presents the new Guidon to the Queen's Royal Hussars, Catterick, 13 June 1997.
RHQ QUEENS ROYAL HUSSARS

1 *The History of the VIII King's Royal Irish Hussars. 1693-1927*. Two Vols Rev R. H. Murray. Heffer & Sons Ltd, Cambridge 1928.
2 As above and Severne Mss.
3 Reproduced in colour, *Cavalry Journal* Jan 1932 and also in *Tradition Magazine* 1965.
4 Reproduced in black and white in J.A.H.R. Vol XXX p6, and also in small format in *Military Drawings and Paintings in the Royal Collection*, A. E. Haswell Miller and N. P. Dawnay, Vol I, Plates 384/5. Phaidon 1964.
5 Published in colour in Murray's *History* although with an incorrect date of 1825.
6 Reproduced in black and white in *British Military Prints* p54, Ralph Neville. Connoiss 1909.
7 Reproduced in colour – *Cavalry Journal* 1930s.
8 Both reproduced in colour in Murray's History.
9 Shown in colour on Ackermann's panoramic sheet which is divided into folds, overall length 66½ feet, the 8th Hussars section part of fold No 7. Another pictorial version of the procession including 8th Hussars, in black and white on double-page spread. *Illustrated London News*, 27 November 1852.
10 All recipients recorded in: *Honour the Light Brigade*, Canon W. M. Lummis and K. G. Wynn, J. B. Hayward & Son, 1973.
11 *Little Hodge. His letters and diaries of the Crimean War 1854-1856*, edited by The Marquess of Anglesey. Leo Cooper, 1971.
12 Reproduced in colour in Murray, also J.A.H.R. Vol XXII, p43.

PART TWO ■ THE REGULAR REGIMENTS ■ INFANTRY

Irish Guards

Lieutenant and Quartermaster J. Fowles, 1900. 'Ginger' Fowles had rapid promotion: Enlisted in Grenadier Guards 30 June 1879, Lance-Corporal 1880, Corporal 1881, Lance-Sergeant 1881, Drill-Sergeant, Grenadiers' Depot 1882, Colour-Sergeant in Battalion 1883. To 3rd Bn 1885. To Egypt with 1st Bn 1887. Warrant Officer 3 November 1890. Lieutenant and Quartermaster Irish Guards 24 May 1900. His medals are for 1887 Jubilee, Egypt, Sudan, Khedive Star and the Khedive Sudan Medal.

AMOT

The Irish Guards were raised in 1900 by order of Queen Victoria, following an initial suggestion from Lord Wolseley

> 'that the Queen should now order all her Irish regiments to wear the "shamrock" in their headdress on the 17th instant (March), to be worn by all her Irish regiments in future years on St Patrick's Day as a mark of Her Majesty's appreciation of the daring display by her loyal Irish soldiers in the recent operations near Ladysmith.'

The Queen accepted this suggestion and the wearing of the shamrock was duly authorised. On 28 February 1900 a letter from an Irish MP was printed in *The Times* praising the conduct of certain Irish regiments and finishing with the sentence: 'There are Scotch Guards and English Guards – why not add to the roll of glory a regiment of Irish Guards?' The same subject was raised in the House of Commons next day going one step further in suggesting that the proposed new regiment should bear the title 'The Royal Irish Guards', and that Lord Roberts should be its first Colonel. Her Majesty, who had in fact been considering the question of a regiment of Irish Guards, approved. No time was lost and by Army Order No 77, 1 April 1900 the regiment was created:

> 'Her Majesty the Queen having deemed it desirable to commemorate the bravery shown by the Irish Regiments during the operations in South Africa in the years 1899-1900 has been graciously pleased that an Irish Regiment of Foot Guards be formed to be designated the "Irish Guards".'

At a time when the fortunes of the British Army in South Africa were at a low ebb, Field Marshal Lord Roberts was appointed to take over as Commander-in-Chief, January 1900. Up to that time there had been defeat after defeat culminating in the 'Black Week' of December 1899. There had been little to cheer apart from the heart-warming bravery displayed by the British soldier and that of certain Irish regiments, the Inniskilling Fusiliers, the Dublin Fusiliers and the Connaught Rangers had particularly distinguished themselves. Things began to improve after Lord Roberts's arrival – Cronje, the Boer Commander surrendered at Paardeberg on 27 February, Ladysmith was relieved about the same time, and Bloemfontein, capital of the Orange Free State, was occupied on 13 March.

So to the finest compliment that Her Majesty could pay her Irish soldiers, the formation of a regiment of Irish Guards, was added yet a further honour, that so distinguished a soldier and Irishman as Field Marshal Lord Roberts be appointed Colonel of the Regiment, 17 October 1900.

Major R. J. Cooper, 1st Bn Grenadier Guards was appointed the first Commanding Officer 2 May 1900 and 200 Irishmen from the same regiment were transferred as a substantial nucleus. Colour Sergeant Conroy from the Royal Munster Fusiliers was given the Regimental

Number 1, whilst a new recruit, James O'Brien from Co Limerick was Number 7. A 'transfer-in' from the 88th Connaught Rangers, was Private Jordan, six feet six and a half inches tall.

Colonel V. J. Dawson, CVO, 3rd Bn Coldstream Guards, was appointed Officer Commanding the Regiment and Regimental District in September 1900, and by this time the regiment was really underway with 400 rank and file.

Hostilities in South Africa ceased on 31 May 1902, Lord Roberts, 'Bobs', whose Generalship had turned the tide of battle in 1900 and was instrumental in boosting morale, handed over to Lord Kitchener in November 1900. From then on, until his death on 14 November 1914, he took the greatest interest in all regimental activities and events. (The regiment last saw him when he came to bid the guardsmen God speed on 11 August 1914, when the Battalion paraded at Wellington Barracks before embarkation for France.)

Two of Lord Roberts's ADCs, Lord Settrington – 3rd Bn Royal Sussex Regt and Lord Herbert Scott – 3rd Bn Royal Scots, were ordered to transfer, whilst from the 3rd Bn Royal Fusiliers came Captain Charles Fitzclarence, VC. Other Guards officers transferring included the Earl of Kerry, DSO – Grenadiers, Lord Oxmantown – Coldstream Guards and Major S. Vandeluer, DSO, from the Scots Guards. The all important appointments, Adjutant and Quartermaster were filled by Lieutenant H. F. Crichton and Quartermaster J. Fowles respectively, both from the Grenadiers. Fowles was an Irishman who had enlisted in the Grenadiers in 1879 and earned rapid promotion, achieving warrant rank in 1890. He was selected as Quartermaster of the new regiment and received the appointment on the last birthday of Her Majesty, 24 May 1900. This led to an occurrence which at that time was probably unique. Mr Fowles trooped the Colour on that day as Sergeant-Major of the Grenadiers, although he was actually at the time Quartermaster of the Irish Guards. It was probably the only time on record that a commissioned officer of one regiment had done duty as a warrant officer of another. (Having instilled into recruits and young soldiers for years that the finest regiment in the British Army was the Grenadiers, one wonders how then he overcame the problem resulting from a sudden switch of allegiance to his new regiment?) He was a great promoter of boxing, athletics and most sports, and served on in the Irish Guards as

Mr C. H. Hassell, first Bandmaster of the Irish Guards, a position he held until 1929.

Colour-Sergeants of the four regiments of Foot Guards, c1900, just after formation of the Irish Guards. Left to right. Grenadier Guards, Scots Guards, Irish Guards and Coldstream Guards. The Sergeant of Irish Guards was probably a transfer from the Grenadier Guards and is believed to be of the Irish Guards Mounted Infantry Company.

Quartermaster until February 1914, retiring with the rank of Hon Captain.

Another of the initial appointments was that of bandmaster for which there was keen competition. The candidate chosen from more than 100 was Mr C. H. Hassell. Mr Hassell was born in 1866 and enlisted in the old 95th Foot (2nd Bn Sherwood Foresters) in 1878 at the age of twelve, attending a course at Kneller Hall during the following year as a pupil on the clarinet. On return to his regiment he was appointed solo clarinet, and in 1889 Band-Sergeant. After a further course at Kneller Hall he was appointed bandmaster of the 4th Bn King's Royal Rifle Corps in 1892 and so was to become first bandmaster of the Irish Guards in 1900. During his early army career he had served in Gibraltar, Egypt and India. He took the Irish Guards band to Canada in 1905 and 1913 and during the First World War the band made three visits to the regiment in France and once to Italy. He was promoted Lieutenant – Director of Music – 1 March 1919, and retired from the army and regiment on 13 March 1929 as Captain, handing over to his successor, Lt J. J. Hurd, one of the finest bands in the Brigade.

It is believed that a few individual officers managed to find their way to South Africa during the war but by November 1901, as a section of the Guards Mounted Infantry Companies, Irish Guardsmen also sailed for South Africa, and were consequently the first other ranks to see active service.

Ceremonial uniform followed the pattern of the other Foot Guards, black bearskin, scarlet tunic and blue trousers; the distinguishing features of the Irish Guards – the St Patrick's blue plume, the shamrock on each end of the collar and the buttons in front arranged four, four and two. For the soldiers the normal day-to-day uniform around barracks, apart from fatigue dress, was the white drill jacket. This was a plain garment with eight regimental buttons down the front and one on each cuff. NCOs wore chevrons on the right sleeve of this garment and Colour sergeants had their scarlet sashes over the right shoulder. Worn in conjunction with most orders of dress was the much maligned Brodrick cap, made of blue cloth with a green band, at first plain but later with the regimental badge in front. Photographs show that from the beginning the 'Micks' managed to wear this cap in their own particular style. One observer recorded his first reaction on seeing the cap in wear, on the London streets:

'When I first saw some of the new Guardsmen the other evening in the streets, I quite thought that we must have been secretly invaded by Russia, so like the Czar's soldiery did the new form of fatigue cap in conjunction with the Guards' great-coat make them look. I do not think I like this new cap; it savours too much of the Fire Brigade or the Bakers.'[1]

The regiment's first official duty was to provide a party, one officer, one sergeant, 24 privates and a drummer, to form part of the Duke of York's escort at the Inauguration ceremony in Australia. This party, under the command of Lt R. C. A. McCalmont, left on board SS *Britannic* in November 1900, was photographed before leaving in their white drill jackets and again in scarlet full dress. The officer appears in both pictures. He wears the undress frockcoat and the peaked cap, when posing with the white clad party, but seated amongst the Guardsmen in full dress, he appears in the blue serge frock without collar badges, buttons in fours, and has a Brodrick cap without badge. The undress cap

Lieutenant H. F. Ward, South Africa 1902, attached Younghusband's Horse. He wears khaki service dress with the 4 button arrangement on tunic peculiar to the Irish Guards. His slouch hat is turned up on the right and he has a plume, (pale coloured, light blue or white?).

he wears with the frockcoat is described in a tailor's book: Forage cap, blue with blue welt round the crown and blue welt to top of band, band 1¾in in black mohair military braid, gold infantry peak.

With so many troops in South Africa the regiment had to be ready to take its share of ceremonial duties in London and the first guard was mounted on 3 March 1901; the King's Guard was commanded by Lt Lord Settrington, the Buckingham Palace Guard by Lt Lord H. Scott and the Bank Picquet by Lieutenant the Earl of Kingston. *The Household Brigade Magazine* of March 1901 noted that

> 'It was generally agreed by officers and others interested in the Brigade that the appearance of the men and their smartness on sentry were well up to the traditions of the older Regiments and we feel confident that the proverbial efficiency of the Guards will lose nothing in the hands of their Celtic comrades.'

Peter Verney on the other hand states in his book:

> 'By all accounts this Guard was not a great success, for the men presented a motley appearance as the uniforms were by no means complete, and certain items of ceremonial equipment were still awaiting issue.'[2]

He no doubt referred to one section who were without bearskins and wore full dress scarlet, with Brodrick cap. This first Guard Mounting duty was performed without Colours, but in May 1902 the regiment, with a year's hard work behind it, was able to parade as a battalion on Horse Guards Parade to receive its first Colours from HM King Edward VII, who wore the uniform of his Irish Guards, and who was accompanied by Lord Roberts. After the presentation, the ceremony concluded with the Trooping of the Colour.

Bandmaster C. H. Hassell and bandsmen, 1910. Mr Hassell now has four medals, the Royal Victorian Medal, Egypt, Meritorious Service Medal and the Khedive Star. His MSM was awarded by Army Order No 8 of January 1910.

Group from Corporals Mess on St Patrick's Day, c1910. Note, by this date the peaked cap was in wear with the brass edging to peak, but the Brodrick still in use; Shamrock fixed below cap badges.

In August of that same year the Irish Wolfhound Club made the generous offer to present to the regiment a prize dog for a regimental mascot, an offer which was accepted by Lt-Col Cooper. There were ten competitors and after a painstaking examination a fine specimen, with the grandiose title of 'Rajah of Kidnal', was chosen and handed over with due ceremony. Needless to say this unwieldy title was soon altered to 'Paddy', later revised to 'Brian Boru' and given the Regimental Number 1463. From then until the present day one of these beautiful hounds has accompanied the regiment on most ceremonial occasions, all with names unmistakably Irish, 'Leitrim Boy', 'Doreen', 'Cruachan', 'Shaun', 'Fionn', 'Cormac (of Tara)' and 'Connor'.[3]

It will be remembered that Queen Victoria had authorised the wearing of a shamrock sprig on St Patrick's Day. These sprigs were at first a generous gift from Queen Alexandra, in later years from Princess Mary, the Princess Royal, and now (1989) Queen Elizabeth the Queen Mother has maintained the custom.

The 1904 manoeuvres included an attempt to stage an amphibious landing at Clacton-on-Sea. The regiment's role was to defend a ford over the Colne at Wivenhoe, but in the event were almost spectators, as the invasion fleet was soon in trouble. The large pontoons used as landing craft capsized, toppling men, horses and guns into the mud off Clacton. Irish Guardsmen wore khaki service dress for this exercise, the headdress a slouch-hat with brush plume attached to the up-turned brim on the right side.[4]

A more unpleasant type of duty occurred in August 1911. Within weeks of the Coronation celebrations in June, when the regiment took part in all parades, street-lining etc, troops were required in great numbers and at short notice, during the railway strike. Fortunately the strike was settled without violence, and quickly, but all precautionary measures were taken, with troops guarding railway stations and signal boxes, as well as coal depots and escorting other forms of transport around London. For this work the battalion appeared in London for the first time in khaki, but wearing with it the most unlikely head-wear, the busby.

Dress Regulations for the Army were printed in 1911. We publish those for the Foot Guards, for general comparison, in full:

FOOT GUARDS

FULL DRESS

Cap   Black bearskin, with a plain taper chain with black leather lining.
For officers not exceeding 5ft 6in in height, 8½in
For officers not exceeding 5ft 9in in height, 9in
For officers not exceeding 6ft 0in in height, 9½in
For officers exceeding 6ft 0in in height, 10in

Plume   Grenadier Guards – White goat's hair, 6in long, on the left side. Coldstream Guards – Scarlet cut feather, 6in long, on the right side. The Scots Guards wear no plume. Irish Guards – St Patrick blue cut feather, 6in long, on the right side.

Helmet, Foreign Service   Abroad, the white Wolseley helmet with white pagri is worn instead of the bearskin cap.

Tunic   Scarlet cloth; blue cloth collar and cuffs; the collar embroidered in front and round the top; at each end, the badge of the regiment embroidered in silver; the cuffs round, 3¼in deep, embroidered round the top. Blue flap on each sleeve, 6in long at the seam, 6¾in at the points, 2¾in wide at the narrowest part, and at the points, 3½, 3¼ and 3¾in respectively, beginning at the bottom

of the cuff; scarlet flap on each skirt behind, reaching within ½in of the bottom of the skirt; 2 buttons at the waist behind, about 3in apart. The front, collar, cuffs and flaps edged with white cloth, ¼in wide; the skirts lined with white. Blue cloth shoulder-straps, embroidered with two rows of embroidery, except at the base. Small button at the top. Field officers and captains have embroidery round the bottom of the collar, round the flaps on the sleeves and skirts, and a second bar of embroidery round the cuffs.

The Grenadier Guards have 9 buttons in front, at equal distances; and 4 bars of embroidery, at equal distances, on each skirt and sleeve flap.

The Coldstream Guards have 10 buttons in front, 2 and 2; and 4 bars of embroidery, 2 and 2, on each skirt and sleeve flap.

The Scots Guards have 9 buttons in front, 3 and 3; and 3 bars of embroidery, at equal distances, on each skirt and sleeve flap.

The Irish Guards have 10 buttons in front, 4, 4 and 2. Four bars of embroidery on the skirt and sleeve flaps, grouped towards the centre.

Embroidery   Gold, of special patterns; that round the collar, cuffs and flaps to be ½in wide.

Lace   Gold, of regimental pattern.

Buttons   Regimental pattern.

Trousers and Pantaloons   Blue cloth, with scarlet stripes, 2in wide.

Boots

Leggings   Dismounted officers, black leather.

Spurs   Brass.

Sash   Worn round the waist with buckle on left hip. On State occasions, gold and crimson net, 2¾in wide. Over the buckle a bow of gold and crimson net 6in

An Irish Guardsman in khaki service dress, worn in conjunction with the busby, on sentry duty during the railway strike, August 1911. This was the first time khaki was worn in London by the regiment. Here seen guarding the London/Brighton Company's electric line at Grosvenor Road.

Two officers in frock coats c1913. The officer on the right is Lieutenant Hon H. R. L. G. Alexander, later Field Marshal and Colonel of the Regiment.

Regimental Sergeant-Major c1913. Thought to be Sergeant-Major J. Kirk. Date of appointment 3 May 1913. His medals are for Coronation 1911, Queen's Sudan Medal 1896, Queen's South Africa Medal, King's South Africa Medal, Long Service and Good Conduct Medal, King Edward VII.

The drummers of the 1st Battalion who went to France in 1914.

long, ends 3½in wide, centre tie 2in and attached thereto is a pair of gold and crimson heads and tassels, the rear tassel being ½in longer than the front one. The bottom of the front tassel should hang 7in below the bottom edge of the tunic skirt of an officer 6ft in height, and for other officers proportionately to their stature. The tassels to hang immediatley in rear of the front sling of the sword belt. At other times, a sash of crimson silk net of the same dimensions.

Sword   Blade as for Infantry; steel hilt, with regimental device pierced and chased in the guard; black fish-skin grip, bound with silver wire; the blade embossed with battles and devices according to regimental patterns.

Scabbard   Steel, lined with wood, with German silver mouthpiece.

Sword Belt   Web, with dees for slings.

Sword Slings   Gold lace, lined with crimson morocco leather 1 inch wide. No metal furniture.

Sword Knot   Gold cord and acorn.

Great Coat and Cape   Milled Atholl grey cloth, lined with Wellington red, double breasted, to reach within a foot of the ground, two rows of gilt buttons of regimental pattern down front, ending at waist, 5 buttons in each row, the top ones 13in and the bottom ones 6in apart. Collar, 2in stand and 8¼in fall, fastened with 2 hooks and eyes. Shoulder-straps of same cloth, 2⅝in wide, small gilt buttons a top. Cuffs, turned back 7½in deep. Pockets, 2 in front below waist, slightly diagonal, with flaps. Sword slit 4in long across waist with pleat and loop to hip button. Inverted expanding pleat 6in wide down centre of back, fastened down 3in from collar, closed by a cloth strap at waist (2in wide and 9 to 10in long with button holes at each end) fastened by two gilt buttons at hips, slit behind 24in long.

Cape, same cloth as coat, lined Wellington red, and long enough to cover tunic, fastened at neck with gilt clasp and chain, 3 small gilt buttons below.

UNDRESS

Forage Cap Blue cloth, universal pattern, with embroidered peak and plain chin-strap, band 1½in wide, and regimental badge in front. The Grenadier, Coldstream and Irish Guards wear a band of plain black mohair braid, the Scots Guards a regimental check band and a gold cord round the edge of the crown. No chin-strap or buttons are worn in the Scots Guards.

Frock Coat Blue cloth, braided according to regimental pattern. Shoulder-straps of the same material as the garment, edged with ½in black mohair braid, except at the base; black netted button at the top.

Frock Serge Blue, full in chest, lined in front only, stand-up-collar and shoulder-straps of same material as the garment; the shoulder-straps with small regimental button at the top. Six medium regimental buttons down the front. A band, 1½in wide, round the waist, with special pattern buckle 2in long and 1¼in wide in front. A patch pocket with shaped flap and small button on each breast, and similar pockets without a button below the band. A slit at the cuff with small buttons and button holes – in the Grenadier Guards, 2; the Coldstream Guards, 2 pairs; in the Scots Guards, 3; and Irish Guards, 4.

Sword Belt Web.

Sword Slings Buff leather, 1in wide.

Sword Knot Buff leather with gold acorn.

Sash Crimson silk net.

Other articles as in full dress.

SERVICE DRESS, HOME SERVICE

Cap Universal pattern.

Cap Comforter

Left. Guardsman of the Irish Guards in Guards Machine Gun Corps, c1918. Note wound stripe on left cuff.
R. J. MARRION

Lieutenant G. Y. L. Waters, 2nd Battalion, Guards MG Coy. This officer was killed in action at Ginnechy on 15 September 1916.
B. TURNER

Pipers of 1st Battalion, c1916. The uniform consists of khaki caubeen with a large St Patrick's Star badge on green cloth backing, khaki cut-away jacket, no skirt pockets. Saffron kilt, green hose and khaki garter flashes. There are several pipers in this group wearing wound stripes on left cuff below service chevron. (2nd Battalion Pipers had a cloth shoulder title, green with yellow print, and two green upright bars of cloth below indicating 2nd Battalion.)

Stretcher-bearers of the 2nd Battalion (note the two green bars below the shoulder title) 31 July 1917, tending a wounded German soldier. The soldier with his back to the camera, is wearing a chain-mail visor, meant to be worn in front of the helmet to protect the eyes. These soldiers of the 2nd Guards Infantry Brigade, Guards Division.
IWM

A trio of 2nd Battalion wearing German plate body armour which they have picked up off the battlefield, July 1917. They examine a German 1908 pattern machine gun.
IWM

Jacket Universal pattern. Bronze buttons.

Breeches Mounted officers, universal pattern. Dismounted officers, knickerbocker pattern.

Trousers Drab mixture.

Leggings Mounted officers, brown, Stohwasser pattern.

Putties Dismounted officers.

Boots Brown ankle.

Spurs Mounted officers, jack, steel.

Belt 'Sam Browne'.

SERVICE DRESS, ABROAD

Khaki Drill Jacket

Khaki Helmet

Khaki Drill Trousers

Remaining Articles As on home service.

REGIMENTAL STAFF

The Adjutants wear the uniform of their rank.

The Medical Officers wear the regimental uniform of their rank, substituting a cocked hat for the bearskin cap.

The Quartermasters wear the regimental uniform of their rank with cocked hat instead of bearskin cap. Sash, crimson silk net.

The Bandmasters holding commissioned rank wear the regimental uniform of their army rank.

Cocked Hat For Medical Officers and Quartermasters with loop of one inch gold lace.

Plume Medical Officers, black cock's feathers, 6in long, drooping from a feathered stem, 3in long. Quartermasters, upright swan's feathers, 5in long;

Sentries of the regiment at the Porte de Mons, Maubeuge, 11 November 1918.
IWM

Passing Cologne Cathedral on their way to change guard, 10 February 1919.
IWM

white in the Grenadier and Scots Guards; red in the Coldstream Guards; and St Patrick blue in the Irish Guards.

Inspection by HM King George V on 21 April 1922, prior to the battalion leaving for Constantinople. Seated on HM's left is Colonel R. C. A. McCalmont, DSO, and then HRH The Duke of York in RAF uniform. On HM's right is Major the Hon H. R. L. G. Alexander, DSO, Commanding Officer. (Major Alexander's date of promotion to Lt-Colonel was 14 May 1922.) On his right Major-General G. D. Jeffreys, General Officer Commanding London District. (General Jeffreys' ADC, Lieutenant The Earl of Brecknock, Scots Guards, is standing at left of group.)

MESS DRESS

Mess Jacket Scarlet cloth, with garter blue collar and cuffs. Roll collar; regimental badge on collar, 5in from seam of shoulder. Cuffs pointed; Field Officers have on each sleeve, three rows of small gold cord forming an eye at the top. Captains two rows and Lieutenants and Second Lieutenants one row.

Mess Vest Garter blue cloth, with roll collar; 4 mounted regimental buttons for Grenadier Guards and Coldstream Guards; 3 for the Scots Guards; 4 for the Irish Guards. In the Coldstream Guards the buttons are in pairs.

Trousers As in full dress.

Boots Wellington; mounted officers, box spurs, brass.

Badges

Regiment	On Buttons	On Collar of Tunic, Mess Jacket and Frock Serge	On the F.S. Helmet and Forage Cap	On the Service Cap in Bronze
Grenadier Guards	The Royal Cypher reversed and interlaced, surmounted by the Crown; a grenade beneath the Cypher in the centre.	*Tunic:* A grenade in silver embroidery on a gold lace ground. *Mess Jacket & Frock:* A grenade in gold embroidery.	On forage cap: A grenade in gold embroidery. On the foreign service helmet: in gilt metal, the Royal Cypher reversed and interlaced on a ground of red enamel within the Garter, surmounted by the Crown. The motto pierced on a ground of blue enamel.	A grenade as on forage cap.
Coldstream Guards	The Star of the Order of the Garter.	*Tunic:* In silver embroidery on a gold lace ground, the Star of the Order of the Garter, the Garter and motto in gold; the cross in scarlet silk. *Mess Jacket & Frock:* A similar badge, but not on a gold lace ground.	In silver, the Star of the Order of the Garter. The Garter and motto in gilt metal, over blue enamel, the cross in red enamel. This badge is worn on the foreign service helmet, but larger.	The Star of the Order of the Garter as on forage cap.
Scots Guards	The Star of the Order of the Thistle, with Crown in place of the upper point of the Star.	*Tunic:* The Thistle in silver embroidery on a gold ground. *Mess Jacket & Frock:* The Star of the Order of the Thistle in silver embroidery.	In silver, the Star of the Order of the Thistle; the circle with motto and the centre in gilt metal.	As for forage cap.
Irish Guards	The Harp and Crown.	*Tunic:* A shamrock leaf in silver embroidery on a gold ground. *Mess Jacket & Frock:* A star as for forage cap, embroidered in silver and colours.	The Star of the Order of St Patrick in silver, the motto and circle in gilt metal on a blue enamel ground; within the circle the cross in red enamel, the Shamrock in green enamel and the crowns in gilt metal.	The Star of the Order of St Patrick as on forage cap.

HORSE FURNITURE

Saddle Universal pattern, with plain stirrups and blue girths.

Wallets Brown leather, with black bearskin covers.

Saddle Cloth Blue cloth, edged with gold lace an inch wide; 3ft long and 2ft deep in the Grenadier and Coldstream Guards; 3ft long at the bottom and 2ft 2in at the top, and 1ft 9in deep, in the Scots Guards. The Field Officers have a second stripe of lace and the badges of rank, embroidered in silver, at each hind corner.

Bridle   Brown leather.

Browbands and rosettes of blue silk in review order. On other occasions of leather.

The bridoon reins are attached to the bridoon by buckles of regimental pattern instead of being sewn on.

In the Grenadier Guards the buckles used on the bridle are of the double Greek pattern, and are in three sizes, viz:

> 2 buckles, 2½in long, with 1in opening.
> 2 buckles, 2¼in long, with ⅞in opening.
> 4 buckles, 1⅞in long, with ⅜in opening.

The bit is the branch bit with a gilt metal boss at each side, ornamented with the Royal Cypher, reversed and interlaced, within the Garter surmounted by a crown.

The bosses on the bit and on the breast plate are identical.

In the Coldstream Guards the 'sham Hanoverian bit' is used.

In the Scots Guards the Star of the Order of the Thistle is worn on the bit, below the frontlet, and on the breast plate.

In the Irish Guards the buckles are rectangular with the Cross of St Patrick in the ends.

Informal group, Spring 1922, showing: Lt-Colonel Hon. H. R. L. G. Alexander, DSO, MC, (4th from left) and Captain Hon. W. S. P. Alexander, DSO, (6th from left). The Padre is Father McGinness and next to him stands RSM C. Harradine, MBE, DSC, whilst the officer at extreme right is thought to be the Battalion Adjutant Captain J. S. N. FitzGerald, MBE, MC.
IWM

When new colours were presented to the 1st Bn on 28 June 1913, a composite service was used for the consecration, the Chaplain-General of the Forces took the first part, and a Roman Catholic chaplain the remainder. The ceremony took place on the lawns of Buckingham Palace, the presentation made by the regiment's Colonel-in-Chief King George V, and the Colonel of the Regiment, Lord Roberts also attended wearing his Irish Guards full dress.

Although 14 years old, the battalion of Irish Guards which left Wellington Barracks on the 12 August 1914 for France, was as fine a regiment as any in the British Army, with almost all of the 32 officers and 1,100 other ranks – Irish. The regiment landed at Le Havre as part of the

4 (Guards) Brigade, 2nd Division. By early September the regiment had received its baptism of fire. In what would otherwise have been an enjoyable glorious summer, the battalion was continually marching, eventually covering the retreat from Mons to the Aisne and engaged in a fierce action at Landrecies on 23 August, during which the commanding officer, Lt-Col Hon G. H. Morris was killed. After this opening phase of warfare and with the onset of winter the regiment, with the remainder of the British Expeditionary Force, became bogged down in trenches.

A 2nd Bn was formed at Warley Barracks in July 1915, joining the 2 Guards Brigade in August. Both battalions spent the remainder of the war years in France and Flanders.

Stories of the bravery and fighting spirit of the Irish Guards during those grim years of war are legion, but the exploits of L/Cpl Michael O'Leary, which gained the regiment its first Victoria Cross and became a legend, must be told, albeit in the unembroidered language of the official citations:

'O'Leary, No 3556, L/Cpl Michael. 1st Battalion. Date of Act of Bravery: 1 February 1915. When forming one of the storming party which advanced against the enemy's barricades, he rushed to the front and himself killed five Germans who were holding the first barricade, after which he attacked a second barricade about 60 yards further on, which he captured after killing three of the enemy and making prisoners of two more. L/Cpl O'Leary thus practically captured the enemy's position by himself, and prevented the rest of the attacking party from being fired upon.'

London Gazette, 18 February 1915.

Drums, fifes and pipes, c1932. The Pipe-Major, seated, is P. M. Tommy Atkins. The regiment's wolfhound can be seen at centre.

Then in 1917 two other Guardsmen received the Victoria Cross, John Moyney and Thomas Woodcock, both during the same attack at Ney Copse, Belgium, in September 1917. L/Sgt Moyney's party was surrounded by the enemy but they held out for 96 hours, drove off an enemy attack and then managed to retreat to the British lines without loss.

Men of the Irish Guards and tanks make their way along a road near St Martin des Besaces, Normandy, 1944.

IWM

An officer, Lt, Acting Lt-Col, J. N. Marshall, MC, whilst attached to and commanding 16th Bn Lancashire Fusiliers at the Sambre – Oise Canal, near Catillon on 4 November 1918, was awarded the Victoria Cross, posthumously, for his bravery, determination and leadership on that day.

A 2nd (Reserve) Bn was formed in 1914, becoming 3rd (Reserve) Bn in July 1915, but it remained at Warley. During the war years of 1914-18 the regiment suffered 115 officers and 2,235 other ranks killed or died of wounds; wounded 195 officers and 5,541 other ranks; prisoners of war 246. Apart from the three VCs, also won for the regiment by the gallantry of its members: 67 MCs, 77 DCMs and 244 MMs.

Pipers were added to the regiment in 1916, but one may make reference here to the regiment of Irish Guards formed in 1662, although no relationship is claimed by the present regiment. Amongst the establishment of that old regiment, which eventually went over to French service, was a 'Piper to the King's Company'.

In 1919 the 2nd Bn was put into suspended animation, whilst the 1st Bn was stationed at Woking. Full dress was taken into wear again in 1920 and on St Patrick's Day 1921 the pipers made their first appearance in full dress. Just a year later, however, the battalion received order to proceed overseas – to Constantinople, and from that time on Guards Regiments (with the exception of the Household Cavalry) took their share of overseas postings, but not to India. HM King George V inspected the battalion on 21 April 1922, and it sailed four days later under the command of Major Hon H. R. L. G. Alexander, DSO, (Lieutenant-Colonel from 14 May 1922). Harold Alexander, an Ulsterman, had joined the 1st Bn in September 1911 and went with the regiment to France, was wounded three times and was much decorated. He attended Staff College in 1926, became Officer Commanding

Regiment and Regimental District in 1928 and by 1938 was a Major-General commanding the 1st Division. He was one of the British Army's outstanding generals during the Second World War, greatly admired and immensely popular with all troops who served under him and adored by the Irish Guards. A Field Marshal in 1944 he remained Honorary Colonel of the Regiment from 1947 until his death in 1969.

After Turkey the battalion moved to Gibraltar for six months before return home to Inkerman Barracks, Woking, in 1923. From then until the next tour of overseas duty in 1936, the regiment resumed the peacetime role of a Guards Battalion, the principle parade of the year – the Sovereign's Birthday Parade. The Trooping of 3 June 1935 was to be King George V's last: on that day, his 70th birthday, he rode on parade wearing the uniform of the Irish Guards and was accompanied by his four sons, an event which had not happened before. The Prince of Wales was in the uniform of the Welsh Guards, the Duke of York – Scots Guards, Prince Henry of Gloucester – 10th Royal Hussars and the Duke of Kent – Queen's Own Royal West Kent Regiment. (George Stone, Irish Guards and formerly Garrison Sergeant-Major relates that the Derby Dinner was usually held on the evening of the Birthday Parade. 'The then Pipe Major of the Irish Guards (Thomas Atkins) told me the King said to him after the dinner, "My old horse likes to get up among the pipers (on the ride back to the Palace), especially during the playing of *The Wearing of the Green*."')[5]

During the 1939-45 war there were three battalions, the 1st Bn fighting in Norway and later in North Africa as part of the 1st Army. It was at a

Pipe-Major, officer in review order and Guardsman in jungle dress, 1960s. From a drawing by A. E. Haswell Miller.

position called Dj Bou Aoukaz in Tunisia on 28 April 1943, that L/Cpl J. P. Kenneally charged at German lines, where the enemy was preparing to attack, running forward alone, firing his bren gun from the hip, so surprising the enemy that they broke in disorder. Accompanied by a sergeant of the Reconnaissance Corps and although wounded, he repeated his charge again, frustrating an enemy attack. He was awarded the Victoria Cross.

The landing and fighting on the beach-head at Anzio resulted in some of the most bitter fighting of the war. Lt-Col B. W. Webb-Carter, commanding a battalion of the Duke of Wellington's Regiment sent to relieve the Irish Guards, summed up the scene as he found it.

'As the tall guardsmen filed out, leaving us the heritage of death and desolation they had borne so long, a peculiar sense of isolation struck us. In all the long drawn out crucifixion of the beach-head, no positions saw such sublime self-sacrifice and such hideous slaughter as were perpetuated in the overgrown foliage that sprouted in the deep gullies.'[6]

Another outstanding deed of heroism occurred when the 2nd Bn was driving its way into the heart of Germany in April 1945. Guardsman Edward Charlton literally attacked a Battalion of Panzer Grenadiers single-handed, armed with a Browning from his knocked out Sherman tank. He kept the enemy pinned to the ground, and even when severely wounded, with his shattered left arm, he propped his machine gun on a fence and continued firing. He was eventually captured but was so severely wounded he died. Charlton, an Englishman, and Irish Guardsman since 1942, was awarded the Victoria Cross, posthumously.

After the War, the Regiment rapidly lost its 3rd and 2nd Battalions (1946 and 1947 respectively). The 1st Battalion has served throughout the world during the intervening years with public duty tours in London being interspersed with service in the Far East (Hongkong and Malaysia), the Middle East (Palestine, Libya, Egypt, Aden and Cyprus), Belize, Kenya and Germany, on several occasions.

Since the Second World War the Battalion has received New Colours in 1949, 1966, 1978, 1988 and 1997. Its Colours have been trooped on six occasions, most recently in 1996. Since 1987 Her Majesty Queen Elizabeth II, the Colonel in Chief, has ridden in an open carriage whereas previously she rode 'Burmese', a black horse presented by the Royal Canadian Mounted Police.

Field Marshal The Lord Alexander of Tunis remained Colonel of the Regiment until his death in 1969 when General Sir Basil Eugster took over. HRH Jean, The Grand Duke of Luxembourg, who served in The Micks during the Second World War, succeeded to the appointment in 1984.

The Regiment's eleventh Irish Wolfhound 'Cuchulian' began his military career on St. Patrick's Day 1994 at Chelsea Barracks and is arguably the best known of all the Army's regimental mascots.

The Regiment treasures its special relationship with Her Majesty Queen Elizabeth The Queen Mother who has presented in person Her gift of Shamrock to the Battalion and Regiment annually since 1966. This has, on several occasions, involved Her Majesty travelling overseas to visit the Battalion.

Although individuals from the Regiment have served in Northern Ireland since the resurgence of sectarian violence in 1969, it was not until 1993 that the 1st Battalion as a whole undertook an operational tour. Both that period and a second deployment in 1995 were undertaken effectively and without casualties.

The Battalion was serving in Berlin in 1990/91 as both Communism and the Warsaw Pact collapsed. The Berlin Wall came down and guardsmen were able to share in the widespread euphoria of that historic time.

In the year 2000 the Regiment, with the Battalion stationed in Germany equipped with Warrior APCs, will celebrate its Centenary. In that period, short as it may be compared with other famous Regiments, the Irish Guards have built themselves a most enviable reputation.

Irish Guardsmen in the Falkland Islands, 1996.
RHQ IRISH GUARDS

---

[1] *Navy & Army Illustrated*, 17 May 1900 and *Black and White Budget*, 24 November 1900.

[2] *The Micks. The Story of the Irish Guards* by Peter Verney. Peter Davis – London 1970.

[3] Delightful coloured photos of 'Connor' with other official service mascots, appeared in an excellent Colour Supplement, *Sunday Express*, 13 July 1986.

[4] Full page illustration – *Illustrated London News*, 17 September 1904.

[5] *A History of the Sovereign's Birthday Parade by the Household Troops*, by Lt-Gen Sir Michael Gow, KCB, Scots Guards. Booklet published by the Household Division, c1980.

[6] *The Micks* (as footnote No 2).

The Royal Irish Regiment (18th Foot)

The oldest of the Irish regiments was raised from the independent companies of foot regimented on the Irish Establishment *c*1683-4, under the command of Arthur, Earl of Granard. It went through the actions against King James in Ireland, the siege of Carrickfergus, the Battle of the Boyne, the siege of Limerick, the capture of Athlone and the engagement at Aughrim. It subsequently came over to England and in 1693 served with the fleet as marines and landed in Flanders the same year. It gained its reputation as a fighting unit after the storming of the citadel at Namur, a regimental officer writing:

> 'The King saw this action from a rising ground at the back of Salsine Abbey, and took particular notice of the behaviour of our regiment, for ours only mounted the top of the breach and we planted our colours thereon.'

Another account states that:

> 'On the 20 August 1695, it was called upon to support the Grenadiers of the army, who in accordance with the custom of the time, were to lead an attack on the breach. The regiment was however, stationed half a mile away and before it could arrive on the scene, the Grenadiers had been beaten back by the tremendous fire of the defenders. Undaunted however by the failure of those whom they were to support, the Irishmen swept forward and pressing through the tempest of fire, and surging over the ruins of the breach, they never paused until the colours of the regiment were waving triumphantly from the summit of the breach, amidst the cheers of the survivors.'

Casualties were heavy. The corps was honoured with the title 'Royal Regiment of Ireland' and also the badge of the Harp and Crown as well as the right of bearing the Lion of Nassau and the motto *Virtutis Namurcensis Praemium*. George B. Short[1] describes the motto as

> '"The Reward of Valour at Namur", being an allusion to the Harp and Crown and Lion of Nassau badges placed on the colours by King William III in recognition of the distinguished conduct of the regiment at the siege of Namur, and which were the first battle-honours borne by any British regiment.'

'The Namurs' was one of the regimental nicknames acquired after this assault, but the less complimentary 'Paddy's Blackguards' probably relates to the early days in Ireland.

During Marlborough's campaigns in the Low Countries, the regiment served with distinction at Blenheim, Ramillies, Oudenarde and Malplaquet. These became the principal battle-honours although it was not until 1882 that permission was given to carry them on the colours, nor did they appear in the Army List until that year. Similarly, it was as late as 1910 before 'Namur' appeared in the Army List. Before leaving the regiment's service in the Low Countries it should be added that there were a further nine battle-honours awarded for sieges and other actions between 1701 and 1715. The regiment was back in Flanders by 1745 but for most of the intervening years was stationed on Minorca 1718-42, from there sending a detachment to assist in the defence of Gibraltar against the Spaniards.

It arrived too late to share the victory of Culloden in 1745 and subsequently spent several dreary years road-making in Scotland.

It was about 1751 that the official title was changed to the 18th (or Royal Irish) Regiment of Foot, Col John Folliott. Accurate information concerning the uniform of this time is supplied by the Clothing Warrant of 1751, also from the series of fine paintings by David Morier. Included in his series of Grenadiers Morier shows the back view of a drummer of the 18th. The Grenadier's mitre cap is shown as the standard pattern of red with a little flap at the front, white edgings surrounding the motto *Nec Aspera Terrent* around the flap, and the white horse, also on the red ground. The remainder of the face of the cap is blue with an embroidered harp and ornamental scrolls either side, crown above, and a blue and white tuft at the top. The turn-up at the back of cap is blue having a grenade embroidered in the centre and the figures 1 and 8 with ornamental scrolls on either side. The infantry coats of 1751 were red, the facings of the 18th royal blue with its own design of lace, waistcoats of red, breeches of blue and long white gaiters. Drummers had a red coat with blue facings, profusely ornamented with a special drummer's lace of blue and yellow, hanging sleeves of red on the back of the shoulders, with chevrons of lace and yellow tassels at the end of the sleeves. Displayed on the front of the drummer's cap, a trophy of drums and colours in place of the harp and crown and the usual flap with white horse badge and motto.[2] Morier also painted a picture entitled 'Conversation Piece *c*1763' in which he shows the back view of a drummer of the 18th Foot as well as a mounted soldier of the 6th Inniskilling Dragoons.[3]

In 1767 the regiment arriving from Ireland, landed at Philadelphia, the next year descending the Ohio and Mississippi rivers to Fort Chartres, where it remained for four years. Whilst there the establishment was increased from nine to ten companies by the addition of 'a company of Light Infantry, to consist of two sergeants, one drummer, three corporals and 38 privates, in common with all other regiments of infantry'. Having returned to Philadelphia in 1773 the Grenadier company was later despatched to Boston and was present at the Battle of Bunker's Hill on 17 June 1775. Five companies during the early part of 1775 were quartered in the City Barracks, New York, but were becoming numerically weaker all the time by desertions, the Americans constantly offering the attraction of land for cultivation, although found later to be dishonouring their promises. 100 men of the 18th went over to the other side and in December 1775 it was ordered that all private men of both the 18th and 59th Regts be sent to other corps at Boston, the officers, NCOs and drummers to return home to re-form. This left the Light and one battalion company still at Fort Gage, Illinois, and on 19 July 1776 all privates fit for service were drafted into the 8th Regt.

By 1783 the regiment was in the Channel Islands but any man joining about this time would have seen much varied service and movement during the next eighteen years. The travelogue begins in 1783 at the conclusion of the siege of Gibraltar. The regiment formed part of a small

Top left. Shoulder-belt plate 18th Regiment
c1800.
Top right. Shoulder-belt plate before 1850,
thought to be other ranks' pattern.
W. Y. CARMAN FSA (Scot)

Bottom left. Officer's gilt shako
plate c1855-61.
W. Y. CARMAN FSA (Scot)
Bottom right. Other ranks' gilt metal helmet
plate centre, 1881-1902, for wear on blue
cloth helmet.

Oil painting of an unidentified officer,
18th Regiment, c1845.
WALLIS & WALLIS LTD

force sent to Toulon in 1793 and which held that town for two months against an enemy four times its strength. It has also been said that at the siege of Toulon, Napoleon Bonaparte, then an officer of artillery, made his first acquaintance with the British soldier and was wounded by a bayonet thrust received in one of the sorties.

In 1794 the regiment was in Corsica, at Elba in 1796, 1797 to Tuscany and later that year served as marines in the battle off Cape St Vincent; on to Gibraltar and Minorca before leaving for Egypt and the capture of Cairo, and present at the surrender of Alexandria. Leaving Alexandria in October 1801 the 18th returned returned home to Ireland after a sojourn at Malta.

A second battalion was formed in Ireland at the beginning of the century and both battalions, each of 1,100 men were sent to the West Indies. Before leaving however, new colours were issued to the 1st Bn at Armagh on 12 June 1802, carrying the badge of the Sphinx and the word 'Egypt'. It was also about this time that we find a superb example of a manufacturing silversmith's craft, an officer's shoulder-belt plate. The oval plate had a matted gilt surface with a beaded rim and the harp and shamrock on a blue enamel ground within a gilt crowned garter inscribed *Virtutis Namurcensis Praemium* in pierced gilt letters on a blue ground.[4]

The 1st Bn served in the expedition to San Domingo in 1809 before return to Jamaica. The total period of service in the West Indies extended from 1805-17 and during this 12-year tour the 1st Bn lost 50 officers and about 3,000 men from sickness and disease. Little wonder that soldiers would go to any lengths to avoid drafts to these fever-ridden islands, in spite of running the risk of the harshest punishment. The skeleton of the 2nd Bn was back in this country by 1810 and finally disbanded there in 1814.

Between 1817 and 1840 there was service in the Mediterranean, Malta and Ionian Isles, home service in the 1830s, Ceylon in 1837. Whilst at Ceylon new colours were presented at Colombo on 1 October 1838 by Lt-Gen Sir John Wilson. Prior to the actual presentation he made the obligatory speech which appears to have been an elaborate regimental history of the past 150 years and which occupied four pages of close print when reported in the *United Services Journal* the following year. How this speech was received by the scarlet-clad troops, parading in the tropical sun, is not recorded.

After Ceylon the regiment was stationed in Madras for a short while before going on to China where it played a prominent part in the 1st Chinese War of 1840-2.

For its part in this campaign the badge of the Dragon and the right to carry the word 'China' on the colours and appointments, was granted. Although returning to India after the war, it went back to China for the operations on the Canton river in 1847, returning again to India before the Burmese War of 1851-2, subsequently adding the battle-honours 'Burmah' and 'Pegu' to the colours.

It went through the hardships of the Crimean Campaign from December 1854 and was present at the siege of Sevastopol, and returned home in July 1856. In June 1855, however, an officer of the regiment Capt (later Lt-Col) Thomas Esmonde, during and after the attack on the Redan on the 16th, performed many acts of outstanding bravery and was awarded the Victoria Cross. The *London Gazette*, 25 September 1857 gives the following citation.

> 'For having, after being engaged in the attack on the Redan, repeatedly assisted, at personal risk, under a heavy fire of shell and grape, in rescuing wounded men from exposed situations; and also, while in command of a covering party, two days after, for having rushed with the most prompt and daring gallantry to a spot where a fire-ball from the enemy had just been lodged, which he effectually extinguished, before it had betrayed the position of the working party under his protection – thus saving it from a murderous fire of shell and grape which was immediately opened upon the spot where the fire-ball had fallen.'

One of the two celebrated photographers at the Crimea, James Robertson, took a splendid group photograph of the officers on a sunny day in May 1856 and it is obvious that they made a special effort to look their best for the occasion. The group is taken in front of a substantial hut, plenty of drink appears to be available. All wear undress, either frockcoat or shell jacket and the undress cap with peak, having the Harp and Crown badge on the gold embroidered shamrock wreath. The veteran commanding officer, Lt-Col A. Edwards, CB, seems to have worn his dress tunic with medals. He had a reputation as a stern

Photograph of an unidentified officer, c1855-61.

disciplinarian and one soldier described him thus:

'Our old Colonel was a very proud man and he would glory in seeing a man flogged, especially if he thought he was a bit stubborn, and while the flogging was going on he would growl and grumble at the flogger for not hitting harder.'[5]

The Earl of Carlisle, Lord Lieutenant of Ireland, presented new colours to the regiment at Dublin in 1856. A new 2nd Bn was formed in 1858 of volunteers from the Irish Militia and was sent to New Zealand in 1863. This new unit fought during the Maori Wars of 1863-6 and although due to leave in 1869 was unable to do so because of fresh outbreaks of raids by outlaw Maoris and remained until 1870, the last of the 14 British battalions to have served in that country. It was on the 24 January 1865 that a captain of the regiment distinguished himself by an act of bravery and was subsequently awarded the Victoria Cross. He was Capt Hugh Shaw who became an ensign at the age of 16 in 1855, a lieutenant in the 1st Bn, 25 September 1857; that year proceeding from the Curragh to Bombay and for two years served in the field under Sir Hugh Rose. He was adjutant from 1859 to 1864 and on promotion to captain, 2 April 1864, joined the 2nd Bn in New Zealand. The official citation from The *London Gazette*, 28 November 1865, is as follows:

'For his gallant conduct at the skirmish near Nukumaru, in New Zealand, on the 24 January last, in proceeding under a heavy fire, with four privates of the regiment, who volunteered to accompany him, to within 30yd of the bush occupied by the rebels, in order to carry off a comrade who was badly wounded. On the afternoon of that day, Capt Shaw was ordered to occupy a position about half a mile from the camp. He advanced in skirmishing order, and when about 30yd from the bush he deemed it prudent to retire to a palisade about 60yd from the bush, as two of his party had been wounded. Finding that one of them was unable to move, he called for volunteers to advance to the front to carry the man to the rear, and the four privates referred to accompanied him, under heavy fire, to the place where the wounded man was lying, and they succeeded in bringing him to the rear.'

Capt Shaw eventually rose to be a Major-General in the army.

Six private soldiers received Distinguished Conduct Medals for bravery in the New Zealand campaign, whilst after the Crimean War, one sergeant, two corporals and 11 privates received similar decorations.

On the very day that the 18th embarked for India, 11 November 1857, a Portsmouth local newspaper printed a short paragraph reporting the story of one man who had no wish to join his comrades on a voyage to India, and paid a heavy price for 'missing the boat'. Under the heading 'Flogging British Soldiers', we learn that –

'Cornelius O'Brien, a private in the 18th Royal Irish Regt, was condemned to receive fifty lashes for theft. The troops were paraded to witness the execution of the sentence; a file of men was sent to escort him from the guard-room, when it was discovered that he had escaped. He was recaptured however before he had enjoyed many hours of liberty, and the sentence was immediately after carried out. He is now in hospital; when he recovers he will be tried for the attempt to escape.'

The actual tour of Indian service lasted until 1866 followed by a few years at home and then, after a two-year stay in Malta, back to India again. Stationed at Ferozepore in the Punjab during December 1879 the

1st Bn was on hand to join the Reserve Division for the invasion of Afghanistan. As the Royal Irish was the only Irish infantry regiment to participate in the campaign it may be of interest to relate the official report of the regiment's record of service:

'In December 1879 the 1st Bn Royal Irish received its orders to proceed to Peshawar. The regiment marched on 4 January 1880, arriving at its destination on the 25th, was posted to the Reserve Division of the force operating on the Khyber line.

'On the Reserve Division being broken up in March 1880, the Royal Irish was detailed to garrison Peshawar, where it remained till it received orders, in the ensuing month, to proceed on service into Northern Afghanistan.

'The battalion arrived at Landi Kotal on 2 May 1880 and was posted to the 1st Section Khyber Line Force. Shortly afterwards one company was detached to Daka, but in the month of June it was withdrawn and rejoined Headquarters, the post being considered too unhealthy for prolonged occupation by European troops.

'The regiment remained at Landi Kotal during the whole summer, performing convoy and other duties. On the return of the troops from Kabul, it was detailed to form part of the newly constituted Khyber Brigade, and with the other units of that force was employed for several months in holding the country from Jamrud to Landi Khana, the only part of Northern Afghanistan retained by the British after the evacuation of Kabul.

'It being considered advisable, during this period, that British troops should be quartered at Ali Musjid, in consequence of the tribes in the neighbourhood constantly harassing convoys etc, one company of the regiment was detailed to that post.

'On the final evacuation of the Khyber on 18 March 1881, the Royal Irish returned to India. During the period of its service in the war, the battalion suffered heavily from the unhealthy nature of the climate in which it was employed, losing from disease over sixty-two non-commissioned officers and men, including Quarter-Master Richard Barrett, who had been 26 years in the regiment.'[6]

Sergeant, full dress, 1st Bn Royal Irish Regiment, Colchester 1891.

The 2nd Bn, after several years at home, embarked at Portsmouth 11 August 1882 on passage to Egypt aboard the Transport *City of Paris*. The battalion was up to full strength of nearly 900, and together with 100 men of the 2nd Bearer Coy arrived at Alexandria on 21 August, whilst another Transport *The Arab*, with the 1st Bn Royal Irish Fusiliers, came into Ismailia on 23 August. Both regiments formed part of the 2nd Infantry Brigade of the 1st Division. It was to be a long, hot and arduous campaign. Under the command of Lord Wolseley the regiment was in the night march across the desert to Tel-el-Kebir and stormed the Egyptian trenches, earning the praise of Lord Wolseley. Although the campaign came to a satisfactory conclusion with the Khedive's authority restored, British troops had to remain to guard and keep open the Canal.

By 1884 the 1st Bn was in Egypt from India, whilst the 2nd Bn moved on to Malta. Towards the close of the year the 1st Bn had joined the River Column in the unsuccessful attempt to relieve General Gordon at Khartoum. It was however awarded Lord Wolseley's prize, being the first regiment up the Nile. The reminiscences of a 1st Bn officer of the 1884-5 river expedition and desert campaign provides the most elaborate description of dress, arms and equipment.[7]

1884
Men's
rowing kit
Extract of an officer's reminiscences of the Royal Irish:
'Greatcoats and nothing else was the favourite kit with the men of my

Group, 2nd Battalion, Mhow, c1899. The Commanding Officer, Lt-Colonel J. B. Forster and Captain H. N. Kelly, Adjutant, with senior NCOs and the old Colours.
S. D. EAGLE

Khaki drill

boat, who prided themselves on their dress and were anxious to save one good suit of khaki in which, they said, they would march into Khartoum. It was a handy costume when you stuck on a sandbank or struck upon a rock, as you could be overboard in a second to shove the boat off. Very often my men used to row in their "birthday suits"!'

28.1.85
Men's fighting kit

Officers' fighting kit

Men's arms and equipment

Kit with transport

No tents

'In the afternoon of 28 January 1885 the battalion paraded for Lord Wolseley's inspection, dressed in the fighting kit devised for them by a former commanding officer, Col M. J. R. MacGregor. It consisted of a khaki-coloured frock and trousers of cotton drill, a helmet covered with the same material, grey woollen putties, a woollen shirt, socks and ammunition boots; spine protectors, cholera belts and drawers had been issued, but were not in general use among the rank and file; all hands carried haversacks, wooden water-bottles and rolled greatcoats. The officers wore "Sam Browne" belts, which supported their swords and field glasses, revolvers and cartridge-pouches; the non-commissioned officers and men were equipped with braces and waist-belts, pouches containing seventy rounds of ammunition, three-edged bayonets (longer than those in use at the present day) and Martini-Henry rifles. As in previous campaigns it had been discovered that when these rifles were fired fast, the barrels became so hot that it was almost impossible to grasp them, they were fitted with leather hand-guards, tightly laced round the stock and barrel behind the back-sight, to enable the men to get a firm grip of their weapons. The remainder of the campaigning kit was carried on transport camels; to every ten men was allotted one animal, which was loaded with their camp kettles, a blanket and a waterproof sheet apiece, and one or two sea-kit bags, each of which contained sets of the following articles, viz: one flannel shirt, two pairs of socks, a tin of grease, a canteen, a towel, soap, and a hold-all, complete. The troops were allowed no tents.'

New colours were presented to the 1st Bn at Devonport on 7

Band of 2nd Battalion, Mhow, Central India, c1899. The Commanding Officer seated in centre, Bandmaster A. J. Cunningham on his right.
S. D. EAGLE

September 1886 by Lady Albertha Edgcumbe but these were lost by fire at Colchester in July 1891, so a new stand was presented on 14 November 1892 at the Curragh, by Lady Wolseley.

The pattern of distribution of the two battalions between the 1880s and 1914 is interesting. After service in the Egyptian campaign 1884-5 the 1st Bn remained at home until 1900 followed by the South African War and from then until 1914 was abroad – whilst the 2nd Bn was abroad from 1882 until 1902, the following twelve years spent at home.

A mounted infantry detachment took part in the expedition organised to put down the rising of the natives in Rhodesia in 1896 and the following year the whole battalion was called to active service for the Tirah campaign, taking part in the relief of Fort Lockhart and the operations on the Samana and in the Bara Valley.

On 20 July 1898 Field Marshal Lord Wolseley, known to the regiment as General Commanding-in-Chief of the expedition to Egypt in the 1880s, became its Colonel-in-Chief.

On 4 December 1899 the 1st Bn was ordered out to South Africa as part of the 6th Division, arriving early in January 1900. By February the regiment was in action around the area of Rensburg – Slingersfontein, Orange Free State, where the Boers were in strength astride the road from Rensburg, the Inniskilling Dragoons and some Australian Horse covering the troops falling back. The Royal Irish Regt, 2nd Bn Bedfordshire Regt, 2nd Bn Wiltshire Regt and 2nd Bn Worcestershire Regt all from the 6th Division and 2nd Bn Berkshire Regt already serving in South Africa, this Brigade under General Clements, suffered defeat at the hands of superior numbers of Boers, two companies of the Wiltshire Regt being surrounded, sustained about 50 casualties and 100 were forced to surrender. So the Royal Irish Rifles gained its first experience of warfare against the Boers, their only consolation being that they had helped to keep a superior force of the enemy so occupied that they were unable to press on to the north in aid of their General Kronje. A year later the nature of the war had changed, the stronger British forces now experiencing hit and run attacks on garrisons and other outposts. One particularly heavy engagement in which 60 men of the regiment were involved whilst at an outpost outside Belfast, the attack so heavy when the Boers took advantage of fog just before dawn to close on the Irish and make their assault. Fierce hand to hand fighting followed, the 18th using bayonets and knives and refusing to surrender, eventually reduced to 20 uninjured men before reinforcements arrived. One officer and 13 men were killed, 43 officers and men wounded and 80 captured – but Boer casualties were even more severe.

The *London Gazette* of 8 August 1902 announced the award of a posthumous Victoria Cross to No 3733 Barry, Pte J.:

'During the night attack on the 7/8 January 1901, on Monument Hill, Pte Barry, although surrounded and threatened by the Boers at the time, smashed the breach of the Maxim gun, thus rendering it useless to its captors, and it was in doing this splendid act for his country that he met his death.'

The Cross was handed to relatives at a later date. During the South

A studio portrait of a private soldier, Mhow, c1899.
R. J. MARRION

Captain and Colour-Sergeant, 2nd Battalion, c1908. (Photograph believed taken at Buttevant.)

African War the Distinguished Conduct Medal was awarded to Sergeant-Major J. Bergin, also to three sergeants, four corporals and lance-corporals and five private soldiers. The battle-honour 'South Africa 1900-1902' was added to the colours.

In November 1904 the colours presented to the old 2nd Bn in 1858 were laid up, as a new stand had been presented on 6 August of the preceding year by King Edward VII at Beaumont Park, Cork.

It may have been about this time that a photograph of a full dress parade, thought to show the 2nd Bn Royal Irish Regt, was taken at The Barracks, Cork. Although not a particularly clear picture it is interesting as it shows that there are a few pipers at the head of the band. These pipers are clad exactly as the remainder of the band, blue helmets, scarlet tunics with blue facings and without any apparent distinguishing dress features. The pipes have two drones and no pipe-banners are in evidence either on this occasion or by 1st Bn pipers in India before 1914, detail from a photograph taken at Jhansi c1912-14, showing three drummers and seven pipers of the 1st Bn.

The description of dress uniform is reproduced here from the Dress Regulations of 1911. With the exception of badges etc, it also applies to the following Irish regiments: The Connaught Rangers and The Leinster Regt.

INFANTRY OF THE LINE
FULL DRESS

Helmet Plate In gilt or gilding metal, an eight-pointed star surmounted by a crown; on the star a laurel wreath; within the wreath a garter inscribed, *Honi soit qui mal y pense*; within the garter the badge approved for the regiment. On the bottom of the wreath a silver scroll with the designation of the regiment. The dimensions of the plate are – from the top of the crown to bottom of plate back measurements, 5¼in; extreme horizontal width of star, back measurement, 4¼in; the bottom central ray of the plate comes halfway over the cloth band of the helmet.

Helmet, Foreign Service Abroad, the white Wolseley helmet with white pagri is worn as the full dress headdress.

Tunic Scarlet cloth, with cloth collar and cuffs of the colour of the regimental facings. The collar ornamented with ⅝in lace along the top and gold Russia braid at the bottom, with badges; the cuffs pointed with ⅝in lace round the top extending to 7½in and a tracing in gold Russia braid ⅛in above and below the lace, forming an Austrian knot at the top extending to 9½in from the bottom of the cuff, and a small eye at the bottom. Eight buttons down the front. The skirt closed behind, edged with white cloth on closing seam with a three-pointed slash at each side, a button at each point. The front, collar and slashes edged with white cloth ¼in wide. Twisted round gold shoulder cords, lined with scarlet. A small button of regimental pattern at the top.

Facings Cloth of the colour authorised in the Army List.

Lace *For Tunics:* gold, ⅝in wide. Rose pattern for English and Welsh regiments, shamrock pattern for Irish regiments. In the following regiments a black line is introduced at the top and bottom of the lace and in the shoulder cords: The Norfolk, Somersetshire Light Infantry, East Yorkshire, Leicestershire, East Surrey, Loyal North Lancashire, the York and Lancaster and the Connaught Rangers.

Trousers and Pantaloons Blue cloth with a scarlet welt ¼in wide down each side seam.

Sash Crimson silk net backed with leather, without plaits, width 2¾in, fastened with a 4-bar buckle fitted with horizontal overlapping loops. To be

Dress parade, the barracks, Cork c1903-8. (Almost certainly the 2nd Bn Royal Irish Regiment after return to Ireland in 1902 and before moving to Blackdown in 1908.) Note pipes and drums in front of the band, normal full dress uniform.

worn round the waist, the tassels over the left hip, to hang 4in below the tunic, and immediately in rear of the front sling of the sword belt.

Sword Slings   Gold lace, Infantry pattern, ⅞in wide, on red morocco leather 1in wide, gilt billet studs, oval wire buckles.

Sword Knot   Gold and crimson strap, with gold acorn.

Sword Belt Web

Great Coat   Universal pattern. Shoulder straps edged with ⅛in scarlet cloth.

UNDRESS

Forage Cap   Universal pattern. Royal Regiments and regiments styled *Kings* other than Light Infantry, blue cloth with scarlet band and welts. Light Infantry, green cloth with band of black oakleaf lace and green cloth welts. The Connaught Rangers, blue cloth with green band and welts. Other regiments, blue cloth with band of black oakleaf lace and scarlet welt round crown.

MESS DRESS

Mess Jacket   Scarlet cloth, roll collar; pointed cuffs, 6in deep at the point and 2¾in behind; four small buttons and button holes down the front. Shoulder straps 1½in wide at the base, tapering to about 1in at the points, rounded points fastened with a small button. The shoulder strap to be sewn in at the shoulder.

   The jacket is edged all round with white piping, the cuffs, collar and shoulder straps are similarly edged. Badges of rank in metal. Collar badges worn on the lapel.

Mess Vest   Open in front, fastened with buttons of regimental pattern.

Overalls   As in full dress.

Boots   Wellington; mounted officers, box spurs.

Jacket				Vest
Colour	Shoulder Straps	Cuffs	Piping	
Blue cloth	Blue cloth	Blue cloth	White	Blue cloth, roll collar, 4 buttons

Badges

On Buttons	On Collar of Tunic, Mess Jacket and Frock Coat	On Helmet-Plate	On F.S. Helmet and on Forage Cap	On the Service Dress	
				On the Collar in Bronze	On the Cap in Bronze
Within a shamrock wreath, a circle inscribed 'Virtutis namurcensis præmium'. Within the circle, the Harp; the circle surmounted by the Crown. In the cap and mess dress buttons the circle is omitted. The mess dress button mounted, design in silver.	In silver, an Escutcheon of the arms of Nassau, with a silver scroll below, inscribed 'Virtutis namurcensis præmium'.	In silver, on a scarlet ground, the Harp and Crown within a wreath of shamrock. On the universal scroll, 'The Royal Irish Regiment'.	In silver, the Harp and Crown, with a scroll below inscribed 'The Royal Irish Regiment'.	As for forage cap.	As for forage cap.

Young soldiers' rifle team, 1st Battalion. Photograph believed to have been taken at Nisarabad, India, c1913. All ranks wearing coloured walking-out caps together with khaki drill uniforms. Note ammunition pouches on leather waistbelts, additional to bandoliers.

In March 1913 Field Marshal Sir John French became the regiment's new Colonel-in-Chief. It was also about this time that an alliance was formed with a regiment of the Dominion of New Zealand: The 7th (Wellington West Coast) Regt.

During the First World War, in addition to the two regular battalions there were a further eight battalions wearing the Harp and Crown regimental badge. The principal recruiting areas were Counties Tipperary, Kilkenny, Waterford and Wexford.

The 1st Bn left India in October 1914 and after two months re-forming at Winchester landed in France just before Christmas 1914. As part of the 27th Division it was in action almost at once at St Eloi. One account states that:

'In spite of the decidedly adverse climatic conditions to which it and the other two Irish regiments – namely the 2nd Bn Royal Irish Fusiliers and the 1st Bn Leinster Regt, had been accustomed, these three battalions advanced in a driving sleet over a squelching morass and captured a formidable line of entrenchments under the famous Mound of Death, after a fierce hand to hand encounter with those tenacious fighters, the Bavarians.'

The commanding officer Lt-Col G. F. R. Forbes, who was killed in this action, was a descendant of the first Colonel of the regiment – Arthur Forbes, Earl of Granard. The 1st Bn left France in 1915 for the Middle East serving thereafter at Salonika, Egypt and Palestine etc.

The 2nd Bn was in France, from their last station at Devonport, by October 1914, and was to spend the whole of the war years, 1914-18, in France and Flanders. This battalion, too, was almost immediately in action, where at the battle for Le Basse, October 1914, a German officer later reported that hardly an unwounded man of the 2nd Royal Irish survived, whilst several hundred, all dead, were found in the main trench.

A Victoria Cross was awarded to a private of the regiment in 1917, The *London Gazette*, 17 October 1917, recorded:

'ROOM, No 8614, Pte (Acting L/Cpl) Frederick G. For most conspicuous bravery when in charge of his company stretcher-bearers. During the day the company had many casualties, principally from enemy machine guns and snipers. The company was holding a line of shell-holes and short trenches. L/Cpl Room worked continuously under intense fire, dressing the wounded and helping to evacuate them. Throughout this period, with complete disregard for his own life, he showed unremitting devotion to his duties.

'By his courage and fearlessness he was the means of saving many of his comrades' lives.'

Uniform insignia as worn by the 2nd Bn in France was as follows: No markings on steel helmets. Covers made of sandbags, so cut as to closely fit the helmet until the practice was forbidden owing to the shortage of material.

No distinguishing marks were worn on the jacket until the battalion put up the badge, common to the 16th Division, from October 1916, viz, a green shamrock worn on the top of each sleeve. No variation in case of officers. After joining 63rd (RN) Division, May 1918, a patch 2½in × 1½in of regimental colours, blue, red, green, was worn on the shoulder by all ranks. Company colours 1½in square patch as follows: 'A' Coy: red; 'B' Coy: blue; 'C' Coy: yellow and 'D' Coy: green. On joining 63rd Div a patch 2½in × 1½in of regimental colour, blue, red and green, was painted on left side of helmet.

After the war the 2nd Bn was in Delhi, India, moving to Dehra Dun in 1922. The 1st Bn was in Germany and by January 1920 had been redirected to Allenstein in East Prussia to help maintain order whilst the Plebiscite was taken, moving from there in August.

So to the last sad days in July 1922 when the colours were handed over to King George V in the St George's Hall, Windsor, and the regiment was finally disbanded after nearly two and a half centuries of continuous service.

Lieutenant D. K. J. Chisholm, 1st Battalion, c1909. Full dress with blue cap, red band. (This officer later transferred to the 114th Mahrattas, Indian Army, was awarded The Military Cross during the First World War.)
AMOT

[1] *Records and Badges of the British Army*, H. M. Chichester and G. Burgess-Short. W. Clowes & Sons, London 1895.
[2] *A History of the Uniforms of the British Army* by Cecil C. P. Lawson, Vol II. Peter Davies, London 1941. Colour plate of Drummers 1751 including 18th Foot.
[3] J.S.A.H.R. Vol XIX, p63. Colour plate 'Conversation Piece 1763'.
[4] *Shoulder-belt plates and buttons* by Major H. G. Parkyn. OBE, Gale & Polden 1956.
[5] Photograph reproduced in *Crimea 1854-56* by Lawrence James, Hayes Kennedy 1981.
[6] *The Afghan Campaign of 1878-1880 (Historical Division)* by S. H. Shadbolt, pub 1882.
[7] *Campaigns and History of the Royal Irish Regiment 1684-1902* by Lt-Col G. le M. Gretton. Blackwood 1911.

THE REGULAR REGIMENTS ■ INFANTRY

The Royal Inniskilling Fusiliers

The early history of this distinguished regiment runs parallel with that of the 6th Inniskilling Dragoons. On 20 June 1689 Major Zachariah Tiffin received his commission as Colonel of a Regiment of Foot raised for the defence of the town of Inniskilling. The men were already hardened fighters after the bitter struggles of the preceding months.

Whilst it is thought that the earliest uniforms were grey, and shown as such in the Regimental History and elsewhere, there is now a suggestion that red coats with blue breeches were worn, certainly from 1689.[1] The colour of facings for this early period are not known but by 1742 were buff, and remained so until the changes of 1881.

Throughout King William's Irish campaigns, from the Boyne to the fall of Limerick, the regiment, at times armed with little other than scythes and reaping hooks, fought with great bravery, earning the right to carry the badge of the Castle of Inniskilling flying St George's banner. The regiment was transferred to Scotland for employment during the Jacobite rising of 1715-16 and subsequently received permission to carry the Horse of Hanover with motto on colours and appointments.

Left. Grenadier, c1751. Right. Officer c1809. After P. W. Reynolds.
W. Y. CARMAN FSA (Scot)

Six hundred men of the regiment set sail for the West Indies in 1739 and were engaged at Porto Bello on the Isthmus of Darien. At the conclusion of this duty just nine men were able to return, the remainder victims of climate, fever and the general unhealthy conditions. A later spell of service in that area came in 1796 and resulted in the regiment's first battle-honour, 'St Lucia'. It left England in November 1795 as part of the expedition under the command of Sir Ralph Abercromby, but after seven weeks at sea was forced to return to Portsmouth through bad weather. After a refit the fleet reached Barbados in April 1796. A principal objective was to capture a strongly held hill on the landward side of the harbour at St Lucia called the Morne, nearly 900 feet high and held by a force of 2,000 coloured men under French officers. Under the command of a Brigadier, Sir John Moore, later of Corunna fame, the force landed in a bay just north of the harbour, marched through thick jungle and occupied a nearby height so that guns could be brought to bear on the French. Brig-Gen Moore led the Inniskillings against the enemy, storming the position and capturing the important citadel of St Lucia. Sir Ralph Abercromby's general order was as follows:

> 'The 27th Regt, under the command of Brigadier-General Moore, will this day at twelve o'clock take possession of Fort Charlotte (Morne Fortuné), the present garrison having first marched out and laid down arms on the glacis. Brigadier-General Moore will then plant the colours of that regiment on the fort, to be displayed one hour on the flag-staff previous to hoisting the usual Union flag.'
>
> 'The behaviour of the Enniskillen Regt of Infantry was so worthy of praise that it deserves the Commander-in-Chief's highest approbation. To Col Gillman,, (commanding 27th) the officers and men of that gallant regiment, he also returns his best thanks.'

Nothing had improved during the fifty years since the decimation of the regiment during its previous service. The losses from yellow fever were appalling. After the capture of the Morne in 1796, Sir John Moore was left in command, in June, of 4,000 men. In November the force had been reduced to 1,000 for duty and 1,000 sick. Fortescue, in his *History of the British Army*, speaking of the campaign in St Lucia from 1793-6, said it resulted in the total of 80,000 soldiers lost to the service, including 40,000 actually dead. The latter number exceeded the total losses of Wellington's army from all causes from the beginning to the end of the Peninsular War. In 1794 men were dying at the rate of 300 a month, due to bad housing and food. The home government were largely to blame. General Gray wrote letter after letter home ending with this pathetic sentence: 'You seem to have forgotten us.'[2]

During the fifty years between 1745 and 1796 the regiment was most active, 1756 to Canada and America, 1761-2 to Grenada and Martinique and the siege of Havana, returning home for a brief spell before the American War of Independence and staying in America until 1778.

The Royal Warrant of 1751 abolished the old system of using its Colonel's name to identify a regiment and numbering according to seniority was adopted, thus becoming the 27th (or Inniskilling) Regt of Foot. Inspection returns provide a few facts concerning dress and music:

26 June 1769: A Band of Music is recorded.

 7 June 1775: First mention of numbered buttons – buttons with badge and number of regiment.

21 June 1789: Men's hat-lace too narrow and not according to regulation.

12 June 1792: Drums and Fifes. 10 Music; 6 young and unserviceable.

Volunteers from the Donegal and Fermanagh Militias formed the basis of a 2nd Bn in May 1800, and whilst the 1st Bn remained at Malta it was mainly this new 2nd Bn which accompanied Sir Ralph Abercromby to Egypt. In May 1801, now joined by the 1st Bn, the two took part in the Siege of Alexandria, thereby earning the distinction of the Sphinx superscribed 'Egypt' to be placed on the colours. Wholesale reductions in the army upon the signing of the Peace of Amiens in 1802 resulted in the disbandment of the 2nd Bn but it was soon to be needed again. In 1804 men from Fermanagh, Armagh and Down enrolled in this new 2nd Bn and the following year a 3rd Bn was raised. From 1805 until 1817 all three battalions were continually on the move or fighting in Spain under Lord Wellington.

It is interesting to follow the separate movements of the three battalions during the Napoleonic Wars and to see how they were brought together but once, separating again almost immediately.

1st Battalion

1805 Remained at Malta since return from Egypt, served in the expedition to Naples under Sir James Craig and afterwards to Sicily.

1806 Battle of Maida.

1807 Sicily.

1808 Sicily.

1809 Expedition to Bay of Naples, then back to Sicily joining 2nd Bn and remaining together until 1811.

1811 To the east coast of Spain remaining there till end of war.

1814 Met the other two battalions at Bordeaux in April and joined the

Duke of Wellington's army. Embarked for Canada. Plattsburg, mouth of Mississippi river.

1815   Returned to Portsmouth. To Belgium – Waterloo. Joined Wellington's army on 16 June in time to be present at Waterloo on 18 June. Out of 698 men, the regiment lost 480 at Waterloo, having been blown to pieces when standing in square above the sandpit on the Charleroi road. Remained in France until 1817, before return home.

2nd Battalion

1805   To Hanover with Lord Cathcart's army.

1806   Sicily.

1807   Malta.

1809   Expedition to Bay of Naples, then to Sicily until 1811, (with 1st Bn).

1811   To east coast of Spain, together with 1st Bn, until end of war.

1814   Met with 3rd Bn. To Ireland, provided drafts for 1st Bn.

3rd Battalion

1805   3rd Bn raised, recruited in Ireland at Belfast, Omagh and Enniskillen and embodied in Scotland.

1808   Portugal.

1809   Cadiz. Joined Wellington's army near Badajos. This battalion remained with the army through all the campaigns until the peace. Capture of Badajos, battles of Salamanca, Vittoria and actions in the Pyrenees, battles of Orthez and Toulouse.

1814   Met 1st and 2nd Bn at Bordeaux in April. To Canada.

1815   Landed at Ostend from Canada in July.

1816   Returned to Ireland and was disbanded.

Silhouette portrait of Major T. P. Touzel, 27th Foot, 1850. Signed, Herve, 145 Strand. (Charles Herve 1756-1866.) Major Touzel served in the regiment as Ensign 1829, and up to 26 May 1854 when he obtained his majority. He wears the blue undress frock-coat. (Note castle seen on left shoulder scale.)
CHRISTIE'S

Naturally, stories of the wars from a regiment such as the 27th, which saw so much fighting, are legion. One remarkable tale vouched for by Napier, occurred during a lull in the battle of Castalla in 1813. A French officer called across 'no mans land' challenging any British officer to fight a duel and Capt John Waldron of the 1st/27th accepted, fought his opponent and killed him.[3]

The senior lieutenant at the Battle of Waterloo, who was to rise to high rank and distinction in later life, was Lt George M'Donnell. He changed his name to George Macdonald, lived to be the 'Father of the British Army' and was Colonel-in-Chief of the 16th Foot. He entered the army in 1805, joined the expedition to Hanover in 1805, the army in Sicily in 1806, expedition to Naples in 1810 and was present at the capture of Ischia and Procida, returned to Sicily in 1811, was subsequently employed in Spain and was present at the battle of Castalla and siege of Tarragona, afterwards served in Canada. He was wounded three times at Waterloo. He was promoted through every rank from Ensign to General by 1871.

At the other end of the rank scale was Pte Thomas Kerrigan, one of the few of the regiment who escaped being blown to pieces when standing in square on the Charleroi road, 18 June 1815, he died at Calkey near Enniskillen, 3 December 1862 and is said to have attained the great age of 108.

The *Regimental Journal* tells a curious story about a button, one that was found on the equipment of an officer killed at Alcot 1813.[4]

It will be remembered that an Inspection Return of 1775 describes a 'button with badge and number of regiment', this being the Castle of Inniskilling with the word Enniskillen above and numerals 27 below.

Group of senior NCOs 27th Regiment, c1879.
ROYAL INNISKILLING FUSILIERS MUSEUM

Allowing for the variation in spelling, ie Inniskilling, this pattern of button remained in wear until 1881. The pattern on the haversack of Capt Parsons however, shows an interesting variation, the word Enniskillen and numerals 27 above and below but the centre design shows the Enniskillen Watergate instead of the Castle. It is known that in 1804 the officer commanding the 1st Bn, an Inniskilling man, Sir Galbraith Lowry Cole, had the badge on the Regimental Colour changed from the traditional heraldic Castle to a representation of the actual Watergate, and so it is assumed he had the buttons designed at the same time, although the haversack button is the only known specimen. However, the innovation was short-lived as a report of 1807 indicates that Lord Moira, Colonel of the Regiment directs 'that it be altered for the original one as granted by William III'.

A writer from the Royal Military College Sandhurst, sent to the *United Services Journal* of 1829 a couple of anecdotes concerning the exploits of an unnamed regimental officer below the heading: An Enniskillener.

'An ensign of the gallant Enniskillen Regt (the 27th), who had just been gazetted, was travelling by the mail in Ireland to join his corps. Hearing a passenger on the coach make some comments on the regiment, which he did not relish – "You thief of the world" says he, "is it after abusing my own regiment ye are, and me sitting here to hear it. Guard, lend us your pistols and stop the coach." The accommodating guard obeyed orders and the combatants had a round at each other by the side of the road. The same officer, when advanced to the rank of field-officer, had a servant, "a nate boy from sweet Tipperary". On going into action one fine morning, he ordered Pat to remain in the rear to look after his baggage. In the heat of the action a spent ball struck the Major, which stunned him; on recovering his senses he

Group of senior NCOs 108th Regiment, Portsmouth, 1879. (Note the Sergeant-Major, seated centre, has a pistol – but where does he carry it?)
S. J. KRETSCHMER

Private soldier of the 108th Foot, Portsmouth 1879/80. The numerals 108 in centre of helmet plate.
S. J. KRETSCHMER

found Pat in the middle of the square and trying to stuff him into a sack. "Thunder and 'ounds! what are we doing here, ye born rascal; didn't I tell ye to remain with the baggage?" – "Sure, and I thought ye'r honour was kilt, and I only wanted to give ye Christian burial."'

In 1835 the regiment was sent to the Cape of Good Hope and participated in the Kaffir War that year. In 1841 a detachment of the Inniskillings under Capt Thomas Smith, a Peninsular and Waterloo veteran, was sent on the long overland journey from Grahamstown, Cape of Good Hope, to Port Natal, near to the present town and seaport of Durban, there to re-assert British authority. Arriving at Congella, a camp near Port Natal, after an arduous march, the garrison became surrounded by Voortrekkers, disgruntled Boer farmers who had trekked north into what is now Natal. The British force was hemmed in for a month but under Capt Smith refused to surrender and, although suffering privations and loss, held on until relieved by troops under Col Sir A. Cloete, transported by the ships of the Royal Navy, *HMS Southampton* and the schooner *Conch*. Smith's plight however, would not have been known but for an historic ride undertaken by a settler named Dick King, who volunteered to take despatches, on horseback, to the Cape, a marathon ride of 600 miles in ten days.

Various accounts help us to gain a picture of conditions, arms and the dress of the soldiers under siege – which apart from the 27th included one officer and eight other ranks Royal Artillery, one officer and four other ranks Royal Engineers and three officers and fifty other ranks of the Cape Mounted Rifles. Lt Bartholomew Tunnard of the 27th made a series of sketches showing the march-up and the laager at Durban Bay, whilst a Capt J. F. Lonsdale, also of the regiment, in letters home was able to add to the picture. The following are notes taken from these sources:

'During this campaign the 27th took with them their full dress and undress and wore both as occasion demanded. The officers are shown in one sketch wearing an undress cap, wide at the top going straight up from the head with perpendicular lines running up the deep head-piece, another in the same sketch wears a shako. A sentry wears a shako with cover, and both light and dark trousers are shown. The large pouch and cross-belts and flint-lock arms are carefully drawn in. The CMR were asked by Pretorius (a leader who made a name for himself in warfare against the natives; Pretoria is called after him) during the interview of 9 May to be ordered to let down the carbine hammers on the nipples for fear of the men shooting him. They were therefore carrying percussion-lock arms. None of the caps of other ranks have peaks, though the officers' do. The Grenadier Company, 27th, OC Capt Durnford, wore their Grenadier caps.'[5]

Capt Smith received full public credit given in a lengthy appreciation in the *Illustrated London News* of 8 October 1842. As his career was an interesting one it is reproduced in full:

'We are glad to perceive by the *London Gazette* that Capt Smith of the 27th Regt has been promoted to a brevet majority for his gallant and successful resistance and ultimate defeat of the rebel Boers at Port Natal. This appropriate and well timed reward is, we are assured, the Duke of Wellington's spontaneous and unsolicited act. The promptitude with which his grace has conferred this well merited mark of distinction upon Capt Smith, and the spirited and exemplary conduct which it is intended to

Types of the Royal Inniskilling Fusiliers, c1893. Watercolour by R. Simkin. Note 'jam-pot' cuffs on Fusilier and Drummer.
THE PARKER GALLERY

reward, are alike honourable to the donor and the recipient. It may not perhaps be generally known to our readers that Capt Smith commenced his professional career in the navy, from which he transferred his services into the 27th Regt in June 1813. At that period his father was a surgeon of that corps, and his sister, Mrs Tucker, married to one of its captains, circumstances which no doubt had their full weight in determining Capt Smith to exchange his blue for a red jacket.'

The regiment stayed on in Africa and participated in the later Kaffir War of 1846-7, arriving back home in 1848. 'South Africa 1835' and 'South Africa 1841-47' were added to the regiment's already impressive list of battle-honours.

It is always interesting to see how the uniforms of the musicians differed from the remainder. Drawings of a contemporary artist, R. Ebsworth and those of the eminent historian and the artist responsible for illustrating the Regimental History, P. W. Reynolds,[6] give comprehensive details for the 1850s and 60s. A drummer of 1850 wears the Albert shako with ball tuft, white over red, scarlet coatee with eight loops of white, with strands of red thread running through diagonally, across front of garment, the shoulder-belt plate of brass carrying the

Below left. Sergeant-Drummer Cook, 1st Battalion, Victoria Barracks, Portsmouth 1890.

Fusilier on sentry duty. 1st Battalion, Tiensin, 1909. Scarlet serge frock, blue collar, no pockets.

Pipers from the Regimental Depot, Omagh, Co Tyrone, at the Bournemouth Centenary Fete, 6-16 July 1910. The first appearance of regimental pipers outside Ireland.
S. J. KRETSCHMER

numerals XXVII with crown above. The collar and cuffs are buff, four button patch on cuff, on the shoulders the large worsted wings of red, white and pale blue interwoven, drummer's lace (before 1866) of white with narrow blue edging and scarlet broken chevrons running through the centre. Trousers of a pale blue shade. By 1868 the drummer wears the normal scarlet tunic, with red thread ornamenting the white drummer's piping, the shoulder wings now reduced in size and of red and white alternate bars within white edging. A bandsman is also shown in the white band tunic which has red collar and cuffs and piping, three button red patch on cuff, each button mounted on a small white backing cloth.

The regiment sailed for India in 1854, suffering a tragic loss en route when the transport *Charlotte* was wrecked off the Cape of Good Hope with the loss of 98 lives, men, women and children. For its work during the Mutiny the battle-honour 'Central India' was awarded, probably appearing for the first time on new colours presented on 19 July 1869 by the Countess of Inniskilling at Chatham, the regiment having returned to this country in December 1867.

During the 1870s, in common with most infantry regimental bands, the 27th had a German bandmaster, Herr Louis Werner. An interesting photograph made up of 50 individual portraits of all 47 musicians, Herr Werner, the commanding officer as well as a picture of a stand of instruments including a 'Jingling Johnny', was taken whilst the regiment was at Malta in 1876.[7] Mr E. Wallace was the regiment's first Warrant Officer bandmaster, date of warrant 1 July 1881.

Another illustration shows a group of senior NCOs of the regiment and one private soldier, these individuals selected as all had served as boys at the Royal Hibernian Military School, taken about the same time as the band picture. It can be seen that whilst the two sergeants have the normal three bar chevron each on right arm, the gymnastic instructor

The Colours, 2nd Battalion, Aldershot 1912.

sergeant has crossed swords with a crown above and the colour sergeants the single bar chevron, crossed swords with flag and crown above. All but one of these NCOs have the red sash across the right shoulder whilst a forage cap has the numerals 27 at the front.

The Cardwell reforms of 1881 occurred whilst the 27th Regt was stationed at Hong Kong, too far from home to have any immediate effect. The regiment with which it was to be permanently linked was the 108th (Madras Infantry) Regt, then stationed at Portsmouth. An immediate compliment to the new regiment was that of becoming Royal, always an honour but it is said that the 27th were loath to part with their cherished buff facings which had to be replaced by blue. Also, that the designation became Fusiliers and so the blue infantry pattern helmet would go, to make way for the fusilier racoon skin cap. All these uniform changes would no doubt have taken time to come about as the 27th did not return home after service in the Straits Settlements, China and South Africa, until 1888.

The 108th Regiment(s)

Two regiments carried the number 108 for a short period during the 18th century. The first was raised in 1760 and disbanded in 1763, the second known to have been raised in Ireland in 1794, served at Gibraltar for a short while before broken up, the men transferred to the 64th and 85th Regiments.

The last regiment numbered 108 began life in India in 1853. A General Order issued on 18 November 1853 allowed the European troops in the Hon East India Company's service to be increased and the 3rd Madras

European Regt was raised. Large drafts of recruits were sent out from Ireland. On paper the British officer's full dress was to be scarlet with yellow facings and gold lace, but no portraits have come to light to show this elaborate dress in wear. A fine officer's shoulder-belt plate is known however; the design shows the numeral 3 in the centre of a garter which carries the title MADRAS EUROPEAN REGIMENT, the garter surrounded by a wreath of laurel and mounted on a frosted star, all on a rectangular gilt plate.

The regiment distinguished itself in the suppression of the Mutiny and was awarded the battle-honour 'Central India'. In 1859 it was serving with the Field Division under General Whitlock and subsequently stationed at Jubbulpore in December 1859 and Jaulnah in 1860.

In 1861 the regiment was transferred to the Crown and became the 108th (Madras Infantry) Regt with scarlet uniform and yellow facings. Colours were presented at Bombay on 23 December 1863. Up to the late 1870s it served in Madras and Bombay respectively and did not come to England for the first time until December 1876, being stationed at Colchester, its first tour of duty in Ireland from 1882. It was at Aldershot in September 1886 that it ran into trouble. It appears that a large draft under immediate orders to join the 1st Bn in South Africa, not at all keen on the prospect, was responsible for an affray in the streets of Aldershot. A report in a local paper of October 1886 states:

'A serious military riot, which at one moment threatened to assume the proportions of a mutiny, happened in the streets of the town about 7 o'clock last evening. At that hour about 150 men of the Inniskilling Fusiliers, part of a draft under orders to proceed this morning to join the 1st Bn in South Africa, collected in the High Street. Some of them were armed with the legs of iron bed cots used in barracks, and soon began to use them freely. The disturbance quickly assumed formidable proportions and the military police and picquets had to be reinforced. The former, under the command of Capt Broockes, Provost-Marshal, grappled with the rioters with the greatest gallantry and several of them were badly wounded in the desperate struggle

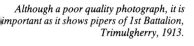

Although a poor quality photograph, it is important as it shows pipers of 1st Battalion, Trimulgherry, 1913.

Pipe-Major T. Fisher, Omagh, 1922-4. Believed to show the first version of full dress for pipers after the war.

Top left. A small drum and bugle band with four pipers, France, c1918 by a Paris photographer.
S. J. KRETSCHMER

The 1st Battalion Band, Shorncliffe, 1926. Bandmaster Mr. W. C. Windram.

which ensued. Ultimately the rioters were overpowered and no fewer than 41 were arrested and taken to the cells. The casualties sustained by the military police included Cpl Stone, head cut open and Pte Harrison, cuts and bruises. The corporal is now in the Cambridge Hospital. It is worthy of notice that the publicans of the town co-operated with the civil and military authorities by closing their premises as long as the disturbances lasted. The riot, which is understood to have been due to dissatisfaction at being sent on foreign service, was the most serious that has ever been witnessed at Aldershot.'

We later learn that

'The whole of the rioters have been sent off with their comrades by train to Southampton, where they are to embark on board the *Praetoria* for Natal, to join their linked battalion.'

Imaginative reporting is not confined to the 20th century. In June 1889 a lengthy story appeared in the columns of a local newspaper, reporting a 'Military Riot at Portsmouth', – 'Nine soldiers of the 1st Bn Inniskilling Fusiliers badly wounded and a strict investigation ordered by General the Hon Sir Leicester Smyth, Commanding Southern District.' The whole affair was put into true perspective in a subsequent report which read as follows:

'We are informed by credible witnesses of the disturbance between soldiers, which took place in Warblington Street, Portsmouth, on Monday night, that the circumstances have been grossly exaggerated. There was an ordinary public-house brawl, and the military police intervened and secured three men (not nine as stated), and removed them to the guard-room. There is not one word of truth in the statement that one of the men, in the course of the fracas, seriously bit the thumb of one of the policemen, the fact being that some time later a drunken prisoner, who had nothing to do with the disturbance in question, bit the finger of one of the escort. As a matter of fact there were only seven military prisoners arrested that night throughout the entire garrison.'

One is reminded of Kipling's words:

'For it's Tommy this, an' Tommy that, an'
"Chuck him out, the brute!"
But it's "Saviour of 'is country" when the guns
begin to shoot;'

When the battalion had returned from South Africa in 1888 a witness recorded that he had seen the regiment and noted at that stage they had not received home service clothing. The uniform consisted of a white helmet, 'the new pattern' with ventilator cap instead of spike, brown leather chin-strap, grey horse-hair or brush plume on left side and at front a brass grenade badge, slightly smaller than that subsequently used for busby. The red serge tunic had no coloured cuffs but blue collar, sergeants had white piping and knot, also white buff belts. By the time the battalion moved into Victoria Barracks, Portsmouth, fusilier full dress was in wear, but at that stage without the busby plume. (A splendid example of this dress is to be found amongst our illustrations of Sgt Drummer Cook, who wears medals awarded for the Egyptian campaign, indicating his transfer from another regiment.) At this date the Drum-Major's sash, or scarf, was of a fairly plain design, but at the top of his staff the Castle of Inniskilling, beautifully worked in silver.

A pleasant year was spent on the Isle of Wight, then to Dover before return to Ireland for five years. In the meantime the 2nd Bn was in India

Warrant Officers, Staff-Sergeants and Sergeants, 5th Inniskilling Dragoon Guards and 1st Battalion Royal Inniskilling Fusiliers. Aldershot, 19 April 1934.

and Burma. Photographs appearing in the *Navy & Army Illustrated* in February 1898 show the Inniskilling Fusiliers' lines in camp at Bara, on the North West Frontier, during the Afridi War. All troops wear khaki service dress, the Inniskillings however had been issued with the extra large khaki cover and neck protector for the tropical helmet.

The 1st Bn was sent to the war in South Africa, both battalions eventually there in 1902, the 1st returning home to Inniskilling whilst the 2nd going on to Egypt. It was at Cairo on 3 November 1906 that new colours were presented to the 2nd by HRH The Prince of Wales.

In the meanwhile, the 1st Bn was at Londonderry and in 1903 it was called upon at short notice to provide Guards of Honour for HM King Edward VII, one at Londonderry and another at Belfast. It was on 11 April 1903 that intimation was received from the War Office that HM the King had been graciously pleased to approve of The Royal Inniskilling Fusiliers being permitted to wear, in their sealskin caps, a plume of grey colour. His Majesty took the opportunity of presenting the King's South Africa Medal to all members of the regiment who had served in that campaign, including officers and men from the depot and from the 4th and 5th Battalions.

By 1907 the battalion was at Crete, and then for three years in Tiensin, China, present during the Chinese rebellion of 1911 and 1912, and proceeding from China to India by 1913. After Egypt the 2nd Bn spent the intervening years before 1914 in Dublin, Aldershot and Dover.

Pipers were added to the band strength before 1914. A photograph taken around that time during Indian service shows six pipers and three drummers, all are dressed in hot-weather white. The drummers' cords with tassels are looped on the left breast, whilst similar cords for pipers are looped on the right.

At home between 6-16 July 1910, pipers of the regiment made what was claimed to be their first appearance out of Ireland at the Bournemouth Centenary Fetes. The *Daily Telegraph* of 7 July 1910 gave

Dancers of 2nd Battalion, Catterick, 1 June 1939.
IWM

Soldiers of 6th Battalion returning to the rear after suffering terrible conditions at the Battle for 'Two Tree' Hill, Tunisia 1943.
IWM

the event a full report and devoted the following paragraph to the pipers:

> 'This was the first public appearance, for the first time out of Ireland, of the pipers of the Royal Inniskilling Fusiliers. Some six or eight of them there were altogether, direct from the regimental depot at Omagh, Co Tyrone, and a brave show they made. At first sight it seemed rather odd to see pipers who wore no tartan, either in the form of kilt or trews, but this impression would doubtless have been removed if these Inniskilling Fusiliers had worn the national uniform or kilt and plaid, which is part of their outfit. The critical in these matters would, no doubt, observe that the Irish bagpipe which these men played had fewer "drones" than the Scottish variant of the instrument, and the result, as it seemed, was that the airs the pipers discoursed stood out more prominently from the groundwork of the drones than is the case with the Scottish pipes. Before saying whether that is an advantage, it would probably be necessary to consult a Highland piper. But drones or no drones, the Inniskillings made excellent music as they footed it proudly in front of the grandstand, the bags of their instruments covered in royal blue, and a strip of blue ribbon of the St Patrick Order streaming gaily from each drone.'

Dress Regulations 1911, also appropriate for: Royal Irish Fusiliers, Royal Munster Fusiliers, Royal Dublin Fusiliers.

FUSILIERS

The uniform and horse furniture are the same as for other regiments of Infantry of the Line, with the following exceptions:

Cap   Short bear skin or black racoon skin.
For officers not exceeding 5ft 6in in height, 8in high in front
For officers not exceeding 5ft 9in in height, 8½in high in front
For officers not exceeding 6ft 0in in height, 9in high in front
For officers exceeding 6ft 0in in height, 9½in high in front
These measurements must not be exceeded. Burnished chain, lined with black leather.

Plume   Cut feather, with gilt two-flame socket. Grey. 6½in height. Left side.

MESS DRESS

As for other regiments of Infantry of the Line.

Jacket				
Collar	Shoulder Straps	Cuffs	Piping	Vest
Blue cloth	Blue cloth	Blue cloth	None	Blue cloth, roll collar, 4 buttons

Badges

On Buttons	On Collar of Tunic, Mess Jacket and Frock Coat	Ornaments for Bear-skin or Racoon-skin Caps	On F.S. Helmet and on Forage Cap	On the Service Dress	
				On the Collar in Bronze	On the Cap in Bronze
A castle with three turrets with St George's colours flying superscribed 'Inniskilling'. For the mess dress the castle is in silver – mounted on a plain gilt button. For the cap, the same design, die-struck.	A grenade in gold embroidery; the Castle, in silver, on the ball.	A grenade in gilt or gilding metal; the Castle mounted in silver, on the ball.	As for full dress head-dress, but smaller. Below the Castle a scroll in silver, inscribed 'Inniskilling'.	As for forage cap.	As for forage cap.

During the First World War the regiment, apart from the two regular battalions and the 3rd and 4th Battalions (Reserve) raised eight service battalions, most in 1914. The 1st Bn sailed from India arriving in England in January 1915 and joined the 29th Division, Expeditionary Force Mediterranean, and landed at Gallipoli on 25 April 1915, this desperate but heroic landing the subject of a spirited painting by L. A. Wilcox. Evacuated to Egypt in January 1916, and by March 1916 arrived at Marseilles and spent the remainder of the war years in France. The

2nd Bn from its station at Dover, landed at Havre in August 1914 and remained in France for the duration of the war.

Battle insignia as worn by these two regular battalions was as follows:

1st Battalion

An oblong green painted patch 2in × ½in on the left side of the helmet – discontinued about September 1916. Helmets were subsequently coloured bright brown.

During the Gallipoli campaign, a patch of cloth of green material 2in × ½in was worn on the back of the collar parallel to the lines of the shoulders, by other ranks, at right angles by officers. On arrival in France these patches were worn by officers in the same way as other ranks, ie, as above.

The red elongated patch of the 87th Brigade, 29th Division, was worn from June 1916 until joining the 36th Division in February 1918. In May 1915, recognised badges of rank of Warrant and NCOs were discarded and the ranks of individuals were shown on the shoulder strap with a marking of indelible pencil. The wearing of the green patch was discontinued, also the 29th Divisional patches, on joining the 36th Division. A blue patch of 2in × ½in was then taken into wear on the point of each shoulder.

2nd Battalion

Patches, same as worn on service dress jacket, were painted on the left side of the steel helmets during the time the battalion served in the 32nd and 36th Divisions.

Sicily 1943. Men of the 6th Battalion 'mopping up' in a Sicilian town.
IWM

*6th Battalion men take up position to cover
the road to Paterno, Sicily.*
IWM

Recognition marks were worn on the upper part of the sleeves of
service dress jacket when serving in the 32nd and 36th Divisions, red
triangle with four bars same colour in 96th Infantry Brigade, 32nd
Division from March 1916 but in 1917 the four red bars worn under the
red triangle were altered as under:

Battalion Headquarters	4 Black Bars
'A' Company	4 Red Bars
'B' Company	4 Green Bars
'C' Company	4 Yellow Bars
'D' Company	4 Blue Bars

These markings were done away with on joining the 109th Brigade,
36th Division, in February 1918 and the markings of the disbanded 10th
Battalion adopted. In August 1918, these were discontinued and a red
oblong patch worn.

The grimmest day in regimental history occurred on 1 July 1916, one
of the First World War's bloodiest battles, the Battle of the Somme. On
that one day alone the Royal Inniskilling Fusiliers suffered 2,208
fatalities, more than any British regiment has ever suffered in a single
day of action. 'Their very valour was their destruction' it has been said.

Seven soldiers of the regiment were awarded the VC during the years
1914-18:

Capt G. R. O'Sullivan	1.7.1915. Krithia, Dardanelles. Killed in action.
Sgt James Somers	1st/2nd. 7.1915. Gallipoli.
Capt E. N. F. Bell	9th Bn. 1.7.1916. Thiepval, France. Killed in action.
2nd Lt J. S. Emerson	9th Bn. 6.12.1917. Killed in action.
Pte J. Duffy (stretcher bearer)	L.G. 27.2.1918.
L/Cpl E. Seaman	2nd Bn. L.G. 15.11.1918. Ypres Sector. Killed in action.
Pte N. Harvey	20.10.1918. Ingoyghen.

The 1st Bn was posted back to India again after the war, to Sialkot in 1921 and 1922 and then to Iraq and the Middle East. The 2nd Bn came to Portland, then back for duty with the British Army of Occupation on the Rhine before return to Portland in 1922, to suffer the same fate as the Southern Irish regiments – disbandment.

A press photograph shows the officers of the 1st Bn, Lt-Col C. Ridings, DSO, OBE, commanding, on return home to England in 1925; the caption points out that the battalion had been abroad for eighteen years on foreign service, ie since 1907 – Crete. In the photograph all officers have their khaki tropical helmets, prominent on the left side of each is the grey hackle plume from a scarlet cloth triangle. This red triangle, the Ace of Diamonds halved, was the sign of the 29th Division and was kept in wear to commemorate the gallant but forlorn attack on Scimitar Hill on 21 August 1915.

Pipers had been officially authorised for Irish line regiments by Army Order 548 of 1920, one sergeant piper and five pipers, although of course the Inniskillings had actually had them before 1914. For many years the regiment wrestled with the problem of dress, and photos of the 1920s show the various stages before the new approved version, Dress Regulations published in 1927. The details:

6th Battalion Fusiliers escort a batch of about 40 German prisoners captured at Cassino 1944.
IWM

'which aim at embodying as many of the distinctive features of the regiment and ancient Gaelic costumes and decorations as possible, combining them with regimental badges, colourings and requirements of the present-day

uniform. The choice of colours was limited to blue, grey, saffron and green. The last named was eliminated, as it has never been associated with the regiment. A combination of the three remaining colours was therefore, decided upon. The headdress is to be royal blue, while the tunic, of smooth face Atholl grey cloth will be slightly cut away in front. The two inch collar, of royal blue and with silver castle badges, will be trimmed with silver cord. The shoulder straps, of the same colour, are to have small silver-plated castle buttons. The side pockets will have pointed flaps, fastened with one small silver button. The cuffs of royal blue are to be buttoned and silver braided. The buttons will be full sized regimental pattern, five of which will show above the belt. The colour of the Brat, which will be unlined is to be grey, having an antique design decoration in silver braid, while the brooch is of special design after a well authenticated Irish pattern. The waist belt of black braid will have a silvered buckle, and the chevrons will be silver. The saffron kilt, pleated all round: the badger bag with silver-mounted tails and hung by small silver chains; the stockings of Atholl grey with saffron cross gartering and flashes and black brogue shoes complete the dress. A cross belt of black leather over the right shoulder will be worn by the sergeant piper only. The pipe bag cover will be the same shade as the headdress and facings, and the ribbons will be blue and grey.'

About the same time as the Pipers' Dress Regulations, a War Office letter dated 3 March 1927 authorised changes in regimental badges, for example, the cap badges.

'To conform to the castle design submitted. In silver for the forage cap and in bronze for the service dress cap.'

The same document then sets out futher details of badges for tunic and mess jacket collar, fusilier cap badge (full dress headdress), service dress collar badge, buttons. Concludes with the instruction that cap and collar badges for other ranks will follow the pattern approved for officers, but supplies of the new patterns will not be available until the present patterns are exhausted.

In April 1934, whilst the battalion was stationed at Bordon, the 5th Inniskilling Dragoon Guards were at nearby Aldershot and in view of

HM The Queen Mother inspecting the 5th Battalion (TA) at Enniskillen, April 1962. Troopers of the 5th Royal Inniskilling Dragoon Guards in the foreground.
CENTURY NEWSPAPERS LTD, BELFAST

their close association, social celebration functions were held and some historic photographs taken. The Dragoon Guards were to move out later that year and by the following year the Inniskilling Fusiliers were in Shanghai. At home, early in 1938, a 2nd Bn, disbanded in 1922, was re-raised at Catterick Camp, Yorkshire, and a pleasant ceremony took place there in February when a side-drum, found on the battelfield of Le Cateau by a French peasant, was returned to the regiment. In March 1937 HRH The Duke of Gloucester, Earl of Ulster, became Colonel-in-Chief of the regiment and was to meet the 2nd Bn at Catterick on 1 June 1939 to present new colours. At Singapore during the preceding year, 25 June 1938, Sir Thomas Shenton, Governor, presented a King's Colour only, to the 1st Bn, the old 1869 Regimental Colour to be carried with this. On the same day that the Duke of Gloucester presented the colours at home, a new Regimental Colour was presented to the 1st Bn at Wellington, Madras, by the Governor of Madras. By request, and gracious permission, both this Colour and Regimental Colour of the 2nd Bn, were buff, the old and cherished facing colour of pre-1881.

Twenty-three years after this presentation the Duke of Gloucester again presented new colours to the 1st Bn, then stationed at Templer Barracks, Kenya. (*Soldier* magazine covered this event and provided a fine colour picture on their cover of the May 1962 issue.) From this picture it can be seen that the King's Colour is buff, that all ranks wear white tunics together with caubeens, still with the red triangle below the regimental cap grenade badge, from which the grey hackle is attached, and that the band is in full dress (scarlet) with busbies.

It was *Soldier* magazine which also published in September 1963, an article in 'Your Regiment' series, this article containing a succint précis of the 1939-45 war history in the following words:

'In World War II the 1st Bn fought with great courage in both Burma campaigns, ending the first with a grim trek of 500 miles through the most pestilent and malarial country in the world.

The 2nd Bn fought on the retreat to Dunkirk and in 1943 took part in the invasion of Sicliy and Italy. In November 1943, the 'Skins' were only 12 miles from Isernia when word came that the Germans were withdrawing. The Americans were racing for the town but the 2nd Inniskillings, determined not be outdone, sent off a lightly equipped patrol with a pot of paint and a huge stencil of the regimental cap badge. When the Americans arrived they found the Castle of Enniskillen inexplicably confronting them from every available wall.'

So to the end of the Regiment's separate history, and the start of a new one. On 1 July 1968, on the anniversary of their first becoming The Royal Inniskilling Fusiliers, the regiment joined the remaining regiments of The North Irish Brigade to become The Royal Irish Rangers (27th (Inniskilling), 83rd and 87th). See page 175.

[1a] Uniform plate by P. W. Reynolds in – The Royal Inniskilling Fusiliers, being the *History of the Regiment from December 1668 to July 1914*. Compiled under the direction of a Regimental Historical Records Committee. Constable & Co. Ltd. London 1928.

[1b] C .C. P. Lawson shows grey in a painting depicting the scene outside the Castle of Inniskilling on Sunday 16 December 1688.

[1c] W. Y. Carman provides the evidence in Richard Simkin's Uniforms of the British Army (*The Infantry Regiments*). Page 56. Webb & Bower, Exeter 1985.

[2] The Regimental Journal. The *Sprig of Shillelagh* 1932.

[3] Impression of the scene reproduced in the *Sprig of Shillelagh* Spring 1945.

[4] *Sprig of Shillelagh* Spring 1945.

[5] *Journal of the Society for Army Historical Research* Vol. XXXIX Page 106.

[6] *History of the Regiment 1688-1914* (as footnote 1).

[7] *Sprig of Shillelagh* 1941.

THE REGULAR REGIMENTS ■ INFANTRY

The Royal Irish Rifles

83rd (County of Dublin) Regiment

The first regiment to carry the number 83 was raised in Ireland on 14 October 1758. After service in Portugal in 1762 it returned to Ireland to be disbanded in 1763.

The second regiment was Scottish, the 83rd (Royal Glasgow Volunteers) Regt of Foot, formed during the American War of Independence in 1778, in Glasgow. Five Companies of the regiment were stationed at Fort Henry at Grouville, 3½ miles from St Helier in the Channel Islands in 1781, being under the command of a Capt William Campbell when the French invaded Jersey, and consequently played its part in the battle of that name.[1] From the Channel Islands the regiment went over to New York but was disbanded in 1783, its colours believed at one time to be in the possession of the City of Glasgow.

The regiment raised in Dublin in 1793 by Col William Fitch, has, under four different titles, remained on constant service up to the present day. It is said of Col Fitch that he was a brave soldier with an attractive personality and was revered by his men. The latter acquired the title of Fitch's Grenadiers, believed because of their diminutive stature. The regiment was soon sent on active service – to Jamaica where it fought a guerilla war against the Maroons and where Col Fitch was killed in 1795.

The uniform for that year is described as: Uniform red faced yellow, men's lace white with a red and green stripe, gold metal for the officers and square ended loops by pairs for the men.

A 2nd Bn was raised by the 83rd, mainly men from the County of Middlesex, and volunteers from the 3rd Royal Lancs Militia. It was this battalion which was to gain the following battle-honours for the regiment between the years 1809 and 1814: 'Talavera', 'Busaco', 'Fuentes d'Honor', 'Ciudad Rodrigo', 'Badajos', 'Salamanca', 'Vittoria', 'Nivelle', 'Orthes, 'Toulouse', and 'Peninsula'. With the exception of 'Peninsula' which was granted beforehand, the remaining battle honours were granted after submission to the Sovereign dated 4 August 1819.

In 1805 the 1st Bn was despatched to the Cape of Good Hope where, as part of the army under Sir David Baird, it took part in the recapture of that colony. Eleven years were spent on garrison duty at the Cape. Inspection reports during this period give an impression of the dress and general conditions at that station:

'Cape. May 1808. Field officers and adjutant well mounted but horse furniture not in accordance with the King's Regulations. Greatcoats nearly worn out. Packs in good order. Accoutrements much worn, arms serviceable for the effective strength. No pioneer appointments (they appear to have had 10 aprons however). Canteens and haversacks mostly good.'

'Wynberg, Cape. May 1809. Mounted officers not provided with horse furniture, but it has been ordered.'

'Capetown. October 1811. (1st Bn 83rd Foot. General James Balfour Colonel, Lt-Col Jacob Brent in command.) No Grenadier caps shown as "delivered" or "wanting" (complement 100). Clothing in wear of 1810; none sent out for 1811, compensation to be paid.'

An interesting footnote concerning dress comes from a War Office Order dated 29th August 1811:

'Infantry serving in Spain and Portugal to wear long grey pantaloons and short grey gaiters, instead of white breeches and long gaiters. The price of the pantaloons is 7/6d. and the short grey gaiters 2/3d.'

Although ordered home the regiment actually proceeded to Ceylon and did not return for many years. When it did it was stationed in Southern England, to Ireland Castlebar and Limerick from 1832-3, Dublin 1834, and then to Halifax, Nova Scotia in 1834. At this time Canada was a wild country and service for the British soldier, hard. One expedition undertaken by two Companies of the regiment in 1838 for instance meant a journey of 600 miles on sleighs, in temperatures of 30deg below zero, followed by a charge across the ice to dislodge a party of bandits. When successfully concluded it was named 'the action at Fighting Island', to be followed later by an attack on Pelée Island in Lake Eerie. Accompanied by Red Indians an advance of 15 miles across ice had to be made on this occasion.

Service in Canada ended in 1843 and the regiment returned to England where R. Ebsworth made some notes and sketches of bandsmen he saw at Chatham in 1846 – his uniform descriptions are interesting. The Drum-Major, with a private soldier, both wear the large undress cap with black peak, chin-strap under chin, scarlet coatee with yellow collar and cuffs, the Sergeant-Drummer has three silver chevrons mounted on red cloth on the right sleeve, with an embroidered drum above. The white shoulder-belt carries a brass regimental belt-plate. A crimson sash is worn around the Drum-Major's waist, the trousers are white. A Band Sergeant has a similar cap but a white coatee with yellow collar and cuffs, the latter with a scarlet line of braid. Chevrons are silver on scarlet cloth backing and twisted knots are worn on the shoulders, crimson sash and white trousers complete a colourful dress. The bass drummer has a leopardskin apron over the all-white uniform front, a special peak-less cap of white, with scarlet band and welt and an intricate pattern of scarlet tracing on crown, the numerals 83 with a sphinx badge above at centre front, the cap held in position with a chinstrap. A boy soldier completes the group, his task to collect the music stands and he is shown carrying one, as well as a pair of cymbals and a bugle. He wears the scarlet coatee with yellow collar and cuffs, white trousers but an all blue cap, numerals and sphinx in front and a pompon of red with white at the top. Drum hoops are of yellow with narrow scarlet border lines with a scarlet worm between.

Two years were spent in England prior to a move to Ireland in 1845 and embarkation in 1849 for the regiment's first tour of Indian service. It was stationed at Deesa when the Mutiny flared up and the left wing was ordered to proceed to Nasirabad, 237 miles by route march, a march accomplished in 17 days at the hottest time of the year – and not a single man fell out. Later the whole regiment concentrated at Nasirabad and in 1858 became part of the Rajputanan Field Force commanded by Sir Hugh Rose. In the same Force was an Irish cavalry regiment, the 8th King's Royal Irish Hussars; nearly one hundred years later in 1950 the

Miniature of an officer, 83rd Regiment of Foot, 1794. By George Lawrence (1758-1802). Uniform scarlet, facings buff, lace silver, shoulder-belt plate with silver grenade and the figures 83 below, epaulettes of the Grenadier Company.
PHILLIPS

Left. Officers' shoulder-belt plate, c1800. 83rd Regt. Right. Shoulder-belt plate c1840-50, 83rd Regt. Another pattern shows the 'Cape of Good Hope' honour at the top, below crown.

two regiments were to be grouped together again in 29 Infantry Brigade in Korea. Much hard work faced the regiment throughout the period of the Indian Mutiny; one of the tasks towards the end, with the rebels on the run and the 83rd part of a Force commanded by General Roberts, entailed pursuit of rebels from Jaipur. Marches during the hot weather period were responsible for many deaths from sunstroke, but two decisive actions completely routed the enemy before return of the regiment to Nasirabad at the end of August 1858.

In 1859 by HM Queen Victoria's Pleasure, approval was given for the title of the 83rd to be The County of Dublin Regt in recognition of the connection with their birthplace. A year before leaving India in 1862 a frock of scarlet serge and a wicker helmet covered with grey linen was ordered to be worn to replace the old shell jacket and shako. Sailing from Bombay the regiment arrived home in May to be stationed at Dover, Shorncliffe and then various other locations in England.

At Shorncliffe in 1863 some interesting photographs were taken showing dress at that time, whilst others were taken four years later when the 83rd relieved the 86th (Royal County Down) Regiment at Gibraltar.[2] Colours were presented by Lady Airley, wife of the Governor, at Gibraltar in May 1867. In 1873 both the 83rd and 86th became linked regiments but it took another five years before a permanent depot for both was established at Victoria Barracks, Belfast, (then known as Queen Street, Barracks).

So to the reforms of 1881, and by GO 41, 1 July 1881, the 83rd (County of Dublin) and 86th (Royal County Down) Regts of Foot, were joined together and became the 1st and 2nd Bns. The Royal Irish Rifles respectively.

Group of senior NCOs, 1863, Shorncliffe. Note, most sergeants have a small 83 on cap but a Band-Sergeant, left side of group, and several others have larger embroidered numerals.
AMOT

Sergeant-Major E. Corbett, 83rd (County of Dublin) Regiment, 1863. (Seen as central figure seated, in previous group.)
AMOT

Glengarry badge, 83rd County of Dublin Regiment, 1874-81.

86th (Royal County Down) Regiment

The first regiment carrying the number 86 did have an Irish connection, raised in that country in November 1756, but was disbanded at Winchester in 1763 after service in Africa. The second regiment, 1778-3, was raised in England and sent to the West Indies. Two Companies, detached to Tobago, were captured by the French in 1781. Two years later the regiment returned home and was disbanded at York in April 1783.

By the 1790s, up to 50 additional regiments of foot were needed, most raised in 1793 under the threat of hostilities, and one of the first corps embodied was General Cuyler's Shropshire Volunteers – although most of the men came from the counties of Yorkshire, Lancashire and Cheshire. The following year these newly raised corps were numbered, and this regiment received the designation 86th or Shropshire Volunteers. General Cuyler succeeded in the Colonelcy by Lt-Gen Russell Manners, the regiment in the meantime having travelled to Ireland. Returning to England in 1795 the 86th was inspected at Newport, Isle of Wight by, HRH The Duke of York, and brought up to strength by drafts from the 118th and 121st Regts. The men from the 121st apparently just liberated from a French prison. In 1796 the 86th embarked for the Cape of Good Hope landing on 22 September. It was to be 23 years before returning to England, during that time there was continuous movement and fighting, in India, Egypt, the Island of Bourbon, India again, Ceylon in 1818, return to India and finally home by 23 October 1819. Only two soldiers who had embarked in June 1796, returned with the regiment in 1819, Major D. Marston and Quartermaster R. Gill, the latter having gone out as a private soldier.

The uniform throughout this time was red faced yellow, men's lace white with two black and two red stripes, the black ones as edging. This may have been the description according to regulations but on active service a very different appearance could be expected. After Bhurtpore in 1805 for instance, the regiment was inspected by Lord Lake who expressed his satisfaction at the bearing of the troops. One regimental historian[3] describes the scene as follows:

'The soldiers of the 65th and 86th presented a motley appearance, their worn-out uniforms were patched with various colours, or replaced by red cotton jackets, many of the men wore sandals in the place of shoes, and turbans instead of hats, but beneath this outward war-worn appearance, the innate courage of Britons still glowed.'

In the year 1806 the designation was changed to 86th or Leinster Regt of Foot, but this title was short-lived as in May 1812 royal authority was given for the corps to be styled the 86th or Royal County Down Regt of Foot; at the same time the facing was changed from yellow to blue, the lace from silver to gold, the Irish 'Harp and Crown' was placed on the buttons, and the 'Harp' was added to the distinctions displayed on the regimental colours. In 1823 the regiment was in Armagh when authority was received 'for bearing the word "India" on the colours and appointments, in consideration of the distinguished conduct of the regiment during the period of its service in India from the year 1799, to the year 1819.'

An interesting picture of the period is worthy of mention here, in this instance one recorded by the Isle of Wight silhouettist Buncombe, an artist who must have had officers from most British regiments call at his studio in Newport. One of his portraits shows an officer of the 86th Foot wearing an 1812 'Waterloo' pattern shako of white. Other contemporary evidence of the wearing of white tropical headdress at the period are the plates by Charles Hamilton Smith, showing 8th, 22nd and 24th Light Dragoons and the York Light Infantry Volunteers. There is also a Knötel plate of an officer of the Hanoverian Feld-Bn Benningsen, 1814-15, wearing a white 1812 pattern cap with gold lines and brass or gilt plate. Presumably the 86th officer was about to join the regiment abroad.

A further note concerning the white cap appears in a subsequent War Office Order dated 12 October 1813:

> 'White caps of Infantry serving in the East and West Indies, being liable to damage by mildew and moth, are to be given up for black caps.'

The regiment sailed for Barbados in 1826 and remained abroad until 1837. Prior to embarkation an Inspecting General said of it, in a letter to Lt-Col Sir Michael Creagh, that he had 'reported the 86th as about to embark for England, after ten years' service in the West Indies, in a state of hardy, soldier-like efficiency, fit, if necessary for immediate service in the field; a circumstance alike creditable to the commanding officer and to the corps.' Nevertheless, the regiment had lost five officers and 299 soldiers during the period abroad, bringing back 424 'effective men'.

The time at home was comparatively short – five years, and by 1842 the regiment was in India, there acquiring the nickname of 'Irish Giants' because of the height and good physique of the soldiers, that is before the climate began to take its toll. During the Crimean War the regiment was transferred to Aden on a stand-by duty, but returned to Bombay after the outbreak of the Mutiny. From then until February 1859 the Royal County Down Regt was heavily engaged in the suppression of mutineers, actions of varying severity at Betwa, Jhansi, Koonch, Gowlowgee, Calpee and finally Gwalior on 19 June 1858.

One of the most outstanding engagements in the history of the regiment took place at Jhansi at the end of March, beginning April 1858, when the fortress was stormed, a most formidable undertaking made more difficult by the untimely arrival of a force of 22,000 under the efficient command of the rebel leader Tantia Topee. For outstanding bravery in this particular assault Lt and Adjutant Hugh Stewart was awarded the Victoria Cross, whilst Lt H. E. Jerome Cochrane was similarly decorated for his gallantry on 3 April. He led the main storming party and during the engagement, assisted by Private James Byrne also awarded the VC, managed to rescue, although under heavy fire, Lt Sewell who was severely wounded. Lt Jerome was himself badly wounded in action on 28 May, on the Jumna River. Yet another soldier of the 86th, Pt J. A. S. Pearson, was to receive the Victoria Cross for his gallantry during the storming of the walls at Jhansi, and for later rescuing Pt M. Burns of the regiment whilst under heavy fire, although Burns later died of his wounds.

The defeat of Tantia Topee at Jhansi had not actually broken his army, which was reinforced by troops of the Ranee of Jhansi. It fell to the regiment to attack a cantonment at Morar, and during this engagement the Ranee herself, dressed as a cavalry soldier, was killed. Sir Hugh Rose's main force then concentrated on Gwalior and so the 86th took part in two main attacks on the city and thus the final defeat of the rebels.

In the course of the campaign the regiment captured, as a trophy of

Glengarry badge, 86th Royal County Down Regiment, 1874-81.

Miniature of an officer of the 86th Regiment, c1798. The number 86 appearing on both shoulder-belt plate and buttons.

war, a rebel drum, which became known as the Jhansi drum, said to have been taken on parade by the regimental band on one special occasion. The uniform of the 86th worn during the eventful years in India have been faithfully recorded in a contemporary account of 1857-8:

'Red shell jacket mainly worn and with blue cotton drill trousers, not white but dyed dark blue. Coatee (tunic) very seldom worn and never with the forage cap; which had no peak and was of felt made in one piece and kept in shape by being blocked occasionally. The Grenadier Company wore a red tuft in the cap, the Light Company a green one, Battalion Company red and white. The cap was plain black with 86 in front. Officers had a leather helmet which they had made in Bombay, with a white cover of cotton, the back part being rounded, the crest part of the helmet was for ventilation. On the march during the day the men used to wear their belts over their grey shirts, but when marching at night or early morning the jackets were worn, for it was often very chilly until after sunrise. Officers wore a white sword-belt, their forage caps had a red band and straight peak with badge and number worked in front in embroidery. Badges of rank on collar of shell jacket. Dark navy facings.'

In 1859 the regiment returned to England after 17 years abroad, and was rewarded by five years at home before leaving for Gibraltar. It was

Four soldiers of the 86th Regiment and a Royal Artillery gunner at the Europa Advance, Gibraltar 1864.

here in February 1867 that new colours were presented to replace those last given in 1833 by Lord Kilmorey, one time Colonel of the Regiment. The 1867 presentation was considered important enough to warrant a half-page account and illustration in the *Illustrated London News* of 9 March 1867. The presentation was made by Lady Airey, wife of Lt-Gen Sir Richard Airey, Governor of Gibraltar, who made the obligatory speech prior to the regiment marching back to barracks to the accompaniment of the band playing the old regimental song, 'The Royal County Down'. As the four verses of this song represent a potted regimental history and invites the singers 'to fill their glasses to the brim' and later to toast again 'with 3 times 3', one may be forgiven for wishing to join in and at least provide the words of this convivial song.

> Come fill your glasses to the brim,
> Ye lads that love renown,
> And toast until that gallant Corps
> That wears the Harp and Crown,
> I mean the 'Bourbon Heroes', the Royal County Down.
>
> When George the Third of 'Bourbon' heard,
> He answered with a smile,
> 'Egad they are a gallant band,
>   Those lads of Erin's Isle
> Their colour shall be Royal blue,
>   They'll wear the Harp and Crown,
> And be called the Bourbon Heroes, or the Royal County Down.'
>
> Come fling our Colours to the breeze
>   And let them flutter free,
> That 'Central India' on our banner
>   Proudly we may see,
> For 'Gwalior Fort' and 'Jhansi' to
>   The bravery redounds
> Of Ireland's favourite fighting sons –
> The Royal County Downs.
>
> Now fill your glasses once again,
>   And toast with three times three:

Here's 'Honour' – it's our password,
    And we shall honoured be:
'Honour' is the password that
    Has led us to 'Renown':
Here's 'Honour' to the men who added
    Bourbon to the Crown.

The 86th Regt was in Bermuda in July 1881 when it became officially the 2nd Bn. The Royal Irish Rifles and the 83rd Regt, then in Natal, duly became the 1st Bn. For two redcoat regiments of the line to be transposed to the status of Rifles was an honour granted by Royal favour, but the new role was to need time for adjustment with much to be learnt. Uniform of course had to change, the scarlet, blue and gold giving way to dark green with dark green facings, the blue covered helmet exchanged for one of similar design but covered with dark green cloth instead of the blue, with bronze/black fittings etc. Ten years later this helmet was exchanged for a rifle busby of black lambskin for officers, the latter with black over green feather plume, whilst the soldiers had a brush plume, again black over green. Officers had a black patent leather shoulder-belt with a very fine silver badge or plate mounted upon it, in the absence of regimental colours, battle honours of both former regiments were displayed on this plate, official description: 'In silver, a shamrock wreath intertwined with a scroll, bearing the honours of the regiment; within the wreath the Harp; above the Harp a scroll inscribed *Quis separabit*; below the Harp the Sphinx over Egypt; below the Sphinx a bugle with strings. Over the strings of the bugle a scroll inscribed "Royal Irish Rifles". The whole surmounted by a Crown. "Whistle and chain of special pattern", and on the pouch itself, "In silver, a bugle with strings surmounted by the Sphinx over Egypt.' Mounted officers had to have completely new saddlery and horse furniture including bits. When khaki became day to day dress, buttons, belts, lanyards etc. were all of dark colour. Bayonets from then on had to be called swords. A corps of bugles replaced the old drums and fifes but a regimental band was still maintained.

The colours of the 83rd were laid up in St Patrick's Cathedral, Dublin, joining the old regimental stand of colours, but the colours of the 86th stayed with the 2nd Bn until 1894 when they too were laid up, in Downpatrick Cathedral, an officer and escort party bringing them home from Malta.

Apart from the various changes of station, generally with one battalion at home and the other abroad, the war in South Africa became the all-important event for the 2nd Bn, the 1st Bn being in India from 1899 and remaining there until 1914.

The men of the 2nd Bn were soon in action; after arriving in November the whole battalion was engaged by mid-December at Stormberg Junction. During this initial action, in the company of the 2nd Bn Northumberland Fusiliers and some Mounted Infantry, the regiment lost its commanding officer, Lt-Col Eager, killed, and four officers and 216 NCOs and men taken prisoner. Drafts were immediately sent to build up the battalion which was back in action within weeks. As part of a force, again under the command of General Gatacre, and again together with the 5th Fusiliers and Mounted Infantry, the Fusiliers and Rifles were once more overwhelmed by the Boers under Commandant de Wet, and for the second time suffered heavy losses, mainly as prisoners of war, six officers and 382 soldiers. General Gatacre was subsequently relieved of his command and sent home, and for a second time the battalion had to be brought up to strength, over 100 of the new men coming from the London Irish Rifles. One report of these two unfortunate episodes reads:

'But the soldiers of the Northumberland Fusiliers and the Royal Irish Rifles in this hour displayed a steadiness above all praise – a stubbornness and endurance which proved their splendid quality, and showed them equal to any work when well led.'

From this time onwards the war situation improved, the London Irish men went home and were eventually replaced by some more volunteers from that regiment together with a fine draft of trained soldiers from the 1st Bn Royal Irish Rifles from India. The battalion was kept fully occupied with work throughout the guerilla war period as well as supplying men for Mounted Infantry. The regiment returned from South Africa in January 1903 and was stationed in Dublin for three years, the remaining time before 1914 spent in various garrisons in England.

On return to Ireland the khaki drill uniforms were exchanged for khaki service dress for all ranks, the soldiers, in common with those of most other regiments at home, were compelled to wear the 'Brodrick' cap for a year or two, until it was replaced about 1905 by a khaki peaked cap or a green forage cap with patent black peak. This cap, in conjunction with a plain rifle-green tunic with bronze buttons, black waist-belt and green/black trousers, combined to make a smart walking-out dress.

The Dress Regulations 1911 for Rifle Regiments include those for The King's Royal Rifle Corps and Rifle Brigade, obviously neither regiment Irish but not entirely inappropriate as regular officers from these two

Young Citizens Volunteers of Belfast [became 14th Bn Royal Irish Rifles (Young Citizens Volunteers)]. A parade marching along Bridges End, East Belfast, c1913–14. (A volunteer organisation 'To assist as an organisation, when called upon, the civil power in the maintenance of the peace'.)
S. J. KRETSCHMER

Left. Unidentified officer in khaki service dress, Belfast, c1914.
R. HEASLIP
Right. An enlarged photograph of the right collar badge.

regiments served as Adjutants, 8th Carlow and 9th North Cork Bns of the KRRC and 6th Royal Longford and West Meath Bn of the RB respectively.

RIFLE REGIMENTS
(Except Scottish Rifles)

Busby   Black Persian lambskin, height in front 5in, rising to 6in in the centre of each side of the busby and sloping back to the bottom edge. The crown of rifle-green cloth, with figured ornament. Black silk square cord plait in front, carried up to a small bronze bugle at the centre of the top of each side with two rows of square silk cord at back, ending in a knot, to which is attached a bronze ring. A black corded oval boss on the top in front. Royal Irish Rifles, a round dark green boss. Chin strap of black patent leather. Black silk square body line with swivel to attach to the ring at the back of the busby, black egg moulds and sliders.

Plume   King's Royal Rifles, scarlet ostrich feathers with black vulture feathers below. Royal Irish Rifles, black ostrich feathers with dark green vulture feathers below. Rifle Brigade, black ostrich and vulture feathers. Bronze corded ball socket, three upright flames. The height of the plume from the top of the busby is 7in.

Foreign Service Helmet   Abroad, the white Wolseley helmet with white pagri is worn instead of the busby.

Tunic   Rifle-green cloth, edged all round, except the collar, with black square cord. King's Royal Rifles, scarlet cloth collar and cuffs. Royal Irish Rifles, dark green cloth collar and cuffs. Rifle Brigade, black velvet collar and cuffs. The collar edged with 1in black braid with a tracing of braid below; the cuffs pointed, an Austrian knot on the sleeve, with a tracing of plain braid round it, extending to 8½in from the bottom of the cuff. The skirt rounded off in front, closed behind, and lined with black. On each side of the breast, 5 loops of black square cord, with netted caps and drops, fastening with black olivets and hooks and eyes down the front. On each back seam a line of the same cord, forming a

Ration party of the Royal Irish Rifles resting in a communication trench, 1 July 1916.
IWM

Soldiers of the 1st Battalion, Eil Camp, Germany, April 1921. Note large regimental badge stencilled on to the steel helmet.
R. J. MARRION

crow's foot at the top, passing under a netted cap at the waist, below which it is doubled ending in an Austrian knot reaching to the bottom of the skirt. Shoulder cords of black chain gimp, with small button of regimental pattern at the top. No collar badges.

Braid   Black mohair.

Buttons and Badges

Trousers   Dark rifle-green cloth, with 2in black braid down the side seams.

Pantaloons   Dark rifle-green cloth, with stripes as on the cloth trousers.

Boots and Spurs

Sword   Steel hilt, with device of bugle and crown.

Scabbard   Steel.

Sword Belt   Web.

Sword Slings   Black patent leather, 1in wide; square silver buckles with the corners slightly rounded.

Sword Knot   Black leather strap and acorn.

Shoulder Belt   Black patent leather, 3in wide.

Pouch   Black patent leather.

Gloves   Black leather.

Great Coat   Universal pattern, shoulder straps edged with ⅛in scarlet cloth. Buttons and badges of rank in bronze.

UNDRESS

Forage Cap   Universal pattern, green cloth. King's Royal Rifles and Rifle Brigade, band of black mohair braid. Royal Irish Rifles, band of black lace, shamrock pattern. Welts of black cord.

Patrol Jacket   *King's Royal Rifle Corps*   Rifle-green cloth, 28in long from the bottom of the collar behind, for an officer 5ft 9in in height, with a proportionate

Lt-Colonel D. J. O. K. Bernard, CMG, DSO, (later Lt-General Sir Dennis Bernard) with band, 1st Battalion Royal Ulster Rifles, Aldershot 1929. Bandmaster W. Allen, LRAM and ARCM.
S. D. EAGLE

variation for any difference in height; rounded in front; collar and pointed cuffs of the regimental facings. 1in black mohair braid down the front, at the bottom of the skirts, and on the slits; the mohair braid traced inside with Russia braid, forming eyes at each angle of the slits. The back seams trimmed with 1in mohair braid, traced on both sides with Russia braid, forming three eyes at the top and two at the bottom. On each side in front, five loops of black square cord fastening with olivets. Each loop forms an eye above and below in the centre and a drop at the end. A cap on each drop. Cuffs edged with 1in mohair braid, traced with Russia braid, forming a crow's foot and eye at the top and an eye in the angle at the bottom. Collar edged all round with 1in mohair braid, traced inside with Russia braid forming an eye at each end. At the back, below the centre of the collar, the tracing forms a plume, 6in deep; a crow's foot and eye at the bottom. Black lining, hooks and eyes. A pocket on either side below the fourth loop, and one inside the left breast. Shoulder cords as for tunic.

Royal Irish Rifles   As for King's Royal Rifle Corps, but with dark green cloth collar and cuffs.

Rifle Brigade   Rifle-green cloth, of the size and shape described for King's Royal Rifle Corps, with collar and cuffs of black velvet. 1in black mohair braid down the front, at the bottom of the skirts, and on the slits. The mohair braid traced inside with Russia braid, forming eyes at each angle of the slits. The back seams trimmed with 1in mohair braid traced on both sides with Russia braid, forming three eyes at the top and two eyes at the bottom. On each side, in front, five loops of black square cord, fastening with olivets. Each loop forms an eye above and below in the centre, and a drop at the end. A cap on each drop, cuffs pointed with 1in mohair braid, traced at the bottom with Russia braid, forming an eye in the angle. Collar edged with 1in mohair braid; a tracing below the braid, and on the collar seam, forming an eye in the corners. At the back, below the centre of the collar, the tracing forms a plume 6in deep; black lining, hooks and eyes. A pocket on either side below the fourth loop, and one inside the left breast. Shoulder cords as for tunic.

Trousers   )
Sword   )
Sword Belt   )   As in full dress
Sword Slings   )

Boots   Wellington; with box spurs for mounted officers.

The pouch belt is not worn in undress.

SERVICE DRESS, HOME SERVICE

Cap   Universal pattern.

Cap Comforter

Jacket   Universal pattern, black buttons.

Breeches   Mounted officers, universal pattern; dismounted officers, knickerbocker pattern.

Trousers   Drab mixture.

MESS DRESS

Mess Jacket   Rifle green cloth with roll collar and pointed cuffs as in table below. Royal Irish Rifles and Rifle Brigade, cuffs 6in deep at the points and 2¾in behind, a 1in slit at the seams. King's Royal Rifles, cuffs of scarlet cloth

*Band c1930, Aldershot, now in Rifles
full dress.*
S. D. EAGLE

RSM M. J. Westmacott, 2nd Battalion, Catterick, 27 October 1937. (Medals: 1st and 2nd, British War Medal and Victory Medal; 3rd, Jubilee 1935; 4th, Coronation 1937; 5th, Military Long Service Medal, Regular Army.)

S. D. EAGLE

trimmed with 1in black mohair braid and tracing braid. King's Royal Rifles and Royal Irish Rifles, shoulder straps of cloth the same colour as the jacket, 1½in wide at the base tapering to about 1in at the point; rounded points fastened with a button; the shoulder strap to be sewn in at the shoulder. Rifle Brigade, shoulder cords of double square edged black cord. Badges of rank in metal; miniature in the Rifle Brigade. No buttons on the front of the jacket.

Mess Vest   Rifle-green cloth, open in front, fastened with four ½in buttons. No collar.

Overalls   As in full dress, except in the King's Royal Rifle Corps, in which they will be of same shade of rifle-green cloth as the mess jacket.

Boots   Wellington; mounted officers, box spurs.

Regiment	Jackets				Vest
	Collar	Shoulder Straps	Cuffs	Piping	
King's Royal Rifle Corps	Rifle-green cloth	Rifle-green cloth	Scarlet, trimmed with black braid	None	Rifle-green cloth, 4 buttons
Royal Irish Rifles	Dark-green cloth	Rifle-green cloth	Dark green cloth	None	Rifle-green cloth, 4 buttons
Rifle Brigade	Black silk	Black cord, square-edged, ¾in wide, ¼in deep	Black velvet	None	Rifle-green cloth, 4 buttons

Badges

On Buttons	On Collar of Mess Jacket	On Busby	On the F.S. Helmet and Forage Cap
Scalloped edge; within a scroll with shamrock leaves issuing from either end, the Harp and Crown. On scroll, 'Royal Irish Rifles'.	In silver, badge as on forage cap boss.	In black metal the Harp and Crown; below the Harp a scroll, inscribed '*Quis separabit*'. On a round boss, the Sphinx over Egypt; below the Sphinx, a bugle with strings.	On F.S. helmet, a badge as for busby. On forage cap, a green cord boss with a Harp and Crown in silver, across which is a scroll inscribed 'Royal Irish Rifles'.

At the outbreak of war in 1914 the 1st Bn was in Aden, and the 2nd at Tidworth; both battalions spent the entire four years of war in France and Flanders. The momentous events and deeds of the regiment, including the Service Bns and Reserve (in all 21 battalions, most with the 36th Ulster Division) during these years have been recorded in detail in Regimental Histories.[4] Suffice to say that 46-honours were added to an already splendid record, three Victoria Crosses were awarded, but the regiment's casualties were heavy: over 7,000 officers and men had died.

Pte William McFadzean from Lurgan, Co Armagh, 14th Bn, on 1 July 1916, France, threw himself on a box of bombs as two of the safety pins fell out, thereby sacrificing his own life but saving those of his comrades in the trench at the time, only one man being injured.

Pte Robert Quigg from Ballycastle, Co Antrim, 12th Bn, on 1 July 1916, France. For conspicuous gallantry whilst leading his platoon in three separate assaults, and later making seven separate forays into 'no man's land', rescuing a wounded soldier on each occasion.

2nd Lt Edward De Wind from Co Down, 15th Bn, 21 March 1918, France. For holding an important post for seven hours, repelling attack after attack until finally killed.

All three awarded the Victoria Cross, two posthumously.

During the war years when khaki caps were worn the 1st Bn had a black regimental cap badge and the 2nd a similar but in white metal. From 17 November 1917 the 1st Bn, whilst in the 8th Division, had the divisional sign on both sides of the steel helmet and from 1918 that of the 36th Division. A black and green cloth patch was worn 1in below each shoulder, the patch consisting of four squares, each of ¾in size, green and black over black and green.

On 1 January 1921, Army Order 509 of 1920 proclaimed that:

'The title of The Royal Irish Rifles be changed to "The Royal Ulster Rifles"; and the shoulder-strap badge ordered to be changed from "RIR" to "RUR".'

Both battalions were taken completely by surprise when the news of this impending change had leaked out. Even Field Marshal Sir Henry Wilson, Chief of Imperial General Staff and Colonel of the Regiment, was unable to intervene successfully. (The Field Marshal was murdered in London eighteen months later by a Sinn Feiner.)

Two good stories are told, the first can be vouched for by word of mouth and photographic evidence, the second – just a good story. During 1920-1 the 1st Bn was stationed at Albany Barracks, Parkhurst, Isle of Wight, and on 1 January 1921 there was a battalion parade, led by the band playing Chopin's funeral march. Then came two parsons, odd looking characters in top hats, dark glasses and white surplices, followed by a coffin draped with a Union Jack borne by NCOs, then a firing party with arms reversed and finally the remainder of the battalion. An hilarious episode followed during which 'ashes' in an orange box were buried in a grave, into which a Warrant Officer promptly fell, and when solemnity was restored three volleys were fired and the Last Post sounded. A wooden cross carrying the inscription 'Sacred to the memory of the Royal Irish Rifles. Departed this life on 1 January 1921, after a brief but glorious existence, aged forty years – RIR, RIP, RUR,' was placed at the head of this grave, later replaced by a small permanent gravestone. It remained in this position for many years but as later it was within the complex of HM Prison, Albany, it was removed for safe keeping to the Regimental Museum, Belfast.

The 2nd Bn was in Mesopotamia when it received the disturbing news, and Col Corbally in his History recounts this anecdote:[4a]

'In far away "Mespot" a company commander (of the old school) summoned to his tent his groom (also of the old school) and said to him:
    "Reid!"
    "Sorr?"
    "To what Regiment – I say to what Regiment – d'ye belong?"
    Proudly Rifleman Reid drew himself up to his full diminutive stature.
    "The Royal Irish Rifles, sorr. Av coorse."
    (Stabbing a finger) "Ye do not."
    (Indignantly) "I do, sorr."
    "Ye do not. Ye belong – now get this – to The Royal Ulster Rifles – now get that."
    "Be jabers!"
    A very stiff five fingers from his "master's" whisky bottle was required, it is believed to assist Rifleman Reid to recover from his shock.'

The years between the wars were spent in normal garrison duties around the world, the 1st Bn leaving the Isle of Wight for the Army of the Rhine, back home for a year or two before Palestine, Egypt, Hong Kong and India by 1938. The 2nd Bn, already in the Middle East in 1921 was then posted via Egypt to Constantinople followed by India, but home during the early 1930s. Before leaving for Palestine in 1938 the battalion took part in the Northern Command Tattoo and was also on street lining duty at the Coronation.

During the 1920s an alliance was formed between the Royal Ulster Rifles and the Halton Rifles, an old Canadian militia regiment dating back to 1866, but this regiment amalgamated with a Canadian highland unit in 1931, then to be known as the Lorne Rifles (Scottish), both based

An unidentified officer, c1942, also seen as a Rifleman on the half title page.
R. J. MARRION

1st Battalion on the banks of the Issel.
IWM

Two walking wounded of 1st Battalion,
River Issel.
IWM

at Georgetown, Ontario. Yet another change of title on amalgamation took place with the allied regiment in 1936, the new title The Lorne Scots (Peel Dufferin and Halton Regt), with headquarters at Barrie, Ontario. All this was changed in 1947 when HM King George VI approved an alliance with The Irish Regt of Canada, to replace the pre-Second World War alliance. During the war the two regiments had fought alongside each other in Italy and a strong link between them was established.

During the Second World War the regiment earned ten hard won battle-honours:

'Dyle', 'Dunkirk, 1940', 'Normandy Landing', 'Cambes', 'Caen', 'Troarn', 'Venlo Pocket', 'Rhine', 'Bremen', 'North-West Europe, 1940, '44-5'

each and every one a story in itself and only the full length histories can do them justice.[5a]

Soon after normal routine peacetime soldiering in Ireland had been resumed, when an amalgamation parade was held at Ballykinlar in the summer of 1948 and the regiment was reduced to a single battalion – 1st Bn The Royal Ulster Rifles (83rd and 86th), North Irish Brigade.

The numerical strength of this battalion was well below that of a battalion on the war establishment, so when the 29th Independent Infantry Brigade Group of which it was a part, was ordered to the Far East, where a war had broken out in Korea, 400 Reservists were called upon, mainly from the North Irish and Lancastrian Groups. The Group, together with other British Army formations, was badly needed to augment American and South Korean forces against the aggressive armies from the North and the United Nations Organisation also agreed to send troops. From November 1950 until October of the following year the regiment remained, and fought in that hostile country, enduring harsh conditions and suffering 65 officers and men killed and over 30 missing.[5b] The battle-honours 'Seoul', 'Imjin', 'Korea, 1950-1', were added to the appointments.

For the first time ever in battle the regiment was accompanied by its own pipes and drums, the pipes having been added to the strength in 1948 after becoming a single battalion, in order to bring the Rifles into line with other Irish regiments. From the nucleus of the old London Irish Rifles, the new regimental pipe band was formed under Pipe-Major T. Woods, the first Pipe-Major of the Royal Ulster Rifles. Since Korea the regiment has served at such scattered stations as Hong Kong, Colchester, Germany and Cyprus etc. The pipes and drums have given displays, as well as in this country, in Cyprus, Belgium, Hong Kong, France and Germany, not forgetting the Royal Tournament at home and the massed Irish Pipe Bands on 8 June 1981 on Horse Guards.

In 1968 the regiment joined the other two surviving Irish Infantry regiments to become The Royal Irish Rangers (27th (Inniskilling), 83rd and 87th). See page 175.

Officers' shoulder-belt plate as worn on black patent leather shoulder-belt, Royal Ulster Rifles. Battle-honours include Korea 1950-1.
L. V. ARCHER

[1] *The Battle of Jersey* by Richard Mayne. Phillimore & Co.
[2] Original photographs in the archives of the Army Museum's Ogilby Trust, two reproduced in this volume.
[3] *Historical Record of the Eighty-Sixth or The Royal County Down Regiment of Foot. From formation 1793-1842.* John W. Parker, London 1842. (Cannon's Historical Records Series.)
[4a] *The Royal Ulster Rifles, 1793-1957.* Lt-Col M. J. P. M. Corbally, Glasgow. The Paramount Press, 1959.
[4b] *History of the Royal Ulster Rifles.* Vol.III by Charles Graves, pub. by The Royal Ulster Rifles Regimental Committee, 1950.
[5a] *The Normandy Campaign, 6 June 1944 to September 1944.* Booklet published by the Regiment c1945-6.
[5b] *The Royal Ulster Rifles in Korea.* Wlm. Mullan & Son Ltd, Belfast 1953.

THE REGULAR REGIMENTS ■ INFANTRY

Princess Victoria's (Royal Irish Fusiliers) 87th (Royal Irish Fusiliers) Regiment of Foot

Silhouette by Buncombe. Officer 87th Regiment, c1807. Scarlet uniform, facings green, green tuft on hat.

The 87th (Prince of Wales's Irish) Regt of Foot was raised by Col Sir John Doyle in Ireland, dating from 8 September 1793, but there were two previous 87th Regts. The first, 1759-63 was a Highland corps with a good reputation and record – 87th (Highland) Regt of Foot, known as Keith's Highlanders. The second regiment had an equally short service record from 1779-83.

Two extracts from West Midlands newspapers provide valuable detail about the newly raised corps of 1794.[1] From the Aris's *Birmingham Gazette*, Monday 17 February 1794:

'Deserted from the Prince of Wales's Regiment of Foot, commanded by Colonel Doyle, on their March through Chester, SERJEANT GRAVES in his full Uniform, an Hussar Cap, and open Cloth-Trousers; took with him two Recruits he had enlisted from Birmingham, called JESSON and REW. The Serjeant is above five Feet nine Inches high, well made and has a very smart Military Appearance, with dark Eyes and Hair; formerly served in the Tenth Regiment of Foot. They are supposed to have gone to Birmingham.

'Whoever will apprehend the above mentioned Deserters, and lodge them in any of his Majesty's Gaols shall receive from the Printer hereof, or from Mr Thomas Honeyborn, near Stourbridge, Two Guineas Reward over and above what is allowed by Act of Parliament for apprehending Deserters.'

From the *Shrewsbury Chronicle*, Friday 18 April 1794.

'The 87th (The Prince of Wales's Irish) Regiment of Foot, 1794 – On Wednesday last 350 recruits belonging to His Royal Highness The Prince of Wales's Own Irish Regiment, arrived in this town, and this morning proceeded on their route for Hilsey Barracks, near Portsmouth. They embarked from Dublin on Thursday Evening the 10th instant, and dined at Parkgate next day. They appear to be brave, hearty boys, and are mostly armed with Shelalehs.'

A fuller description of the early dress is provided in Cannon's Historical Record 1793-1853:

'A much laced scarlet coatee, of closer fit than at that time was worn, with collar and cuffs of deep green, the latter pointed with an Austrian knot of lace in the present style, green overalls, strapped, and tucked into Hessian boots, black leather cross-belts, and a black leather helmet with bearskin crest and green hackle feather. The regimental badge was the Harp and Crown.'

Most of the regiment was made prisoner at Bergen-Op-Zoom in 1795 and a new regiment was re-formed at home before service in the West Indies. Following a further spell at home it went to the Cape in 1810, duty on the Island of Mauritius until 1815 and was then sent to India.

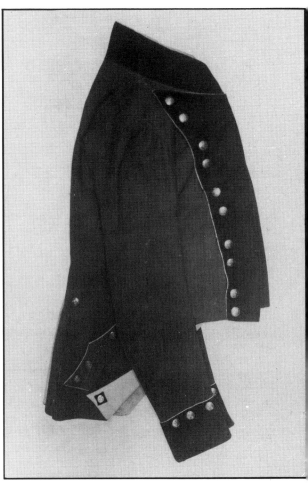

A 2nd Bn was raised in Ireland in 1804 by Sir Charles Doyle, son of the Colonel of the Regiment, and served with great distinction until 1817 when it was disbanded. In 1809 the regiment embarked for Portugal and was in most of the battles throughout the Peninsular War. It took part in the operations before Oporto, the battle of Talavera where it suffered forty per cent casualties, and assisted at the defence of Cadiz. It was at the battle of Barrosa on 5 March 1811 that the 2nd/87th, under its gallant commander Hugh Gough, distinguished itself when part of a small attacking force, which was instrumental in turning an impending defeat into victory, and capturing the first French eagle in the Peninsular War. In the midst of the engagement Ensign Edward Keogh saw the eagle of the 8th French Light Infantry on its pole and went for it – was killed in the struggle, but his sergeant, Patrick Masterson, snatched it up and secured it in spite of the desperate efforts of the enemy to regain it. For this day's work the regiment was directed, through their patron, the Prince Regent, that it should be entitled to style itself the 87th (Prince of Wales's Own Irish) Foot and to be granted the badge of the imperial French eagle and wreath above a tablet inscribed '8', the Harp and Crown and the Prince's plume. The victory at Barrosa was gained without the assistance of the Spanish general, La Péna, (who had merely looked on, but later claimed victory himself) consequently the casualties were heavy, 1,200 British officers and men killed or wounded, although the French losses were almost double. Sgt Masterson was promoted to ensign, and again to lieutenant in the regiment 17 November 1813.

A further example of promotion from the ranks to commissioned

Two officers, Drum-Major and drummer, 87th Regiment, called 1826. By R. Simkin. The Drum-Major figure is based on the print by Hull, 1829.
THE PARKER GALLERY

status without purchase (such promotions generally at the discretion of the commander-in-chief or some other high authority), is that of Capt John Shipp of the 87th Regt. In later life Shipp recorded his experiences and left a very valuable and descriptive document.[2] Shipp was a workhouse orphan who enlisted as a boy of 12¾ years into the 22nd Regt in January 1797. At the siege of Bhurtpore 1804-5 he showed such gallantry that Lord Lake gave him an ensigncy in the 65th Regt, and he was promoted almost at once to a lieutenancy in the 76th Regt. Returning to England he sold out in March 1808, re-enlisted in the 24th Light Dragoons and by 1813 had been promoted to sergeant-major. In India two years later he won a commission for the second time, was given an ensigncy in the 87th Regt by Lord Hastings, governor-general and commander-in-chief; by 1821 he was a lieutenant. It is also worthy of note that a paper written by Shipp in 1831 against 'the barbarous and degrading system of flogging soldiers and sailors' is claimed to have greatly influenced Sir Francis Burdett, MP, in his campaign against flogging.

To continue with the Peninsular record – after Barrosa the regiment distinguished itself at the defence of Tarifa. One historian records that it was during the fighting at Tarifa that the pipes and drums played 'St Patrick's Day' and 'Garry Owen'.[3] Before return home the battalion took part in the battles of Vittoria, Bidassoa and Nivelle, Orthez and Toulouse, but was eventually disbanded in 1817.

In India meanwhile the 1st Bn was fully employed by an expedition to, and war in, Nepaul 1815-16, and later against the Pindarees. Due home

in 1820 it found itself re-directed, and later fighting in the 1st Burmese
War 1825-6, with subsequent return to England in 1827.

On 16 July 1827 the battalion was made a fusilier corps and the title
changed to 87th (Prince of Wales's Own Irish Fusiliers) Regt of Foot,
but this clumsy title was changed again in November to 87th (Royal Irish
Fusiliers), facings altered from deep green to blue. The description of
the colours presented after the change to Fusiliers is given as follows:

> 'The regimental colour was blue, cantoning the Union, and having
> LXXXVII in the centre of the latter in letters of gold. In the centre of the
> colours was the Eagle and Laurel Wreath, with the Harp and Crown below it,
> and the Plume of Feathers above, all on a blue ground, enclosed within a
> Union Wreath and surmounted by the Crown, with the battle-honours on
> scrolls on either side of the Wreath.'

In September/October 1828, three prints were published from the
original drawings of Edward Hull, showing a private, officer and drum-
major respectively, in the new 'fusilier' dress. Then in 1833, as one of his
long series of 100 paintings for King William IV, A. J. Dubois Drahonet
painted a magnificent study of Capt J. S. Doyle of the regiment, signed
and dated 1833.[4] (John Sidney Doyle son of Charles William Doyle who
raised the 2nd Bn, married Susan, Baroness North in 1838, and assumed
the name of North, Rt Hon). Purely from the viewpoint of sartorial
splendour this uniform would take some beating; as a practical and
serviceable dress, however, it would have had many defects. Dress
Regulations for the Army 1831 and 1834 both stipulate a bearskin cap
14in deep, but Doyle's would most certainly top this measurement by
several inches, suitable only for a gentle mild day, but misery in a high
wind or on a very hot day. The scarlet coatee is tailored to show a very
tight waist and little freedom of movement in the sleeves. There are
grenade skirt ornaments, the blue facings, since November 1827, can be
seen on the cuffs, but the gold lace ornamentation completely covers the
blue on the collar. The coatee has two rows of gilt buttons set in pairs, on
the shoulders a pair of the most ornate wings, each having three rows of
gilt chain set on gold lace backing, gold wire fringe, central device of an
eagle over harp within a wreath on a circular metal base, and on the strap
a large gilt grenade. A white sword-belt crosses the right shoulder and
upon this belt a gilt metal rectangular plate with a grenade worked upon
it. Around the waist a narrow crimson girdle terminating in two long
cords with tassels suspended from a button at the front. White tight
fitting summer trousers complete a uniform of quite magnificent
appearance. Hull's drum-major also wears a busby, a scarlet coatee and
white trousers, but otherwise there are many differences. The busby of
this NCO and for the bandsmen is broad at the top, has a tall white
plume from a small grenade holder at top central position, from which
ornamental cords are suspended. His scarlet coatee is single breasted,
gilt buttons in five pairs down the centre and with double bars of chest
ornamentation. He, too, wears the white shoulder-belt with the
rectangular plate with grenade, also has shoulder wings and a band
aiguillette attached to the right shoulder and falling across the chest,
terminating in two metal tags. There are three bar chevrons on each
arm, blue cuffs each with three bars of lace, and he too has a narrow
crimson waist sash terminating in two cords, with large tassels falling to
the left knee. The white trousers are wide fitting, quite the opposite to
those of Capt Doyle. The drum-major's staff has an ornate silver eagle
mounted at the top.

*Watercolour signed and dated J. Thomas
1847. 87th Fusiliers. Blue coat and trousers
gold buttons, lace grenades and epaulettes
with silver eagle and grenade. Cap-band
scarlet*

Above: Kettle-drummer of the 1st Regiment of Horse, 1781. R. Simkin.

Below: Captain John Cummings, 8th Light Dragoons. Captain in Regiment 16 May 1805 to 1811. Miniature by Engleheart.

Above: 5th (or Royal Irish) Dragoons. Officer, 1798. Showing the early green Standard. Print dated March 1800.

Below: The black Regimental Colour of the 89th Regiment. Presented by HM Queen Victoria, 5 April 1866.

Above: 8th The King's Royal Irish Dragoons (Hussars). In camp, Chobham, Surrey, 1853. R. Ackermmann's Chobham series. Plate 5 in the series, published 21 October 1853.

Far left: 'On Despatch'. Trooper of 4th Royal Irish Dragoon Guards. Study by Harry Payne, c1890s.

Left: A captain of the 4th Dragoon Guards in mounted review order, 1890s. From a tailor's book. Study by R. Simkin.

Opposite page
Top left: A corporal of the 8th King's Royal Irish Hussars. A final polish to his leather sabretache before parade. Early Christmas card, 1890s, by Harry Payne.

Top right: Trooper of the 5th Royal Irish Lancers. A watercolour after Harry Payne's early Christmas card, c1890s.

Bottom left: Officer's shabraque of the Londonderry Militia, c1870s. Royal Inniskilling Fusiliers Museum.

Bottom right: The Drums of the Inniskillings. From a painting by B. Granville Baker, c1920s.

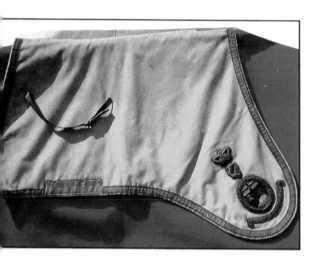

TYPES OF THE IRISH REGIMENTS
STUDIES FROM CIGARETTE CARDS, MOSTLY PRE 1914 VINTAGE

Top	*Left to Right*	Centre	*Left to Right*	Bottom	*Left to Right*
Drum-horse	4th Dragoon Guards	Trooper	5th Lancers	Trooper	8th Hussars
Trooper	4th Dragoon Guards	Lieutenant	6th Dragoons	Officer	8th Hussars
Colonel	5th Lancers	Drum-horse	6th Dragoons	Guardsman	Irish Guards
Drum-horse	5th Lancers	Drum-horse	8th Hussars	Drummer with wolfhound	Irish Guards

Top	Left to Right	Centre	Left to Right	Bottom	Left to Right
Private	Royal Irish Regiment, tropical uniform	Private	Royal Irish Rifles	Sergeant	Royal Dublin Fusiliers
Private	Royal Inniskilling Fusiliers	Private	Royal Irish Rifles, with bulldog mascot	Private	Royal Munster Fusiliers
Drummer and Fifer	Royal Inniskilling Fusiliers	Private	Royal Irish Fusiliers	Pipers	London Irish Rifles
Private	Royal Irish Rifles	Private	Connaught Rangers	Lieutenant	London Irish Rifles

"SHAMROCKS."

18th County of London.
London Irish.

Above left: An Edwardian greetings card. Officer of the Irish Guards, with lady, St Patrick's Day.

Above right: Private of the London Irish Rifles, *c*1910.

Left: Officer of the North Irish Horse. Mounted review order, *c*1913. From painting by B. Granville-Baker.

Opposite page
Left: Present Arms. Sentry of Royal Dublin Fusiliers in camp, 1890s, by Woolen.

Centre: The Adjutant, Royal Inniskilling Fusiliers, *c*1904, by E. A. Campbell.

Right: The Adjutant, Connaught Rangers, *c*1898, by E. A. Campbell.

Bottom row
Left: Pipe-Major of the Irish Guards, 1930s. Windsor Castle in background.

Centre: Pipe-Major, Royal Irish Fusiliers, 1923, by E. A. Campbell.

Right: Pipe-Major, Royal Inniskilling Fusiliers, 1929, by E. A. Campbell.

Above: Piper, Queen's Royal Irish Hussars, Hanwell, 1974. S. D. Eagle.

Below: Trumpeter, 5th Royal Inniskilling Dragoon Guards. Edinburgh Castle Tattoo, 1978. S. D. Eagle.

Above: Band-Sergeant, Queen's Royal Irish Hussars. Cavalry Memorial Parade, May 1981. R. J. Marrion.

Below: 'Brian Boru', wolfhound, Royal Irish Rangers, Tidworth 1972. D. W. Quarmby.

Captain John Hallowes, 87th Fusiliers, c1862. Cap has embroidered figures 87 with grenade above. Hallowes was a Captain in 1857, Major 1866 and retired as Lt-Colonel 1870.
J. V. WEBB

The regiment was abroad until 1842 and on its return was seen at Edinburgh Castle, and later in Glasgow by R. Ebsworth in 1844. His first remarks concern the size of the men, 'their height augmented by their bearskin caps'. From his sketches one can see that an officer has a uniform similar in most particulars to that of 1833, and it is noted that the gold grenade ornaments on the skirt are mounted on blue cloth backing. A regimental sergeant-major is also shown, his dress similar to the officer but he has of course a four bar chevron on each arm, the chevrons of silver mounted on blue with a crown above. The group includes a drum-major, band-sergeant and band-corporal, as well as a drummer. With the exception of the drummer, whose coatee has lace ornamentation on the chest and drummer's lace on the arms, spaced between the cuffs and the white shoulder wings with five inverted lace chevrons, all others have much as before. All have a brass grenade on the tall headdress, the coatee has two rows of buttons in pairs and all chevrons are silver on blue cloth backing. The drum-major's dress belt or sash has the unusual distinction of having a large grenade in the centre of the back, his staff now has an Irish harp, wreath and laurel in silver at the top. The band-corporal has an all white uniform, white wings on the white coatee with a blue collar and large white cloth grenades on either side of the opening, also on the blue skirt turnbacks: blue cuffs. Carried on the waist-belt is a black music case with a brass grenade badge on it.

The regiment embarked for Bengal in April 1849 but was doing duty on the North West Frontier at the time of the Mutiny. New colours were presented by Lady Canning at Ambala on 19 January 1860, replacing those presented in 1838 by Lady Nicolay, whilst the regiment was at Port Louis, Mauritius. After India the regiment was sent to China and was at Hong Kong for a period before return home in May 1861. The stay at home was short and by 1865 was at Gibraltar prior to moving on to Malta, and eventually Nova Scotia.

A glimpse at the domestic side of soldiering can be gathered from the reminiscences of the Master Tailor (whose name strangely enough is given as Mr. A. Taylor) and covers the period when the regiment garrisoned Gibraltar, 1865-6.

Left. Soldiers' shoulder-belt plate, 89th Regiment, c1810. Right. Shoulder-belt plate, 89th Regiment, c1830. Frosted plate, mounts of silver.
W. Y. CARMAN FSA (Scot)

'When the 87th arrived in Gibraltar in 1865, I was conducting the principal tailoring business on the Rock. The officers of the regiment patronised our establishment, and I was fortunate enough to give them complete satisfaction, I was asked by many of them, including the colonel, to join the regiment as Master Tailor. After consideration I decided to do so, and must say I never had cause to regret my decision, for a finer lot of fellows, happy, jovial, and best of sportsmen, it has never been my fortune to meet. From the beginning I was kept very busily employed, my first great business being the conversion of the blue frock coat (the wearing of which had just been abolished) to patrol jackets. At this time the pay of the soldier was extremely small, in fact might be considered nil, the men parading at noon each day to receive the magnificent sum of 1d. I am afraid this small pay was caused mainly by the insufficient supply of clothing issued to them, the yearly issues being one tunic, one pair of trousers (winter), and one pair of boots. All extra clothing such as shell jacket, summer trousers and cap, and all small kit had to be provided by the men themselves.

'The only badges worn were "87" and a grenade on the cap. At my suggestion, and with the consent of the men to pay for the addition, Col Lyons permitted the wearing of a white cloth grenade on the collar of the shell jacket and tunic. That instrument of torture (how I remember the discomfort of it even after this lapse of years), the "stock" was discontinued, a leather tag being substituted for it at the expense of the men. I believe I am correct in saying that the 87th was the first regiment to discontinue the wearing of the stock, not by regular authority, but solely by permission of the commanding officer.'

The regiment was at home again by 1876 and at Aldershot when the Army Order of 11 April 1881 was received, announcing the linking with the 89th Regt, with future designation – 1st Bn Princess Victoria's (Royal Irish Fusiliers), Depot – Armagh.

89th (Princess Victoria's) Regiment of Foot

There were three British regiments with the number 89, and whilst our interest is concerned with the third in succession – the 89th Foot which became Princess Victoria's Regt, brief mention of the earlier regiments may be permitted. The first, the 89th (Highland) Regt of Foot 1759-65, during its short existence did good work in India suppressing a mutiny and fighting at Buxar 1764. A silver plated shoulder-belt plate with gilt mounts, ie the words ROYAL ABERDEENSHIRE above the numerals LXXXIX, and HIGHLANDERS below, has survived.

The next regiment known as the 89th Worcestershire Volunteer Regt of Foot was raised, as its title suggests, at Kidderminster, Worcestershire in 1779. Most of its service seems to have been in the

West Indies before disbandment in 1783. A particularly generous sounding bounty of three guineas, with a further three guineas after twelve months' service without deserting, was offered. The trick was apparently to enlist, accept the bounty and then desert and enlist into another corps – very risky but rewarding if successful. The reward for apprehending a deserter on the other hand was an equally generous one guinea.[5]

The third 89th Regt was raised in Ireland by Maj-Gen William Crosbie in 1793 and was placed on the Establishment of the Army in December that year, and numbered 89. The facings were ordered to be black; black velvet for officers. Almost without training the new regiment was hurried off to Holland and was severely mauled at Boxtel before retreating and return to England. An interesting note concerning dress is contained in a letter dated 21 January 1796:

'Commander-in-Chief out letter. Adjutant-General to Thomas Fauquier Esqre. W.O. 3/28, p.127.

    'The coats of the Drummers and Fifers of the 50th, 58th, 64th, 70th and 89th Regiments, are in all future clothings of the said Regiments, to be made of white cloth, instead of black, according to former regulation; and to have black cuffs, collars, and facings. The waistcoats, and breeches are to be white.'[6]

Officer 89th Regiment, c1805. Miniature by Buck, c1810. Red uniform, black facings and gold lace, gilt shoulder-belt plate of the earlier pattern. Note, this officer wears the Egypt Medal of 1801.
CHRISTIE'S

The following year the regiment went over to Ireland and was there in 1798 when the rebellion broke out, and was present at the battle of Vinegar Hill where the rebels were defeated. After service in Egypt under Sir Ralph Abercrombie the 89th was ordered to join the expedition to Holland in 1805 – but their ship was wrecked, many losing their lives whilst colours, band, mess plate etc, were all lost, although some survivors were taken prisoner by the Dutch. Back in England the following year, the prisoners returned by exchange, new colours to replace those lost at sea were received, and the regiment then embarked for South America. After the failure at Buenos Aires the 89th was sent to the Cape, a year later to Ceylon and eventually to India. It was from Madras in 1811 that a portion of the regiment set out to participate in the capture of Java, thereby securing another battle-honour, to join 'Egypt', on the colours. During this campaign half of the battalion under Major Richard Butler was formed into a Rifle Bn dressed in green, and served as an advance guard to the army under the command of Maj-Gen Gillespie. Authority for the word 'Java' to be borne on the colours was granted on 24 June 1818.

The silhouette artist Charles Buncombe of Newport, Isle of Wight, made an interesting study, original now in the Regimental Museum, interesting inasmuch as it depicts a surgeon wearing the white shako of 1812-16. This officer is named as John W. Brown, Assistant Surgeon to the 1st Bn 89th Regt, 1810-16. His uniform follows the pattern of the regiment, red coat, black facings and gold lace but is single breasted, and he wears a narrow black waist-belt, the latter two items of dress peculiar to a staff officer in a regiment or medical staff.[7]

A 2nd Bn of the regiment was formed in Ireland in 1803 – after some

Left. Brass Glengarry badge, 89th Regiment, 1874-81. Right. Music pouch badge after 1881.

time spent at Gibraltar it was sent to North America and by 1812 was stationed at Halifax, Nova Scotia. A relic of service in Canada, an oval shoulder-belt plate with numerals 89 within a crowned star, was found at Fort George, Niagara-in-the-Lake, Ontario.[8] This was probably from the Light Company of the regiment, the remnants of which, after the hard campaigning and actions of 1813-14, was sent to form the garrison of Fort George and Mississaga. The 2nd Bn embarked for England in June 1815 and was disbanded in Novembr 1816, all fit men being handed over to the 1st Bn. During its short lifetime this battalion had earned for the regimental colours the battle-honour 'Niagara'.

The 1st Bn did not return home until 1831, serving for many years in India and Burma, from 1817-19 employed against the Pindarrees, before return to Quilon, a coastal station in Madras. It was here in May 1820 that a new pair of colours was presented. In 1825-6 the regiment was part of the army during the 1st Burmese War, returning to Madras in October 1826, where it received the following despatch:

'In consideration of the distinguished part borne by the regiment in the war in Burmah, His Majesty was pleased to issue his Royal authority under date 29 November 1826, that the 89th Regt should thenceforth bear the word 'Ava' on its Colours and Appointments.'

During a two-year spell spent at Devonport 1831-3, an important event occurred. The young Princess Victoria, whilst visiting the West Country, consented to present new colours to the regiment. This was her first public duty, taking place on Plymouth Hoe, 3 August 1833. There was to be a sequel to this presentation in later years.

The next tour of overseas duty took the regiment to the West Indies and Canada; home again in 1847 for nine years. The 89th embarked for Gibraltar on 20 April 1854 and from there on to the Crimea, joining the army before Sevastopol and taking part in the assaults of 18 June and 8 September 1855. Before leaving the Crimea in 1856, Roger Fenton photographed a group of the regiment in various orders of dress, this picture recognised as one of his most interesting studies. The officers in the group wear undress, others sheepskin coats and heavy winter clothing, whilst one has the new pattern tunic which replaced the coatee. A sergeant of the Light Company is shown in full dress.[9]

After many long years spent in Africa and India the regiment returned home eventually in August 1865, and during the early months of the following year was attached to the 3rd Infantry Brigade at Aldershot, quartered in huts at the North Camp. In the flowery language of the day one historian[10] tells of the circumstances leading to the important parade of 5 April 1866:

'It having been humbly represented to the Queen by the commanding officer, through HRH the FM Commanding-in-Chief, that the colours which she herself had presented to the regiment in 1833 were completely worn out and required to be replaced, Her Majesty was graciously pleased to intimate her intention of presenting new colours in person, and appointed the 5 April for the occasion,'

and on 23 April 1866

'The Queen has been graciously pleased to command that the 89th Foot may henceforth bear the title of "Princess Victoria's Regiment", in commemoration of the recent presentation of new colours, to replace those presented 33 years ago by Her Majesty when Princess Victoria.'

A minor change in dress in 1866 is recorded: The Oxford grey tartan trousers which were issued in 1866, in place of blue serge, were not found to wear well, and summer trousers (Oxford mixture) of a somewhat improved material were issued this year to the regiment. Eleven years later when stationed at Rangoon, the same time as the Martini-Henry rifles were issued to the regiment in lieu of the snider pattern,

> 'Her Majesty was pleased to sanction the "Princess Victoria's Coronet", the regimental badge, to be worn on the collars of the tunics, instead of the universal crown, hitherto worn by men of the regiment.'

It is interesting to note that a photogrpah of the officers taken at Rangoon in 1879, shows that an embroidered coronet, upon a dark rectangular cloth patch, was worn on the left side of the white tropical helmet.

The regiment was still in Burma in 1881 when it received the Horse Guards General Order No 41 of 11 April 1881:

> 'The 89th Princess Victoria's Regt to be localized with the 87th Royal Irish Fusiliers, and to become the 2nd Bn Royal Irish Fusiliers (Princess Victoria's). The facings to be blue, the pattern of the lace shamrock. The number of the regimental district to be 87th. By a subsequent G.O. No 70, dated 30th June 1881, the name of the regiment was changed to Princess Victoria's (Royal Irish Fusiliers).'

THE REGULAR REGIMENTS ■ INFANTRY

Princess Victoria's (Royal Irish Fusiliers)

On 8 August 1882 the new 1st Bn embarked for Egypt and was present at the Battle of Tel-el-Kebir, returning to England during the same year but embarking for India in 1883. The 2nd Bn was on its way from India in 1884 after 14 years abroad, when it was stopped at Aden and took part in the Sudan campaign of 1884, earning the new battle-honours 'Egypt, 1882, 1884' and 'Tel-el-Kebir' to be added to the colours. New colours were presented to the 2nd Bn in 1889, again by Queen Victoria, and so the battalion had the proud distinction of having colours presented by Her Majesty on three successive occasions. The ceremony took place at Windsor on 3 June 1889 and by this time all ranks were in the complete fusilier uniform.

The 1st Bn had adopted the new headdress from 1866, sealskin busby, later changed to racoon skin with grenade badge in front, introduced into the 2nd Bn no doubt on return from its travels in 1884. The Monogram of HRH The Princess Victoria was ordered to be worn as a collar badge by the 89th, and on amalgamation both the grenade with eagle on the ball, as well as the Monogram and Coronet with sphinx above, were displayed on either side of the collar-opening by both battalions. In 1894 the Monogram and sphinx badge was replaced by a large Coronet, still displayed together with the grenade badge, the distinction of having two badges on the collar enjoyed by only one other regiment – the Seaforth Highlanders.

Lt-Col George Cox, commanding 2nd Bn, is said to have formed a pipe-band during the period 1892 until the South African War.

Both battalions saw service in the war, the 1st arriving in time to fight in that first section of the war at Talana Hill on 20 October 1899. In this engagement the Irishmen advanced uphill in the face of heavy fire, and succeeded in putting the Boers to flight. Ten days later at Nicholson's

In spite of its poor condition, an historic photograph of 2nd Battalion Royal Irish Fusiliers, 1886. It shows the three stands of colours, all presented by Queen Victoria, one in 1833 when she was Princess Victoria, the second in 1866, whilst in the centre the stand presented in that year.
S. J. KRETSCHMER

2nd Battalion officers in review order. Kilkenny, 1895. The officer with medals is Major C. R. Money.
S. J. KRETSCHMER

Nek, however, the Fusiliers were surrounded by vastly superior numbers and although they held on for nine hours, suffered many casualties, either men killed or captured. The 2nd Bn was at the Battle of Colenso and later at the final defeat of the Boers, not without much hard marching, skirmishing and suffering casualties. The commanding officer of the 2nd Bn, Lt-Col J. Reeves, received a most curious gift from a Boer farmer while on trek in the Transvaal – a five-horned ram. This peculiar beast was photographed, surrounded by soldiers of the regiment, but there is no record of what became of it![11]

After the war a photograph of the presentation of war medals in Belfast 1902, shows the men wearing khaki service dress with tropical helmet, the green brush plume prominent on the left side of the helmet. Later in 1902 an observer, seeing a dress parade of the regiment, remarked on the extraordinarily high busbies worn by the officers, with particularly vivid green flashes.

Dress Regulations of 1911 stipulate that for Fusiliers (except the Royal Scots Fusiliers): The uniform and horses furniture are the same as for other regiments of Infantry of the Line, with the following exceptions:

Cap Short bear or black racoon skin.
For officers not exceeding 5ft 6in in height, 8in high in front.
For officers not exceeding 5ft 9in in height, 8½in high in front.
For officers not exceeding 6ft 0in in height, 9in high in front.
For officers exceeding 6ft 0in in height, 9½in high in front.
These measurements must not be exceeded. Burnished chain, lined with black leather.

Plume Cut feather, with gilt two-flame socket. Colour of plume green, height 6½in worn on the left side.

The band of the 1st Battalion, Aldershot, c1910. Bandmaster Mr A. J. Dunn, in frock-coat.

Mess dress as for other regiments of Infantry of the Line.

Badges

On Buttons	On Collar of Tunic, Mess Jacket, and Frock Coat	Ornaments for Bearskin or Racoon-skin Caps	On the F.S. Helmet and Forage Cap	On the Service Dress	
				On the Collar in Bronze	On the Cap in Bronze
Scalloped edge; an Eagle with a wreath of laurel; below the Eagle a small tablet inscribed with the figure '8'. For the mess dress, plain edge with the eagle and tablet in silver – mounted. For the cap, as for mess dress, but die-struck.	1st Badge: Coronet of HRH the Princess Victoria in silver, worn nearer to the opening of the collar. 2nd Badge: A grenade in gold embroidery, with badge on ball as for buttons, but in silver.	A grenade in gilt, or gilding metal. In silver on the ball, the Eagle with a wreath of laurel. Below the Eagle, a small tablet inscribed with the figure '8'.	1st Badge: The coronet of HRH the Princess Victoria. 2nd Badge: A gilt or gild-metal grenade with the Harp surmounted by the plume of the Prince of Wales in silver, on the ball. The 1st Badge is worn over the 2nd one.	As for forage cap.	As for forage cap.

In October 1910 HM King George V honoured the regiment by becoming its Colonel-in-Chief.

From time to time throughout the history of British Army music, there have been family names which have become legendary, one such name is to be found in the musical annals of the Royal Irish Fusiliers; that name is Dunn.

One – Thomas Dunn – joined the army, the 33rd (Duke of Wellington's) Regt of Foot, in 1863. He was at that time a skilled musician and gained swift promotion in the band, eventually to band sergeant, which rank he held until leaving the service in 1886. He had three sons, the first, Augustus John, was born in the regiment in 1872 and enlisted in the Royal Field Artillery in 1886 at the age of 14. He was already an accomplished pianist and organist and received rapid promotion in the band attaining the rank of sergeant in just four years. He attended a Kneller Hall course in 1894 when he won the 'Gold Baton'. On 1 November 1897 he was appointed to the 1st Bn Royal Irish Fusiliers as bandmaster and stayed with that regiment until May 1918 when he transferred to the Royal Artillery (Mounted) Band. During this twenty-year period 'Dandy' Dunn's band became one of the topmost in the army. He volunteered for active service and served with his regiment in South Africa, was captured together with most of the battalion at Nicholson's Nek but eventually escaped from the Boers, returned to Ladysmith and was present during the siege. It was actually just after he had decided to retire from the army in April 1920 that an acceptance came through for the bandmastership of the Coldstream Guards but, alas – too late.

Another of Thomas Dunn's sons was William James, also a gifted musician choosing the army for a career. After many years as bandmaster of the 60th Rifles, he was appointed Director of Music, Royal Horse Guards (The Blues), retiring as Lieutenant-Colonel in 1935. His son, Vivian Dunn, was appointed to the Royal Marines Band, Eastney, in 1931, by 1953 was promoted Lieutenant-Colonel and Principal Director of Music, Royal Marines. He retired in December 1968 and was knighted in January 1969.[12]

Very little is recorded about pipers since that short period during the 1890s, but a newspaper in January 1913 printed a photogrdaph of pipers of the regiment at the funeral of the Duke of Abercorn, MP, 1st Life Guards (Reserve).

During the First World War, apart from the two regular battalions there was in addition the two former militia regiments, ie 3rd and 4th Reserve – also 7 Service Battalions and 3 Garrison Battalions were raised, making 14 in all. As well as service in France and Flanders the regiment also served in the Middle Eastern theatres of war, Gallipoli, Macedonia, Egypt and Palestine. At the outbreak the 1st Bn was at Shorncliffe, embarked for France straight away and landed at Boulogne 23 August 1914 as part of the 10th Infantry Brigade, 4th Division. A green cotton patch, 2in square, was worn by the battalion whilst in this

Drummers of 1st Battalion, Aldershot, St Patrick's Day, 1908.

Stand of Colours, drums, staff, bugles, tiger skin and a Regency shako as ornament. 2nd Battalion, Ferozepore, 1908.

Young soldier in his first walking-out dress,
1st Battalion, c1910.
S. J. KRETSCHMER

Drum-Major and Pipe-Major,
full dress, c1928.
GEORGE POTTER & SONS

brigade, but on transferring to the 107 Brigade of the 36th Division in August 1917, wore a green cotton inverted triangle on the left shoulder. The 1st Bn remained in France and Flanders throughout the war. The *London Gazette* of 22 May 1915 announced the posthumous award of the Victoria Cross to Pte Robert Morrow of the battalion:

'For most conspicuous bravery near Messines on the 12 April 1915, when he rescued and carried successively to places of comparative safety, several men who had been buried in the debris of trenches wrecked by shell fire. Pte Morrow carried out this gallant work on his own initiative, and under very heavy fire from the enemy.'

Sad to say Morrow, a 24-year-old regular soldier from Co Tyrone was killed two weeks later at St Jan, Ypres Salient on 25 April.

The 2nd Bn was stationed at Quetta, due for Madras, in August 1914, but left in October for the United Kingdom joining the 82 Brigade, 27th Division in November, and landing in France just before Christmas; the

Soldiers of 5th Battalion Royal Irish Fusiliers with the 10th Division in the trenches, Gallipoli, 1915-16. Official caption is marked as 'Teasing a Turkish sniper'. The figure 5 is just visible on lower portion of puggri on the topee held above trench.
IWM

charge of the 'Faughs' at St Eloi in 1915 is commemorated in a graphic painting made by 'Snaffles'. In November 1915 the battalion transferred to the 10th Division in the Middle East and remained with that Division, and in that theatre until the end of the war.

A posthumous award of the Victoria Cross was made to an officer of the 9th Bn, Lt G. St George S. Cather:

'For most conspicuous bravery. From 7pm till midnight he searched No Man's Land, and brought in three wounded men. Next morning at 8am he continued his search, brought in another wounded man, and gave water to others, arranging for their rescue later. Finally, at 10.30am, he took out water to another man and was proceeding further on when he himself was killed. All this was carried out in full view of the enemy, and under direct machine-gun fire and intermittent artillery fire. He set a splendid example of courage and self sacrifice.'

London Gazette, 9 September 1916.

The 2nd Bn returned home and was at Dover Castle during 1921 and 1922 when the reductions and amalgamations were announced, but the regiment had offered to sacrifice a battalion and so, on 16 September 1922, Army Order 341 promulgated the amalgamation of the 1st and 2nd Bns.

Throughout the whole of the 1920s and up to 1934 the regiment was abroad, firstly Egypt and then on to India before a return home to Bordon Camp by November 1934. The battalion was nevertheless represented at the massed military band displays at the British Empire Exhibition, Wembley, 1924-5. A photograph of Directors of Music, bandmasters, drum and pipe-majors at Wembley includes Bandmaster L. P. Bradley, LRAM, and the drum-major, both in scarlet full dress but with peaked forage caps in place of bear skin caps. Attention had also been paid to the dress of the pipe-band, both the drum-major and pipe-

The anti-tank platoon of 1st Battalion at gun drill, Dury, Fauntaine Les Croiselles.
BEP 1940.
IWM

Drum Major of the 1st Battalion, Palestine 1945.
IWM

Forward position of 'D' Coy. 1st Battalion, observer position in the Hitler Line, Italy 1943.
IWM

major appear in a photograph of 1928 in full dress. The pipe-major by this time having a green caubeen, with plume of a lighter and brighter shade of green, affixed below a large silver metal harp and crown badge. The green tunic has ornamental piping across the front, wings on the shoulder and is of a cut-away design at front. The kilt is saffron and hose dark green. The pipes are the two drone variety with green ribbons and bag.

On return to this country in 1937 Brig-Gen A. B. Incledon-Webber, CMG, DSO, DL, Colonel of the Regiment, presented nine officers at a Royal levée at St James's in June, all officers in the regimental full dress. In the same year the 2nd Bn was re-raised, and in November HRH The Duke of Gloucester presented new colours to both battalions, also at St James's.

During the Second World War there were four battalions. After return from Dunkirk and reorganisation, the 1st Bn went to North Africa, fought in the desert war and through to Sicily and Italy. From Malta the 2nd Bn was sent to the Dodecanese in 1943 as part of the garrison of the island of Leros, sought after by the Germans for its excellent harbour. After a four-day battle from 12 to 16 November, which included heavy dive bombing and eventual landings by paratroops and seaborne forces, the garrison of 8,500, including the whole of the 2nd Royal Irish Fusiliers, was taken prisoner.

Garrison duty after the war included a spell of Guard Mounting at British HQ at Schonbrünn Palace, Vienna. Photographs of this ceremony show 1st Bn soldiers in neatly pressed battle-dress bearing the 78th Divisional sign above a green cloth shamrock on each sleeve. The regimental cap badge with green plume was worn on the khaki caubeen.

The two battalions were amalgamated once again after the war and the round of peacetime garrison duties resumed. In Germany in July 1963, after a three year tour of duty in Tripoli and Libya, new colours were presented by Field Marshal Sir Gerald Templer at Celle. The band, pipes and drums, had previously appeared in all their finery at the Royal Tournament, and the following year were greatly admired when, in the company of the Royal Inniskilling Fusiliers and the Royal Ulster Rifles, they toured Canada and the USA. It is interesting to note that Bandmaster L. F. Marks and four others of the Royal Irish Fusiliers band were English, the pipe-major came from Scotland but all others of the 40-strong band were Irish. There would of course have been none other than Irish way back in 1793 when a Dublin paper of 7 September reported that:–

> 'Major Doyle announces that it is his intention to introduce into his newly formed Regiment the peculiar music of Ireland, the pipes, an introduction that appeals to the Irishman very strongly, and marks that warm affection of everything concerned with his native soil which has always characterised his conduct.'

In the November of that year it was announced that a War Pipe Band had been established.

Once more in July 1968 the Royal Irish Fusiliers joined company with the other two Ulster regiments, the Royal Inniskilling Fusiliers and the Royal Ulster Rifles, to form the new Corps, the Royal Irish Rangers (27th (Inniskilling) 83rd and 87th).

Left. Officers with Colours, 1st Bn Royal Irish Fusiliers, Cannon Street Station, London. On return from Austria, en route Belfast, 1 May 1947. Centre figure is General Sir G. Templer welcoming home the regiment.
S. D. EAGLE

1 J.S.A.H.R. Vol.LV, p.123 and LVI, p.121.
2 *Memoirs of the Military Career of John Shipp, late a Lieutenant in His Majesty's 87th Regiment.* Written by himself. London 1843.
3 *The British Army and Auxiliary Forces*, by Col C. Cooper-King, RMA, late Professor of Tactics at the Royal Military College. Cassel & Co 1897.
4 Original in the Royal Collection: reproduced in colour in the J.S.A.H.R., Vol.XXXI, p.95.
5 J.S.A.H.R. Vol.LVII, p.117.
6 *British Military Uniforms, 1768-96.* Hew Strachan. Arms and Armour.
7 See colour plate and article by W. Y. Carman. J.S.A.H.R. Vol.XLIX, p.191.
8 Photograph in *History Written with Pick and Shovel*, Calver and Bolten. New York Historical Society 1950.
9 Photo reproduced in J.S.A.H.R. Vol.XVIII and also *1854-6 Crimea*, by Laurence James. Hayes Kennedy Ltd 1981.
10 *Historical Record of the Eighty-Ninth, Princess Victoria's Regiment.* R. Brinckman. Gale & Polden, Chatham 1888.
11 Photograph reproduced in the *Black and White Budget*, 27 October 1900.
12 *Fanfare.* Journal of Kneller Hall. Vol.1, No.10 1977.

THE REGULAR REGIMENTS ■ INFANTRY

The Royal Irish Rangers

The Royal Irish Rangers was formed on 1 July 1968 from the amalgamation of The Royal Inniskilling Fusiliers (27th and 108th), The Royal Ulster Rifles (83rd and 86th) and the Royal Irish Fusiliers (Princess Victoria's) (87th and 89th).

On its formation, the regiment consisted of three Regular Bns, one Territorial Bn and the Regimental Depot at Ballymena in Northern Ireland. The 3rd Bn was disbanded on 12 December 1968 and the 5th (Volunteer) Bn was raised on 1 April 1971. Prior to the formation of the regiment, The North Irish Militia (4th Bn) was formed on 1 April 1967, from the amalgamation of the 5th Bn The Royal Inniskilling Fusiliers (TA), the 6th Bn The Royal Ulster Rifles (TA), the 5th Bn The Royal Irish Fusiliers (TA) and the 1st Bn The London Irish Rifles (TA). The four rifle companies of the North Irish Militia wear the respective collar badges of the former regiments.

Battalions of the Royal Irish Rangers were posted to Gibraltar, Bahrain and Cyprus in addition to regular tours in the United Kingdom and BAOR. They took part in training exercise in Libya, Sharjah, Muscat and Oman, Denmark, Canada and Fort Hood in Texas. The 2nd Battalion was the Demonstration Battalion at the School of Infantry twice and the 1st Battalion once.

The rank of a private soldier, previously Rifleman, was altered to Ranger.

During the post-war years the regiment could boast four separate musical sections in its band, ie Military Band, Pipes, Bugles and Drums. Following the custom of rifle regiments the bass drummer wears an apron of black bearskin. In the 1970s and 80s an Irish wolfhound mascot was owned by the regiment, often accompanying the band on parade. Each hound was named in succession 'Brian Boru', by 1983 the proud title held by Brian Boru III.

In 1969, to commemorate the Rangers' service on The Rock, Gibraltar issued a postage stamp featuring a piper in full dress together with the regimental Badge. The Regiment ran its own newspaper *The Irish Ranger*.

In 1992 the Royal Irish Rangers were amalgamated with the Ulster Defence Regiment to form The Royal Irish Regiment (page 283) with the parade being held at Warminster, the Infantry's home. The new Regiment retains the Rangers' custom of owning an Irish wolfhound named 'Brian Boru'.

Bandmaster (WO 1) A. W. Healey, 2nd Bn Royal Irish Rangers, frock-coat, in conversation with the Director of Music, Mr P. A. Cave, ARCM, Royal Barbados Police and Harbour Band, at the Royal Tournament 1973. Bugle Major J. J. W. Maxwell is on the left of the group.
W. BOAG, MA

THE REGULAR REGIMENTS ■ INFANTRY

The Connaught Rangers

88th (Connaught Rangers)

There were two regiments which carried the number 88 before September 1793 when The Connaught Rangers was raised. The first was a Highland regiment, 88th (Royal Highland Volunteers) Campbell's, raised in 1760. It served on the continent as a linked battalion with the 87th Highlanders, but was disbanded at Linlithgow in July 1763.

The next regiment was raised in October 1779 and numbered 88th Foot, Keating's, but subsequently disbanded in 1783.

The third regiment raised in 1793 in Connaught, and named immediately – The Connaught Rangers, the facings yellow, the Irish Harp and motto *Quis Separabit* adopted, although was not recorded in the 1794 Army List.

Badges were not officially sanctioned until 1830 and appeared in the Army List for 1831. In that same List one finds that the regiment had earned a most impressive number of battle-honours, only surpassed by four or five other regiments. The first battle-honour was awarded for Egypt 1801 and on 28 August 1817 followed by the Peninsular War honours:

'Talavera', 'Busaco', 'Fuentes D'Honor', 'Ciudad Rodrigo', 'Badajoz', 'Salamanca', 'Vittoria', 'Nivelle', 'Orthez', 'Toulouse', 'Peninsula'.

The following notes record dress changes from 1793:

1793 Officers' uniform scarlet, facings yellow, epaulettes and buttons silver. No lace. Gorget silver. Hat black, no lace. White breeches. Black gaiters. Silver plate, ornaments gilt, the numerals 88 surrounded by the motto *Quis separabit* with crown above and harp below.

Men. Uniform red, faced yellow, lace white with yellow, black and red lines. Buttons by twos, laced barred. Coat lined white, waistcoat white, white cross belts. Button pewter, engraved 88. White breeches and black gaiters. Hat black, no white lace.

Sergeants. With sashes of yellow and crimson and probably epaulettes, but plain white lace. Half pike.

1795-6 Privates' coats to be single breasted and buttoned up. Waistcoats of men not seen. Officer's swords to have a brass guard and the sword knot to be crimson and gold. Gorgets to be gilt with the King's cypher and crown engraved thereon. Rosettes of the colour of the facings.

1796 Plain hats in the Infantry of the Line and in the Guards. White feathers in them. A cord of yellow and white round the crown.

1800 Cocked hat for the men to be discontinued and a shako introduced, plume red and white, cockade of leather with regimental button in centre, brass plate.

1801 Plates on Grenadier caps changed from white to yellow.

1802 Chevrons for NCOs introduced.

1808 Queue abolished, hair to be cut short to the neck.

1809 Officers now wear the felt caps with the men. For service,

officers generally wear grey pantaloons with hessian boots.

1810 (GO) Officers' rank. Colonel, crown above a star. Lt-Colonel, a crown. Major, a star. Captains and Lieutenants, one epaulette on the right shoulder. Flank Companies wore wings with grenades and bugles on them.

An officer, William Grattan, Ensign in the regiment from 6 July 1809, recorded interesting facts and anecdotes from his service during the Peninsular War.[1] The author mentions a soldier of the 88th at Busaco being killed by a bullet which passed through the plate of his cap. Black Cymbalmen of the 88th mentioned in September 1811. In 1812 at the Storming of Badajoz:

> 'the soldiers, unencumbered with their knapsacks, their stocks off, their shirt collars unbuttoned, their trousers tucked up to the knee, their tattered jackets so worn out as to render the regiments they belonged to barely recognisable, and their faces with huge whiskers and bronzed.'

1813 On arrival of Grattan and some other officers at Portsmouth he writes:

> 'We were all splendidly dressed with braided coats, handsome forage caps, rich velvet waistcoats appended to which were a profusion of Spanish silver buttons (some wore gold ones), and our pantaloons bore the weight of as much embroidery as poor Fairfield* once said would furnish a good sideboard of plate. Thanks to the old German tailor in Lisbon for this. But as

The officers, 88th Connaught Rangers, Portsmouth 1872

Left. Lt-Colonel R. Jeffreys, CB, c1858. He held all ranks in the 88th from Cornet 1825, to Colonel 1858.
S. J. KRETSCHMER

Private, 94th Regiment. Walking-out dress, c1875, Belfast.
S. J. KRETSCHMER

we landed we saw the garrison of Portsmouth in their white breeches and black gaiters and their officers in red coats, long boots and white shoulder belts. We must have appeared to them as they did to us, like men who had arrived from a different nation.'

*(John Fairfield, Ensign in the regiment from 5 July 1809)

The regimental historian Lt-Col H. F. N. Jourdain, CMG,[2] provides the story of the 'Jingling Johnny', a unique trophy captured by the regiment and treasured right through to disbandment:

'The original "Jingling Johnny" was made partly of brass and partly of silver, the stem and the Crescents being of brass, the Bells and the attachment rings of silver. The plumes which hang from the two ends of the Crescents were made of red and black horse-hair. The Napoleonic eagle on the top of all was of brass.

'Originally it was carried in battle by the Moors, partly as a musical instrument and partly as a Rallying Colour for the Moorish warriors.

'It is uncertain at what date it was captured by the French from the Moors, but from accounts rendered to the 88th by French Officers during the occupation of France, after the Battle of Waterloo, by the British Army of Occupation, of which the 88th was a part, it is certain that it had already been some years in the possession of the French Regt from which it was captured in 1812.

'It is certain that the French captured it from the Moors, and that the French surmounted it with an Imperial eagle after its capture.

'The 88th captured it from the French, probably the 101st Regt of the Line, at the Battle of Salamanca, on 22 July 1812.

'This regiment, which had three battalions present at the battle, was in the 7th Division under Thomieres.

'The 101st Regt was engaged by the 88th and the trophy was taken during the charge on 22 July, most probably from that regiment.

'For many years it was an accepted tradition that it had been captured from the French 88th Regt of the Line, but this regiment was not present at the Battle of Salamanca, and without doubt the story of the capture of the "Jingling Johnny" by the 88th, and the meeting of the 88th (Connaught Rangers), with the French 88th Regt of the Line in the following year had become somewhat intermixed. (The 88th Regt of the French Army was in a brigade in the 1st Division in May 1813, and in July 1813, in the 8th Division.) At the Battle of Salamanca, this interesting relic of the gallantry of the 88th Connaught Rangers was taken in the historic charge of Wallace's Brigade, and has since then always been with the regiment both at home and abroad. It has invariably been carried on parade by the tallest man in the regiment, and always at the head of the regiment in front of the Band and Drums.'

A soldier from the Infantry Depot at Chatham in 1833, Pte Owen Sweeny, was the subject chosen by the artist A. J. Dubois Drahonet. It will be recalled that Drahonet was commissioned to paint 100 pictures for King William IV, illustrating the dress of the Army and Navy at that time, this painting confirming the uniform as red with yellow facings, the

88th Connaught Rangers. A battalion parade, Portsmouth 1872. Band in white tunics at rear.

lace white with a green stripe and the shako plume white.[3]

The following year 1834, the regiment was stationed at Corfu and on 27 February, the anniversary of the battle of Orthes, new colours were presented by Lady Woodford, wife of Maj-Gen Sir A. Woodford, commanding troops in the Ionian Islands. The ceremony was reported at length in the *United Services Journal* of June 1834 from which the following description of the parade is taken:

'The regiment being assembled and drawn up in line, at about eleven o'clock, Lady Woodford arrived in her carriage, attended by the Major-General and his staff on horseback; and on her Ladyship's descending in front of the line, the regiment presented arms, the band playing "God Save the King". The Grenadier company then moved from the right, and drew up facing the centre of the battalion: having opened its ranks, it presented arms to the old colours, of which it took charge, and escorted them to the Citadel, the regiment presenting arms to them. Shortly afterwards the Grenadiers returned with the new colours that had been consecrated on the previous Sunday, and had remained ever since in the Garrison Chapel. These were delivered by the Rev Charles Küper to the Major and the senior Captain, by whom they were borne to the Parade, where those Officers placed themselves on either side of Lady Woodford, continuing to hold the colours unfurled. The Grenadiers having resumed their place on the right of the line, the regiment formed three sides of a square, leaving the fourth open to the public.'

Then addressing Col O'Malley, officers and NCOs and privates of the regiment, Maj-Gen Woodford made a speech to which the Commanding Officer replied. The remainder of the day was treated as a holiday, a splendid dinner was provided for the troops and a ball given by the officers that night.

The regiment served in the Mediterranean, the West Indies and North America up to 1851 and after three years at home sailed for active service in the Crimea. An amusing story is told of the embarkation of the 88th at Halifax, Nova Scotia, on 18 June 1851. Whilst in Canada it appears that a bear had been adopted as a pet and had become a great favourite with all ranks. The regiment was to travel home aboard *HMS Resistance* and the ship's Captain had issued the strictest instructions that no wild animals would be allowed on board. The troops embarked without their bear, but a fatigue party was stopped by a naval officer in the act of rolling a large barrel aboard. 'What on earth have you got there?' he requested of the sergeant in charge, who stood at attention and replied 'Warm winter clothing for the regiment, sir.' This apparently satisfied the officer and the barrel was safely stowed away, even though the animal was about the size of a small donkey. It appears that Bruin had been given a sleeping draught beforehand by the Medical Officer and was curled up and sleeping peacefully, the NCO's quick thinking and answer prompted by the fear he later confessed, that the naval officer might look through the bung-hole and see the fur! The beast had a very friendly disposition borne out by a further story about a guest night after arrival in England. Stationed at Parkhurst Barracks, Isle of Wight, a young gentleman who was entertained in the mess and who had partaken freely of wine, was later missing, and it was assumed had made a discreet and unnoticed departure. When the bear's keeper visited his charge next morning with breakfast, however, he found the bear curled up comfortably, whilst in deep slumber with his head upon the bear's soft fur was the young visitor of the previous evening!

Between the years 1853 and 1857 Richard Ebsworth saw and sketched soldiers of the regiment, at Chobham and the Isle of Wight in 1853, and later in 1856 and '57 at Aldershot and Canterbury. In 1853 he saw the band and noted that the Drum-Major wore a scarlet coatee with yellow facings and four silver chevrons on right arm, but the 24 bandsmen as well as the Bandmaster wore white, faced yellow. The 'Jingling Johnny' was carried by a private, the bass drum was large size emblazoned with the Royal Arms, battle honours and yellow hoops. The Drum-Major's sash was edged with gold lace, an embroidered crown of gold, and below this the Harp and Crown badge. The staff was black encircled with silver cord, the head of silver surmounted by a silver Harp and Crown.

The regiment left England for the Crimea in 1854 and remained throughout the campaign, fighting at the Alma and Inkerman and the siege of Sebastopol.[4] During a brief respite in England before embarkation for India, new colours were presented on Southsea Common on 3 July 1857 by Sir William Codrington. The regiment was in India during the Mutiny, and was eventually granted the battle honour 'Central India'; then after many long years in India returned home again in December 1870, South Africa was the next destination for the spell of overseas service, this time active service in the Kaffir War of 1877-8 and in the Zulu War of 1879. A very brave action by Major Hans Garrett Moore on the 29 December 1877, resulted in that officer being awarded the Victoria Cross. The citation, *London Gazette* 27 June 1879, reads as follows:

> 'For his gallant conduct in risking his own life in endeavouring to save the life of Pte Giese of the Frontier Armed Mounted Police, on the occasion of the action with the Gaikas, near Komgha, on 29 December 1877. It is reported that when a small body of Mounted Police were forced to retire before overwhelming numbers of the enemy, Major Moore observed that Pte Giese was unable to mount his horse, and was thereby left at the mercy of the Kaffirs. Perceiving the man's danger, Major Moore rode back alone into the midst of the enemy and did not desist in his endeavour to save the man until the latter was killed, Major Moore having shot two Kaffirs and received an assegai wound in the arm during his gallant attempt.'

In 1879 the celebrated artist Lady Elizabeth Butler, wife of the distinguished soldier General William Butler, painted that delightful picture 'Listed for the Connaught Rangers'. In her autobiography she tells how she made studies for this painting in Glencar:

Colour-Sergeant, 1st Bn Connaught Rangers, 1891.

> 'I had splendid models for the two Irish recruits who are being marched out of the glen by a recruiting sergeant, followed by the "decoy" private and two drummer boys of that regiment, the old 88th, with the yellow facings of that time. The men were cousins, Foley by name, and wore their national dress, the jacket with the long, white homespun sleeves and picturesque black hat which I fear is little worn now. The deep richness of those typical Irish days of cloud and sunshine had so enchanted me that I was determined to try and represent the effect in this picture, which was a departure from my former ones, the landscape occupying an equal share with the figures, and the civilian peasant dress forming the centre of interest. Its black, white and brown colouring, the four red coats and the bright brass of the drum, gave me an enjoyable combination with the blue and red-purple of the mountains in the background, and the sunlight on the middle distance of the stony Kerry bog-land.'[10]

The regiment moved on to India in 1879-80 and remained until 1891. Whilst at Mooltan in 1881 the designation was changed to 1st Bn

Connaught Rangers. Although previously linked with, and sharing a depot with, the 87th Fusiliers, the regiment which became the 2nd Bn Connaught Rangers was actually the 94th Foot. At Meerut in 1885 new colours to replace the much travelled and worn 1857 pair, were presented by HRH The Duchess of Connaught on 6 February 1885.

The 94th Regiment of Foot

The 94th Regt of Foot, which was to eventually become the 2nd Bn The Connaught Rangers, was raised in December 1823. To follow the sequence of regiments numbered 94 one has to go back to 1793 when a corps, believed to be Irish, was raised by Col the Hon J. Hely Hutchinson, afterwards Earl of Donoughmore. (This was the third corps to be so numbered, the previous two being short lived, 1760-3 and 1779-83.) The life of Hely Hutchinson's regiment was of even shorter duration; it joined the Duke of York's army on the Waal where it was drafted into other units in 1794.

In 1793 King George III commanded ex-officers of the Old Scots Brigade 1572-1783, formerly in Dutch service, to raise a regiment in Glasgow to be known as 'The Scotch Brigade', this regiment to be later classified 94th in place of Hely Hutchinson's regiment which had disappeared from the Army List. Hence the Scotch Brigade became the fourth titled 94th. The regiment was a Highland corps wearing Mackay tartan kilt. In November 1795 it sailed for Gibraltar and in 1796 for the Cape, from there to India in 1798, and remained in India until 1807. Back in England in 1808 to recruit, it proceeded eventually to Portugal, Spain and France, coming home once again in 1814 and was disbanded in Belfast in 1818.

Left. Glengarry badge, rank and file, 1890-4.
Right. Cap badge, rank and file, 1894-1903.

During the years spent in India the regiment fought at Malavelly and the storming and capture of Seringapatam, 4th May 1799, and is shown in H. Singleton's famous painting of this event, although in this painting the regiment dressed not as Highlanders but in white gaiter trousers. P. W. Reynolds states that this would almost certainly be the dress worn by Highlanders, instead of the kilt, in India at that time.[5]

On return home from the wars in 1814 the regiment went to Ireland and remained there until disbandment. The regimental colour, laid-up in St Giles's Cathedral, Edinburgh, was dark green bearing the Scottish Thistle on a crimson centre surmounted by the crown, together with the Elephant badge and battle-honours, 'Seringapatam' and 'Peninsula'. The officers' shoulder-belt plate of the period 1814-18, was very fine, gilt with silver mounts:– The Elephant with battle honour scroll 'Peninsula' between it and the crown above, the numerals XCIV surrounded by a wreath of thistle and the title Scotch Brigade on a scroll below the central device. The Elephant badge awarded to this regiment was without a howdah.

The fifth and final regiment styled 94 had a similar beginning to the regiment disbanded in 1818. As was the case with the raising of the Scotch Brigade in 1793, ex-officers of the old 94th were invited to raise the new regiment, which was then recruited from Glasgow. The new battalion embarked for Gibraltar soon after formation and received its first colours whilst at that station. The 94th Regiment of Foot appears in the January 1824 Army List, the Colonel, Lieutenant-Colonel, two

94th Regiment. At the capture of Seringapatam, 4 May 1799.

Majors all with date of appointment 1 December 1823, the remaining officers and Adjutant, with the earlier dates from the half-pay list, mainly 94th Scotch Brigade.

A magnificent portrait in oils of the Colonel, Maj-Gen Sir Thomas Bradford, KCB, 1823-9, and a watercolour of a Colour-Sergeant c1828, provide fullest details of the uniforms worn when the regiment was raised on 1 December 1823.[6] Both have the Regency shako, bell-topped and of black felt, the Colonel's with a star plate, gold lace at the top and a twelve inch plume, white out of a red base. The Colour-Sergeant's is roughly the same but without any gold lace decoration and in place of the star a brass domed disc badge, surmounted by a crown and with a scaled strap connecting the badge with a black cockade to which a brass plume-holder is attached. The coatee is scarlet, the Colonel's with green collar, cuffs, and curved lapels with bands of gold lace and buttons in pairs. The NCO has bastion-shaped loops of lace across the front, but the facings are more of a blue shade than green. Both wear crimson sashes, the Colour-Sergeant's has a central stripe of green running through, his trousers are white, the Colonel's black. Col Bradford wears no shoulder-belt, but the Colour-Sergeant does, with a rectangular brass plate. His rank is denoted by a single chevron or silver or white lace surmounted by crossed swords with a Union Jack on a central stave, with gold crown above.

Still on the subject of dress, valuable correspondence relating to the making of a Drum-Major's belt for this regiment was located in the Public Archives of Canada.[7] Lt-Col G. W. Paty writing from Birr Barracks, 21 July 1837, sets out the requirements for the new belts:

'Gentlemen,
'The Dress Belt of the Drum Major which was given to the Corps by Sir Thomas Bradford, at its formation in 1823, having become completely worn out, and the Regiment being in daily expectation of a Removal to Dublin, where this article will be much used – I have the honour to request that you will be pleased to obtain the sanction of the Colonel that a new Belt may be supplied as soon as possible.

'New Drum Sticks will not require to be furnished, the old ones which are of Ebony and mounted with Silver being sufficiently good.

'The following are the dimensions etc.,

Length of Belt _____ 5 feet
Breadth of it _____ 5½ inches

'To be bordered with two rows of broad gold Lace, and from the points where the belt is joined, is to be placed a long Bullion Tassel, or a rich Bullion Fringe – 5¼ inches below the Centre of the Belt is to be placed a Crown, and underneath X_{CIV}^{VR} surrounded by a wreath of the Rose Thistle and Shamrock the whole in Embroidery – and the space this is to occupy to be 6¾ inches on a ground of Scarlet Cloth: the Belt to be made of Scarlet and Green Cloth but as little of the Green to appear as is consistent with the Style of Belt required, in Consequence of its being liable to fade so soon, and the extreme edging of the Belt to be of Scarlet Cloth. It will be necessary to forward a small quanity of the same Lace as the Border to make the Loops to admit the Drum Sticks which can be put on at the regiment, and it may be proper to remark that the Belt is to be worn by the Drum Major over the left Shoulder.

'I have not sent the old Belt as I do not consider it worth the carriage, and I hope that a new one may be forwarded as soon as possible as we really are exceedingly in want of it.

'I have the honour to be
(Signed) . . . . . . Paty.
Commg. 94th Regt.'

The article concludes with a footnote relating to the band of 1854:

'R. Ebsworth on observing the band of the regiment at Windsor Castle during 1854, noticed that the Drum-Major, Van Maanen wore a 'scarlet scarf-belt, not green' and he also saw what he considered was a strange 'leaden hue' of the regimental green facings. He surmised that this was attributable to the affects of the sun as the regiment had just come from a long tour of duty in India.'

Ebsworth saw the band again in 1854 at Chatham. About this time the band was under the direction of a foreign bandmaster, as most were in those days. He was Carl von Fröenherdt, a Saxon who came to England under the sponsorship of the Prince Consort. Although his command of the language was poor, he was nevertheless highly efficient, and during his time with the regiment established a fine band. He went on to become one of the leading bandmasters in the British Army, to the 2nd Life Guards 1856-72 and then to the band of the Plymouth Division, Royal Marine Light Infantry, 1872-90.

The regiment in the meanwhile carried on with the normal round of garrison duties, at home and abroad. During a tour of India in 1862 new colours were presented at Jullundur by Maj-Gen Sir Sidney Cotton, on 19 November. Returning home in 1868 the 94th were to enjoy a ten-year spell of home service, much of it in Ireland. Whilst at Belfast in 1875 the regiment learned that Queen Victoria was pleased to allow the 'new' 94th to bear all the battle honours of the previous unit numbered 94, to revive the badge, 'The Elephant', and according to one authority, to adopt the diced band to the infantry shako, the distinctive mark of Lowland Scottish regiments. The· forage cap badge for an officer between 1874 and 1881 was an ornate embroidered device, the Elephant above the numerals 94 with the battle honour Seringapatam on a scroll below. Soldiers had a brass glengarry badge, the numerals 94 within the open centre of a circlet bearing the word REGIMENT, crown above.

Between February 1879 and 1882 the regiment served in Zululand, and in the Zulu War, against Sekukuni in the Transvaal, and subsequently in the Boer War of 1880-1. There were many examples of heroism shown during this campaign in South Africa, three soldiers being awarded the Victoria Cross. Pte Thomas Flawn and Pte Francis Fitzpatrick were both decorated for bravery on 28 November 1879. The citation reads as follows:

'In recognition of their gallant conduct during the attack on Sekukuni's Town, on the 18 November last, in carrying out of action Lt Dewar, 1st Dragoon Guards, when badly wounded. At the time when he received his wound Lt Dewar had with him only Privates Flawn and Fitzpatrick, and six of the Native Contingent, and being incapable of moving without assistance, the natives proceeded to carry him down the hill, when about 30 of the enemy appeared in pursuit about 40 yards in the rear, whereupon the men of the Native Contingent deserted Lt Dewar, who must have been killed but for the devoted gallantry of Privates Flawn and Fitzpatrick, who carried him alternately, one covering the retreat and firing on the enemy.'

Also, during the fighting in the Transvaal L/Cpl James Murray, from Cork City:

'For gallant conduct (with Trooper John Danaher of Nourse's Horse) during an engagement with the Boers of Elandsfontein on 16 January 1881, in advancing for 500 yards, under a very heavy fire from a party of about 60 Boers, to bring out of action a private of the 21st Foot, who had been severely

Band of 1st Battalion at Sheffield 1896. Note the Jingling Johnny held aloft by a bandsman in the back row.

wounded; in attempting which Lance Corporal Murray was himself severely wounded.'

Mention must also be made of some brave women of the regiment. As early as 1810, in the Peninsular War, the wife of a Sergeant in the 94th, Mrs Reston, actively assisted the surgeon in attending the wounded during the defence of Fort Matagorda, drawing water although under heavy fire, and tearing up her own and her husband's linen for bandages. At Bronkhuist Spruit in the Transvaal in 1880, Mrs Smith, wife of the bandmaster and Mrs Fox, wife of the newly appointed Quartermaster, George Fox, both tended the desperately wounded under fire, Mrs Fox being herself severely wounded. She was later decorated by Queen Victoria with the Order of the Royal Red Cross, but died from the effects of her wounds in 1888.

A strange story emerges from the action and ambush at Bronkhuist Spruit. On the morning of the attack, 20 December 1880, the 94th had 'outspanned' for breakfast near a farm which contained a number of peach trees. During the halt some of the men wandered around, discovered the orchard and proceeded to help themselves to peaches, those not consumed on the spot carried away in haversacks. The march resumed and three or four hours later the ambush occurred. Those killed were buried as they had fallen, in clothing and equipment, the peaches still in their haversacks. Twenty years later, young officer of the 4th Hussars serving in South Africa came across the graves of the officers,

Private soldier, 1st Battalion, Punjab,
c1909.
R. J. MARRION

NCOs and men who fell in 1880, and was curious when he discovered that the graves of the men were in a veritable orchard of peach trees. It was later established that there were no such trees at Bronkuist Spruit in 1880, proved by photographs of the graves taken some short while later. The orchard thus became a remarkable and fitting memorial for brave men.

It is claimed that the colours of the 94th, those presented in India in 1862, obtained their baptism of fire at Ulundi on 4 July 1879, and that in December 1880 they were in action again, 'the last occasion that a British regiment ever carried colours in the field'.[8] These colours were taken from their poles and smuggled into Pretoria by a Sergeant Bradley and Conductor Eggerton, who were sent for medical aid. Those not killed during the ambush were forced to surrender. At Pretoria the colours were given into the custody of the 2nd Bn 21 Royal Scots Fusiliers; these colours were returned at a ceremonial parade held in Pretoria on 5 April 1881. They were marched under the escort of 'G' Company, 94th Regt, whilst the band of the 21st played them off to the regimental march of the 94th, 'Blue Bonnets'.

The regiment returned home in March 1882, having now become the 2nd Bn The Connaught Rangers, so no longer with any Scottish connection.

This battalion came over from Ireland in 1888 to be stationed in Portsmouth as a jumping-off station for overseas, embarking in July 1889 for Malta. Before that however the regiment had the misfortune to be in garrison with old antagonists, the old 40th (Second Somersetshire) Regt. An affray did take place and thirteen Connaught Rangers were taken into police custody, actually to prevent really serious trouble and no charges were preferred against them, although much was made of the event in the local newspaper. A resident, who was also an eyewitness, wrote the following enlightening remarks:

'The account on this page of a riot betwen the 40th East Lancashire Regt and the 94th, 2nd Bn Connaught Rangers is erroneous. The 40th was a very quarrelsome regiment and the year the riot occurred was the worst conducted regiment in the army, although before it became the South Lancashire it was a crack corps, known as the 40th Second Somersetshire. The 94th was one of the best regiments that had been in the Portsmouth Garrison for years, was exceptionally well conducted, having a good backbone of NCOs and veterans who had served in the South African 1871-89, Boer 1881 and the Egyptian Sudanese affairs 1882-4. In the ranks of the 94th there was a VC man, his award was for gallantry in the Transvaal. I was an eyewitness throughout the riot and no one was molested excepting the offending regiment. Whilst on the war-path the Connaught Rangers passed the barracks where the 54th Dorset Regiment were stationed and cheered them, being very friendly and on good terms with the "Flamers".'[9]

Two years after the 2nd Bn sailed the 1st returned, having served 14 years overseas, almost all in India. After a spell at home this battalion sailed for South Africa, landing in December 1899 and forming part of

A company of the 1st Battalion, Jullundur, North West Frontier, c1920.

the 5th, the famous Irish Brigade under Maj-Gen Hart. It served throughout the whole South African Campaign and its participation in most major engagements is reflected in the sad list of casualties sustianed, 104 NCOs and men killed or died of wounds, disease etc, 16 officers and 252 NCOs and men wounded. A few years to recuperate in Ireland and then off to India again by 1908, whilst the 2nd Bn returned from the sub-continent about the same time.

A note in a tailor's book of 1902 gives an entry for the officers' forage cap as blue, green cloth band and green welts (Regimental green), whilst on 3 January 1907 and 10 March 1908, the tailor' note for service forage cap reads:–

'Special service serge, bronze badge of harp, crown and motto. Chin strap, buttons – khaki bone with – C.R.'

Dress Regulations were published in 1911, and those for the Connaught Rangers are similar to those laid down for the Royal Irish Regiment, although it should be noted that a black line is given in the lace, with the forage cap as previously stated being blue with green band and welts.

Mess Dress

Collar	Shoulder straps	Cuffs	Piping	Vest
Green cloth	Green cloth	Green cloth	White	Green cloth, the pockets, front and bottom to the side seams, edged with ⅛in gold cord, 5 buttons.

Badges

On Buttons	On Collar of Tunic, Mess Jacket, and Frock Coat	On Helmet Plates	On the F.S. Helmet and Forage Cap	On the Service Dress	
				On the Collar in Bronze	On the Cap in Bronze
Scalloped edge. Within a wreath of shamrock, the Harp surmounted by a Crown; on the lower part of the wreath a scroll inscribed *Quis separabit*. For the mess dress, the letters 'C.R.' on a lined button with a raised edge.	On tunic and frock coat: The Elephant, in silver. On mess jacket collar: The Harp and Crown in gold embroidery, strings in silver.	In silver, on a dark green velvet ground, the Harp, with scroll, inscribed *Quis separabit*. A sprig of laurel issues from either end of the scroll. On the universal scroll, 'The Connaught Rangers'.	In silver, the Harp and Crown; below the Harp a scroll inscribed 'Connaught Rangers'.	As for forage cap.	As for forage cap.

Both battalions received new colours in 1911, those for the 1st Bn had been issued in 1906 but in the event not presented until King George V's tour of India after his Coronation, the actual ceremony taking place on 11 December at Delhi. Earlier those for the 2nd Bn had also been presented by King George on 11 July 1911 at Dublin.

At the outbreak of war in 1914 the 1st Bn was in India and the 2nd in Aldershot, but their war histories were to be almost identical as the battalions amalgamated at Le Touret, north east of Bethune in December 1914, and served together for the remainder of the war. In addition to these two regular battalions there were the two former Militia battalions, ie 3rd (Reserve) Bn and 4th (Extra Reserve) Bn and in addition two Service Battalions, the 5th and 6th.

In 1916 Pte (later Corporal) Thomas Hughes from Carrickmacross, Co. Monaghan, was awarded the Victoria Cross:

'For most conspicuous bravery and determination. He was wounded in an attack, but returned at once to the firing line after having his wounds dressed. Later, seeing a hostile machine gun, he dashed out in front of his company, shot the gunner, and single-handed captured the gun. Though again wounded, he brought back three or four prisoners.'

London Gazette, 26 October 1916.

Soldiers of the 5th Bn Connaught Rangers guard two Bulgarian prisoners captured near Calkali, 28 November 1915.

[1] *Grattan's Adventures with the Connaught Rangers*. First published 1847 and reprinted early in the 20th century.

[2] *The Connaught Rangers* by Lt-Col H. F. N. Jourdain and Edmund Fraser. London. R.U.S.I., 3 Vols, 1924, 1926, 1928.

[3] Illustrated in colour in Jourdain, Vol.1, and in black and white, Plate 417, *Military Drawings and Paintings in the Royal Collection* by A. E. Haswell Miller and N. P. Dawnay. Phaidon Press 1966.

[4] The uniforms of the 88th Foot, as well as those of the 18th and 89th Regts, as worn during the Crimean Campaign, is set out in detail in *Crimean Uniforms* by M. Barthorp. Historical Research Unit, pub. 1974. Further photos and drawings, Barthorp/Turner. *Military Illustrated* No.6, April/May 1987.

[5] See J.S.A.H.R. Vol.XIV, p.237/8.

[6] See J.S.A.H.R. Vol.XXX, p.1 and XXX p.47.

[7] Correspondence published, an explanatory article by John Gilinsky in *Bulletin of Military Historical Society* November 1982, p.67.

[8] The Regimental Journal – *The Ranger*. September 1925.

[9] Copy of letter in author's possession.

[10] *An Autobiography* by Elizabeth Butler. Constable & Co. London 1922.

[11] *The Times*. 25 November 1920.

An Army Order of 1924 published the battle-honours; these of course were collective for all the combatant battalions. The 1st and 2nd sailed for the Middle East in December 1915 but were replaced by the 6th Bn in France where the latter remained until April 1918. The Regimental battle-honours are as follows:

'Mons', 'Retreat from Mons', 'Marne 1914', 'Aisne 1914', 'Messines 1914, '17', 'Armentières 1914', 'Ypres 1914, '15, '17', 'Festubert 1914', 'Givenchy 1914', 'Neuve Chapelle', 'St Julien', 'Aubers', 'Loos', 'Somme 1916, '18', 'Guillemont', 'Ginchy', 'Cambrai 1917, '18', 'St Quentin', 'Bapaume 1918', 'Hindenburg Line', 'Selle', 'France and Flanders 1914-18', 'Kosturino', 'Struma', 'Macedonia 1915-17', 'Sulva', 'Sari Bair', 'Scimitar Hill', 'Gallipoli 1915', 'Gaza', 'Megiddo', 'Sharon', 'Palestine 1917-18', 'Tigris 1916', 'Kut al Amara 1817', 'Baghdad', 'Mesopotamia 1916-18'.

At the conclusion of hostilities, both the 1st and 2nd Bns were reconsituted at Dover. The 1st Bn went to India in October 1919 and the 2nd to Upper Silesia in May 1921. In June 1920, mutiny broke out amongst the 1st Bn at Jullundur and Solan following reports from Ireland of Black and Tan atrocities. Two of the mutineers died at Solan whilst attacking the armoury and 69 men were later court-matialled: 14 were sentenced to death, but only the ring-leader at Solan, Pte J. Daly, was executed.[11] The battalion was then sent to Rawalpindi and at the next General's inspection declared to be a first-rate battalion again.

Both battalions had returned to the United Kingdom by June 1922 for the final laying-up of colours at Windsor, followed by disbandment on 31 July 1922.

THE REGULAR REGIMENTS ■ INFANTRY

The Prince of Wales's Leinster Regiment (Royal Canadians)

100th and 109th Regiments of Foot

This regiment had its origins in India and Canada, and from 1881, Ireland, when the former 100th and 109th Regts of Foot were joined as 1st and 2nd Bns The Prince of Wales's Leinster Regt, respectively.

Between 1761 and 1818 there were as many as five regiments which carried the number 100 for varying periods of time, all comparatively short, but only two of these corps were Irish. One, during its fourteen years of service had a fine record. It was raised in Ireland in February 1805, all officers and men were Irish and it was transferred to the British Establishment from 25 March 1805, its title The 100th County of Dublin Regt. On 19 March 1805 it left Ireland for the Isle of Wight, proceeded from there to Haslar Barracks (Gosport) in June, and thence to Canada in August. Between November 1805 when it arrived at Quebec, until

Uniforms at formation of the 100th (Prince of Wales's Royal Canadians) Regiment. From left to right: sergeant, private, lieutenant, corporal in fatigue dress and three privates. (Illustrated London News 24 July 1858.)

Alexander R. Dunn, VC, Major 29 June 1858, Lt-Colonel commanding 25 June 1861. In the uniform of the 100th Regiment of Foot. (His regiment formerly 11th Hussars.)

May 1812 its Headquarters moved many times, Montreal, Fort George, Three Rivers and back to Quebec. During May 1812 the title was changed to The 100th or HRH The Prince Regent's County of Dublin Regt. During the war with the United States it fought many engagements, served as marines and distinguished itself at the capture of Fort Niagara and was subsequently granted permission to carry the battle-honour 'Niagara' on its colours, from May 1815. After Waterloo when the 95th Rifles was taken out of the Line, the regiment was renumbered 99th, and so remained until the final disbandment on return to England in July 1818. The uniform of the corps was red coat with deep yellow facings, silver lace for officers and white with red and blue lines and square-headed loops for soldiers, white breeches.

Major H.G. Parkyn's book, 'Shoulder-belt Plates and Buttons', provides illustrations of both officers' and soldiers' shoulder-belt plates, the former of silver, oblong rounded corners with the Prince of Wales's coronet, plume and motto, all within a garter inscribed County of Dublin Regt. The Soldiers' plate of brass, again oblong with rounded corners and the design stamped '100' below a crown. The Prince of Wales's coronet motto above the numerals 100 also appear on the other ranks' pewter button.[1]

The next forty years there was no regiment numbered 100. During the Crimean War an offer was made by Canada to the British Government, to send troops for service in the Crimea, but this was thought unnecessary at the time.

When, during the Indian Mutiny a futher offer to raise a regiment was made, it was accepted. Permission was given therefore in March 1858 to raise an infantry regiment to be designated The 100th (or Prince of Wales's Royal Canadian) Regt, and by the end of May, 1,200 men had been recruited. The new regiment was quartered in the citadel of Quebec. The Assistant Quartermaster-General in Canada, Baron George de Rottenburg, CB, was chosen as the first Lieuenant-Colonel Commanding in May, and he was assisted by Major R. A. Dunn, VC.

It will be recalled that as a lieutenant in the 11th Hussars, Alexander Roberts Dunn was awarded the VC 'For having, in the Light Cavalry Charge of 25 October 1854, saved the life of Sgt Bentley, 11th Hussars, by cutting down two or three Russian lancers, who were attacking him from the rear, and afterwards cutting down a Russian hussar, who was attacking Pte Levett, 11th Hussars.' The records tell us that Lt Dunn was the only officer to win the decoration in the Valley of Death, but won it twice over. He was decorated by Queen Victoria on 26 June 1857. A man of fine physique, he was six feet two inches in height, he sold out after the war, and being a wealthy man retired to his estates in Canada. In 1858 he was gazetted Major in the 100th Foot, eventually succeeded to command by purchase, 29 June 1861, and was then the youngest Lieutenant-Colonel in the army. He exchanged to the 33rd Foot in December 1864, and died commanding that regiment during the Abyssinian War the same year. After his death, at an auction sale at Sotheby's, his Victoria Cross, Crimean medal with clasps and Turkish medal, together with a portrait by Chevalier Desanges were sold for £155! (Today a five-figure sum would be expected for the group of medals alone.)

Left. Shako plate c1869-78
F. Y. CARMAN FSA (Sco
Right. Glengarry badge post 1881
MRS L. RYAI

By the time the regiment arrived at Liverpool in July 1858 – in three detachments, almost 500 men on each transport, the Mutiny was over. The men had to be clothed in what was available in Canada at the time and on arrival were wearing Kilmarnock forage caps, without diced borders, coatees of 1837 with short tails – 'too short to sit upon', with blue facings and epaulettes. Sent down to Shorncliffe in August the regiment was thoroughly equipped and was later inspected by HRH The Duke of Cambridge who was 'agreeably surprised at its magnificent appearance'.

On 10 January 1859 HRH The Prince of Wales attended Shorncliffe Camp to present the first set of colours to the regiment. This was the first public ceremony performed by the future king. A contemporary record states that:

> 'The youthful Prince performed his part in a most able manner, the whole tenor of his bearing being cool, manly, and dignified, such as would have done credit to one over whose head forty summers had passed', and that 'it made a great impression upon every officer and man in the regiment.'

The battle-honour 'Niagara', awarded to the old 100th (Prince Regent's County of Dublin) Regt, was emblazoned on this first Regimental Colour. In addition to the press reports where the Prince's presentation address to the regiment was recorded in full, there were several pictures made of the event.[2] One interesting painting shows 'types' of the regiment grouped together after the parade. The commanding officer and adjutant are mounted and seen giving instructions to a dismounted officer in frock-coat, the two officers with the colours are 'at ease' and chatting to the Quartermaster who wears a cocked hat. On the right of the group is a bearded pioneer conversing with a private soldier in parade order, on the left five members of the band in white coats. The Sgt-Drummer has a four-bar chevron on his right sleeve, the sash is of fairly plain pattern, probably the Ordnance issue belt. R. Ebsworth saw

the regiment at Shorncliffe during 1859 and made the following note about the band, to accompany his two sketches. His note covers the period 1859-73.

'Bandsmen – these wore white cloth tunics; the cuffs, shoulder-straps, and collars were piped round with red cloth; the seams of the sleeves back and front were piped likewise as well as the back seams of the coat. Gold lace Good Conduct badges, and badges of rank on blue facing cloth, on red cloth. The round forage-caps were worn, of the same cloth as the sergeants'; on the top of the cap was a button covered with red cloth; the caps were stiffly "blocked"; on the front of the caps, the regulation brass "number", but nicely polished and filed up. The Band Sergeant wore the same cap as an officer, i.e. dark blue cloth, with red band, and the "100" with Plume (blue "Ich Dien" scrolls) above, both embroidered in silver and gold lace respectively. He wore his gold lace stripes on blue facing cloth, and this in turn on scarlet cloth.'

By this time the regiment was to undertake the peace-time duties of any other infantry battalion, and so embarked on 7 May 1859, and followed the stay in Gibraltar by one in Malta until 1866 and thence to Canada, where it received a tremendous welcome, returning to England on 11 November 1868. Photographs of officers and men during the

Private's tunic from c1861-81. White facings and the numerals 109 in brass on shoulder straps.
F. Y. CARMAN FSA (Scot)

Pioneer section, 1st Battalion, India, 1880s. Note Pioneer Sergeant's elaborate embroidered Prince of Wales's crest on a red backing as cap badge. Also, detachable crossed axes 'trade' badges on red backing.
AMOT

Canadian winter of 1867 show the special clothing worn, an officer with a large fur cap and fur-lined greatcoat, and a Colour Sergeant who had mounted a regimental(?) badge on his fur cap, had wound a check pattern scarf around his neck and wears his normal scarlet tunic, padded trousers and fur-lined boots. He carries snow shoes on his back.

Returning home again in November 1868 the next six years were spent in England, before moving over to Dublin in 1874. The first tour of Indian duty commenced in 1877 and was to last for 17 years.

Whilst in India in 1881 the designation of the regiment became the 1st Bn The Prince of Wales's Leinster Regt (Royal Canadians), Depot – Birr. A fascinating note written by a sergeant about uniform worn during the 1882-3 period, describes the introduction of khaki and the feelings about it.

'In cold weather we wore red on all occasions and in hot weather – white. When khaki came in we were ordered to dye our white suits. Abolition of white for walking out was unpopular. The men took no pride in themselves when dressed in bazaar dyed abominations and gave up walking out, loafed about barracks and the canteen, and crime increased. During the cold weather of 1883-4 white was reintroduced.'

Whilst stationed at Fort William, Calcutta in 1887, new colours were presented by the Countess of Dufferin. The old colours were sent over to the Dominion of Canada and were deposited and displayed in the Library of Parliament, Ottawa.

Dominion Day, 1 July, was always regarded as a holiday with special celebrations. Large quantities of maple leaves were sent out annually from Canada to be worn in headdresses on that day.

The battalion returned home in December 1894.

109th (Bombay Infantry) Regiment

Between 1761 and 1795 there were two regiments numbered 109, neither were Irish. The first was raised in 1761 and disbanded two years later, the second was a Scottish regiment: The 109th (Aberdeenshire) Regt of Foot, raised in 1794 and disbanded in 1795.

The third regiment to eventually carry the number 109, the last incidentally in the numerical list of Line battalions and followed only by the Rifle Brigade, was originally the Honourable East India Company's 3rd Bombay European Infantry. The 3rd was made up of men from the 1st Bombay Fusiliers and 2nd Bombay Light Infantry, plus recruits from the Warley depot in Essex, between 1853-8. One of the early nicknames of the corps was 'The Brass Heads', referring to the fine physique of the men, seasoned by life in India.

The regiment was soon to receive its baptism of fire, joining the Central India Field Force under Sir Hugh Rose in 1857. During the Mutiny it was present at, and fought encounters with, mutineers at the following locations: Rathghur, Baroda, Saugur, Garracota, the Pass of Muddenpur, Betwa, Jhansi, Loharee, Koonch, Muttra, Garowtee, Calpee, and Gwalior. It is said that at Koonch the temperature ranged from 115 to 130 degrees.

The *London Gazette*, 21 October 1859, announced the award of the Victoria Cross to Pte Frederick Whirlpool:

> 'For gallantly volunteering, on 3 April 1858, in the attack on Jhansi, to return and carry away several killed and wounded, which he did twice under a very heavy fire from the wall; also for devoted bravery at the assault of Loharee, on the 2 May 1858, in rushing to the rescue of Lt Doune on the regiment, who was dangerously wounded. In this service Pte Whirlpool received seventeen desperate wounds, one of which nearly severed his head from his body. The

Pipes and drums – 2nd Bn The Leinster Regiment, c1912, Cork.
S. J. KRETSCHMER

gallant example shown by this man is considered to have greatly contributed to the success of the day.'

The battle-honour 'Central India' was awarded for the regiment's service during the Mutiny period.

Early in the 1860s the regiment was brought up to strength, the reinforcements gained from an unusual source, men from the force known as the British German Legion, recruited in Germany and sent to England in 1855 for eventual service in the Crimea. Very few got to the Crimea, the remainder, ie two regiments of Light Dragoons, three of Rifles (Jägers) and six battalions of Light Infantry, were spread around various garrison towns in southern England between 1855 and 1858. Most eventually left for South Africa, England glad to be rid of them as there was much friction between British garrison troops and those returning from the Crimea. It was also soon evident that they would not make good colonists in South Africa, and in September 1858, 1,400 were sent to India. With the Mutiny suppressed, soldiers of the Legion were invited to volunteer for the East India Company's regiments, or return to South Africa. By 1862 nearly 500 men of the Jägers had been accepted for the new 109th Foot, including their own German officers, some of the latter were to do well in British service. It was to be expected therefore that this unusual reinforcement would attract some ribald nicknames, 'The German Mob' and the 'Jägers', two examples.

A later-day officer of the Leinster Regt, Major N. H. C. Dickinson, DSO, left some valuable notes concerning the early dress of the band, covering the period 1862-75:

> 'Bandsmen – these wore round, red cloth caps with a white cloth band round them; with a white button and white braid crossing on crown and over the sides to the band; regulation brass numeral "109" in front; badges of rank and Good Conduct badges, gold lace on red cloth. Band Sergeant same forage cap as an officer. The bass-drummer always wore a very fine leopard-skin lined with red on white facing cloth. The head and paws were well "set up" (made as life-like as possible) and so slung that when the skin was in use they hung close up on the drummer's shoulders behind.'

The regiment was sent abroad in 1864, to Aden, and was engaged in some action against an Arab enemy in which a German contingent

Staff-sergeants, 2nd Battalion, c1912, Cork
S. J. KRETSCHMER

Four soldiers of the 2nd Bn The Leinster Regiment, 24th Division, New Army, France, c1917.

played its part. A glance at the Army Lists of 1864-6 shows German names mingled with the British, Major Valintine, Major August Schmid and the Adjutant Oscar Schmid, Lt Luckhardt and a few others. August Schmid was a seasoned warrior who had served in the Schleswig-Holstein army during the first Danish War, took part in the campaigns of 1848-50 and received the Schleswig-Holstein decoration. After some regimental service in the 109th he served in the Adjutant-General's Department, but returned to take over command of the 109th in July 1878 to August 1879 when he retired on pension, the only foreigner who commanded a Queen's Regt during Queen Victoria's reign. Whilst at Aden on 23 January 1866 colours were presented to the regiment by Mrs Raines, wife of the General Officer Commanding, Aden. That year the regiment moved back to India. For the next eleven years spent in India there was still a strong German contingent, although the German language was forbidden.

HRH Edward Prince of Wales visited India between 1875-6. 450 rank and file and the band entrained from their station at Bankipore in Bihar for Calcutta, on 17 December 1875, to provide a Guard of Honour when HRH arrived on the 24 December. The Prince later visited the regiment when the gift of a handsome panther was made by the Sergeant's Mess; a photo appeared in the *Illustrated London News*, 25 March 1876.

In December 1877 the regiment embarked for England and was stationed at Gosport, with further moves to Aldershot and Preston before being ordered to Ireland in 1883. By this time the composition of the regiment had become predominantly Irish, with only a sprinkling of

Soldiers of the regiment with captured enemy gun, Dead Horse Valley, Palestine.
IWM

Germans left, most seeking permission to return to Germany by 1882.

The uniform was the standard pattern for Line Infantry, blue helmet with usual star helmet-plate, the ground in centre of the plate being red, scarlet tunic with blue facings. The 1st Bn in India had a white helmet with the Plume of the Prince of Wales's badge, mounted on red cloth on the puggri at front.

Both battalions saw service in the South African War, the 1st from early days but the 2nd arriving from the West Indies in January 1902. The 1st Bn formed part of Sir Leslie Rundle's 8th Division, together with the 2nd Bn Grenadier Guards, 2nd Bn Scots Guards and 2nd Bn East Yorkshire Regt. The 8th Division was given the difficult task of holding the formidable enemy forces against attack on the right flank of Lord Roberts's Army. So well was this done that Sir Conan Doyle mentions General Rundle's operations in glowing terms:

> 'So well did he select his positions that every attempt of the enemy, and there were many, ended in failure. Badly supplied with food, he and his half-starved men, held bravely to their task, and no soldiers in all that great host deserve better of their country.'

The battle-honour 'South Africa 1900-2' was awarded to the regiment, although a total of 120 casualties were suffered, officers, NCOs and men. The 1st Bn came home, but the 2nd Bn stayed on in South Africa after the war, moving on to India in 1907.

A note from a tailor's book of 1907 tells us that the regimental forage cap 'was as for Royal Regiment, with silver Prince of Wales's plume with gold coronet and motto, gilt buttons etc.'

Whilst at Mauritius in 1906 new colours were presented by the Governor on 2 April.

First mention of pipers comes from the *Regimental Journal* in 1909:

'The pipers have no distinctive features of dress. They wear dark blue forage caps with scarlet welt and band. The scarlet tunics have white piped scarlet shoulder straps bearing the regimental title in white embroidery and white piped dark blue collar and cuffs. The two drones of the pipes are united by a cord ending in a tassel. There are eight pipers, one a sergeant.'

And again:

'On St Patrick's Day 1909 the 1st Bn attended service in the Roman Catholic Cathedral, Plymouth; six Irish pipers were on parade for the first time. At the Sergeants' St Patrick's Ball held at the Stonehouse Town Hall, the music was provided by the Battalion String Band, under the skilful baton of Sgt Reilly, while a novel feature was furnished by the introduction of the Irish pipers (their first appearance in public) who, during two of the intervals, marched up and down the room amidst loud applause, the success of his bantlings bringing a gleam of pleasure to the anxious and fostering eye of Lt Orpen-Palmer.'

At the Southern Command Bronze Medal Tournament held in Portsmouth on 23-24 March 1909,

'The pipers played up and down the course at intervals, and provided a very attractive feature, causing some surpise, for it is curious how few people in England realise that the pipes have been played in Ireland as well as Scotland from time immemorial.'

The Dress Regulations for 1911 for this regiment are the same as those provided for the Royal Irish Regt section, but mess dress, badges etc. are as follows:

Mess Dress

Jacket				Vest
Collar	Shoulder Straps	Cuffs	Piping	
Blue cloth	Blue cloth	Blue cloth	None	Blue cloth, roll collar, 4 buttons, for service at home. White washing, for service abroad

Badges

On Buttons	On Collar of Tunic, Mess Jacket and Frock Coat	On Helmet-Plate	On F.S. Helmet and on Forage Cap	On the Service Dress	
				On the Collar in Bronze	On the Cap in Bronze
A Circle, inscribed 'Prince of Wales's Leinster Regiment'; within the circle, the Prince of of Wales's Plume. For the mess dress the plume in silver – mounted, on a plain gilt button. For the cap, same as mess dress, but gilt, die-struck.	The Prince of Wales's Plume, in silver; the Coronet in gilt or gilding metal.	In silver, on a black velvet ground, the Prince of Wales's Plume over two maple leaves. The Coronet in gilt or gilding metal. On a scroll, beneath the leaves, 'Central India'. On the universal scroll, 'Prince of Wales's Leinster Regiment'.	In silver, the Prince of Wales's Plume, the Coronet in gilding metal. Below the Coronet a scroll, in gilt or gilding metal, inscribed 'The Leinster'.	As for forage cap.	As for forage cap.

During the First World War 1915-18 there were seven battalions of the Leinster Regt, the 1st and 2nd Regular Army, the 3rd Reserve and 4th and 5th Extra Reserve (these being the three former Militia Regts), and the 6th and 7th Service Bns.

The 2nd Bn returned home from India in 1911, was stationed at Cork, so on the outbreak of war came over to England and thence to France, landing at St Nazaire on 12 September 1914. The battalion remained in France and Flanders throughout the war years, most of the time spent with the 24th Division but later for a few months with the 16th Division: 1st February 1918 to April 1918; transferring again, remaining in the 29th Division until the Armistice.

The Colonel-in-Chief, HRH The Prince of Wales presenting decorations to officers and men, 2nd Battalion, Colchester 1919. Seen in the photograph congratulating No 10313, Fagan J. Piper 'D' Company, who is receiving his 1914 Star.
AMOT

Blue and green were the colours favoured by the Leinsters in peacetime, and so cloth (upright) diamond shaped patches of these colours arranged in the following manner, were sewn on to both sleeves, above a yellow square with three inch sides, the square denoting the senior regiment in the Brigade. The diamonds worn by:

'A' Company. Top half of diamond blue, bottom half green.
'C' Company. Top half of diamond green, bottom half blue.
'B' Company. Left side of diamond green, right side blue.
'D' Company. Left side of diamond blue, right side green.
'HQ' Company. Diamond divided sideways into two rectangles, top section blue, bottom section green.
When in the 16th Division the Divisional sign of a shamrock was worn, and later in the 29th the new Divisional sign, a red triangle, was painted on the steel helmet.

Three soldiers of the 2nd Bn were awarded the Victoria Cross. To Cpl John Cunningham from Co Tipperary, for conspicuous bravery on 12 April 1917 at Bois-En-Hache, France. Sadly he died from his wounds on 16 April.

To Pte Martin Moffat from Sligo, for conspicuous bravery on 14 October 1918 at Ledeghem, Belgium, and to Sgt John O'Neill, MM, on the same day near Moorseele, Belgium.

Earlier in the war Lt John Vincent Holland, 3rd Bn, who came from Co Kildare, was also awarded the Victoria Cross for most conspicous bravery at Guillemont, France, on 3 September 1916.

The 1st Bn was in Fyzabad, India, in 1914, and was able to sail from Bombay by October, arriving in the United Kingdom 16 November, and by Christmas had landed in France, part of the 27th Division. Remaining in France for one year it transferred to the Middle East theatre of war in December 1915, to Egypt in September 1917, and to the 10th Division, Palestine towards the end of 1918. Whilst in Egypt it wore the green patch with white maple leaf centre on the helmet from 5 October 1917.

The battle-honours awarded to the regiment for its services during the war are as follows:

'Armentières 1914', 'Ypres 1915-17-18', 'Somme 1916-18', 'Guillemont', 'Vimy 1917', 'Messines 1917', 'St Quentin', 'Macedonia 1915-17', 'Gallipoli 1915', 'Jerusalem'.

On the 4th July 1919 HRH Edward Prince of Wales became the Regiment's Colonel-in-Chief. He paid a visit to the 2nd Bn at Colchester where he presented war medals.

In view of the regiment's bond with Canada an Alliance was formed with two regiments of Canadian Militia: 10th Regt (Royal Grenadiers) from Toronto, Ontario, and the 100th Winnipeg Grenadiers, from Winnipeg, Manitoba.

The 1st Bn went back to India after the war in November 1919 and was in Malabar, Madras, 1921-2, leaving in April 1922 for the United Kingdom. The 2nd Bn was with the Army of Occupation and arrived at Oppeln in Upper Silesia on 5 June 1921. It is recorded that the battalion marched from the railway station led by the pipes and drums, pipers wearing their caubeens and kilts.

Both battalions made their last journey home for disbandment in 1922.

Bandsman Walters, 1st Battalion, 1920-1, India. Note, helmet flash, the maple leaf in red, outlined in white upon a green background. The bandsman's lyre and crown is also on green backing.
BRIAN FORDE

[1] See *Shoulder-belt Plates and Buttons*. Major H. G. Parkyn, OBE. Gale & Polden 1956, and also J.S.A.H.R. Vol.I, p.208.
[2] A full page in the *Illustrated London News* of 27 January 1859, also reproduced in Vol.I *Edward VIII. His Life and Times*. Amalgamated Press 1910.
[3] J.S.A.H.R. Vol.XX, p.54.
[4] See articles, J.A.H.R. Vols.LIV and LXII.

THE REGULAR REGIMENTS ■ INFANTRY

The Royal Munster Fusiliers

101st and 104th Regiments of Foot

Although the reputations of the 101st and 104th Regts, linked in 1881 to form the Royal Munster Fusiliers, were mainly Indian, both could trace predecessors from the 1760s. The history of the 101st can be broken down into three main periods:

1760-1817 during which there were four short-lived regiments numbered 101.

1756-1858/61: The century of service with the East India Company.

Finally from 1861 when control passed from the Company to the Crown, and as the 1st Bn Royal Munster Fusiliers (1881), through to 1922 when disbanded.

From the early regiments only two can claim an Irish connection, the third in succession dating 1794-5 was entitled The 101st (Irish) Regt of Foot, raised by Col William Fullarton in March 1794 but reduced in 1795. The National Army Museum has in its collection a beautiful miniature by Frederick Buck of an unnamed officer of this corps, in scarlet uniform with yellow facings, and the numerals 101 on an oval

Two pictures of Lieutenant David F. Millett Brown, VC, 1st Bengal European Fusiliers. Left, in khaki service dress 1858 and right, in full dress 1861.

1st Bengal European Fusiliers, officers and men, Lucknow, 1858. The officer in full dress standing in centre is 'Lucknow' Kavanagh. There are three officers in khaki service dress, one in 'mufti' and the remainder are NCOs and men. Note medal ribbons on soldier, extreme left.

shoulder-belt plate.[1] The next regiment was raised in 1806, The 101st (Duke of York's Irish) Regt, and saw service in the West Indies and Canada 1813-14. It was disbanded at Haslar, Gosport, in Hampshire on 17 January 1817.

None of the regiments which carried the number 104 were Irish, only two had titles. The earliest from 1761-3 was the 104th (King's Volunteers) Regt of Foot, the next from 1780-3 left no record. In 1794 the 104th (Royal Manchester Volunteers) Regt of Foot was raised and was sent to Ireland. Although this regiment only lasted a year it was presented with colours which were laid up in Manchester Town Hall. The last of these early corps was entitled simply 104th Regt of Foot in 1806, but did see much service in Canada and during the American War of Independence before disbandment in Canada in 1817.

The 101st Royal Bengal Fusiliers and The 104th Bengal Fusiliers

The story of the Bengal European Regiments begins in 1756 with the return of Lt-Col Robert Clive to India, and his successful attempt to suppress the degenerate but powerful Suraj-ud-Daula, who had captured Calcutta and was responsible for the atrocity of the 'Black Hole'. (Two of the 23 survivors of the Black Hole on the 20 June 1756 were Ensigns Walcot and Moran, two of the first officers of the

Sergeants, 101st Fusiliers, India c1865, including several Mutiny veterans still serving.

regiment.) Clive's army consisted of about 900 British: HM 39th Regt of Foot and various companies and detachments already in being and formed into a battalion. The Battle of Plassey was fought and won on 23 June 1757, the 39th Regt gained the motto *Primus in India* and the battle-honour 'Plassey', as did the new regiment The Bengal (European) Regt. In one of the early actions of the regiment at Kuttra in 1774, a Sgt Burrell greatly distinguished himself and was promoted to an Ensigncy in 1779 and subsequently became a Major-General, one of the most distinguished officers of the Company's army.

For the next 100 years this regiment, (for one short period with as many as six battalions), marched and fought throughout the length and breadth of India, was awarded battle-honours for its endeavours at Plassey and down through the years until the Mutiny.

In those early days no consideration was given to clothing suitable for the climate; the same, often unserviceable, apparel worn at home was also endured in India. Records of dress at the time of Plassey are scant and not until 1777 is there a note that officers' hats were 'plain', cocked with gold looping. In 1786 there were six scarlet clad battalions, each with different facings: 1st blue, 2nd black, 3rd yellow, 4th green, 5th buff and the 6th white, and in that year white hats were first allowed on the line of march, or black hats with white linen folded round them. Ten years later amalgamations were effected down to three battalions, the 1st with buff facings as the old 5th, 2nd white from the old 6th and the yellow facings of the 3rd Bn retained, the uniforms of that year given as short jackets with round black hats, officers to wear white linen waistcoats, pantaloons and gaiters.[2] In February 1821 the colour of pompadour was introduced into the regiment for facings but the next year a change was ordered. One can perhaps picture the Regimental Adjutant, sweating it out at some dreary station, and receiving the GOCC of 6 August 1822, with the important news that the facings were ordered to be changed from pompadour to light sky blue!!

In 1839 the regiment became Light Infantry. A rare shoulder-belt plate of this period carries the title Bengal European Light Infantry.

The Bengal Army List of 1840 shows both regiments under the titles 1st and 2nd Bengal European Regts, the 1st with the supplementary title Clark-Ka-Gora (Clark's Corps). This dates back to the beginning of the century when the regiment was named after its then colonel, and was known to natives by that name throughout the existence of the East India Company.

The 1st Regt was divided into two wings, the Left Wing with 28 officers and the Right with 16; as many as 18, however, detailed for duty elsewhere.

When one glances at the list of the officers of the Left Wing one finds that the Colonel, Philip LeFevre was on furlough in Europe since 3 January 1837 and the only Major was also on leave in Van Diemens Land. The commanding officer Lt-Col Abraham Roberts, CB, was the Brigadier in command of the 4th Infantry Brigade in Afghanistan, his Brigade consisting of his own regiment and the 35th and 37th Bengal Native Infantry. (In 1832 his son had been born into the regiment at Cawnpore and was to become one of the most famous commanders in British Army history, Field Marshal Lord Roberts, VC.) Abraham Roberts was eventually to reach full General's rank having been appointed to the Colonelcy of the 101st Regt in 1862.

By a General Order of 11 April 1846 the regiment was to be made

Officers' shoulder-belt plate, 1st Bengal European Fusiliers, c1846-55. All gilt except small crowned garter with title, the numeral and small scroll inscribed 'Fusiliers' below the number, all in silver. 9 battle-honour scrolls. Officers' waist-belt clasp. Lower right. Officers' racoon skin cap grenade from 1869. Above. Small forage cap badge. Extreme right. Other ranks grenade badge for racoon skin cap.

Fusiliers, for gallantry in the Sutlej campaign of 1845-6, and from this time on facings were to become dark blue.

One of the regimental officers in the East India Register of 1851 was William S. R. Hodson, Lieutenant in the regiment from 1 April 1849, but noted as in Civil Employment (ie Assistant Commissioner at Lahore and later Amritsar). In 1852 he was promoted Commandant of the Guides, but on the outbreak of the Mutiny was ordered to raise, and was appointed Commandant of, a Corps of Irregular Horse, this Corps later to become the famous regiment – Hodson's Horse.

On 29 July 1839 a 2nd Regt was ordered to be formed, volunteers from the 1st Regt providing a nucleus, its official title when raised on 8 October 1839 was 2nd Bengal European Regt, its facings initially white. The 1840 Bengal Army List gives 43 officers although 18 were employed elsewhere, three lieutenants for example as Commandant and second in command, etc in the Local Horse.

At the outbreak of the 2nd Sikh War it took part in the battles of Chillianwalla and Goojerat. The regiment was made a Fusilier regiment in consequence of its having captured a village which was the key of the Sikh position at the battle of Goojerat, 1849. The facings were subsequently changed to dark blue in 1851. A march right across India in 1850, prior to embarkation, took the regiment to Burma where it served through the 2nd Burmese War – 1851-3.

Left. Captain T. A. Hunter, a Mutiny veteran from the 2nd Bengal European Regiment.
S. J. KRETSCHMER

Lieutenant L. W. Iredell, Ensign 4 October 1860. Full dress 1860s, 104th Fusiliers.
S. J. KRETSCHMER

Both regiments fought many actions throughout the Mutiny. The 1st Regt was at the siege of Delhi, and it was here that it acquired the famous nickname 'Dirty Shirts', the men fighting in what would now be termed 'shirtsleeve order'. Since the scandal of the inadequate and unsuitable clothing for the troops in the Crimea a few years beforehand, there was a little more concern for the welfare of troops, and although India was still a long way from home – the following homily appeared in an 1857 edition of the *Illustrated London News*:

'Uniforms of Troops before Delhi.

'The farce of dressing up British soldiers in India in exactly the same uniforms as are comfortable and convenient in a European climate, has been played out in this Delhi campaign. Stocks discarded, coats entirely dispensed with or replaced by white jackets, shakos left in barracks and forage caps with white covers and turbans would round them, is the prevailing uniform. HM 75th Regt of Infantry are decked out in jacket and pantaloons of light material dyed and colour similar to the dress worn by the Gurkhas, who can scarcely be distinguished at a short distance. The (Bengal) Fusiliers wear light grey pantaloons and shirt sleeves. The Carabiniers wear cloth jackets and with a thermometer in tent at 120 and in the sun, 140. Hear this ye English public. Few can tell what it is to be not only under a broiling sun with a glare enough to blind you, but to be under the influence of a burning hot scorching wind, that has withered up everything. Let those who have glass hot houses raise the temperature to 140 if they can, and then say if leather stocks and tight clothes are the things for India. Surely the oriental garb might be modified and adapted for English wear as exemplified in the uniform of the Irregular Cavalry – one easy pattern of light and warm material, according to the time of year.'

No fewer than five Victoria Crosses were awarded to soldiers of the 1st Regt, and one to the 2nd. They were Sgt J. McGuire and Drummer M. Ryan for acts of bravery on 14 September 1857, Delhi. Lt T. A. Butler at Lucknow, 9 March 1858. Pte J. McGovern before Delhi, 23 June 1857 and Lt F. D. M. Brown at Narnoul, 16 November 1857. Lt T. Cadell of the 2nd Regt at Delhi, 12 June 1857.

In 1861 the three Bengal European Regts were transferred to the Crown, the 1st and 2nd becoming the 101st Royal Bengal Fusiliers and 104th Bengal Fusiliers respectively (The 3rd – The 107th, later 2nd Bn Royal Sussex Regt). The 101st were entitled to royal blue facings and the 104th dark blue, both entitled to wear a scarlet band around the forage cap for services in India. It is also interesting to note that an officer who was to command the 101st from 1875-80, Lt-Col H. G. Delafosse, CB, was one of the only four survivors of the Cawnpore massacre in July 1857.

Sir Hugh Rose presented colours to both regiments, to the 101st at Multan on 25 February 1862 and the following year to the 104th at Bareilly on 26 February. Earlier colours of the 101st Regt, those carried during the 1st Sikh War and later the Indian Mutiny, were laid up in Winchester Cathedral, alongside a memorial plaque.[3]

The National Army Museum had on exhibition two very unusual items connected with the 104th Bengal Fusiliers, namely a gold replica of the Victoria Cross which was presented to the wife of the commanding officer, Mrs Webber Harris, for 'her indomitable pluck' in the cholera epidemic of 1869. Accompanying this unique item was a miniature of Mrs Harris mounted in a special frame of jewels.

The 101st Regt returned to England in 1869, the first of the old Company's troops to come home and was followed by the 104th on 18

Top. Officers' shoulder-belt plate, 2nd Bengal European Fusiliers, 1850-58. Bottom. Grenade badge for racoon skin cap, other ranks.
F. Y. CARMAN FSA (Scot)

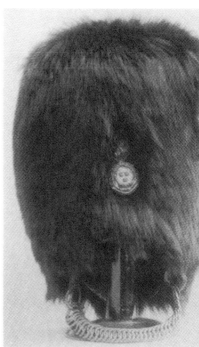

December 1871. For the first three years of home service the 104th was stationed at the Gosport Forts and in barracks at Portsmouth. One important photograph should be mentioned here, a group of the officers taken at High Street Barracks, Portsmouth, 1873. Several are in full dress and one is wearing the new sealskin cap. Others are in undress, most wearing the peaked forage cap with the red band, the numerals 104 with embroidered grenade badge above. One be-medalled officer in full dress, holding his cocked hat, is the Quartermaster Charles Wooden, VC. Wooden was awarded the VC for assisting Dr James Mouat in saving the life of his colonel, Lt-Col Morris of the 17th Lancers after the charge of the Light Brigade at Balaklava. Wooden, then a Sergeant-Major in the 17th, was a German with a ginger beard and was nicknamed 'Tish me – the Devil' from a broken English explanation he made one night when a sentry on the gate failed to recognise him. He was promoted to Quartermaster rank in the 5th Lancers on 21 March 1865 and transferred as Quartermaster to the 101st in November 1871.

In accordance with the Localisation of the Forces Scheme in 1873, the regiment was first connected with Munster, and the counties of Cork, Kerry, Limerick and Clare were assigned to it for a recruiting area, its depot at Tralee.

On 1 July 1881 the two regiments, previously linked, became joined as the 1st and 2nd Bns The Royal Munster Fusiliers. The 1st Bn was away during this period, having left the Isle of Wight in 1874 and after a two-year stay at Malta, proceeded to Nova Scotia followed by service in Bermuda and was in England again by 1884. At Western Heights Dover, on 22 September 1886, new colours were presented to the battalion by Lady Louisa Fielding, wife of the Lieutenant-General Commanding South East District.

A high compliment was paid to the corps in the 1890s. During a conversation on the various merits of the Line Battalions in England, Field Marshal Viscount Wolseley is reported to have remarked 'Well, I have an Irish battalion which can beat the whole lot you mention, and

that is the 1st Bn of the Munsters, now in Ireland.'

The 2nd Bn on the other hand was home in Ireland, at Birr in King's County in 1878, then to Belfast and the Curragh, going abroad again in 1882, firstly to Malta and then off to India. In 1887 it joined the Burma Field Force before return to India where it remained until called upon for active service in South Africa towards the end of the war. The 1st Bn however served throughout the whole of the South African campaign, arriving at Cape Town on 16 September 1899 and was in battle at Belmont on 23 November, and from then continually on the move and in action almost the whole of the next two years. Throughout the war the regiment suffered 5 officers and 63 NCOs and men killed, and four officers and 73 soldiers wounded. The Distinguished Conduct Medal was awarded to 19 NCOs and men.

After the war the 1st Bn embarked for India where the Queen's South Africa Medals were presented in January 1903.

The 2nd Bn came home to Ireland where King Edward presented new colours at Cork on 1 August 1903. The King's South Africa Medals were presented later that year on 5 December but prior to that a communication from the War Office addressed to the Field Marshal Commanding 3rd Army Corps in Ireland, dated 2 December, read as follows:

'I am directed by the Commander-in-Chief to acquaint you that HM The King has been graciously pleased to approve the Royal Munster Fusiliers being permitted to wear in their busbies a plume of green and white colour.'

The particulars were given later as:

'it will be 6½ inches in height and worn on the left side of the Fusilier cap.'

104th Fusiliers, Cambridge Barracks, High Street, Portsmouth, 1873. Several officers in full dress with newly introduced busbies, others in undress. Note grenade badge on cap with 104 below. Figure at top of steps with medals is Quartermaster C. Wooden, VC.
S. J. KRETSCHMER

Officer's busby.

Bandsman and Fusilier in marching order, c1890. The letters R M F in white thread seen on shoulder strap, grenade above. Painting by Harry Payne.

Drum-Major Treaves with drummer and bugler, 1st Bn Royal Munster Fusiliers, 1897, Fermoy. The Drum-Major's sash is of dark blue cloth with oak-leaf pattern scalloped edging. A four-hooped crown above a scarlet garter with Royal Munster Fusiliers round a circlet of blue with numerals 101 in centre. Eleven battle honours each side and one below surrounding a plain gold grenade. Pair of black drum-sticks. (Note, 22 regimental battle-honours pre South Africa, but one is split with date on separate scroll.)

The 2nd Bn took part in the Coronation Day procession in London, June 1911; photographs show the band looking resplendent in full dress. The Sergeant-Drummer's sash was of comparatively plain design compared with that of the 1st Bn, blue with gold edging and embroidery. Drummers' cords were of yellow with red and blue interwoven and terminating in large tassels of yellow, red, blue and white.

The 1911 Dress Regulations describes the Fusilier uniform as for the Royal Irish Fusiliers, the official description of the plume: height 6½in, white above, green below, and worn on the left side. Details for mess dress and badges are as follows: Jacket, shoulder straps, cuffs, blue cloth. Piping none. Vest, blue cloth, roll collar, three buttons.

On Buttons	On Collar of Tunic, Mess Jacket, and Frock Coat	Ornaments for Bear-skin or Racoon-skin Cap	On the F.S. Helmet and Forage Cap	On the Service Dress	
				On the Collar in Bronze	On the Cap in Bronze
Within the designation, 'Royal Munster Fusiliers', a grenade, with the Royal Tiger on the ball. For the mess dress, silver – mounted, on a plain gilt button. Same for cap, die-struck.	A grenade in gold embroidery, with the Royal Tiger, in silver, on the ball.	A grenade in gilt or gilding metal. Mounted on the ball a deep wreath of laurel intertwined with a scroll bearing the honours of the regiment. Within the wreath the Heraldic device for the Province of Munster, the Crowns in gilt or gilding metal, the shield in silver. On the bottom of the wreath, a scroll, in silver, inscribed 'Royal Munster'.	In gilt or gilding metal, a grenade. On the ball, in silver, the Tiger and scroll inscribed 'Royal Munster'.	As for forage cap, in pairs.	As for forage cap.

(Photographs of the 1st Battalion serving at Nowshera at that time show a white over green plume on the left side of the khaki tropical helmet.)

Family Group 1890s. Colonel F. D. M. Brown, VC, Indian Staff Corps, and his two sons, 2nd Lt F. R. Brown, 1st Bn Royal Munster Fusiliers and Lt C. R. Brown, Royal Engineers, c1894.

Lt-Col E. S. Evans and officers of 1st Bn at Fermoy, 1899, in service dress for South Africa.

Between 1909 and 1911 the 2nd Bn was at Tidworth, moving into the Aldershot Command in 1913. In May a Regimental reunion was held, veterans travelling from Ireland and elsewhere to be present and to be inspected by HM King George V. The oldest man on parade was Mr A. Armstrong, who joined the regiment in 1852 and wore an Indian Mutiny medal, whilst also present Mr M. Vaughan who joined in 1854, served 20 years in the regiment, retiring in 1874 with the rank of Sergeant.

Both battalions had formed alliances with Canadian Militia Regts, the

1st Battalion with the 101st Regiment, Edmonton Fusiliers of Edmonton, Alberta, and the 2nd Bn with the 104th Regt, Edmonton Fusiliers of New Westminster, British Colombia.

During the First World War there were eleven battalions of the Royal Munster Fusiliers, the 1st and 2nd Regular, 3rd Reserve and 4th and 5th Extra Reserve from the former three Militia Bns; four service Bns, 6th, 7th, 8th and 9th, also the 1st and 2nd Garrison Bns.

At the outbreak of war the 1st Bn was at Rangoon, leaving in December for England and joining the 86th Brigade of the 29th Division, taking part in the landing at Helles in April 1915. A regular

A military funeral at Tidworth, 1912. In foreground soldiers of 2nd Bn Royal Munster Fusiliers, marching with arms reversed, followed by the band of the 4th Royal Irish Dragoon Guards. The infantry band with white facings is probably 1st Bn Duke of Cornwall's Light Infantry, then comes the coffin on an Army Service Corps wagon, escorted by more Munster Fusiliers, so the deceased was probably from that regiment.

A lieutenant on leave during the war years 1914-18. Note cloth shamrock shaped backing on the cap grenade badge.
B. TURNER

soldier of the battalion, Corporal, later Staff-Sgt William Cosgrove of Co Carlow, was awarded the Victoria Cross:

'For most conspicuous bravery in the leading of his section with great dash during our attack from the beach to the east of Cape Helles, on the Turkish positions, on the 26 April 1915. Corporal Cosgrove on this occasion pulled down the posts of the enemy's high wire entanglements single-handed, notwithstanding a terrific fire from both front and flanks, thereby greatly contributing to the successful clearing of the heights.'

The battalion was so badly cut up that for a short while in April/May there was a temporary amalgamation with the 1st Bn Royal Dublin Fusiliers survivors, the complete battalion called the 'Dubsters' until resuming original identities in late May. The Munsters sailed to Egypt and later on to France to be brought up to strength from their 9th Bn. Before the landing at Helles a green cloth shamrock was worn on the caps below the regimental grenade badge, and a green cloth triangle worn on each shoulder.

From Malplaquet Barracks, Aldershot, in August 1914, the 2nd Bn landed in France as part of the 1st (Guards) Brigade of the 1st Division, later transferring to the 3rd Brigade. The regiment served on in France and Flanders throughout the whole war. A dark green shamrock made of cloth was worn below the cap badge and in the 1st Bn, the various sections wore a small ½in coloured square sewn on the back of the collar, ie yellow for Lewis Gunner, red for Bomber, black for Rifle Grenadier and green for Rifle man. One observer in June 1916 noted a soldier on 'trench-leave' with a cloth rectangular patch on arm below shoulder, circa 2in long by 1in deep, a mauve square alongside a yellow one.

The 2nd Bn suffered heavily in their battles from Festubert, Rue du Bois and later at Passchendaele and St Quentin. The *London Gazette* of 5 August 1916 announced the award of the Victoria Cross to Lt A. H.

Batten-Pooll (3rd Bn) 'For most conspicous bravery whilst in command of a raiding party on the Western Front.' Towards the end of the war C. S. M. Martin Doyle, MM, of the 1st Bn was also awarded the Victoria Cross for conspicuous bravery near Riencourt on 2 September 1918.

Both battalions were abroad in 1922, the 1st in Silesia and the 2nd at Alexandria and both returned to the United Kingdom for disbandment. So a fine old regiment dating back to 1756 was finally stood down, a regiment described as one whose bones came from Bengal but the blood and sinews – Irish.

Opposite page:
Top. Albert shako 1844-55. 1st Madras (European) Fusiliers, later 102nd Foot. A star plate with 12 points, on the main rays left and right 4 battle-honours each, 'Arcot on scroll above and 3 below central device, which has the motto 'Spectamur Agendo' on strap, with Royal Tiger in centre, crown above.

Below. Presentation of medals and clasps to the Bombay Fusiliers, later 103rd Fusiliers, by Mrs Mignan, wife of Lt-Colonel Robert Mignan, commanding, at Poonah, 10 February 1852.
In right foreground two mounted officers of the Bombay Horse Artillery. Print by J. Harris after H. Martens, from a sketch by Captain Thomas Studdert, Bombay Engineers. Pub. 1 Jan 1853.
CHRISTIE'S

Below. Laying up the Colours of the regiment at the Tower of London 15 February 1923, Colour Parties found by the Irish Guards
IWM

---

¹ Illustrated in colour. JSAHR. Vol. XXIV, p.51.
² See W. Y. Carman. *Indian Army Uniforms (Artillery Engineers and Infantry)*. Morgan-Grampian. London 1969.
³ Photograph and notes JSAHR Vol. LIII, p.55/58.

THE REGULAR REGIMENTS ■ INFANTRY

The Royal Dublin Fusiliers

102nd (Royal Madras) Fusiliers
103rd Royal Bombay Fusiliers

The history of this old and famous corps is bound up with India. The two regiments which were in 1881 to become 1st and 2nd Bns Royal Dublin Fusiliers, can trace their individual histories back as far as 1661 (the 2nd Bn) and 1741 – the 1st. Both were built up as East India Company Bns, and later as numbered regiments of the British Line, one to serve its early years as Madras Europeans and the other – Bombay Europeans.

The Madras Europeans were formed about 1748 and claim to have taken part in 72 battles against native forces and the French by 1758. It was increased to a three battalion regiment in 1760 and a 4th Bn was added in 1774. During that sixteen year period it fought further actions, was engaged at Goojerat in 1780 and received the 'Royal Tiger' badge in 1791. By 1841 there were more engagements fought and won, and the motto *Spectamur Agendo* (We are judged by our deeds) was granted. Up to about 1830 the regiment was known as the Honourable East India Company's European Regt, when 'Madras' was added to the title and in

Soldiers of the 1st Madras (European) Regiment standing outside the gateway of the Chota Imambara, Lucknow, summer 1858. The damage to the building was caused by the British bombardment of Lucknow in March 1858. After the capture of Lucknow the British used the Chota Imambara as a magazine.

1839 it became the 1st Madras European Regt, the designation Fusiliers was added in 1843, and finally – simply 1st Madras Fusiliers. In 1860-1 it became a numbered regiment of the Crown: The 102nd (Royal Madras) Fusiliers.

Four previous regiments had carried the number 102 during the period 1760 to 1818, but only one of them was Irish, a corps that existed for just one year between 1793-94, and was known as The 102nd (Irish) Regt of Foot.

Study of General Orders issued towards the end of the 18th century provide a fair picture of the dress: G.O. dated 20 October 1775: 1st Regiment of Europeans to be turned up or faced with buff. (2nd Regiment, black.) 11 May 1785, a new uniform was ordered for the Madras Army, in which blue facings and gold embroidery were directed for the European Infantry. A G.O. of 4 February 1786, however, ordered the facings to be by Brigades: 1 Brigade, blue; 2, green; 3 and 4, yellow; 5, buff; and 6, yellow. There were then, apparently, two European Regiments of two battalions each. These four battalions were assigned one to each of the first four Brigades. On the issue of clothing on 3 December 1786 accordingly: the

    1st   European Bn had blue facings and gold looping
    2nd   European Bn had green facings and yellow looping
    3rd/4th European Bns had yellow facings and white looping

The officers had the number of the regiment (? battalion) on their epaulettes. It was also on the buttons of officers and NCOs.

Commander-in-Chief's Order of 29 February 1788 (apparently General Neill considered this to apply to all battalions of the European Corps):

'Officers' Regimentals A short jacket, yellow lapels, silver embroidery, 9 buttonholes, three and three at equal distances (sic); on cuffs and collars three each. One epaulette on right shoulder. *Hat* Round, white, turned up close on left side; black feather. *Stock* Black leather with linen false collar ¼in deep. *Waistcoat* White linen, cut short, as at present worn. *Pantaloons* White linen, to be made long enough to overlap the hind part of shoe, and to cover the place of the buckle, and to be fitted to the ankle by 7 buttons from the swell of the calf of the leg (lower part of) to the quarter of the foot, to

Colour Party, 102nd (Royal Madras) Fusiliers, Cananore, Madras, c1863.
J. V. WEBB

Senior NCOs, 102nd Fusiliers, Cananore, Madras, c1863.
J. V. WEBB

which the pantaloon is to be kept close by a strap coming from the inner side, under the shoe, and fixing to the lower button. *Sword-Belts* For officers of the battalion companies, black leather, worn across the body, with an oval plate engraved with the company's crest and motto and the number of the battalion. *Officers of the Flank Companies* Distinguished by the King's Arms and (? on) the accoutrements. Scarlet shoulder straps instead of epaulettes. The hats of flank companies to be ornamented as commandants of battalions may direct, but both companies must be uniform. *Officers* To have jackets without embroidery for common duties, pattern as now ordered for full regimentals. Shoes and buckles not to be considered part of officers' dress on duty, but off duty breeches, with stockings and buckles may be worn if preferred. Waistcoats and pantaloons of nankeen recommended for field service. Half boots, uniformly made, for officers in the field.'

From then on there is a record of facing changes until 1843: Buff 1775-6; Blue 1776-8; French grey 1778-1830; White 1830-43; Blue from 1843. An officer's scarlet dress jacket at the National Army Museum has a blue collar and cuffs, the collar with double loops of gold lace and with large embroidered grenades upon it, the grenades on blue cloth backings. The buttons are in pairs, there are ornate shoulder wings of gilt rings and gold bullion mounted on red cloth. The white shoulder-belt has a plate with a crown and the Royal Tiger and motto *Spectamur Agendo* below, whilst separately, and above the plate, a metal grenade.[1]

There are also reliable pictorial sources for the 1840s. An oil painting shows an officer in review order, he stands on steps whilst his charger is being brought round by a syce.[2] Then there is the Ackermann print from the 'Costumes of the Indian Army 1844-49' series, No 26, published 14 April 1847. There are two states of this print, one shows a fusilier with white pompon, the other red. A valuable piece of evidence is provided by a watercolour painted by a Capt T. J. Ryves, *c*1846, which shows a corporal of the regiment on a route march, his uniform: shako with white cover, red jacket with blue cuffs piped white, and his shoulder-belt plate

'Plassey', tiger mascot, Madras, c1869
J. V. WEBB

Pioneers, 102nd Fusiliers, Cananore, Madras, c1863
J. V. WEBB

carries the crown with a tiger below. He is shown walking through a stream, he has turned up his light blue trousers, which have broad red stripes, and carries his shoes. The blue collar of the jacket is turned down showing white lining and his leather stock has been removed and is carried on the end of his firearm.[3]

Yet another contemporary painting, signed and dated July 1856, and believed to show Lt George J. Harcourt of the Madras Fusiliers in summer dress, agrees in detail with the previous paintings of officers, although the white trousers are now worn. This officer has the medal for the 2nd Burmese War 1852-3, a campaign in which the regiment took part, and then remained in Burma till 1857.[4]

Returning to India just ten days after the outbreak of mutiny at Delhi and Meerut, it was engaged at Benares and Allahabad in May and June 1857 and in September in the desperate fighting for the relief of the Residency at Lucknow. It was here that the regiment earned its famous nickname 'Neill's Blue Caps' alluding to the warning given by the rebel leader Nana Sahib to his men to 'Kill all the men in blue caps and dirty shirts', a tribute to the Madras and Bengal Fusiliers whose fighting reputations were renowned and feared throughout India. Neill, the gallant Colonel of the Fusiliers, fell at Lucknow, not only leaving his name to his regiment but was also an historian responsible for recording the complex early history of the corps.[5]

Throughout the Mutiny period four members of the regiment were awarded the Victoria Cross, three of them Irish soldiers who, sadly, died from their wounds. They were Sgt Patrick Mahoney, 21 September 1857. Pte John Ryan, 26 September 1857. Pte Thomas Duffy, *London Gazette*, 18 June 1858. Pte J. Smith, 16 November 1857.

The Band, 102nd Fusiliers, Cananore, Madras, c1863.
J. V. WEBB

The battle-honours earned by the regiment up to the Mutiny are as follows: 'Arcot', 'Plassey', 'Wyndewash', 'Condore', 'Sholinghur', 'Amboyna', 'Ternate', 'Banda', 'Pondicherry', 'Mahidpoor', 'Ava', 'Pegu', 'Lucknow'.

In the reorganisation of 1860-1, the 1st Madras Fusiliers was designated the 102nd (Royal Madras Fusiliers), henceforth no longer a company regiment.

Amongst a fine group of photographs believed to have been taken at Cannanore, Madras, about 1863, is one of a Bengal tiger, the story of this beast is interesting and is related in the *Illustrated London News* of 30 April 1870.

'The Royal Madras Fusiliers, of which the first detachment arrived at Dover on 23rd ult, (an 1870 date) have brought home with them from Lucknow a fine young Bengal tiger, presented to them by its captors, two officers of the 5th (Royal Irish) Lancers, Capts Thackwell and Chaffy. Those gentlemen, while shooting in the Terai last hot season, encountered a tigress with two cubs, and killed the mother, but not before Capt Thackwell's arm had been severely torn and bitten, so that it was afterwards found necessary to amputate the limb; and this operation, we regret to say, caused his death from exhaustion in a few days. One of the cubs did not long survive its arrival at Lucknow; the other was given to the Madras Fusiliers for a regimental pet, which is the more appropriate since the figure of a tiger has for many years formed the emblem of their regiment. 'Plassey', as this young animal is named by his masters, is hardly yet full grown; and though possessing a great strength and a large appetite, has shown no signs of a ferocious disposition. He delights in playing with any men or animals that will go near him. He had a free passage from India to Suez on board the *Jumna*, and from Alexandria to England on board the *Himalaya*, granted him by the kindness of Capt Rickard and Capt Piers. Two leopards were his fellow passengers on the voyage, and their gambols afforded much amusement.'

Left. Grenade, officers's racoon skin cap, pre 1881.
Right. Grenade, other ranks racoon skin cap, pre 1881.

(It is understood that later, at Aldershot, the animal managed to break his chain. By this time he was becoming too difficult to handle and consequently was handed over to a travelling menagerie.)

Whilst still at Cannanore new colours were presented by Mrs de Saumarez, on 26 January 1866.

The regiment came to England for the first time in March 1870 but was only to enjoy six years in this country, stationed at Dover, Parkhurst and Portland, before embarking once more for overseas in April 1876. After two years at Gibraltar the next move was to Ceylon, where it remained until returning home in 1886, moving to Ireland in 1887. So it was abroad when re-designated the 1st Bn Royal Dubin Fusiliers, depot – Naas.

103rd Royal Bombay Fusiliers

This regiment claims a record going back to 1661 when a European corps was formed to garrison Bombay. Although it is known that such a regiment did serve at this early date, details up to about 1748 are sketchy, but it is said that the clothing was scarlet with sea-green facings. What is certain is that it must have been made up with a very 'hard-boiled' collection of desperadoes, deserters from armies from other countries, mercenaries and in general a 'foreign legion'. Conditions of service were of course harsh, little wonder that a nickname, which was to stick, was 'The Old Toughs'. A detachment of this Bombay corps was later to join Clive at the Battle of Plassey, then at Buxar in 1764, before return to its own Presidency.

Colour-Sergeant, 103rd Royal Bombay Fusiliers. Photograph probably taken at Aldershot, 1873.
S. J. KRETSCHMER

The facings were changed to white in 1759 when the lace was silver; in 1840 lace changed to gold and by 1844 the facings were altered to blue.

In the early months of 1834 new colours were presented to the regiment at Poona by the Governor of Bombay, the Earl of Clare. A full report of the ceremony is to be found in the *United Services Journal* of June 1834, the description of the parade is interesting:

'The troops were formed in three sides of a square, in double lines, the Horse Artillery and 4th Light Dragoons forming the rear or second line. The Bombay European Regiment was formed in line thirty paces in front of the centre face of the square. The approach of the Right Honourable The Governor, was announced by a salute of nineteen guns from the Horse Artillery and a general salute from the whole brigade. The Bombay European Regiment was then wheeled back and formed into close columns of wings facing inwards and the space between the two centre companies became the arena for the ceremony. A large drum was placed in the centre, on which Lt-Col Wood, commanding the regiment, placed the colours, and with the two ensigns and the two colour sergeants, awaited the approach of Lord Clare.'

As usual on these occasions, a long speech was given, in essence a history of the regiment and, although no doubt tedious for those forced to listen, the penultimate paragraph of the speech does sum up the story of the regiment during the early years of the 19th century.

'I pass onward from the general pacification of this country in 1818, to the year 1821, when the Bombay European Regt was again employed in active service, under the orders of Sir Lionel Smith, against the Arabs in the Persian Gulf, when you entered their capital in triumph, and by your prowess added to your former honours. In whatever quarter you have been engaged, I find the gallantry and good conduct of the Bombay Regt equally remarkable. Wherever you have been present, I find you have invariably increased your reputation. Bear witness Seringapatam, bear witness the field of Kirkee, bear witness Bennibon-Ali on your colours, and let me assure you that I feel confident, in the event of another war, that you will add to all these honours.'

As the Royal Tiger superscribed 'Plassey' and 'Buxar' belonged to the 102nd, so the Elephant superscribed 'Carnatic' and 'Mysore' are carried on the appointments, badges, etc of the 103rd, this being the numerical title of the regiment on becoming a Queen's regiment in 1860-1, its full title – The 103rd Royal Bombay Fusiliers.

103rd Royal Bombay Fusiliers. An interesting note given on the dress of the period 1862-9 tells how a General Officer offended by ordering the removal of a cherished dress privilege:

'Sergeants and rank and file wore a red cloth band round their regulation round forage-caps. But when the 103rd went to Morar (East Indies) in 1869, Maj-Gen Tombs (there commanding, or when inspecting the regiment) made the regiment take off this red band. (He is reported to have said that he "thought it was a regiment of Grenadier Guards that had suddenly come out from England when they arrived in the station"). The taking away of this red band from off the caps of the rank and file and sergeants, caused intense indignation in the regiment, as it was an old privilege enjoyed by the regiment while they were in the H.E.I. Company's service many years before they became the 103rd. (By the Royal Warrant of Amalgamation, 1861, it was clearly laid down that all the European Corps on their transfer to the Queen's service were to retain all their former distinctions.) A white worsted grenade was worn as a collar badge. Bandsmen – all Good Conduct badges and badges of rank of gold lace on facing cloth. The forage-caps were of fine blue cloth, with a gilt grenade and the number 103 below it, the same as the rank and file.'[6]

The *Illustrated London News* of 1 August 1863, carried a paragraph relating to recruiting for the regiment and informs that a temporary depot had been established at Colchester:

'The recently formed 103rd Regt being short of its full complement, HRH the Field-Marshal Commanding-in-Chief, has directed that volunteers should be supplied by other regiments now in England; and upwards of 200 men have accordingly arrived at the depot, at the camp at Colchester. A draft will leave shortly to join the service companies of the regiment in India.'

Seven years later, in the 209th year of its service, the regiment was brought over to England for the first time, arriving in February 1871. Later that same year, on 19 August, HRH Prince Arthur, later Duke of Connaught, presented new colours at Parkhurst, Isle of Wight.

A domestic story, which paints a vivid picture of life in the ranks of a regiment of very tough, hard drinking men, just returned from years of soldiering in the East, to the green and pleasant pastures of the Isle of Wight, is to be found in a book written by one of them. Robert Blatchford joined the army because he had little other choice, he was

Left. A lieutenant of Royal Dublin Fusiliers in undress. Believed 1st Battalion, Ireland, c1890. Photograph by Andrews, Wexford.

Colour-Sergeant, believed 1st Battalion, c1897-8.

MAJOR A. F. FLATOW TD

Bugler John Dunne in campaign kit, being chaired through the streets of Portsmouth by his father and a blue-jacket. c February 1900.

hungry and without work or money; he is described as solemn, awkward, sullen and sickly, all the wrong qualifications for the soldier's life. Strangely enough as a recruit he was treated well by his barrack-room comrades, 'a blend of respect and half-patronising protection'. So Blatchford grew in confidence, his physique improved and he acquired a broader outlook. His upbringing had taught him to regard all soldiers as foul mouthed, drunken and woman-chasing desperadoes, and although his view remained much the same, he decided to work for promotion, which he gained, and to try and alter things. He had succeeded with promotion; trying to alter the system was a different proposition and even when in later life he became a politician, a pioneer socialist, his books and papers had little effect on War Office thinking, although he did once send in a letter of suggestion to improve musketry instruction, – twenty years later this reform was introduced during the Boer War. But as a sergeant in the 103rd Regt he gained some overnight popularity. Celebrations to mark the return of the regiment to England, coupled with such a complete change of environment, were such that every day a whole company paraded for pack-drill. The Provost-Sergeant, one of the most unpopular NCOs who had smashed dozens of other NCOs with his evidence, 'Drunk Sir' and of whom it was said, nightly bagged his

trousers praying for more crime, fell sick. The nightly picquet duty, to patrol the town of Newport, a short distance from the barracks, was given to Sgt Blatchford, his orders were to arrest 'every man with as much as half a drop of drink in his eye'. Blatchford spent the evening searching every rat-hole in Newport, until he found the Provost Sergeant's four cronies, four men who shared their master's ill fame – and arrested every one of them.

When he left the army he had acquired enough background knowledge to write several books about military life in the 1870s, as well as others on politics. Not an altogether pleasant character, but even on his 90th birthday he told an interviewer, 'To myself I'm always just Sgt Blatchford.'[7]

The regiment enjoyed a good long spell of home service between 1871 and January 1884, when it embarked for Gibraltar. It was stationed at Bradford when, under the reorganisation of 1881 it joined its linked regiment (102nd Fusiliers), to be designated The 2nd Bn Royal Dublin Fusiliers.

In 1899 the 1st Bn Royal Dublin Fusiliers was at the Curragh whilst the 2nd Bn had been in South Africa for several years, so it was amongst the first troops in action on the outbreak of war. The celebrated storming of Talana Hill in the face of a murderous fire, produced one of the initial victories of the campaign, although the Dublins suffered heavy casualties, killed and wounded. One of the wounded was later visited in hospital by a padre who was indiscreet enough to ask him if he had seen

Left. Major H. R. Beddoes. Review order, c1907. Major Beddoes's first regiment was the 7th QO Hussars, 1886, but transferred to the Royal Dublin Fusiliers in 1889. He has medals for service in Burma, 1888-9 and special employment in Central Africa 1898-9, (medal with clasp). He later commanded the 4th Militia Battalion.

Band-Sergeant, 2nd Battalion, c1910.
S. J. KRETSCHMER

Fusilier in walking-out dress, 2nd Battalion, c1910.
S. J. KRETSCHMER

Corporal in service dress, 2nd Battalion, c1910. Probably photographed whilst on leave in Cork.

any dead Boers on the hill, to which the fusilier replied, 'Begorrah, sorr, but the hill was alive wid 'em!'

On 15 December the Battle of Colenso was fought and it was here that the Irish Brigade was engaged in some of the most severe fighting of the war. One of the heroes of the battle was a lad of fourteen, Bugler Dunne of the 2nd Bn. He accompanied the column in the advance on Colenso and whilst in the firing line during the attempt to force the passage of the Tugela, was severely wounded. He was invalided home and recovered his health on the voyage. On arrival at Portsmouth he was chaired through the streets, the subject of a fine painting by Frank Dadd, RI.[8] Again at Tugela Heights on 23 February the brigade had to cross rugged country with a final uphill slope. A charge resulted in heavy casualties, so that all that could be done then was to sit it out under the inadequate shelter of rocks for almost four days, driving off repeated attempts by the Boers to dislodge them, until relieved by Sir Redvers Buller's army; then joining in the final charge which captured 500 Boers. The total losses of the Royal Dublin Fusiliers during the war amounted to 8 officers and 209 NCOs and men killed in action, or died of wounds, disease, etc, and 24 officers and 408 NCOs and men wounded.

During the war years in South Africa, the khaki service helmet was decorated with a pale blue cloth square, 2in square, and stood on its point, fixed to the left side. At the welcome home ceremony to Dublin in 1903 it was noted that the square had been replaced by a plume on the left side of the khaki helmet, the plume powder- blue at top out of a green base. A further most unusual feature was also recorded, that the ventilation button at the top of the helmet was coloured green by the 2nd Bn. The 1st Bn had similar, but coloured blue. A tailor's book for the period 1902-4 notes that the officers' peaked forage cap was of a special light blue shade, which was called Dublin Fusiliers Blue, and made the point of stating that it is 'not as 18th Hussars', presumably referring to the busby bag colour of that regiment. The special light blue was also for the staff caps of the rank and file when introduced about 1905 and so remained.

Presentation of colours took place on 5 April 1907, to the 1st Bn by the Duke of Connaught at Alexandria. The Duke, who had honoured the regiment by becoming its Colonel-in-Chief in November 1903, also presented new colours to the 2nd Bn at Aldershot on 1 July 1911.

The Dress Regulations for 1911 are the same as those already given for the Royal Inniskilling Fusiliers, but with the following exceptions:

Cap   Short bearskin or black racoon skin.

Plume   Cut feather, with gilt two-flame socket. Blue above, green below, 6½in, on the left side.

Forage Cap   Of a special shade of blue cloth.

Mess Dress

Jacket				Vest
Collar	Shoulder Straps	Cuffs	Piping	
Blue cloth	Blue cloth	Blue cloth	White cloth	Blue cloth, roll collar, buttons

Badges

On Buttons	On Collar of Tunic, Mess Jacket, and Frock Coat	Ornaments for Bear-skin or Racoon-skin Cap	On the F.S. Helmet and Forage Cap	On the Service Dress	
				On the Collar in Bronze	On the Cap in Bronze
Within the designation, 'Royal Dublin Fusiliers', a grenade, on the ball of the grenade, the Crown. For the mess dress, the elephant and the tiger on separate buttons in silver, mounted. For the cap, the same design, die-struck.	A grenade in gold embroidery; mounted in silver, on the ball, the Royal Tiger; below the Tiger, the Elephant.	A grenade in gilt or gilding metal; mounted on the ball, in silver, the badge of the City of Dublin; below the shield – to the right, the Royal Tiger, on a silver tablet inscribed 'Plassey', to the left, the Elephant, on a silver tablet inscribed 'Mysore'. Below the tablets a silver scroll inscribed 'Spectamur agendo'. In silver on either side of the shield, a rich mounting of shamrock leaves.	In gilt or gilding metal, a grenade. On the ball, in silver, the Tiger; below the Tiger, the Elephant. Below the grenade, a scroll in silver inscribed 'Royal Dublin Fusiliers'.	As for forage cap, in pairs.	As for forage cap.

The 1st Bn was serving in Madras in August 1914 but sailed for the United Kingdom, arriving home on 21 December. It sailed again for the Middle East as part of the 29th Division, and later in 1917, to France, and joined 16th Division, eventually amalgamating with the 2nd Bn. After April 1915 the 1st wore a square of dark blue cloth on the left sleeve, point upwards. After April 1916 the square was worn on the back of the jacket with another painted on the side of the steel helmet.

The 2nd Bn served in France and Flanders throughout the entire war years having landed at Boulogne in August 1914, served with the 31st

Cardinal Bourne addresses the Dublin Fusilier Brigade from a horse waggon at Ervillers, 27 October 1917.
IWM

Division but at the end of the war was part of the 50th Division. This battalion wore a square cloth patch similar to 1st Bn but of bright green.

In addition to the two regular battalions, the regiment provided a 3rd Reserve Bn and 4th and 5th Extra Reserve from the old 3rd and 4th and 5th Militia Bns, these regiments remaining in England and Ireland and the 5th to Scotland from 1917. There was also an 11th (Reserve) Bn formed at Dublin in 1916, later absorbed by the 3rd Bn. The 6th, 7th, 8th, 9th and 10th were all service battalions, all serving in France and Flanders, whilst the 6th landed at Sulva Bay in October 1915, remaining in the Middle Eastern theatre with transfer to Italy and later France.

Three sergeants serving with the 2nd Bn were awarded the VC during the war, Sgt R. Downie, (*London Gazette*, 25 November 1916), Sgt J. Ockendon, (*London Gazette*, 8 November 1917), and Sgt H. A. Curtis, (*London Gazette*, 6 January 1919). The last mentioned Sgt Curtis, was recommended for his award for conspicuous bravery in the Le Cateau area in October 1918. The citation for Sgt Ockendon is as follows:

'Award of the Victoria Cross to 10605 Sgt James Ockendon, VC, MM, 1st Bn, Royal Dublin Fusiliers.

Return of a hero. Sergeant James Ockendon on return to his home in Warwick Street, Southsea, after presentation of Victoria Cross, winter 1917.
J. R. A. OCKENDEN

In the attack on the morning of 4 October 1917, east of Langemaarke (Flanders), Sgt James Ockendon was acting Company Sgt-Maj. Noticing the right platoon held up by an enemy machine gun which was causing many casualties he, with absolute disregard for his personal safety, immediately rushed the gun, killed two of the gunners and followed and killed the third who was making his escape across No Man's Land. He then led a party to the attack on T. Gord Tervestern Farm. This party was heavily fired on as it advanced. Sgt Ockendon dashed ahead and called upon the garrison to surrender. They, however, continued to fire and with great boldness Sgt Ockendon then opened fire himself. Having killed four of the enemy he forced the remaining sixteen to surrender. During the remainder of the day Sgt Ockendon displayed the greatest gallantry, making many dangerous patrols and bringing back most valuable information as to the disposition and intentions of the enemy.'

Sgt Robert Downie was a Glaswegian whose home was in a short street of humble dwellings, Carleston Street. It has been related that from this little street alone, over 200 men went into the army, 16 were killed and many others wounded; Sgt Downie was able to add a VC hero to its war record.

During the war years a bewildering assortment of Regimental, Brigade and Divisional signs were worn by soldiers of various regiments for varying periods. An observer made some notes of dress he had personally seen in London between 1915 and 1918, and those of the Royal Dublin Fusiliers are added here.

January 1915. An officer with a blue band round khaki cap (much as Northumberland Yeomanry) with gold embroidered grenade in front.

16 May 1916. An officer with bright blue grenade on each arm below shoulder.

May 1916. Grass green below shoulder-strap on each arm.

10 August 1917. An officer in khaki drill with bright blue Austrian

Sergeant James Ockendon, VC.
J. R. A. OCKENDEN

pattern forage cap with grenade in front, no badge at side of cap.

6 July 1918. Ealing Common Railway Station, a lieutenant with a powder blue cap, scarlet band and welt round crown, gold embroidered grenade with silver device on ball and gold scroll under plain black peak. Plain dark blue serge jacket with two gilt stars on shoulder-straps, upright collar, no collar badges, brown Sam Browne belt.

The 1st Bn spent the final years of 1921 and 1922 at Bordon Camp but the 2nd was in India and left Multan for home, and disbandment in 1922.

---

[1] Photographs of an exhibition, National Army Museum, *Illustrated London News*, 10 July 1954.
[2] Painting owned by the Parker Gallery, *c*1979.
[3] Watercolour reproduced in black and white in *Indian Army Uniforms – Infantry*, W. Y. Carman. Morgan-Grampian, London 1969.
[4] J.S.A.H.R. Vol XIII, p194.
[5] *Historical Record of the H.E.I.C.'s 1st Madras European Regiment, 1645-1842*, Brig-Gen J. G. S. Neill. Smith Elder & Co, 1842.
[6] From the notes by Major N. Dickenson. Fmly 100th Foot, J.S.A.H.R. Vol XX, p54.
[7] *Portrait of an Englishman, the story of Sergeant Blatchford*. Gollancz.
[8] Reproduced in black and white. *With the Flag to Pretoria*, Vol I, p96.

PART THREE ■ YEOMANRY, SPECIAL RESERVE & TERRITORIAL FORCE REGIMENTS

The Imperial Yeomanry

During the early months of the war in South Africa – 1899, the pressing need was for trained mounted infantry soldiers who could both ride and shoot. Ireland was at some disadvantage here, being without existing Yeomanry regiments from whence to draw volunteer recruits as in England, Scotland and in Wales.

Irish civilians and former soldiers did come forward, and there were no initial difficulties in forming the Companies, three, four or five of which made up an Imperial Yeomanry Battalion. By the early months of 1900 Ireland was able to provide a very strong battalion made up of the 45th Company (Dublin), 46th and 54th Companies (Belfast), and 47th (Lord Donoughmore's) Company. Under the command of Lt-Col B. E. Spragg, DSO, formerly King's Own Yorkshire Light Infantry – who had seen much service in India and Burma, this battalion was soon in action but suffered heavily – 40 killed and 11 wounded, the Commanding Officer and the remainder of his battalion captured.

Another battalion was raised at about the same time, the 17th, with two Companies of Irish and two of English – the 50th Hampshire, 60th North Irish, 61st South Irish and 65th Leicestershire Companies, this battalion commanded by a former 5th Lancer officer and Master of the Kildare Hounds, Col R. St L. Moore.

The uniform of the Imperial Yeomanry was sensible, comfortable and hard-wearing, generally suited for campaigning, but styles often differing between battalions, or even Companies. The entire dress was of khaki, a slouch hat with turned-up brim on left side, often with an identifying badge or number upon it. The 65th (Leics) Coy for example, had a scarlet rosette with a blue centre and the brass numerals 65 in the centre, whilst the 60th Coy had the Red Hand of Ulster on a white shield (but initially worn on khaki helmet instead of the slouch hat). The tunic was generally the khaki serge pattern with stand collar, with or without pockets, and leg-wear Bedford cord breeches with khaki puttees. Bandoliers were mostly the single cartridge holder pattern. A bayonet was carried from a leather waistbelt, haversack, water-bottle etc. worn about the person, and often the blanket-roll over the shoulder. The horse was well loaded with rifle in bucket, feed bags, spare boots for rider and much else.

These Imperial Yeomanry Battalions gave noble service throughout the war and many veterans later chose to serve in the two newly raised regiments of Irish Imperial Yeomanry. It was Lt-Col R. St L. Moore who had commanded the 17th Bn who became a founder-member and second-in-command of the new South of Ireland Regiment.

The stories of these two new regiments are to be found elsewhere in this volume.

YEOMANRY, SPECIAL RESERVE & TERRITORIAL FORCE REGIMENTS

The North Irish Horse

Soldier in the first pattern khaki uniform, rectangular patch on slouch hat, of green and white. White piping on cuffs and pants, leather covered buttons.
AMOT

The same spirit which prompted Irishmen to volunteer for service with the Irish Imperial Yeomanry Companies during the South Africa War, also prevailed in 1902 when recruits were sought for two new Irish Yeomanry regiments, the North and South Imperial Yeomanries. It is said that the Commander-in-Chief, Ireland, HRH The Duke of Connaught commanded the Earl of Shaftesbury to raise a new regiment for the North, which he did, and became its first commanding officer. Lord Shaftesbury had formerly served as Captain 10th Hussars, and transferred as Captain to the Dorset Imperial Yeomanry, and was to command the North of Ireland Regt until 1912, becoming its Honorary Colonel in June 1913. The first Adjutant was Capt R. G. O. Bramston Newman, 7th Dragoon Guards, and there were several senior NCOs from regular cavalry regiments appointed as Permanent Staff Instructors.

The regiment was raised on 7 January 1902, two squadrons were formed that year and two more in 1903, Regimental HQ and one squadron at Skegoniel Avenue, Belfast; the remainder at Enniskillen, Londonderry and Dundalk.

The regiment was sufficiently advanced to attend annual camp for the first time at Dundalk in July 1903. On the day before leaving for camp, however, a dismounted guard of honour was found on 27 July for King Edward VII at Balmoral Showgrounds.

From 1903 until 1914 camps were held annually at the following locations: 1904 and 1913, Finner, Ballyshannon, Co Donegal; 1905 The Curragh, Co Kildare; 1906 Ballykinlar, Co Down; 1907, 1908 and 1911, Newbridge, Co Kildare; 1909 and 1912, Murlough, Dundrum, Co Down; 1910 Magilligan, Co Londonderry and 1914 Donard Lodge, Newcastle, Co Down.

The first all-purposes uniform of khaki was embellished with an Austrian knot of white piping on cuffs and white welt down the seams of Bedford cord pantaloons, khaki puttees and ankle boots. There were leather buttons on tunic, later replaced by brass, collar badges – the Irish Harp with crown above and regimental title on triple scroll below. A larger pattern badge as cap badge, also worn as sergeant's arm badge above the chevrons. The slouch hat carried a cloth patch on the upturned brim, upright patch, rectangular – two tapes, green and white, green on the left, the undress forage cap of green and white piping.

By 1905 a full dress for ceremonial, and walking-out for other ranks, had been designed and was in wear, a stylish uniform of Lancer pattern but with a unique headdress. The uniform is well described in a letter from a former NCO with pre-1914 service[1]:

'I served in the regiment in the pre-war days and know every detail of the uniform and badges. The tunic was green (lighter or brighter) in colour than riflemen, and was of the Lancer pattern with plastron front, but same colour as the body. White piping on the seams behind and on the seams of the sleeves, the plastron front was not piped. Girdle white, silver for officers, with two green stripes running through, the collar with white gorget patches and the cuffs white and pointed, with an edging of narrow white braid framed into a small ring at point of cuff, two buttons on outer seam of cuff. Burnished shoulder chains mounted on white cloth. Overalls – dark blue with a two inch broad white stripe down the outer seams. Boots – Wellington with swan neck spurs. Pouch or shoulder-belt (officers) silver lace (shamrock design running through lace) silver ornaments and a black patent leather pouch on which was set a silver badge, as cap-badge, but slightly larger. Silver lace sword-slings, backed with pale leather and suspended from a web belt worn underneath the tunic. In mounted full dress Bedford cord pantaloons with a half inch white cloth welt down the seams, brown field boots and jack spurs were worn. Blue pantaloons were not worn. Officers and men wore exactly the same pattern dress, the only difference being in quality of material. Full headdress – a blue felt bowler – crowned hat with a stiff flat brim, cloth on the bottom side, and patent leather (black) on the upper side. A black patent leather band around the bottom of hat and down to the brim, 1½in wide. Black patent chin strap. Plume – green drooping feathers, officers similar to 5th R. I. Lancers and a silver badge set on a white corded ribbon rosette with a ½in green border on outer edge. Diameter of rosette overall, 4in.'

The officer's dress tunic had a 'turn-back' half plastron of white which could be used for levee dress. This uniform was worn at a levee held in Dublin Castle, a photograph of the occasion was published in the *Tatler* of 8 February 1905 and depicts a dazzling full dress occasion, HRH George, Prince of Wales, in the uniform of the Queen's Own Cameron Highlanders, and amongst the military officers in levee dress is Lord Cole, Major in the North of Ireland Yeomanry since July 1903.

In 1908 there was a change of status and title brought about by the creation of the Territorial Force. The legislation did not apply in Ireland

Annual camp on the Curragh, 1905. Senior NCOs. Seated on chairs, third figure from left is PSSM Turner, 'C' Squadron. Captain B. Newman, 7th Dragoon Guards, Adjutant. Lord Shaftesbury, Commanding Officer. RSM Pittaway, PSSM Blakely, 'A' Squadron, PSSM Embry, 'B' Squadron. The sergeant, sixth from left in back row is from the Northamptonshire Yeomanry.
LT-CMDR K. B. HOOK RD

Full dress cap badges. Left up to 1908, right from 1908. All silver with bright centre, raised harp, bright edge to matted circle.

Full dress head-dress, felt bowler. Regimental badge on a white ribbon rosette, with narrow green border.
AMOT

so the two regiments were converted to Special Reserve and re-named The North and South Irish Horse. They were to be found recorded after the regular regiments of cavalry in the Army List, but taking priority in the order of precedence over the Yeomanry regiments of the Territorial Force. During the year 1908 Lord Abercorn, Honorary Colonel since 7 December 1903, was re-appointed with effect from 7 July 1908, and Capt Bramston Newman terminated his period as Adjutant on November 1909 and joined the regiment, with rank of junior Captain.

New Regulations for regimental dress were issued in 1909 to cover both service dress, full dress and mess dress:

Coat Green serge Patrol, with waist seam, White Lancer Front, white cuffs and shoulder pads. Slits at sides. White gorget on the collar 2¾ a 1½ and silver metal collar badges. White piping up the back and down hind arm. Chains stitched on the shoulder pads. Lapels edged No 4 silver and top of cuff edged No 4 forming eye above the point. 7 buttons up each front and 2 above cuffs.

Overalls Green serge, double white stripes.

Mess Jacket Green cloth. White roll collar, green shoulder straps. Metal collar badges silver.

Mess Vest White marcella.

Hat Plume	)	27/6	**Forage Cap**	)	23/6	**Service Cap**	)	20/-
Plated Badge	)		**Plated Badge**	)	Palt	**Bronze Badge**	)	Pt/-
								1.4.09

Service Dress Drab Jacket, Bedford cord Breeches. Slouched Hat, Puttees. Brown ankle boots and spurs.   (Hawkes)

Silver Belt in Full Dress, Sam Browne Belt – undress.   30.3.09.

Note: The words describing coat (white Lancer front) are misleading. The tunic was exactly as before with false Lancer plastron outlined by the buttons. White Lancer plastron for officers' levee dress or ball dress. (Gauntlets worn with levee dress, white wrist gloves for ball dress.)

It is interesting to note that NCOs had their own pattern of mess dress, following closely that of the officers. The regiment had formed a very fine band by 1914, about 30 strong. All bandsmen wore white aiguillettes from left shoulder, looped across left breast and fixed to the tunic by a special detachable white shoulder knot affixed to the shoulder chains. The Trumpet-Major had the crossed trumpets above four inverted chevrons on right cuff with the NCOs arm badge placed below the trumpets but on the tip of the uppermost chevron, the Band-Sergeant and Corporal had theirs in the normal position above the chevrons on the right, upper arm.

The Hon Colonel, the Duke of Abercorn died in January 1913, and the regiment was represented by a party in full dress at the funeral, the cortege led by four pipers lent by another regiment.[2] The Earl of Shaftesbury, formerly commanding officer, succeeded to the Honorary Colonelcy.

The outbreak of war in August 1914 found the regiment fully prepared and able to send 'C' Squadron, commanded by Major Lord Cole to Dublin, sailing from there, and to be joined in France by 'A' Squadron, and a squadron of South Irish Horse, by 22 August; thus the first non-regular regiments to go to France. A day later they were in the thick of one of the initial actions, a half squadron of North Irish Horse found itself fighting alongside the 2nd Bn Royal Inniskilling Fusiliers; became separated in the darkness and was not able to rejoin the regiment until the 28 August. After this sudden plunge by the Irish horsemen 'in at the deep end', they were mainly employed as divisional cavalry up to 1916.

The regiment had expanded to six squadrons by this time, 'A' to 'F', 'F' Squadron was absorbed by 'B' Squadron in May 1916, and by this date all squadrons were in France. 'A', 'D' and 'E' Squadrons then formed the 1st North Irish Horse, remaining as such until the end of the war, but were converted to cyclists in 1918. 'B' and 'C' Squadrons, with a squadron of 6th Dragoons became the 2nd North Irish Horse until August 1917, when converted to infantry; 304 soldiers of the 'B' and 'C' (North Irish Horse) Squadrons being absorbed by 9th Bn Royal Irish Fusiliers (North Irish Horse).

An officer of the regiment, Capt R. A. West, was awarded the DSO and MC, and in 1918 – the Victoria Cross for outstanding bravery during the closing stages of the war – although, sadly, killed in action. The official citation tells part of the story but an officer of the 2nd Bn Suffolk Regt whose Company was in the same sector, supplied the author with a very detailed account, and the fact that this brave officer was buried at Mory Abbey.[3] Citation:

Private in walking-out dress, c1904.

'West, Captain (Acting Lt-Col) Richard Annesley, DSO, MC, (Cavalry Special Reserve) and Tank Corps. For most conspicuous bravery, leadership and self sacrifice. During an attack, the infantry having lost their bearings in the dense fog, this officer at once collected and reorganised any men he could find and led them to their objective in face of heavy machine-gun fire. Throughout the whole action he displayed the most utter disregard of danger, and the capture of the objective was in a great part due to his initiative and gallantry.

On a subsequent occasion it was intended that a battalion of light Tanks under the command of this officer should exploit the initial infantry and heavy Tank attack. He therefore went forward in order to keep in touch with the progress of the battle, and arrived at the front line when the enemy were in process of delivering a local counter-attack. The infantry battalion had suffered heavy officer casualties, and its flanks were exposed. Realising that there was a danger of the battalion giving way, he at once rode out in front of them under extremely heavy machine-gun and rifle fire and rallied the men.

*Sergeant D. C. Campbell, c1910. Mess-kit
for NCOs but rarely seen. As officers',
except for white shoulder cords and collar
badges having scrolls, the badge for officers'
mess dress – a silver harp and crown only.*
AMOT

*Officer in dismounted review order, c1910.
Head-dress with feathers seen on plinth.*
AMOT

In spite of the fact that the enemy were close upon him he took charge of the situation, and detailed non-commissioned officers to replace officer casualties. He then rode up and down in front of them in face of certain death, encouraging the men and calling to them, "Stick out, men; show them fight; and for God's sake put up a good fight." He fell riddled by machine-gun bullets.

The magnificent bravery of this very gallant officer at the critical moment inspired the infantry to redoubled efforts, and the hostile attack was defeated.'

London Gazette, 30 October, 1918

During the years 1914-18, 27 officers and 123 men were killed. There were 60 decorations awarded to the regiment and the battle-honours for the entire regiment are as follows:–

'Retreat from Mons', 'Marne 1914', 'Aisne 1914', 'Somme '16, '18', 'Albert 1916', 'Messines 1917',, 'Ypres 1917', 'Pilckem', 'St Quentin', 'Bapaume 1918', 'Hindenburg Line', 'Epehy', 'St Quentin Canal', 'Cambrai 1918', 'Selle', 'Sambre', and 'France and Flanders 1914-18'.

Although a complete page in every edition of the post-war Army Lists

was given over to the Cavalry, Militia (the South Irish Horse and King Edward's Horse had both been disbanded), the North Irish Horse still appeared, although having been disembodied. The title, battle-honours, Headquarters all continued to appear but the list of Regimental officers gradually decreased until, by the edition of 1938 only two names were recorded, those of the Honorary Colonel and Honorary Chaplain.

One cannot resist making mention of a highly entertaining advertising booklet published in the early 1930s, compiled by a former officer of the Royal Marines.[4] Gifted with considerable artistic talent and coupled with a nice sense of humour, he devoted an entire page of his *Illustrated Army List* to the North Irish Horse, accompanied by five delightful sketches showing the Honorary Colonel in mounted review order and also the Honorary Chaplain, together with the following verse:

> Have ye ivver heard the story of that famous Oirish Regiment,
> The loikes of it was never seen from Larne to Donegal,
> And they look so foine in green and white, though faith oi'll give ye just a hint
> There's not a Captain in it nor a Corporal at all.
>
> There's a Colonel and, begorra, there's an honorary Chaplain, too,
> That's there to tache the bhoys to be a credit to the corps,
> And if they had some shquadrons, sure 'tis foine they'd look and iligint
> With their green plumes all a-wavin' and the Colonel to the fore.
>
> They never sound reveille, faith, they haven't any thrumpeterr,
> And there's divil a liftinint or a sargint in the force,
> But when the bugle blows for the bhoys to go to war,
> They'll be ridin' off to glory on the North Oirish Horse.

The last stanza was to prove prophetic. In 1939 the regiment was reconstituted as a light armoured regiment of the Supplementary Reserve and part of the Royal Armoured Corps. In 1940 it was training in Ireland with Valentine tanks, moving over to England for further training in 1941 and by January 1943 proceeding overseas to Egypt, equipped with Churchill tanks, as part of the 25th Tank Brigade. In April 1944, commanded by Lt-Col The Lord O'Neill, and equipped with

The Band, Donnard Lodge, Newcastle, Co Donegal, 1914. Including The Earl of Shaftesbury, Hon Col and Captain E. M. Dorman, 4th Dragoon Guards, Adjutant, on right and left of Bandmaster respectively. Captain Bramston-Newman (former adjutant and now a captain in the regiment) next to Dorman.

Lieutenant S. B. Combe, 1914. Killed in action 1 October 1914. In the photograph he wears khaki service dress. Note the stiff white collar and black tie, also narrow shoulder chains, black peak to cap and bronze badges.

Sherman tanks, it moved to Italy. Three regiments of the Canadian Army comprising the Canadian 1 Brigade, Princess Patricia's Canadian Light Infantry, the Seaforth Highlanders of Canada and the Loyal Edmonton Regt were supported by tanks of the North Irish Horse, and together fought one of the most bitter battles of the Italian campaign, smashing the Adolf Hitler Line, 23 May 1944. Although the line was broken and the breakthrough exploited, the cost was heavy, the 1st Canadian Division lost 1,000 men killed, wounded and missing, whilst 70 officers and men of the North Irish Horse were killed or wounded. The regiment also lost 25 tanks. A permanent link was thus established with Canada as the North Irish Horse soldiers who participated were entitled to wear a small maple leaf on their Italian campaign ribbons, and soldiers who did not participate would enjoy the Regimental honour of wearing a small metal maple leaf below the title on shoulder, a proud distinction which is still seen with service dress to this day. The fighting record in the Second World War is proved by the battle-honours:

'Hunt's Gap', 'Sedjenane I', 'Tamera', 'Mergueb Chaouach', 'Djebel Rmel', 'Long Stop Hill, 1943', 'Tunis', 'North Africa, 1943', 'Liri Valley', 'Hitler Line', 'Advance to Florence', 'Monte Farneto', 'Monte Cavallo', 'Casa Fortis', 'Casa Bettini', 'Lamone Crossing', 'Valli di Comacchio', 'Senio', 'Italy, 1944-5'.

The regiment has seen many changes since demobilisation in June 1946, firstly reconstituted in September 1947 as an Armoured Car Regt (Yeomanry) of the Territorial Army. Major changes in 1967 saw two squadrons retained, 'D' Squadron (North Irish Horse) Belfast to the

The Minister of Defence inspecting a North Irish Horse armoured vehicle in Belfast, 1960. Note, the metal arm badge now worn on sergeant's chevrons, the maple-leaf emblem below the shoulder title and the 107 (Ulster) Independent Infantry Brigade badge, a green shamrock on a black ground.
AMOT

Royal Yeomanry Regt, with affiliations to 5 RIDG and the QRIH , and 'B' Squadron (Londonderry) becoming 69 (North Irish Horse) Signal Squadron (V). A NIH element of the North Irish Band still remains and is fully up to strength.

In 1960 HRH Princess Alexandra of Kent, the Regiment's Honorary Colonel, presented a Guidon carrying the battle-honours of both wars. On this occasion officers wore a revised version of full dress, with peaked cap of green with white welt around the crown. The uniform colour, now described as piper green for tunic and overalls, the tunic single breasted, plastron front now discarded, white gorget patches on the collar and white cuffs with white piping on back and sleeves, steel chains on shoulders. A dress shoulder-belt of silver lace, double white stripes on overalls, silver lace sword-belt from below tunic, half Wellington boots, spurs. This uniform, together with the full dress headdress, was worn by a mounted officer of the Royal Yeomanry Regt in the Lord Mayor's Show, London, 8 November 1975.

This regiment will have completed its first century of service by the year 2002.

---

[1] Letter in author's possession.

[2] Photograph of the funeral in the *Daily Mirror*, 9 January 1913. 'The Pipers from the Royal Irish Fusiliers'.

[3] Letter in author's' possession from Officer Commanding 'X' Company, 2nd Bn Suffolk Regt, 76th Infantry Brigade, 3rd Division, 20 August 1918.

[4] Described as 'An Illustrated Army List', composed, illustrated, and thrust upon Moss Bros & Co Ltd, by Capt J. S. Hicks, Royal Marines (Retd).

YEOMANRY, SPECIAL RESERVE & TERRITORIAL FORCE REGIMENTS

The South Irish Horse

A mounted trooper, Curragh Camp, 1904.

Trooper Ernest N. Ryan, c1907. A medical student in Dublin but on moving to a London Hospital transferred to the 3rd County of London Sharpshooters Yeomanry. He served during the First World War war as an officer of the Army Medical Corps, attaining the rank of Lt-Colonel. After the Armistice he was attached to the 6th Dragoons in Cologne.

This regiment was raised under similar circumstances to those of the North Irish Horse, the first public announcement appearing 7 January 1902:

> 'HM The King has been graciously pleased to approve the formation of two regiments of Imperial Yeomanry in Ireland, to be designated the North of Ireland Imperial Yeomanry and South of Ireland Imperial Yeomanry.'

The new Southern Irish regiment had its headquarters at Artillery Barracks, Limerick, and the distribution of squadrons as follows:–

'A' Squadron. Beggar's Bush Barracks, Dublin.
'B' Squadron. Artillery Barracks, Limerick.

'C' Squadron. Glen House Ballyvolane, Cork.
'D' Squadron. Beggar's Bush Barracks, Dublin.

The first commanding officer was Lt-Col The Marquess of Waterford, date of appointment 10 February 1902. The Adjutant, Major I. W. Burns-Lindow, 8th Hussars, appointed 7 April 1902, RSM White, also from the 8th Hussars, as were the other PSIs.

Major Burns-Lindow was born in Cumberland in 1868, was commissioned in the 8th Hussars in 1892 and served in South Africa where he was severely wounded. When the term of his adjutancy with the South of Ireland IY terminated in 1904 he retired from the 8th Hussars and was immediately accepted as Major in the regiment. During the First World War he was promoted Lieutenant-Colonel, was mentioned in despatches in October 1914 and again when his Companionship of the Distinguished Service Order was gazetted in 1915. He remained closely associated with the regiment throughout his life and attended a Royal Levee in the full dress of the South Irish Horse in 1934.

The first annual camp was held on the Curragh in the summer of 1903. The service dress uniforms worn were of khaki with some coloured

The RSM and two sergeants, summer 1903.

Winners of the O'Connor Cup, 1906.

Unnamed officer in full dress, c1910.

embellishments, ie stand collar of green with scarlet band and ½in scarlet welt on the Bedford cord breeches and on the khaki slacks. The cap was for dual purpose, green with scarlet below the green band and scarlet welt, but with khaki cloth cover for normal camp duties or drill purposes, otherwise for dress or walking-out.

The dress tunic was green with green and scarlet collar, four patch pockets, plain cuffs, a waist girdle of green with two red stripes running through, or alternative wear on duty, a leather bandolier. In service dress Stohwasser gaiters or khaki puttees for leg-wear, walking-out – green overalls with double red stripes. Officers had brown leather shoulder-belt and pouch for service dress, the pouch with the gilt regimental shamrock badge mounted upon it. There was a special tunic for officers' full dress or levee dress, this was of a finer green material, had scarlet collar with gold lace edging, gold Austrian knots on cuffs and twisted gold shoulder-knots. The gold lace shoulder-belt was of shamrock pattern and the pouch was of black patent leather with the gilt shamrock badge mounted upon it, waist girdle of gold lace with two fine dark green stripes running through. Green overalls with two scarlet ¾in stripes, half-Wellington boots, and nickel-silver box spurs. Officers' swords of ordinary cavalry pattern, special device of shamrock leaf, the letters SIY on leaf, all in gilt metal on hilt.[1] Headdress for full dress uniform was always a vexed question which was never resolved, although there were many suggestions. In the *Regimental Journal* of June 1907 there was a proposal for a pattern closely resembling the helmet worn by Austrian Dragoons, leather with fur crest and badge at front; this and all others discarded, the peaked cap with shamrock cap-badge retained throughout the life of the regiment. It will be recalled that the North Irish Horse had adopted a black hat with broad brim and large drooping plume of cock's feathers, much as that worn by Italian Bersaglieri. It is said that when King Edward VII saw a picture of an officer of the North Irish Horse in full dress he remarked 'Have the South Irish Horse chosen a headdress yet? If not, I want to see it first.'[2]

Sketches of the regiment's second annual gymkhana, held at Beggar's Bush Barracks, Dublin, July 1906. The gymnastic display was given by a team from the 11th Hussars.

On 19 March 1904 Field Marshal His Royal Highness The Duke of Connaught accepted the Hon Colonelcy.

By 1904 the regiment could boast a fine band under the direction of Mr C. F. Allen. This band, 20 musicians strong, claimed to be the first volunteer regimental band formed in Ireland since the Union.[3]

In 1906 there was to be an important duty, the regiment was ordered to provide an escort for HM King Edward and Queen Alexandra during a visit to Waterford. 2nd Lt L. L. Hewson, MVO, was chosen to command, and S. S. M. Prentice, a PSI from the 13th Hussars, to ride on the nearside of the royal carriage. 30 men were drawn from the various squadrons and the horses borrowed from the Gunners at Cahir. The uniform worn by the escort – coloured caps, green tunics, bandoliers, Bedford cord breeches and Stohwasser gaiters. Mounted escort duty was always a worrying business, the escort commander not only had to place himself in the correct position near the offside wheel in order to receive any command from the royal passenger, but to keep an eye on the dressing and spacing of the remainder. In the event the drive went well and Lt Hewson received HM's congratulations for the manner in which the duty was performed and for the splendid turnout. General Pole Carew on the other hand, in charge of the overall arrangements for the visit, confessed afterwards that he had not slept properly for three

Trooper (later Sergeant) Jol Christian, in khaki service dress, 1915.
GLENN THOMPSON (from Mrs Curphy)

weeks through anxiety.

An enterprising undertaking by this regiment in 1906 was the production of a journal called *The South of Ireland Imperial Yeomanry Club Gazette*, which ran for several years.

In 1908 the regiment was transferred to the Special Reserve and title changed to South Irish Horse.

Every opportunity was taken to send soldiers on courses and representatives attended the Hythe School of Musketry. An account from a team member who competed at Bisley one year for the Yeomanry Cup reported that 'To an outsider it must have been a pretty match to watch with all the different Yeomary uniforms, none however smarter than our own.' Horsemanship was another skill that the regiment was proud of, annual sports were held after the training and there was keen competition to gain the prizes awarded for tent-pegging, jumping and flat racing.

The regiment sent a party of 25 rank and file under the command of Capt E. L. Phelps to London for the Coronation of King George V in June 1911.[4]

After mobilisation in 1914 one squadron was able to join the two from the North Irish Horse and proceeded to France almost immediately as part of Field Marshal French's Army; it was involved in one of the initial mounted actions within a day or so of landing, covered the Guards Brigade at Mons and subsequently acquired the nickname 'Lord French's Body Guard'. The remainder of the regiment was employed as divisional cavalry until 1916, then as corps cavalry, and after September 1917 as infantry forming the 7th (South Irish Horse) Bn Royal Irish Regt.

There was a brief mounted action on the Somme. Major H. E. D. Harris in his book,[5] gives the following description:

'As XV Corps Cavalry Regt on 26 September, together with the 19th (Indian) Lancers, they advanced from Hametz, crossing trenches full of British troops, and trotting across open country near Flers. After coming under shell fire, the mounted patrols went into Gueudecourt, and opened fire on enemy there with Hotchkiss and rifles. They held their positions despite an advance of three German battalions until relieved by infantry in the evening.'

An infantry Private of the 1st/5th West Yorkshire Regt, recording his own experiences after the war, remarked 'My strongest recollection: all those grand looking cavalry-men, ready mounted to follow the breakthrough. What a hope!'[6]

In November 1916 'A' and 'B' Squadrons together with the 1st/1st Hampshire Carabiniers formed a composite regiment of IX Corps Cavalry. At this time the regiment was located near Bailleul in huts, with horse standing made from bricks salvaged under shell fire from Ypres.

Two squadrons of the Horse went to Egypt and later took part in Allenby's advance into Palestine. The battle-honours awarded to the regiment are as follows:

'Loos', 'Somme, 1916, '18', 'Albert 1916', 'St Quentin', 'Rosières', 'Avre', 'Ypres, 1918', 'Courtrai', and 'France and Flanders, 1915-18'.

The close wartime association with the Royal Irish Regt was maintained well on into the 1970s when Old Comrades of both regiments joined together for annual reunions and dinner. At one of these

Lt-Colonel I. W. Burns-Lindow (late 8th KRI Hussars) attending a Royal Levee at St James's 1934. He wears the full dress of the South Irish Horse but had introduced a shako which was totally unofficial and which had been obtained from a costumier. It has been said that King George V noticed this unusual headdress and remarked on it!

functions, a Royal guest, King Edward VIII pleased members of the South Irish Horse by remembering and enquiring after Pte Robert Bell of the regiment, a Cavan man, who had served as his orderly in France for two years, and described him as a 'splendid soldier'.

In common with all other regiments from South Ireland the regiment was disbanded in July 1922.

[1] A most comprehensive article on the uniforms of the regiment 1902-22, was written, illustrated in colour also with line drawings and photographs, by F. Glenn Thompson, *The Irish Sword*, Vol.XIII, No.50, Summer 1977.
[2] *Daily Telegraph*, 4 May 1966.
[3] Photograph in *The King, His Navy and Army*, 3 September 1904.
[4] See Booklet No.10 in the Army Museum's Ogilby Trust Yeomanry series.
[5] *The Irish Regiments in the First World War*, by H. E. D. Harris. The Mercier Press, Cork, 1968.
[6] *The First Day on the Somme*, by Martin Middlebrook. Penguin Press, 1971.

YEOMANRY, SPECIAL RESERVE & TERRITORIAL FORCE REGIMENTS

The London Irish

Major Sir Randal Howard Roberts, Bart, c1871. Fought in the Franco-Prussian War 1870 and was awarded the Iron Cross, seen in wear on his London Irish Rifle Volunteer undress uniform. Photo – Paris.

The initial enthusiasm which greeted the inauguration of the new Volunteer Force in 1859 was reflected in recruiting for a London corps of Irish volunteers, the London Irish. In the autumn of 1859 an Irish journalist Mr G. T. Dempsey took the first step by calling together five young men, civil servants, for a meeting held in his rooms in Essex Street, Strand. This was followed by a larger and more representative gathering in December at Morley's Hotel, the Marquis of Donegall in the chair, the meeting resulting in a resolution passed 'that a Rifle Volunteer corps be at once organised under the title of the London Irish Volunteers'. The services of the corps were accepted in February 1860,

George Hamilton Chichester, Marquess of Donegal, KP, GCH. Lt-Colonel of the London Irish Volunteer Rifle Corps. Drawn from life on stone by H. Fleuss, 1860.
AMOT

official title 28th Middlesex (London Irish) Rifle Volunteer Corps, and by 1861 had become a battalion. Field Marshal Viscount Gough became its first Honorary Colonel on 21 May 1861 and the Marquis of Donegall the first Commanding Officer from May of the preceding year. It is said that in the early days the London Irish Volunteers was supported 'by almost every peer on the Irish roll and every Irishman of distinction', and a whole string of names of VIPs of the day added to make the point, also the fact that the Prime Minister, Lord Palmerston, joined as a private. How long he served and how long the interest of these influential gentlemen lasted is not known but in 1862, when it was realised that there was to be no fighting, enthusiasm waned and numbers dropped. This proved to be a temporary hiccup as within a year or two the battalion was up to strength with a total of nearly 1,200, said to be the highest number of any corps south of the Tweed and third in the United Kingdom. (*The Army and Navy Gazette* of 1867 reported that the London Irish, at the Great Review held that year, was by far 'the strongest corps on the ground if not double the strength of any other'.) There was a strict rule that only Irishmen, 'men connected with Ireland by birth, marriage or property', be enlisted. This rule obviously had to be relaxed on occasion although preference was always given to the Irish. At this time there were nine Companies identified by numbers but this was altered to identification by letters, a system maintained to the present day.

The uniform of 1860 was of 'Sardinian' grey, green facings, dark silver lace, a shako with a green cock's-feather plume. The shako-badge of silver, an 8-pointed star surmounted by a crown, in the centre a garter inscribed 'Irish Volunteers' and enclosing a harp. The shoulder-belt plate worn by officers consisted of a harp and crown within a wreath of

The Band of the 16th Middlesex at Queen Victoria's Diamond Jubilee procession, 1897.

Dress uniforms of the 1890s. 16th Middlesex Rifle Volunteers. Three officers, Sergeant Bugler, Corporal, Pioneer and Private. All rank and file in marching order. Photo – F. G. O. Stuart.

shamrock, designed by Samuel Lover, a great Irish poet and author who joined the ranks as a founder member. Mr Lover, although 62 years old, attended all drills with great enthusiasm.

An officer in the uniform of 1860 appears on the well known print entitled 'Metropolitan Rifle Corps in Hyde Park', this picture showing 24 figures in the uniforms worn at the Royal Review of the Volunteer Force by Queen Victoria on 23 June 1860.[1]

There had always been a close association between this corps and the London press, commencing with Mr Dempsey. So during the early days we find that there were many interesting snippets in the *Illustrated London News*, some of which would not merit a mention nowadays even in a local newspaper, only to be found in the *Regimental Journal*. In December 1863 a silver tankard (value 50 guineas) was presented to Capt A. B. Leech by the West End Company during a dinner at the Rainbow, Temple Bar. This vessel had figures of an officer and private engraved upon it, a handsome and valuable gift indeed. As with any other large body of men the regiment could not avoid accepting, unknowingly, an odd crank, and one such was reported in April 1866 – 'Patrick Butler of the London Irish, who was given into custody at Brighton on a charge of having threatened to shoot the Prince of Wales, has been struck off the roll of this regiment.'

In common with other Volunteer regiments, men from the London Irish served as special constables during the Fenian alarm in 1868, and a picture of the 'Swearing-In' of the London Irish Volunteers at the National School Rooms, St Martins in the Fields, appeared in the issue of 18 January 1868. Later, on St Patrick's Day 1868, a Guard of Honour, two companies commanded by Major Ward was found – to receive HRH The Prince of Wales at the Easter Review at Portsmouth. For the Easter Review of 1870 held at Brighton the regiment appeared in a new uniform, the grey now exchanged for rifle green, the pattern similar to that of the Rifle Brigade, and the shako was retained.

A London Irish officer, Major Sir Randal Howland Roberts, Bart, is the subject of one of our illustrations. The photograph, taken in Paris, shows him in the undress uniform of the regiment, he has the regimental harp badge on his peakless cap and is displaying an Iron Cross attached to the frogging of his coat by its scarlet, black and white ribbon. (A companion photograph shows him in the regimental full dress of rifle green, and with leathered overalls.) Major Roberts's career was an interesting one. He was born on 28 March 1837 at Britfieldstown, Co Cork, educated at Merchant Taylors School before service with the 33rd (The Duke of Wellington's) Regt in the Crimea and Indian Mutiny. He served as war correspondent for the *Daily Telegraph* during the Franco-Prussian War 1870-1, and he died in October 1899. He received the Iron Cross of Prussia and was also a Knight of the Legion of Honour and Knight of Saints Maurice and Lazarus (Italy). He was only with the regiment from 1870-2 and was Captain of the London Irish '8' at the Shooting Competition of 1871.

The shako gave way to the spiked cloth helmet in the Regular Army in May 1878 and most Volunteer Battalions followed suit. The new helmet-plate was bronze, a Maltese cross bearing a crowned Irish harp in the centre and the title 'London Irish Rifle Vols' surrounding it, the plate on a green cloth backing. The corps title was redesigned on 3 September 1880 as 16th Middlesex (London Irish) Rifle Volunteers, and in the following year became the 4th Volunteer Bn the Rifle Brigade, (changed once more from 4th to 3rd V Bn 1892).

HRH The Duke of Connaught honoured the regiment in June 1871 by accepting the Honorary Colonelcy, an appointment he held until his death in 1940. He always kept in touch with the regiment, often leading it at an annual review. A spirited picture of such an occasion was published in the *Graphic* of 15 July 1899, showing His Royal Highness, mounted and in full rifle dress, followed by the commanding officer with sword at the salute, the drawing by W. T. Maud.

The Marquis of Donegall died at the great age of 87 in 1883, and command, as Colonel Commandant, was given to James Ward, CB. Colonel Ward had actually been in command since 1868, was described in the Army List as Captain – Antrim Militia, but curiously had held a commission as Captain in the Royal North Lincoln Militia since 1858! He therefore held two commisions simultaneously until the Royal Warrant was issued prohibiting such dual employment. In 1883 he commanded the 4th Column of Volunteer battalions at the annual review and in 1887 was responsible for providing a Guard from the regiment at Buckingham Palace from 28 June, subsequently at the Royal Review at the Palace during the following month. He retired in 1896 and was succeeded by Col Sir Howland Roberts, Bart, VD. Col Roberts had commenced his Volunteer career in the ranks as a private in the 3rd Middlesex in March 1867, transferring as an ensign to the London Irish in 1868, and he had a proud distinction of having been a 'marksman' every year since he joined the Service, and was twice winner of the gold medal as best shot in the regiment.

The important event of 1897 was the Diamond Jubilee, and the

Senior NCO, 28th Middlesex (London Irish) Rifle Volunteer Corps, c1870s. Note shamrock badges on cuffs and collar, also that he probably wears his everyday civilian trousers – not unheard of at that period when visiting a photographer's studio for a seated portrait.

regimental band took its place in the procession through London on 22 June. The strength of the band at this time was between 25 and 30, the uniform similar to the remainder of the corps but with green and black piping, drummers' wings of dark and light green with fringe, black and green drummers' cords looped across the chest to the left. The bass drummer's apron was of black leather. (The regiment had had a band, certainly since 1868, although pipers were not introduced until much later.) NCOs' rank chevrons throughout the regiment were light green and those of senior NCOs worn above the right cuff – silver. It is claimed that 'stretcher-men' had helmet balls instead of the spikes used by remainder.

Although there was no commitment by the Volunteer Force to serve other than in defence of this country and not abroad, there was no lack of volunteers for active service in South Africa 1889. The London Irish did not therefore serve as a unit, but out of the 17 officers and 400 other ranks who did volunteer, 8 officers and 200 NCOs and men were selected, either for the CIV (City Imperial Volunteers) Contingent to be commanded by Capt E. G. Concannon of the regiment or for the Volunteer Service Companies of the Royal Irish Rifles. The latter, under the command of another regimental officer, Capt C. G. Henty, son of the well known author of boys' adventure books, one Company becoming 'K' Company of the 2nd Bn Royal Irish Rifles. Capt Concannon's contingent embarked on the last day of 1899 and was not to return to this country until 26 October 1900. Both of these officers were twice mentioned in despatches whilst Capt Concannon received the DSO.[2] Inasmuch as it mirrors the movements and fighting record of his

A Boer War period group, two London Irish Riflemen in walking-out dress with a 17th Lancer companion and civilian.

Rifleman P. E. Smith, 26 June 1916, Winchester.
D. W. QUARMBY

Regimental Band at Duke of York's Headquarters, Chelsea, 1930.
S. D. EAGLE

contingent it could be of interest to include here an extract from the official citation:

'He served in South Africa with the City Imperial Volunteers, Mounted Infantry, and was present in operations in the Orange Free State, February to May 1900, including operations at Paardeberg (17 to 26 Feb); action at Poplar Grove, Dreifontein, Karee Siding and Hautnek (Thoba Mountain); operations in the Transvaal in May and June 1900 including actions near Johannesburg, Pretoria and Diamond Hill (11 and 12 June); operations in Orange River Colony, including actions at Belfast (26 and 27 Aug), Lydenberg (5 to 8 Sept) and Wittebergen 1 to 20 July).'

The Volunteer Service Companies, Royal Irish Rifles, returned in April 1901. During the South African War the regiment lost 3 NCOs and 7 privates killed in action.[3] Being a rifle regiment no Colours were carried but 'South Africa 1900-02' became its first battle-honour.

On the badges in 1902 the Imperial crown replaced the Royal crown and in addition the inscription on the button was amended to 'London Irish Rifle Volunteers'. The belt buckle had on the upper part of the ring the words 'Irish Volunteers' and at the base two shamrock sprays. The ends of the clasp were also ornamented with shamrocks. In the centre was a crowned harp. The pouch-belt plate was a crowned shamrock wreath enclosing a harp on a solid background.[4] Khaki was now the accepted uniform, rifle green kept for walking-out dress and ceremonial. At annual camp in 1903 the slouch hat was used, but does not seem to have remained in wear for long.

In 1906 Col Roberts retired and Lt-Col Hercules A Packenham, formerly Grenadier Guards and 4th Bn Royal Irish Rifles, was appointed to command, so becoming the first Commanding Officer since the Marquis of Donegall not to have been a regimental Company Commander.

When the Territorial Army came into force in 1908 the title was changed to 18th (County of London) Bn. The London Regt (London Irish Rifles), now forming part of the 5th London Brigade of the 2nd Division, Territorial Force, in London District Command. The title private became rifleman and it was about this time that the rifle busby replaced the helmet. Pipers were introduced by 1906-07 and a newspaper photograph of 1911 above a caption 'London Irish in the Royal Progress' shows a small part of the regiment in full dress uniform, marching through London led by two pipers. Full dress was naturally the dress of the day when HM King George V reviewed the two London Divisions of the Territorial Force in Hyde Park on Saturday 5 July 1913, the regiment again led by their Colonel, the Duke of Connaught, although on this occasion he wore a Field Marshal's uniform. This spectacular event was probably the last of full dress for many a year.

With the 1908 change of status and the Volunteer battalions becoming Territorial Army battalions, changes were also made in the regulations governing the Force, allowing for its soldiers to volunteer for overseas service. The regiment was in camp during the summer of 1914 when mobilisations sent it hurrying back to the Duke of York's Headquarters on 4 August and there is an interesting note on the scene at the headquarters and the varying uniforms of the miscellaneous corps assembled there.[5] The author describes how he saw soldiers of at least six Territorial units there, most seemed to have the regulation khaki, although men of the London Royal Army Medical Corps had only their blue uniforms with dull crimson facings and the Rough Riders kept their drab riding breeches with purple stripe. The London Irish had khaki with the $_1^T8$ over the semi-circular word LONDON, all in black

Annual Remembrance Parade of the Old Comrades Association at the 1914-18 War Memorial to the London Regiment, outside Royal Exchange in 1937. Bugles playing the Last Post.
THE LONDON IRISH

Pipe-banners, presented 1937.
GEORGE POTTER & SONS

Major P. R. Savage. Killed in action 1939-45 war.

metal, on their shoulder straps. All the various units had left the London headquarters by 28 August, the 18th travelling to the St Albans area for training before eventual embarkation in March 1915. The battalion, commanded by Lt-Col E. G. Concannon, DSO, VD, landed at Havre and, from then until the end of the war, remaining in France and Flanders as part of the 141st Brigade, 47th Division. It was continually in the thick of battle, principal honours including Loos, Somme 1916-18, Messines 1917, Ypres 1917, and France and Flanders. A memento in the Regimental Museum recalls how the regiment made history at the Battle of Loos, related by a Regimental historian, Lt-Col M. J. P. M. Corbally.[6] Major C. Beresford led the 1st Bn over the top on 25 September 1915. In the front rank was the battalion football team's captain, Sgt Edwards, who kept a football tied to his pack. Once over the parapet he kicked the ball long and hard towards the enemy lines, then it was continually kicked forward by the men, under fire the whole time, until, finally kicked into the enemy trench, the actual football now preserved in the Regimental Museum. A regimental distinguishing flash was painted on the steel trench helmet of the 1st Bn, a black rectangle with two horizontal green lines and in white the letters LIR, whilst on the sleeves the title $^{LONDON}_{IRISH}$ on a khaki patch. A 2nd Bn was raised in London in August 1914, trained in England and sent to Salonika in 1916 and in June 1917 to Egypt, eventually disbanded in Palestine July 1918, personnel to 1st Bn Royal Irish Regt, Irish Fusiliers and 1st Bn Leinster Regt, all in the 10th Division. A 3rd Bn was formed in 1915, serving in England throughout the war as a Reserve Bn. In total the regiment suffered 1,016 killed, 2,644 wounded and 303 prisoners-of-war. Further figures tell us that decorations included – DSO – 7, MC – 33, DCM – 24 and MM – 101. 24 battle-honours awarded.

In 1919 the regiment was reduced to a cadre but shortly reconstituted. The important events during the years beween the wars were of course the weekly training sessions at the drill hall and the annual camps where training was mixed with sport and where plenty of liquid refreshment was consumed. Ceremonial parades and the changes of uniform patterns are always worth recording. In 1928 the Territorials took on the regular army during manoeuvres, notable for the novel employment of aeroplanes. There was a large turnout at the parade and service held outside the Royal Exchange marking the 15th anniversary of Loos; it was in 1929 also that the regiment was officially affiliated with the Royal Ulster Rifles. When the regiment was on annual training in Ulster in the summer of 1931 they received a visit from HRH The Duke of Connaught, who wore the regimental harp badge on his khaki cap. Prior to 1937 the Permanent Staff Instructors were drawn from any Irish regiment but were now to be taken exclusively from the Royal Ulster Rifles. The RSM was from the Irish Guards. About eleven newly commissioned 2nd Lieutenants attended a Levee on 17 March 1938 and were photographed leaving St James's Palace, all looking incredibly smart, wearing the caubeen with St Patrick blue hackle, together with khaki uniform with plus-four trousers and khaki puttees. The caubeen incidentally was officially sanctioned for wear by all ranks in 1937.

Various changes in uniform had taken place since 1922. In that year pipers were parading in green balmorals, khaki cut-away jackets with green collars and green rounded cuffs, saffron kilts with green hose and black belts. At the 1928 manoeuvres pipers of the regiment on the march were then wearing the caubeen, khaki cut-away tunics and dust-covers over the kilts, whilst at the 1929 Loos Commemoration Parade pipers and buglers were in full dress, the latter with rifle busbies, although the Bugle-Major on this occasion wore his dark green peaked cap. Finishing touches to the full dress of the pipe band came in 1937 with a gift that year of pipe banners. These were of dark green with silver embroidery and fringes, the battalion harp badge surrounded by a wreath of

'Tara', the wolfhound, parading with the Pipes and Drums whilst stationed in Kent during early days of the war, 1939-45.
S. D. EAGLE

Lt-Colonel J. R. J. Macnamara, MP,
Commanding Officer, with a piper and
bugler, winter 1939-40.
S. D. EAGLE

shamrock and with 11 principal battle-honours mounted upon it, whilst
the regimental title was embroidered on a triple scroll below, on the
reverse the donor's arms and crest. A splendid photograph was
published in the *Territorial Magazine* in December 1937 showing
representative uniforms. Capt J. J. D. Reidy in service dress, green
caubeen normal khaki tunic, in his case worn with well-cut khaki
breeches; Company Sergeant-Major J. Daly in green patrols and Pipe-
Major J. Franklin in full dress, the Pipe-Major's green doublet having
four bars of silver lace ornamentation across the front of the garment.

1940 saw the regiment taking proud possession of its first Irish
wolfhound mascot, a beautiful beast with the difficult name of Sean of
Ballykenny but soon re-christened Tara. He was put under the care of
Piper Mulqueen, who had been valet/footman at the German Embassy,
and to whom Ribbentrop, then German Ambassador, entrusted his dog
when he left the United Kingdom to become Foreign Minister in Hitler's
Government. When the London Irish went on active service overseas
Tara was handed over to the 70th Bn London Irish Rifles (Young
Soldiers Bn, formed 1941 and disbanded 1943), and when that unit was
disbanded he was passed on to the 70th (YS) Bn The Royal Ulster Rifles.
When with the latter unit he had the distinction of appearing in the Lord
Mayor's Procession in London in 1943. He died in 1947. The next
wolfhound was presented by a member of the regiment in March 1952
and named Kevin. On ceremonial parades Kevin wore a handsome
green coat, decorated with the Irish Harp with crown over it and within
two sprigs of shamrock, on each side, all in silver embroidery; the coat
was also edged with embroidery. Around his neck he wore a heavily
studded collar from which was suspended on to his chest the badge of the
regiment. He was led by the Dog-Major. He accompanied a detachment

to Belfast when the regiment joined with the Royal Ulster Rifles to receive the Freedom of the City on 6 February 1954.[7]

Back to 1939 when two battalions of the London Irish were mobilised. It is impossible to tell, or do justice to, the story of the regiment during the war of 1939-45 in the space available here but fortunately it has been fully recorded in the History – *The London Irish at War*.[8] After the retreat of the British Expeditionary Force to Dunkirk the 1st Bn volunteered to go over and form part of a bridgehead to cover the evacuation, but shipping could not be spared so instead it was employed on disembarkation at Margate and Ramsgate. During the 'phoney' war period the battalion was fully engaged with anti-invasion and guard duties, as well as most intensive training. In August 1942 it left this country for Iraq, which was to be the start of three year's travel and fighting, from the Middle East with the 56th (London) Division to Egypt, Sicily, and then up through Italy and the horror of the Anzio-beach-head where the battalion suffered grevious casualties before being able to move to a rest area at Naples, and later withdrawal to Egypt. Back to Italy once more and the static warfare prior to the fighting south of the River Po and along the Rivers Senio, Saturno, and Reno, with the 8th Army.

The 2nd Bn's war was equally fierce. After Dunkirk the battalion moved about from the East to South Coasts and was retained in this country training etc, slightly longer than the 1st Bn, but was in action before then, in North Africa in November 1942, with the Irish Brigade, 6th Armoured Division and as part of the 1st Army. The battalion enjoyed the fruits of victory after entering Tunis in March 1943 and the whole battalion with pipers took part in the Victory Parade. Then came Italy and continuous fighting until April 1945, mostly over the extremely difficult country and in atrocious weather. The battalion had had the distinction of playing an important role as part of the 'Kangaroo Army', so called because it was mounted in armoured carriers of the 4th Hussars, backed up by the 9th Lancers, and once out in the open leaping forward with great strides, the 8th, 5th and Allied Armies finally trapping the German forces south of the River Po.

These were the last actions of the war for both battalions, a war in which 1,200 soldiers of the Royal Ulster Rifles and London Irish Rifles had laid down their lives.

From the River Po the 1st Bn moved to Trieste after the war to keep the peace in a disputed area between Italy and Jugoslavia where, in spite of troublesome demonstrations, the Pipes and Drums of the regiment were always popular. The battalion was eventually moved to Rimini where a temporary amalgamation with the 1st London Scottish took place prior to disbandment of the wartime unit in 1946. The 2nd Bn was engaged in combing the Carintia Hills in South Austria for stragglers of war, until January 1946 when the battalion was disbanded and details transferred to the 1st Bn.

So to the post war years. In 1947 the regiment was re-formed at the Duke of York's Headquarters, Chelsea, under the command of Lt-Col The Viscount Stopford, MBE. The parent regiment, the Royal Ulster Rifles, received approval from HM The King to form an alliance with The Irish Regiment of Canada, old friends of the London Irish who had served alongside them in Italy 1944 when the Pipes and Drums of both regiments had managed to perform together during the infrequent periods of respite from the fighting to force the Gothic Line.

Pipes and drums, 1st Bn London Irish Rifles (TA), Folkestone, 3 September 1948.
HASTINGS OBSERVER

In November 1949 Field Marshal The Earl Alexander of Tunis became Honorary Colonel of the regiment, both battalions having been in his command in Sicily 1943.

One of the tasks of the new peace-time regiment was to take in and provide further training for National Servicemen of Irish descent from the London area after their period of service with the three Irish regular infantry regiments.

On 6 February 1954 the Royal Ulster Rifles received the Freedom of the City of Belfast, and a strong detachment, including the band, from the London Irish Rifles was sent over to Ireland for this ceremonial occasion.

At the Beating Retreat ceremony on Horse Guards Parade, 8 June 1981, the London Irish Rifles Association was represented by a lone piper, the distinguished figure of Pipe-Major J. R. Franklin, BEM. Pipe-Major Franklin, already in his 70s, had retired from the London Irish Rifles Regimental Association pipe band, but was specially invited to be the lone piper as a representative of the Second World War survivors. After the parade he was presented to HM The Queen Mother.

The regiment is now part of the Royal Irish Rangers, the latter title dating from 1968 when the Royal Inniskilling Fusiliers, the Royal Ulster Rifles and the Royal Irish Fusiliers were amalgamated. The present title – 'D' Company, (London Irish Rifles) 4th (V) Bn The Royal Irish Rangers, North Irish Militia, and forming part of the King's Division.

[1] Issued as a coloured plate Supplement to the *Illustrated London News* 27 October 1860. Reproduced in colour in the Journal of the Society for Army Historical Research Vol XXXVIII, p.95, and also as dust cover to the 1986 volume, *The Territorial Battalions, A Pictorial History* by Ray Westlake. Spellmount. (The London Irish officer is third figure from the right.)

[2] *The VC and DSO*. Sir O'Moore Creagh VC and E. M. Humphries. c1920.

[3] *The King 8 August 1903 and His Majesty's Territorial Army*. Walter Richards. 1911.

[4] Bulletin of the Military Historical Society. Vol IV No. 22, November 1955.

[5] A Regimental file of notes and pictures at the Army Museums Ogilby Trust. Author the late Mr. L. E. Buckell.

[6] *The Story of the London Irish Rifles 1859-1984*, by Lt-Col M. J. P. M. Corbally and *The Royal Ulster Rifles 1793-1957*. Same author Dec 1959.

[7] As 5. The Regimental file at AMOT.

[8] The London Irish at War. Pub London Irish Old Comrades Association 1949.

YEOMANRY, SPECIAL RESERVE & TERRITORIAL FORCE REGIMENTS

The Tyneside Irish

The story of the Tyneside Irish Battalions is an inspiring one, a story of bravery and loyalty, but ending in tragedy and great sadness. At the outbreak of war in August 1914 the young men of Newcastle flocked to recruiting offices. It is estimated that probably as many as 20,000 volunteered for service with the county regiment, the 5th of Foot, Northumberland Fusiliers, too many in fact for that regiment alone but were readily accepted by other English regiments.

The Lord Mayor of Newcastle, an Irishman, not to be outdone by other cities and towns who had raised regiments of Pals, called a meeting for 14 September. (These units of Pals were formed of men from the same localities and places of work, who knew each other through business or sport.) At this meeting it was agreed to seek permission from the War Office to raise a brigade of Tyneside Irish soldiers, whilst in the same city and at the same time the Scots were doing the same. The request was at first refused but within a month, following a visit to Newcastle-on-Tyne from Lord Haldane, a former Secretary for War, the War Office was persuaded to reverse its original decision. So, given certain conditions, permission was granted. One of the stipulations was that the newly raised unit(s) form part of the county regiment. The results from the recruiting drives were astonishing: during September,

The officers of the 4th Bn Tyneside Irish prior to embarkation for France, 1916.
B. TURNER

Captan Harold Price, MC. Born in Canada, he joined the Royal 22E Regiment ('The van doos') at the outbreak of war as a private but later transferred to the 3rd Bn Tyneside Irish as captain. He went to France with the battalion in January 1916 and was twice mentioned in despatches, and awarded the Military Cross. He was killed on the night of 25/26 June 1916 at La Boiselle. Badges seen in the photograph are those of the parent regiment, the Northumberland Fusiliers.
B. TURNER

October and November 1914 the Scottish had raised four battalions and during the month of November the Irish had raised three full battalions and another followed in January 1915. The titles of the Tyneside Irish battalions were as follows:

24th (Service) Bn (1st Tyneside Irish) Northumberland Fusiliers.
25th (Service) Bn (2nd Tyneside Irish) Northumberland Fusiliers.
26th (Service) Bn (3rd Tyneside Irish) Northumberland Fusiliers.
27th (Service) Bn (4th Tyneside Irish) Northumberland Fusiliers.

Later in July 1915 a Reserve Bn of Tyneside Irish, the 30th, was formed, and yet another in June 1916, the 34th. The subsequent histories of the Tyneside Irish and Scottish were to be closely bound together throughout the war.

The Tyneside Scottish had hoped for a kilted uniform but had to be satisfied with their own distinctive glengarry badge. The Irish were

34th Division Troops of the Tyneside Irish Brigade advancing to the attack on La Boisselle, Battle of Albert, 1 July 1916.
IWM

badged as Northumberland Fusiliers wearing the grenade cap badge, but a crowned Irish harp with title scroll, and the letters N F as shoulder title of brass, was permitted. The pipers of the Irish in the first instance had Irish pipes with two drones, but were ordered to exchange for the three drone pattern. They also had to engage the services of a Pipe-Major and piper from the Tyneside Scottish as instructors, the piper eventually returned to his battalion but Pipe-Major John Wilson, apparently liking the Irish, continued as their Pipe-Major.

In June 1915 the four battalions formed the 103rd Brigade (Tyneside Irish) of the 34th Division, whilst the Scottish, the 102nd Brigade of the same division. After twelve months' training, the last six months on Salisbury Plain, the division embarked for France in January 1916, where the divisional sign was changed to the black and white checkered square. After a spell in the trenches came a move in April to a training area in preparation for the 4th Army offensive, in which 14 divisions, including the 34th, were to be committed.

The story of that offensive of the 1 July 1916 on the Somme has been told and told again, and will not be repeated here. Suffice to say that the enemy seemed well prepared, that the attacking force along an 18 mile front was met with withering machine-gun fire and that by the end of the day the British Army had suffered nearly 60,000 casualties; nearly 20,000 killed and the remainder wounded or missing. The Tyneside Irish Brigade suffered nearly 80% casualties, but a small number struggled on and reached their objective, the village of Contalmaison, only to be overwhelmed by the German occupiers.

The remnants of the brigade, then attached to the 15th (Scottish) Division, took part on another Somme attack in September 1916, and in April 1917, back with the 34th Division, was in the fighting for Arras. It was during this battle that L/Cpl Thomas Bryan, 25th Bn, won the Victoria Cross on 9 April and this decoration was also won by Pte Ernest Sykes, 27th Bn, on 19 April. Both citations were announced in the London Gazette 8 June 1917:

L/Cpl Thomas Bryan, No.22040.

'For most conspicuous bravery during an attack. Although wounded, this non-commissioned officer went forward alone, with a view to silencing a machine-gun which was inflicting much damage. He worked up most skilfully along a communication trench, approached the gun from behind, disabled it, and killed two of the team as they were abandoning the gun. As this machine-gun had been a serious obstacle in the advance to the second objective, the results obtained by L/Cpl Bryan's gallant action were very far reaching.'

Private Ernest Sykes, No.40989.

'For most conspicuous bravery and devotion to duty when his battalion in attack was held up about 350 yards in advance of our lines by intense fire from front and flank, and suffered heavy casualties. Private Sykes, despite this heavy fire, went forward and brought back four wounded – he made a fifth journey and remained out under conditions which appeared to be certain death until he had bandaged all those who were too badly wounded to be moved.

These gallant actions, performed under incessant machine-gun and rifle fire, showed an utter contempt of danger.'

Due to the heavy losses sustained by both 102nd and 103rd Brigades, the 24th and 27th Bns amalgamated in August 1917, then to be known as the 24th/27th Bn Northumberland Fusiliers, 103rd Brigade, whilst the remnants of the 25th joined those of the 22nd Bn (3rd Tyneside Scottish), and the 23rd Tyneside Scottish in the 102nd Brigade. Both these brigades were involved in replacing the March 1918 German offensive and again suffered heavy casualties, so much so that by May the units were reduced to cadre strength.

What remained of all the brave battalions from Tyneside were withdrawn from the line and a few officers and men then became instructors for the newly arrived American force, before final disbandment in 1918.

There can be little doubt that the heavy casualties suffered by the Tyneside battalions in 1916 were instrumental in bringing to an end the recruiting of Pals units.

Battalion colours were laid-up in Newcastle's two cathedrals.[1]

---

[1] The most detailed account of the Tyneside Irish Brigade is to be found in a comprehensive article by Frank Forde. *The Irish Sword*, Vol.XVI, No.63 1985.

YEOMANRY, SPECIAL RESERVE & TERRITORIAL FORCE REGIMENTS

8th (Irish) Bn
The King's Regiment (Liverpool)

Whilst the official date for the formation of this corps is given as 25 April 1860, it is apparent that positive steps had been taken in Liverpool to enable the city to be among the foremost in the new Volunteer Movement. As early as November 1859 we hear that a Capt Bousfield had organised a parade with band through the streets of Liverpool, which did much to stimulate recruiting:

> 'In connection with the Volunteer movement in Liverpool, it may be stated that the Mersey Docks and Harbour Board yesterday week gave permission to their employees to enrol themselves in the various corps now forming. The members of No.1 Company, Captain Bousfield, assembled at their barracks on Saturday afternoon last whence they marched through the town to the Exchange, accompanied by their excellent band. They excited great interest along the whole line of the march, and on arriving at the Exchange the excitement was intense. Their soldierly appearance was highly applauded, and the band striking up the National Anthem was the signal for a loud outburst of enthusiasm.'

(The officer referred to is Nathaniel G. P. Bousfield, 1st Liverpool Brigade; Corps HQ, St Anne Street. Bousfield was promoted Major in May 1860 and Lieutenant-Colonel in 1876).

In response to an advertisement in the *Liverpool Daily Post* of 5 December 1859, an appeal was made to the large Irish population to attend a meeting at the London, Clayton Square, on 7 December, in order to discuss formation of an Irish Volunteer Rifle Corps. Resulting from this gathering it was agreed that a corps be formed, and such was the enthusiastic response that the first drill took place at the Concert Hall, Lord Nelson Street, on 25 January 1860.[1]

The first commanding officer was Lt J. G. Plunkett of the 5th Lancs Militia, soon promoted to Captain, and was assisted by Ensign P. S. Bridwell. Plunkett resigned in November 1860 and Bridwell took over command. He purchased a supply of instruments and enrolled 30 bandsmen, increased the strength from the two Companies he took over to six Companies, with full complement of officers, and he received rapid promotion. By September 1863 he was Lieutenant-Colonel commanding, and had the services of a regular adjutant, G. H. Greaves. Greaves had previous service in the ranks of the 25th King's Own Borderers before transfer to the Donegal Militia as Sergeant-Major, his new appointment carrying the rank of Captain. The unit by this time was designated 64th (Liverpool Irish) Rifle Volunteers (Lancashire).

The annual review was always an important event. In 1862, 4,000 Liverpool Volunteers marched past on the Aintree racecourse, and the

Lord Mayor of Liverpool on that occasion undertook to defray the expenses of refreshments and rail travel for all the troops present.

In 1866 at the march-past before Col Erskine, Inspector General of Volunteers, the 64th formed part of the 3rd Brigade, comprised of the 5th, 65th and 80th Rifles (Press Guard). In 1869:

'The annual presentation of prizes to the successful competitors of the 5th Liverpool Rifle Brigade, took place on Monday evening at the drill-shed in Warwick Street, Toxteth Park. Mr S. R. Graves, MP, presided and distributed the prizes. Mr Graves expressed himself strongly in favour of increased support being given to volunteers by Government. He also thought that greater inducements should be held out to officers, by freeing them from the heavy expense which generally at present they are subjected to, relieving them from the civil obligations of citizens, and allowing them, after they have retired, to retain the rank they held in the force.'[2]

The uniform of the corps was green, at first with shako but later adopting the uniform of the 60th Rifles (King's Royal Rifle Corps), green with scarlet facings, and a helmet. During the 1880s there was a bewildering number of changes of title, in 1880 – 18th Lancashire Rifle Volunteers, July 1881 becoming a Volunteer Battalion with H.Q. at Netherfield Road North, and in March 1888 a new title of 5th (Irish) Volunteer Bn, The King's (Liverpool Regiment) at new H.Q. 50/52 Everton Brow.

Two riflemen of the 5th (Irish) Vol Bn The King's (Liverpool Regiment), 1906-7. Both wear full dress of rifle green with scarlet facings.

A young soldier of the 8th (Irish) Bn The King's (Liverpool Regiment) in khaki service dress, c1915. Although he wears dark rifle buttons and dark leather belt, the cap badge is of white metal.

D. W. QUARMBY

Lt-Col Bridwell who had commanded the corps for over twenty years was elevated to the Hon Colonelcy in July 1887, when Lt-Col Francis Walker assumed command. A full dress group photograph taken during the 1890s[3] shows the almost complete complement of officers. Col Bridwell, by this time a white whiskered gentleman, together with the regimental officers, are wearing full dress of rifle uniform with helmet, the Hon Chaplain in the same dress but with clerical collar from below the tunic collar, and the Medical Officer and Quartermaster in similar full dress but with cocked hats. Small collar badges are visible on the scarlet collars, the shoulder-belts of black patent leather, all carry a fine large silver badge,[4] a crown with circlet below, the interwoven letters LRV within, and above a harp, the whole surrounded by a wreath of shamrock with a scroll at the foot and the motto *Erin go Bragh*.

During the 1890s, from the small beginnings of 1860, the unit possessed a fine band under the direction of Bandmaster Hull. By 1898 the battalion was fully up to strength with eight companies, and consequently when the South African War broke out, 224 all ranks volunteered, most joining the 1st Bn Royal Irish Regiment whilst others went to the Imperial Yeomanry and 1st Bn King's Liverpool Regiment.

In June 1903 one company was disbanded but replaced by a cyclist corps. When King Edward and Queen Alexandra visited Liverpool on 19 July 1904, a long section of the carriage route through the city was lined by the battalion, in rifle full dress. There had been some changes in this uniform since the 1890s, the helmet had been replaced by a rifle-busby and the facings now black, the uniform in fact similar to that of the Royal Irish Rifles.

A photograph taken on the morning after a night raid, 17-18 April 1916, by a raiding party of the 1st/8th (Irish) King's Liverpool Regiment. Two captured German helmets are in evidence and it can be seen that both long and short Lee Enfield rifles are in use. The man in front row extreme left is holding a stick-grenade and a 'jam-tin' grenade is just visible in his left pocket. Minimal equipment is worn.
IWM

In 1908 the battalion was re-numbered, the title now 8th (Irish) Bn King's Liverpool Regt; possessing the battle-honour 'South Africa 1900-02'. A new drill hall at Shaw Street was taken over by the unit in 1912.

Mobilised in August 1914 the regiment formed part of the Liverpool Brigade of the West Lancs Division, but in 1915 joined the North Lancs Brigade at Sevenoaks, Kent. A few months later this brigade was posted to the 51st Highland Division and was in France by the following month. A 2nd Bn was formed in Liverpool in October 1914 and was sent to France in February 1917. The following year this battalion was absorbed by the 1st/8th Bn.

In April 1916, during the fighting at Blairville, France, a 2nd Lt of the regiment won the Victoria Cross. The citation in the *London Gazette* of 26 September 1916 reads as follows:–

Baxter, 2nd Lt Edward Felix
'For most conspicuous bravery. Prior to a raid on the hostile line he was engaged during two nights in cutting wire close to the enemy's trenches. The

enemy could be heard on the other side of the parapet. 2nd Lieutenant Baxter, while assisting in the wire cutting, held a bomb in his hand with the pin withdrawn ready to throw. On one occasion the bomb slipped and fell to the ground, but he instantly picked it up, unscrewed the base plug, and took out the detonator, which he smothered in the ground, thereby preventing the alarm being given, and undoubtedly saving many casualties. Later, he led the left storming party with the greatest gallantry, and was the first man into the trench, shooting the sentry with his revolver. He then assisted to bomb dug-outs, and finally climbed out of the trench and assisted the last man over the parapet. After this he was not seen again, though search parties went out at once to look for him. There seems no doubt that he lost his life in his great devotion to duty.'

A march-past HM King George V – Aldershot, September 1916.

An adventurous story is told by an officer of this regiment. He was taken prisoner at Guillemont in August 1916 after serving with the battalion in the trenches since July 1915. From an Offlag at Augustabad he, and nine other officers, tunnelled their way to freedom, but unfortunately he was recaptured after only eleven days. Transferred to Mannheim and undeterred by his previous experience, he made a second escape attempt, this time a successful one. He managed to cross over into Dutch territory by February 1918, having made a railway journey of 200 miles across Germany, even though his command of the language was poor.

Various patterns of badges as worn by 8th Battalion, 1914 to date.

1 Pattern used when the 5th changed to 8th Battalion, during the First World War probably issued with black finish.

2 Badge issued on reforming, white metal.

3 Badge issued on reforming, on scarlet rosette for officer's cap.

4 Believed to be an alternative officer's cap badge from 1939.

5 Anodized version of No 2, different crown.

6 The left of a pair of collar badges.

P. R. BRYDON ARICS

One of the few happy photographs from the First World War was printed in the British newspapers in October 1918, showing the Liverpool Irish entering Lille and receiving an ecstatic welcome from the inhabitants, long used to German occupation. By this time the regiment was part of the 57th (West Lancs) Division, and wearing the divisional sign of a red semi-circle on a white bar, all upon a black patch on sleeve. On return home the regiment was disbanded on 14 June 1919 and was finally disbanded at Liverpool on 31 March 1922.

By 1939 the services of Liverpool men were again required and the regiment was re-formed and at full strength within a month. Serving at home during the early years of the war, the regiment took part in the Normandy Landing, 6 June 1944. There is an historic photograph, published in the *Regimental Journal*, of the Commanding Officer Lt-Col W. J. Humphry, MC, with General Montgomery, as he then was, taken on the beach, Normandy, June 1944.[6]

Reconstituted in 1947, the new title 626 (Liverpool Irish) HAA Regiment, Royal Artillery, TA; amalgamated in 1955 as 'Q' (Liverpool Irish) Battery, and redesignated in 1964 as 470 (3rd West Lancs) Light Air Defence Regt, RA.

The green caubeen, with cap badge and blue over red hackle, is kept in wear, pipers with the same headwear but with the kilt and brat, or shawl.

[1] 'The Liverpool Irish Brigade by Frank Forde, *The Irish Sword* – Winter 1971.

[2] Reports on the various events in the Illustrated London News for:– 16 November 1859, 13 September 1962, 26 May 1866 and 6 February 1869.

[3] Reproduced in *The Regiment*, 20 February 1897.

[4] This badge illustrated in *The Bulletin*, Military Historical Society, Vol.VIII p.33, November 1957.

[5] *How I escaped from Germany*, by Walter Duncan. Printed for private circulation by Messrs E. Howell Ltd, 83 Church Street, Liverpool.

[6] Published in *The Kingsman*. July 1946.

YEOMANRY, SPECIAL RESERVE & TERRITORIAL FORCE REGIMENTS

The Ulster Defence Regiment

Following the outbreak of severe rioting and prolonged community and inter-sectarian violence in the Summer of 1969, Lord Hunt's Advisory Committee recommended the creation of what was to become the Ulster Defence Regiment. The Regiment was formed by Act of Parliament in January 1970 and became operational three months later on 1 April.

Initially it consisted of a Regimental Headquarters at Lisburn and seven battalions, one in each of the six counties and the seventh in the City of Belfast. Escalation of terrorist violence in 1971 led to the formation of four additional battalions when the Order of Battle read:

1st Battalion (County Antrim) - St Patrick's, Ballymena
2nd Battalion (County Armagh) - Armagh Barracks

Pipers and musicians from the Irish Regiments at Kneller Hall, summer 1986, before proceeding on a massed band tour of Northern Ireland. Left to right: Pipe-Major Ulster Defence Regiment; Royal Irish Rangers; Irish Guards; 5th Royal Inniskilling Dragoon Guards; Queen's Royal Irish Hussars; Royal Irish Rangers; Irish Guards.
ARMY OFFICIAL PHOTOGRAPH.
HQ UK LAND FORCES

3rd Battalion (County Down) - Anderson Centre, Ballykinler
4th Battalion (County Fermanagh) - Coleshill Centre, Enniskillen
5th Battalion (County Londonderry) - Shackleton Barracks, Ballykelly
6th Battalion (County Tyrone) - St Lucia Barracks, Armagh
7th Battalion (City of Belfast) - Palace Barracks, Hollywood (County Down)
8th Battalion (County Tyrone) - Killymeal House, Dungannon
9th Battalion (County Antrim) - Steeple Road, Antrim
10th Battalion (City of Belfast) - Malone Centre, Windsor Park, Belfast
11th Battalion (Craigavon) - Mahon Road, Portadown, (County Armagh)
Regimental Headquarters - Lisburn

Initially the Regiment was to be a part-time military force providing support to the Regular military forces in the Provinces, manning guards at key points, patrols and check points. But this role developed significantly.

In 1973, the first women were recruited into the Regiment. Known as Greenfinches, they quickly became wholly integrated and key elements of their battalions. Another significant change was the establishment of a full time Permanent Cadre. This development coincided with the assumption by the battalions of their own tactical areas of operational responsibility (TAORs) during the late 1970s in support of the Royal Ulster Constabulary.

The 1980s saw some improvement in the security situation, enabling a series of amalgamations which reduced the eleven battalions to seven by 1971. This was achieved by the merger of the County Antrim Battalions (1984), the City of Belfast Battalions (also 1984), the 4th with the 6th and the 2th with the 11th (both in 1991).

Most significantly, as a result of the Options for Change defence review, The Ulster Defence Regiment amalgamated with the Royal Irish Rangers to form The Royal Irish Regiment in 1992 (see page 283).

In its brief but distinguished history, the Regiment earned massive respect for its contribution to the fight against terrorist violence. Indeed it can claim the distinction of having seen more prolonged active service than any other regiment in the history of the British Army.

1UDR manning a vehicle checkpoint on the Co Antrim coast road, 1975.
RHQ ROYAL IRISH REGIMENT

PART FOUR ■ ROYAL ARTILLERY
THE MILITIA AND VOLUNTEER AND SUPPORT GROUPS

Royal Artillery

When the Militia was re-embodied in 1855, certain of the regiments were designated Artillery, those in Ireland recorded in the 1855 Army List as follows:

Antrim. (Distinct from the Antrim Rifles.)

Armagh. (Distinct from the Armagh Light Infantry.)

Royal Cork Artillery and West Cork Artillery (Distinct from the North Cork Rifles and South Cork Light Infantry.)

Donegal. (Distinct from the Donegal Militia.)

Dublin City Artillery. (Distinct from the Royal Dublin City Militia and the Dublin County Light Infantry.)

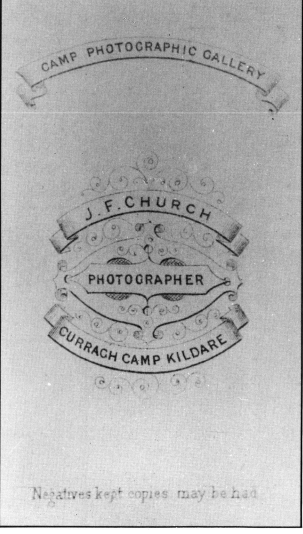

A smart Lance-Bombardier, c1890s. A carte-de-visite taken at the Camp Photographic Gallery, Curragh Camp, Kildare. A later photographer at the Curragh was Charlton and Sons.

*Pipes and drums of 661 Field Regiment
(Antrim) Royal Artillery (TA), 1955.*
S. D. EAGLE

Galway. (Listed but disbanded. Distinct from Galway Militia.)
Limerick City Artillery. (Distinct from the Limerick County Militia.)
Londonderry Artillery. (Distinct from the Londonderry Light Infantry.)
1st or South Tipperary Artillery. (Distinct from the 2nd or North
Tipperary Light Infantry.)
Tyrone. (Distinct from the Royal Tyrone Fusiliers.) Waterford.

Note: A complimentary report on the Tipperary Artillery Militia was
published in the *Illustrated London News* 8 October 1859, and provides
an example of the state of efficiency of a good militia corps of the day:

> 'The Tipperary Artillery Militia, numbering 891 of all ranks, was inspected
> on Monday by Maj-Gen Sir J. Yorke Scarlett, KCB, attended by Col Noel
> Lake, CB, commanding the artillery of the South West District. Having all
> the officers and men of the regiment drawn up in quarter-distance column,
> the General addressed them as follows: "A finer body of men, more cleanly,
> more orderly, more soldierlike, I have never seen. To Lord Donoughmore,
> your Lieutenant-Colonel, to your officers, and to yourselves the greatest
> credit is due, and to all of you I have to express my entire satisfaction. I have
> seen a great many militia regiments, but I can truly say I never yet saw one at
> all equal to this."'

After the South African War the following Royal Garrison Artillery
Militia regiments remained in Ireland, county names given here with
precedence number.

1.	Antrim	27.	Tipperary
4.	Cork	29.	Waterford
8.	Donegal	34.	Wicklow
9.	Dublin City	35.	Sligo
20.	Limerick City	36.	Londonderry
21.	Mid-Ulster	37.	Clare

Each unit had a regular army Royal Artillery Adjutant, as well as
NCO Permanent Staff Instructors, also from the Royal Artillery. •

After 1908 the former Militia Artillery of Ireland was reduced to two Royal Garrison Artillery, Special Reserve Regts under county titles: 'The Antrim' and 'The Cork'. The Headquarters of The Antrim, was at Carrickfergus and J. M. McCalmont, formerly 8th Hussars, was Honorary Colonel from 1908, succeeded in 1913 by the Earl of Shaftesbury. The Cork HQ was at Fort Westmorland, Spike Island, Queenstown Harbour; the Earl of Bandon, the Hon. Colonel since 1908.

In 1938 coast defences at Queenstown, Berehaven and Lough Swilley were handed over to the Irish Free State.

Whilst in 1947 the Territorial Army in Northern Ireland could boast as many as seven regiments of artillery, these units were gradually reduced by amalgamations and disbandments. In 1967, however, a unit was formed with an unusual composition, with headquarters in England and sub-units in Scotland as well as Ireland: The 102nd (Ulster and Scottish) Air Defence Regt, RA, (V).

Standard helmet plate of the Artillery Militia, identifiable as Militia by the M below the gun.

Otto Schulz

Osnabrück   Hasestr. 59.

Photograph of Lieutenant Francis M. Hyde of the 1st or South Tipperary (or Duke of Clarence's Munster) Artillery Militia, 1879. It would be interesting to know how this young officer in the full dress uniform of his regiment came to be photographed in Austria.

D. W. QUARMBY

ROYAL ARTILLERY ■ THE MILITIA AND VOLUNTEER AND SUPPORT GROUPS

The Regiments of Irish Militia

The story of the Irish Militia Regiments is an absorbing one. Each regiment had its own individual history, traditions, uniform and badges, and should be treated separately – there have been in fact numerous Regimental Histories published.[1]

Raised around the year 1793, (although there were earlier units known to have been in existence since 1776), they were stood down (or disembodied) in 1802 following the Irish Revolutionary War, but called upon again in 1803 for periods of varying length until 1816. The Crimean War necessitated re-embodiment for the two years of its duration and in some cases for a further period to cover the years of the Indian Mutiny until its suppression. A long period of peace followed and in 1881 regiments were affiliated to the regular regiments of Irish Infantry, forming 3rd, 4th and occasionally its 5th battalion (Militia).

In 1900 the Militia of the United Kingdom supplied units to serve in Gibraltar, Malta and even South Africa in order to release troops from peace-time garrison duty, for the duration of the South African War. After the war however the Militia served no useful purpose. In 1908 the regiments were transferred to the Special Reserve.

During the First World War the Militia battalions, then known as 3rd (Reserve) or 4th (Extra Reserve) battalions, performed garrison duties,

Left. Wexford Militia. Major John Deverill of Ballywankin, c1801-10. Miniature by Buck. Uniform scarlet, facings yellow, lace silver.
CHRISTIE'S

Kilkenny Militia. A captain, c1815. Uniform scarlet, facings green, shoulder-belt plate – gilt.
CHRISTIE'S

Top left. Gilt shoulder-belt plate of the Royal Downshire Regiment of Militia, c1816-28. Became Royal South Down Militia in 1835.
Top right. County Louth Rifles Militia. Officer's helmet plate, black with polished highlights.
Bottom left. Officer's shoulder-belt plate, Royal Limerick County. Gilt pierced circle with month and date. Gilt crown, gilt title scrolls and gilt back plate. Silver cut star. Light blue enamel backing to circlet, titles, etc.
Bottom right. Dublin County. Officer's shoulder-belt, silver.
L. V. ARCHER

thereby again releasing regular soldiers, although fit Militia men could be transferred to fighting units.

The Irish Militia from the South were disbanded in 1922 at the same time as the parent regiments. Those from the North went into 'suspended animation' in 1921 whilst carrying the title Militia, but were finally disbanded in 1953.

Note: Numerals appearing in brackets after 1793 and 1855 are the precedence numbers.

The Regiments

Antrim
1793	(7)	
1817		HQ Randalstown
1855	(79)	Antrim Militia, (Queen's Royal Rifles)
1879		Uniform Rifle green, facings scarlet
		HQ Belfast
1881		4th Bn Royal Irish Rifles
1921		Redes as 3rd Bn Militia

Top left. Shako of Wexford Militia, c1855-61.
Top right. Plate from bell-top shako of Wexford Militia, c1829. An all-gilt plate.
Bottom left. Shako plate of Londonderry Militia.
Bottom right. Shako of North Mayo Militia, c1869-78.
L. V. ARCHER

Note   In 1798 the Royal Downshire Militia, Antrim and Louth Militias helped to restore order at the time of the rebellion of the United Irishmen. At Tubberneering Drummer Hunter of the Antrims, a boy of 12 was captured by the rebels and ordered by them to beat his drum. He broke the drumheads crying 'This drum shall not beat for rebels.' He was subsequently put to death by the rebels. A well known picture painted by George Joy (1844-1925) shows Drummer Hunter seated beside his drum and surrounded by his captors.[2]

Armagh
1793   (8)
1817   HQ Market Hill
1855   (75) Armagh Light Infantry, HQ Armagh
1879   Uniform scarlet, facings French grey
1881   3rd Bn Royal Irish Fusiliers
Note   At the Battle of Ballinamuck the Armagh Militia captured a Colour of the French 70th Demi-Brigade on 7 September

1798, the only Colour ever taken by a Militia Regiment in Ireland. During the Crimean War the regiment supplied a large draft for the 68th Foot.

Carlow

1793	(23)	HQ Carlow
1855	(70)	Carlow Rifles
1879		Uniform Rifle green, facings black
1881		8th Bn King's Royal Rifle Corps, disbanded 1908

Cavan

1793	(18)	HQ Cavan
1855	(101)	Uniform scarlet, facings black
1881		4th Bn Royal Irish Fusiliers

Clare

1793	(26)	
1817		HQ Clare Castle, Enniskillen
1843		An interesting announcement appeared in the Illustrated London News, 22 April 1843:

'The Adjutancy of the Clare Militia, vacant by the death of C. A. De Ruyvenes, formerly of the 21st Light Dragoons, is in the gift of Colonel of the Regiment, Lord Fitzgerald and Vesci.'

1855	(94)	Uniform scarlet, facings yellow
1879		Uniform scarlet, facings black
1881		7th Clare Brigade. South Irish Division Artillery

North Cork

1793	(34)	
1817		HQ Youghal. To Fermoy
1855	(116)	North Cork Rifles. Uniform green, facings black velvet
1874		HQ Mallow
1881		9th Bn King's Royal Rifle Corps
1908		Disbanded

South Cork

1793	(32)	HQ Rathcormack
1855	(87)	South Cork Light Infantry
		HQ Bandon. Uniform scarlet, facings white
1881		3rd Bn Royal Munster Fusiliers
1908		4th Bn (Extra Reserve)
1922		Disbanded

Cork City

1793	(27)	HQ Cork
1855	(5)	Cork City Regiment
1856		Cork City Artillery
1881		3rd Royal Cork City Brigade, South Irish Divsion Artillery

Donegal

1793	(36)	
1817		HQ Ballyshannon
1855	(102)	The Prince of Wales's Own Donegal Militia

1874   HQ Lifford

1881   3 Brigade North Irish Division Artillery

North Downshire

1793   (9)

1817   HQ Killyleagh, Newtownards

1855   (77) Royal North Downshire Militia (Rifles), uniform green, facings scarlet.

1881   3rd Bn Royal Irish Rifles

Note   In 1796 the regiment force-marched from Drogheda to Bantry to assist in dealing with a French landing, although arrived too late. When in Cork the Commanding Officer of the 33rd Foot wrote to Lord Downshire saying 'Your regiment is as good as my own'. This comment came from Arthur Wellesley![3]

South Down

1793   nil

1797   (24) From Drogheda Militia

1817   HQ Bangor

1831   HQ Hillsborough

1855 (112) Royal South Down Light Infantry, uniform scarlet, facings blue

1874   HQ Downpatrick

1881   5th Bn Royal Irish Rifles

Dublin County

1793 (35) HQ Lucan

1855 (109) Dublin County Light Infantry, uniform scarlet, facings white.

1881   5th Bn Royal Dublin Fusiliers

Dublin City

1793 (12) HQ Dublin

1855 (100) Royal Dublin City Militia (Queen's Own Royal Regiment) uniform scarlet, facings royal blue.

1881   4th Bn Royal Dublin Fusiliers

Fermanagh

1793 (29) HQ Enniskillen

1855 (71) Fermanagh Light Infantry, uniform scarlet, facings buff

1881   3rd Bn Royal Inniskilling Fusiliers

1921   4th Bn (Extra Reserve)

1953   Disbanded

Galway

1793 (11) HQ Ballinasloe

1855 (91) HQ Loughrea, uniform scarlet, facings yellow

1881   4th Bn Connaught Rangers

1908   Redes 3rd Bn

1922   Disbanded

Kerry

1793 (14) HQ Tralee

1855 (107) Uniform scarlet, facings yellow

1881	4th Bn Royal Munster Fusiliers
1908	Redes 3rd Bn
1922	Disbanded

A charming study of Irish Militia by M. Angelo Hayes. (In 1842 M. A. Hayes, 1820-77, was appointed Military Painter in Ordinary to the Lord Lieutenant of Ireland. In 1848 he settled in Dublin.) This picture shows the uniform of the Crimean War period and is undoubtedly a faithful record.
CHRISTIE'S

Kildare

1793	(4) HQ Naas
1855	(88) Kildare Rifles, uniform green, facings black
1881	3rd Bn Royal Dublin Fusiliers

Kilkenny

1793	(20) HQ Kilkenny
1855	(127) Kilkenny Fusiliers, uniform scarlet, facings yellow
1881	5th Bn Royal Irish Regt
1908	Redes 4th Bn (Extra Reserve)
1922	Disbanded

Kings County

| 1776 | Raised as Parsonstown Loyal Independents Volunteer Corps |
| 1793 | (19) On the Militia establishment as King's County Royal Rifles. |

HQ Parsonstown. Changes of HQ before 1838 at Banagher and Kinnitty

1855 (98) King's County Rifles, uniform green, facings scarlet
1881 3rd Bn Leinster Regt

Leitrim

1793 (10) HQ Carrick-on-Shannon
1855 (111) Leitrim Rifles, uniform dark green, facings black
1858 HQ Mohill
1874 HQ Carrick-on-Shannon
1881 8th Bn The Rifle Brigade

Royal Limerick County Militia

1793 (21) HQ St Francis' Abbey
1855 (123) Uniform scarlet, facings blue
1859 Presented with new colours on Southsea Common, August 1859 by Maj-Gen Yorke Scarlett, KCB
1874 Royal Limerick County Militia (Fusiliers)
1881 5th Bn Royal Munster Fusiliers
1900 One of the Irish Militia Regts embodied during the South African War from 10 May 1900 to 10 October 1901, served at Fort Chambry, Gozo, Malta

Limerick City

1793 (13) HQ Limerick City
1855 (20) Limerick City Artillery, uniform blue, facings red
1881 4th Brigade North Irish Division (Artillery)

Londonderry

1793 (16) HQ Londonderry
1855 (95) Londonderry Light Infantry, uniform scarlet facings yellow
1881 9 Brigade North Irish Division (Artillery)

Longford

1793 (15) HQ Newtown Forbes, Longford – The Prince of Wales's Royal Longford Militia
1855 (85) The Prince of Wales's Royal Longford Rifles, originally uniform scarlet, facings blue, with Light Infantry designation, shortly after changed back to The Prince of Wales's Royal Regiment of Longford Rifles with uniform of green faced scarlet.
1881 6th Bn The Rifle Brigade

Louth

1793 (5) HQ Colton
1797 (24) Absorbed Drogheda Militia
1855 (108) Louth Rifles, HQ Dundalk, uniform green, facings black
1881 6th Bn Royal Irish Rifles
1908 Disbanded

North Mayo

1793 (3) HQ Castlebar
1817 HQ Ballina
1855 (120) North Mayo Fusiliers, uniform scarlet, facings white
1881 6th Bn Connaught Rangers

South Mayo

1793	(30) HQ Westport
1855	(15) South Mayo Rifles, uniform Rifle green, facings scarlet
1881	3rd Bn Connaught Rangers
1889	Amalgamated with 6th Bn, as 3rd Bn
1908	Disbanded

Royal Meath

1793	(17) HQ Kells
1855	(119) Uniform scarlet, facings blue
1874	HQ Navan
1881	5th Bn Leinster Regt

Monaghan

1793	(1) HQ Monaghan
1817	HQ Glasslough, Tynan
1838	HQ Monaghan
1855	(121) Uniform scarlet, facings white
1881	5th Bn Royal Irish Fusiliers

Queens County

1793	(25) HQ Maryborough
1855	(104) Royal Queen's County Rifles, uniform Rifle green, facings scarlet
1881	4th Bn Leinster Regt

Roscommon

1793	(31) HQ Boyle
1855	(93) Roscommon Militia, uniform scarlet, facings buff
1881	5th Bn Connaught Rangers

SLIGO

1793	(22) HQ Sligo
1855	(124) Sligo Rifles, uniform green, facings green, (later changed to black)
1881	8th Brigade North Irish Division Artillery

Tipperary

1793	(28) HQ Clonmell
	Title (Duke of Clarence's Munster) Tipperary Militia
1855	Two regiments
	(27) 1st or South Tipperary Artillery
	(105) 2nd or North Tipperary Light Infantry, uniform scarlet, facings dark green.
1881	1st to Artillery Militia.
	Light Infantry became 4th Bn Royal Irish Regt

Tyrone

1783	(2) HQ Caldeon
1793	(2) Royal Tyrone Militia
1855	(80) Royal Tyrone Fusiliers, HQ Omagh, uniform scarlet, facings dark blue
1855	(28) Tyrone Artillery. HQ Moy, to Artillery Militia
1881	Fusiliers became 4th Bn Royal Inniskilling Fusiliers

An officer of the 2nd or North Tipperary Militia Light Infantry. Photograph taken at Clonmel, c1880. On his cap he has an elaborate embroidered badge consisting of a Light Infantry bugle over a crown with the harp below, and the word Tipperary on a scroll below that again.

Pipe-Major Barnes and Sergeant-Drummer Young of the 5th Bn Donegal Militia (Royal Inniskilling Fusiliers). This photograph was taken at Dover, 1901, during the time the battalion was embodied for service during the South Africa War. Both men wear the normal full dress scarlet tunic and blue trousers, but in conjunction with the khaki slouch hat. The 4th Bn (later 3rd) Royal Tyrone Fusiliers, (Royal Inniskilling Fusiliers) was one of the first to introduce pipers, as early as 1887.

Westmeath
1793   (6) HQ Mullingar
1855   (114) Westmeath Rifles, uniform Rifle green, facings black
1881   9th Bn The Rifle Brigade

Waterford
1793   (33) HQ Waterford
1855   (29) Waterford Artillery
1881   6th Brigade South Irish Division Artillery

Wexford
1793   (38) HQ Wexford
1855   (99) Wexford Militia, uniform scarlet, facings yellow
1881   3rd Bn Royal Irish Regt

Wicklow
1793   (37) HQ Wicklow
1855   (92) Wicklow Rifles, uniform green, facings black
1881   7th Brigade North Irish Division Artillery

---

[1] The Histories of 18 Irish Militia Regts listed in *A Bibliography of Regimental Histories of the British Army* by A. S. White. Pub. by Society Army Historical Research in conjunction with Army Museums Ogilby Trust, 1965.
[2] The actual drum used by the artist for his painting, now in the author's possession.
[3] *The Royal Ulster Rifles. 1793-1957.* By Lt-Col M. J. P. M. Corbally. Glasgow Press, Glasgow 1959, The Paramount Press 1959.

ROYAL ARTILLERY ■ THE MILITIA AND VOLUNTEER AND SUPPORT GROUPS

Volunteer Support Units of Northern Ireland

In addition to the units of the regular army, the following is a representative list of volunteer support units, beween the years 1945 and *c*1980. It makes no claim to be comprehensive – with yet further changes of title, amalgamations and disbandments within or after this period.

Corps of Royal Engineers
591 (Antrim) Independent Field Squadron, RE, (TA)
146 (Antrim Artillery) Corps Engineer Regt
          Royal Engineers (TA)
74 (Antrim Artillery) Engineer Regt, Royal
          Engineers (V)

Royal Corps of Signals
66th (Ulster) Signal Regt (TA)

Royal Corps of Transport
601 (Ulster) Squadron, Royal Corps of Transport
  (TA)
931 (Ulster) Company RASC (TA)
112 Transport Column RASC (TA)
68 (Northern Ireland) Regt, Royal Corps of
  Transport (TA)
152 (Ulster) Regt Royal Corps of Transport (V)

Royal Army Medical Corps
107 (Ulster) Field Ambulance, RAMC (TA)
253 (Northern Ireland) Field Ambulance, RAMC (V)
4 General Hospital, RAMC (TA)
204 (Northern Irish) General Hospital, RAMC (V)

Royal Army Ordnance Corps
107 (Ulster) Ordnance Field Park RAOC (V)

Royal Electrical and Mechanical Engineers
107 (Ulster) Infantry Workshop REME (TA)

Corps of Royal Military Police
Northern Ireland Command Provost Company

Intelligence Corps
Numbered units of:–
Field Security Section
Counter Intelligence
Air Photography Interpretation Section (APIS)

Photo Interpretation Company (V)
Port Security Platoon (V)

Women's Royal Army Corps

The Queen's University Officers Training Corps

Army Cadet Force

The Royal Irish Regiment

The Royal Irish Regiment was formed on 1 July 1992 by the amalgamation of the Royal Irish Rangers (27th (Inniskilling), 83rd, 87th) and the Ulster Defence Regiment and immediately became the largest Infantry Regiment in the British Army.

Uniquely, on formation it consisted of two General Service Infantry Battalions (the 1st and 2nd), six Home Service Battalions and the 4th and 5th Volunteer Territorial Battalions.

The Home Service Battalions, namely 3rd (Co Down & Armagh), 4th (Co Fermanagh & Tyrone), 5th (Co Londonderry), 7th (City of Befast), 8th (Co Armagh & Tyrone) and 9th (Co Antrim), were formerly the Ulster Defence Regiment (see page 268) and are restricted to operational service in Northern Ireland.

The Regimental Headquarters and Depot at St Patrick's Barracks, Ballymena provided the administrative and training base.

On formation the 1st Battalion was stationed in Warminster and the 2nd in Lemgo, Germany. In 1992 a Company of the 2nd Battalion deployed to Bosnia supporting 1st Battalion The Cheshire Regiment during a particularly difficult and dangerous period of that confict. Later that year the 1st Battalion moved to Cyprus and, as part of the Army's restructuring, merged with the 2nd Battalion in 1993.

At the same time the two Territorial battalions amalgamated to form the 4th/5th Battalion, The Royal Irish Rangers (Volunteers).

First Presentation of Colours to the 1st Battalion Royal Irish Regiment by the Colonel-in-Chief of the Regiment, HRH The Prince Andrew CVO ADC at Alma Barracks, Catterick on 29 June 1996. Left to right: Major A. K. Cullen, HRH, 2Lt C. S. O'Hara, Major R. G. Russell, Lt S. J. Shirley.

RHQ ROYAL IRISH REGIMENT

In 1995 the 1st Battalion moved to Catterick from where it sent a Company detachment to Bosnia, and conducted a six month tour in Northern Ireland, at which point all of the Regimental Battalions were serving together in the same theatre for the first time.

On a second Northern Ireland tour in 1996 the entire Regiment was under operational command of the Colonel of the Regiment, General Sir Roger Wheeler, the then GOC Northern Ireland.

The Home Service Battalions continue to play a key role in maintaining law and order in support of the Royal Ulster Constabulary. The courage and commitment of the men and women of these battalions, whether full or part time, are amply demonstrated by more than one thousand honours and awards received since the formation of the Ulster Defence Regiment. Sadly 197 serving officers and soldiers including four Greenfinches have been killed by terrorists and some 450 wounded or injured. Forty seven former soldiers have been murdered, in some cases several years after leaving the Regiment.

Since formation the new Regiment has quickly established its professional reputation. It has enjoyed success in Army football, cross country running and shooting, exemplified by the distinction of having won the prized Methuen Cup three years running (1995-97).

1st Battalion The Royal Irish Regiment. Pipe Major B. Kidd, Drum Major R. A. Stewart, Bugle Major D. A. Young, piper and handler with Brian Boru, the Regimental Mascot, Catterick 1996.
RHQ ROYAL IRISH REGIMENT

A Private, Royal Irish Regiment (Home Service), manning a Vehicle Check Point (VCP) in Ulster. He is wearing the current 90 pattern webbing and is armed with an SA 80.
RHQ ROYAL IRISH REGIMENT

Bibliography

(Additional works consulted)

The Regimental Records of the British Army by John S. Farmer, pub Grant Richards London 1901.

The Victoria Cross (The Empire's Roll of Valour), compiled by Lt-Col R. Stewart, MVO, pub Hutchinson & Co *c*1928.

An account of the Territorials in Northern Ireland 1947-1978 by Col I. B. Gailey, Col W. F. Gillespie and Lt-Col J. Hasset, Belfast 1979.

Collecting Miniatures by Daphne Foskett, pub by the Antique Collectors' Club 1979.

Churchill and the Irish Marshals by Patrick Marrinan, pub Pretani Press 1986.

The British Soldier in the 20th Century by Mike Chappell, pub Wessex Military Publishing 1987.

The Road to the Somme by Philip Orr pub the Blackstaff Press, 1987 Army Lists.

Index